SPORT PSYCHOLOGY

Psychology: The Key Concepts provides the most authoritative, e-ranging and up-to-date A to Z guide available to this fascinating . Cross-referenced, with suggestions for further reading and a full x, it offers a highly accessible introduction to the vocabulary of t psychology, its central theories and its contemporary relevance. r 160 entries cover such diverse terms as:

- Arousal
- Celebrity
- Cognition
- Emotion
- Fear
- Home advantage

- Left-handed
- Mental toughness
- Pain
- Sex
- Streaks
- Zone

A comprehensive guide to an increasingly important field, whether for students, athletes, journalists or fans, this book is an essential resource for all those with an interest in sports.

Ellis Cashmore is Professor of Culture, Media and Sport at Staffordshire University, UK, and author of *Making Sense of Sports* and *Sports Culture – An A–Z Guide* (both Routledge).

ROUTLEDGE KEY GUIDES

Routledge Key Guides are accessible, informative and lucid handbooks, which define and discuss the central concepts, thinkers and debates in a broad range of academic disciplines. All are written by noted experts in their respective subjects. Clear, concise exposition of complex and stimulating issues and ideas make *Routledge Key Guides* the ultimate reference resources for students, teachers, researchers and the interested lay person.

SPORT PSYCHOLOGY

The Key Concepts

Ellis Cashmore

London and New York

First published 2002
by Routledge
11 New Fetter Lane, London EC4P 4EE

Simultaneously published in the USA and Canada
by Routledge
29 West 35th Street, New York, NY 10001

Routledge is an imprint of the Taylor & Francis Group

© 2002 Ellis Cashmore

Typeset in Bembo by Taylor & Francis Books Ltd
Printed and bound in Great Britain by TJ International Ltd,
Padstow, Cornwall

British Library Cataloguing in Publication Data
A catalogue record for this book is available from the British Library

Library of Congress Cataloging in Publication Data
A catalog record for this book has been requested

ISBN 0–415–25321–7 (hbk)
ISBN 0–415–25322–5 (pbk)

CONTENTS

INTRODUCTION

The seven deadly virtues

Imagine that genetic technology has progressed to the point where we can create the world's greatest pound-for-pound athlete by cloning from the DNA of anyone we choose. We are invited to take our pick from recent history, selecting the strongest features of any set of living athletes. For example, we could take the lightning speed of Maurice Greene or the sure touch of Wayne Greztsky. The bullish power of Marshall Faulk would be perfect, as would the hand-to-eye co-ordination of cricketer Steve Waugh and the agility of Tara Lipinski. Marion Jones' reactions, Michael Jordan's dexterity, Derek Jeter's consistency and Tegla Loroupe's durability might also feature in our genetic e-kit construction. And for vision, who can compare with Zinedine Zidane? Selecting the best physical components from the world's best would provide us with a formidable athlete, a genuine 'dream athlete'. Tempting as it sounds, the sport psychologist would probably have different ideas.

An alternative set of attributes drawn from a completely different group of athletes could contribute to the psychologically ideal athlete. This time, we might begin with the all-round **mental toughness** of Michael Schumacher, without doubt one of the most psychologically interesting athletes ever, as we will see in this book (throughout the book, words in **bold** have entries of their own). For strength of **motivation**, Lance Armstrong, who recovered from testicular cancer to win three Tours de France, takes some beating. How about the focusing capacity of pole-vaulter Stacy Dragila, who seemed to respond to every centimeter the pole vault bar was raised with an extra step into her own **zone**? Or the **aggressiveness** of arguably the most tenacious swimmer ever, Ian Thorpe?

For supreme **confidence** (occasionally bordering on over-confidence), Roy Jones Jr has few equals. Andre Agassi seems a logical choice for **concentration**: in training and **competition**, he is known to be proficient in eliminating extraneous thought – and not just for short periods, either. Agassi reached the semi-finals of the US Open in 1988, when aged 18, and for the next thirteen years continued to compete at the premier level of men's tennis, collecting all four Grand Slam titles. Permitted a choice for **intelligence**, we would need someone not necessarily high on the IQ scale but who demonstrates a keen sense of strategy, **decision making** skills, and preferably **leadership** capability. Peyton Manning would be a sensible selection. And **composure**? Tiger Woods has many of the qualities necessary for the psychologically ideal athlete, but his ability to remain calm and arrange his thoughts, behavior and even expression for a specified purpose and refuse to be fazed by activities around him sets him apart. The seven deadly virtues may not appear on the fan's list of criteria, but the sport psychologist is looking for different qualities.

The rationale behind picking psychological components instead of purely physical ones might run as follows. Improvements in diet, hygiene and medical science have led to the healthiest, most physically robust population ever known. Add to this the understanding we now have about athletic conditioning, training and all-round preparation and the technology at our disposal for implementing that conditioning and you have a generation of near-equals. Athletes today are stronger, hardier and more resistant than ever in history. So much is known about how to keep our bodies hale and healthy that every sport has taken advantage. Golfers in the 1980s never went near a gym; today's pros work out regularly. Women tennis players have enough upper body strength to blow away the men's top players of twenty-five years ago. In other words, while athletes are not equal physically, they are considerably more equal than they ever have been. Take all the NBA players in the league and subject them to a series of physical tests, then compare them with each other, and there would not be much deviation from a norm. Compare this with senior college players and again there would be differences, but not huge ones. Same goes for the world's elite sprinters: physically, they resemble each other more than at any time in history.

The phrase *primus inter pares* means 'first among equals', and it is not a self-contradiction. Even when athletes of identical physical mettle meet, there is always difference. This is why we have an Olympic 100 meters champion rather than a mass dead heat. Advantages always exist. This raises questions. What are the sources of the advantages and how do some athletes acquire them? How do others negate them? Why do they work in some events yet not in others? How can we procure those advantages? The answers lie in the realms of sport psychology.

Mutant concepts

It is a sure sign of a discipline's maturity when dictionaries, encyclopedias and A–Zs on its subject matter start appearing. This book is actually none of these, though it shares with a dictionary an alphabetical arrangement, concise definitions of every item and brief etymologies, unless the origins of a term are glaringly obvious (as in **body language** or **comeback**, for instance). It also has common ground with encyclopedias, providing information on many branches of knowledge: each entry is an essay in its own right. Of course, the term 'encyclopedia' has connotations of comprehensiveness, and while I have tried to capture many of the central terms in the sport psychology lexicon, there are inevitably some omissions.

My defense is that this book's title is *Sport Psychology: The Key Concepts* and I have concentrated on exactly that: the *key* concepts. These include terms that are part of the basic conceptual equipment of any sport psychologist – **burnout, focused, goal setting, self-efficacy, zone** and so on – plus terms that are germane to psychology and have specific relevance to the study of sports. Here I am thinking of the likes of **anxiety, emotion, identity, instinct, perception**, etc. Some concepts have clear application not only to psychology but to public discourse: **doping, race, gay, religion, sex** and several other terms that command widespread attention. I have looked at them from the perspective of sport psychology. Then I have included technical terms that apply to styles of analysis, such as **mimetic, nomothetic** and the **Premack principle**. I should at this stage confess to having indulged myself with some other inclusions. I have covered some terms because they lead to interesting discussions. This is a judgement call, of course, but I hope the reader will agree that some terms simply deserve closer inspection since they excite fascinating questions. For example, why are we enthralled by **celebrity** sports stars? Do **left-handed** athletes enjoy an advantage over right-handers? What role does **luck** play in sports? Are we natural **risk** takers? Sport psychology has partial answers to these questions and I augment them with answers from other subject areas.

One further question that is in a way implicit in this book is: where are the frontiers of sport psychology? The subject has come a long way since Norman Triplett started watching how cyclists improved their performances when in the company of others way back in 1897/8.

There is dispute over whether this was, in fact, the first ever insight into the psychology of sports (the **Ringelmann effect** had been discovered earlier), but it was a milestone research project and began at least one line of investigation into the **social facilitation** of **skill performance**. Over the decades the discipline grew and expanded, its focus widening with new theoretical contributions and research findings. John M. Silva's illuminating essay 'The evolution of sport psychology', published in 2002, shows that, if the 1960s and 1970s were decades of rapid growth and development, the 1980s and 1990s were ones of consolidation. 'As the visibility of sport psychology increased in academic settings, it was simply a matter of time before individuals from psychology, the media, and the public became more interested,' writes Silva, adding that this caused tension as it was thought that 'many "academic" sport psychologists were not closely attuned to developments taking place in the applied aspects.'

The academic response to the expansion of sport psychology was to establish methods of regulating access, training and accreditation. Yet, in many ways, attempts to close ranks and **control** the **discipline** were never likely to succeed totally: the subject was already migrating into popular discourse. Coaches, journalists, fans and almost anyone with a serious interest in sports now have some degree of knowledge about sport psychology and its contemporary value. How often have we heard or read about **cohesion**, **intensity**, **motivation** or **psyching**? These are all key concepts, and while their casual use may offend some purists there is no denying that they and many other terms have escaped into the public domain. Sport psychology, like the aphoristic toothpaste, has been squeezed out of the tube.

The benefit of this is that sport psychology has spread far and wide, though the cost is that many of the key terms have been misused, abused and sometimes plain subverted. One of my aims in this book has been to round up many of the terms in popular use and give them a more explicit technical meaning. Not a meaning that is unrecognizable to users, I should emphasize, but one which accommodates both popular use and academic theory and research. A term like **aggressiveness**, for example, is now used everywhere in a way that suggests that it has become synonymous with what psychologists have for years called assertiveness. A vocabulary is a moving phenomenon and the discipline has to accept that many of its key concepts have been appropriated, altered and are still being changed. To stick with Silva's idea of the discipline's evolution, we might say that its concepts are *mutating*.

I am not a preservationist when it comes to language: my preference is to accommodate and clarify rather than resist mutations. As such, I have applied a more multidisciplinary approach than many other psychologists to the study of sport. The reader will notice the presence of anthropology, biology, cultural studies, history, philosophy and sociology in many of the entries, and perhaps a trace of neurology and political science in a few others. I make no apology for this: my belief is that sport is a social activity that takes place in actual settings; as such, it should not be severed from its historical and cultural foundations. The athlete actualizes, embodies, reflects, personalizes and resonates with multiple influences. Any meaningful psychological project needs to account for this or **risk** producing sheer artifice.

All writers or compilers of dictionaries and comparably exhaustive volumes are fallible and, as one, I have probably made many errors of omission – and possibly a few of inclusion. Like the terminology of the subject area itself, this book is subject to evolutionary processes. So, to those readers who will take the trouble to bring to my **attention** my shortcomings and so help the improvement of this project in future editions, I express my thanks in advance.

LIST OF CONCEPTS

Achievement ethic
Achievement motive
Adherence
Adrenaline rush
Aggression
Aggressiveness
Aging
Androgyny
Androstenedione
Anger
Anxiety
Applied sport psychology
Arousal
Attention
Attribution
Autogenic
Automaticity
Autotelic
Biofeedback
Body image
Body language
Burnout
Catharsis
Celebrity
Centering
Character
Choke
Cognition
Cognitive–behavioral
   modification
Cohesion
Comeback

Commitment
Competition
Composure
Concentration
Confidence
Control
Coping strategies
Death wish
Decision making
Dependence
Depression
Deviance
Discipline
Doping
Drive
Dropouts
Eating disorders
Egocentrism
Electroencephalogram (EEG)
Emotion
Emotional
Endorphins
Equality
Eustress
Expectancy
Eyeballing
Fandom
Fear
Feedback
Flow
Focused
Gating

Gay
Gender
Goal
Goal orientation
Goal setting
Group dynamics
Halo effect
Home advantage
Hypnosis
Identity
Idiographic
Imagery
Incentive
Information processing
Injury
Instinct
Intelligence
Intensity
Intervention
Inventory
IZOF (individual zones of
    optimal functioning)
Knowledge of results
Leadership
Learned helplessness
Left-handed
Life course
Luck
Mastery
Memory
Mental practice
Mental toughness
Metamotivation
Mimetic
Modeling
Momentum
Mood
Motivation
Negativity
Nervous
Nervous system
Nomothetic

Obedience
Obsession
Overtraining
Pain
Parenting
Participation motivation
Peak performance
Perception
Performance enhancement
Personality
Personality assessment
Premack principle
Profile
Psyching
Psychological skills inventories
Race
Reaction time
Rehabilitation
Reinforcement
Relaxation
Religion
REM
Retirement
Reversal theory
Ringelmann effect
Risk
Self-actualization
Self-efficacy
Self-esteem
Self-handicapping
Self-talk
Sex
Skill
Skill acquisition
Skill performance
Slump
Social facilitation
Social loafing
Socialization
Stimuli
Streaks
Stress

SPORT PSYCHOLOGY

The Key Concepts

ACHIEVEMENT ETHIC

A moral code that guides conduct toward individual attainment or self-improvement, the achievement ethic has its origins in seventeenth-century England (though the term is formed from the French *achèvement*, derived from the phrase *à chef*, to a head, and *éthique*). It rests on the principle that the individual is the best judge of his or her own interests and, given the opportunity, will try to maximize those interests through initiative, endeavor and, if necessary, abstinence. This was precisely the principle that supported and gave purpose to what we now recognize as sports. The term 'achievement ethic' is analogous to, though broader than, the Protestant Ethic which evolved during the Protestant Reformation of the sixteenth century in the context of Calvinism and which promoted the values of **goal orientation**, asceticism (self-discipline), thrift and, crucially, individual achievement.

After the sixteenth century, the ethic of individual achievement was embraced by those seeking freedom, whether economic freedom from statutory restrictions on free enterprise, political freedom from would-be autocratic rule or religious freedom from the Roman communion. The offshoots of the Christian sects that separated from Rome during the Protestant Reformation promoted individualism, particularly in its application to self-fulfillment: enterprise, labor and self-improvement were exalted. Achieving as much as one's ability allowed was regarded as a virtue; idleness was discouraged. This was enshrined in a series of statutes that decreed for 'sturdy beggars,' vagrants and men refusing to work, such punishments as whipping, branding, imprisonment and, during one period, slavery or death.

Against the older paternalistic teaching that behavior must be guided and contained by religious, moral or social obligations, the doctrine declared the individual to be a free self-determining agent who should be allowed to pursue his or her interests relatively unhindered. The economic implications of this are clear: an open market of competing interests was encouraged and the only role for a central agency or state was in enforcing contracts and suppressing fraud.

But while the achievement ethic was highly individualistic, it was not necessarily opposed to forms of collectivism, and organizations such as churches, fighting units and, of course, sports teams were seen as embodying the ethic. In these organizations, the individualistic impulse remained dominant, but was pursued through collective means.

One important consequence of the spread of the achievement ethic was the realization that one's fate was not sealed. Earlier conceptions of destiny as linked in some way to structures of class, **religion** and power gave way to newer perceptions: far from being actors in a divinely ordained script, individuals believed they could affect their life chances. The Enlightenment of the seventeenth century ushered in a new attitude of mind that emphasized the power of reason, rationality and, above all, individualism. And, as if to provide evidence of the efficacy of human reason when allied to action, the French Revolution of 1789 exposed the erroneous belief that individuals were cast by nature to a station where they would remain fixed for their whole lives like mice on treadmills.

Across Europe, opportunities in education, industry, politics and elsewhere provided a ladder for individuals of lower orders to climb. Improving or bettering oneself became an active ideal to be aspired to, whether as an individual or as a member of a collectivity. This change in mentality brought with it an inducement to strive for success, what we now call an **achievement motive**. Without the achievement ethic there would be no motive: the two are inseparable.

The competitive activities that became sports mirrored changes in society and in consciousness. Benjamin Franklin's autobiography and, later, Samuel Smiles' *Self Help* were key texts, lauding hard work and perseverance. **Talent** and effort were the keys to success in rivalries; and the rivalries themselves were bound by rules that facilitated rather than restrained free expression. Outcomes were necessarily unequal, reflecting differences not only in aptitude but also in application. This was true in both sports and the economy; the values of enterprise and work became central.

In the mid-nineteenth century, at the height of British imperialism, a reviewer of Thomas Hughes' novel *Tom Brown's Schooldays* introduced the term 'muscular Christianity' to describe a Christian lifestyle in which young men would develop a strong **character** to complement their healthy bodies. This chimed perfectly with the achievement ethic with its stress on hard work, competitiveness, goal orientation and achieved (rather than ascribed) status. The creed of muscular Christianity was exported to many areas of what was then the British Empire. Religious organizations were extremely influential in disseminating muscular Christianity and, by implication, sports to all the colonial territories. The achievement ethic and the values, attitudes and behaviors it inspired became embedded in distant and diverse cultures.

The achievement motive proliferated in cultures that defined success and failure in terms of individuals' or groups' attainment of goals. While it may sound obvious, the achievement motive is meaningless in cultures where achievement is not positively evaluated or encouraged; where life is understood as an unstoppable cycle over which individuals have no power (for example, in many Pacific islands); or where individuals strive not to achieve but yield to nature, as in Australian aboriginal cultures. Such environments do not facilitate the development of an achievement ethic nor of the organized sports it has nurtured (though there is evidence of playful ball games in these parts, documented by Kendall Blanchard in *The Anthropology of Sport*, 1995).

Further reading

Lukes, S. (1973) *Individualism* Oxford: Blackwell.
Money, T. (1997) *Manly and Muscular Diversions: Public schools and the nineteenth-century sporting revival* London: Duckworth.

ACHIEVEMENT MOTIVE

Striving for success is often seen as a manifestation of an achievement motive (or **motivation**), something that induces a person to direct his or her behavior toward the attainment of certain goals. Motive is from *motus*, Latin for move. When that motive becomes established in a set of moral principles and regarded as a virtuous rule of conduct, it becomes an **achievement ethic**. The whole field of sports is guided by an achievement ethic: victory is sought after and defeat is to be avoided in every endeavor. Competitors are energized by an achievement motive in the sense that they personally seek success rather than failure and are prepared to defeat others in their pursuit of that goal.

The motive and the ethic coexist, of course: were victory and the striving for it not seen as worthy, the motive to pursue it would have little purchase. As it is, sports have prospered in cultures that have honored success. It is no accident that cultures that extol the virtues of **competition** and rivalry have produced high achievement-motivated individuals who excel in sports. There is unlikely to be an achievement motive at an individual level outside cultures that do not value success over failure.

The influential research of John W. Atkinson – especially with D.C. McClelland, R.A. Clark and E.C. Lowell, in *The Achievement*

Motive, published in 1953 – sheds light on the composition of the achievement motive. It is the combination of two personality constructs: the motive to approach success and the motive to avoid failure. According to Atkinson, all humans have both; it is the way in which they combine which affects whether one person will be achievement-motivated. Atkinson's research involved testing subjects for both the motive to succeed and the motive to avoid failure. For example, would they look for challenges, show persistence, remain unafraid to lose and blame themselves when making the **attribution** for success or failure? Or would they try to avoid failure, dodge challenges – preferring to compete against easy opponents – dislike being evaluated by others and attribute their performance to external factors, such as **luck** or hard opponents? Those who scored big on the first scale were said to have an achievement motive.

Situations also factor into Atkinson's model, which rates probability of success from 0 (no chance) to 1.00 (certainty) and builds in an incentive value (the lower the chance of success, the greater the incentive). An achievement-motivated kicker faced with a 50-yard field goal chance to win a game and no time left on the clock would relish the opportunity. A kicker without a strong motive would prefer either an easier, more certain task, such as a 25-yard attempt, or an impossibly tough kick from outside field goal range to avoid being blamed for the failure. So the type of situation determines whether the behavioral tendencies of the achievement-motivated player will come to the fore. As many situations in sport have a mid-range chance of success without a very high **incentive** value, the high achievement-motivated athlete is not always an asset; many situations demand a more conservative performer – a 'safe pair of hands.'

M.L. Maehr and J.G. Nicholls rejected many of Atkinson's assumptions about the invariance and objectivity of success and failure. Instead, they proposed that they are much more subjective, based on the **perception** of reaching or not reaching goals. There is, according to Maehr and Nicholls, 'cultural variation in the personal qualities that are seen to be desirable.' In other words, success and failure will be viewed differently in different cultures. While they do not examine the relationship between the achievement ethic and the achievement motive, Maehr and Nicholls acknowledge that it is necessary to understand the meanings of achievement rather than assume there is a single definition that holds good for all. Their interest was in exploring how, for example, winning may be the only criterion of achievement for some, while pleasing a coach by performing well may constitute achievement for others. Different goals give rise to different perceptions of success and failure. But, significantly, all individuals use goals of some kind to evaluate their achievements.

Achievement goals can be grouped into three kinds, according to Maehr and Nicholls: (1) to demonstrate ability; (2) to be task-involved (mastering a competence rather than assessing oneself against others); and (3) to seek social approval. The same competitor may have a different goal for each different sport, or at different times in his or her life, or may even have several goals at once. Michael Jordan was presumably motivated to achieve a successful outcome during his basketball career (1), but, while his venture into baseball was generally considered a failure, he may well have set himself a different goal, perhaps to master the sport rather than win anything (2).

Further reading

Maehr, M.L. and Brascamp, L.A. (1986) *The Motivation Factor: A theory of personal investment* Lexington MA: Lexington Books.

Maehr, M.L. and Nicholls, J.G. (1980) 'Culture and achievement motivation: a second look,' pp. 221–67 in Warren, N. (ed.) *Studies in Cross-Cultural Psychology* New York: Academic Press.

ADDICTION *see* dependence

ADHERENCE

Behaving according to a plan is adherence, from the French *adhérer*, to stick. 'Stickability' is a valuable quality in any athlete. 'It is imperative,' write Kerry Mummery and Leonard Wankel, 'that an athlete conscientiously *adhere* to the prescribed program of training and preparation in order to gain maximum benefit from his or her efforts.'

This raises questions, such as: what makes some athletes stick to their programs, while others shirk? While many people adhere to health-related exercise as a leisure time activity, training for **competition** is different. Its **goal** is not to enrich **body image** or lifestyle, but to improve performance. This is an instrumental objective, though participation sport also involves an **emotional** component – athletes enjoy competing, at least initially. At higher levels, a **commitment** to the utility of training is a more reliable predictor of adherence.

Consistent with the *theory of reasoned behavior*'s proposition that the main precursor of behavior such as exercise is intention, Mummery and Wankel's study of swimmers revealed that adherence to training (measured in terms of frequency, volume and **intensity**) was greatest among athletes who held strong intentions to participate in and complete prescribed training. A combination of the attitudes held toward a specific behavior and subjective norms (what the subject thinks others think) affects intention. The *theory of planned behavior* extends the previous theory and introduces behavioral **control** to the account. Volitional control in training for competitive sports is problematic: subjects do not actually choose to do thirty 60-meter sprints or nonstop crunches for three minutes or to get up at 4.00 a.m. to get to the training pool before it gets busy.

The swimmers in the study believed in the utility of their training: the outcome of their efforts would be improvements in performance. They also believed that other individuals who were important to them thought that they should complete their training. Swimmers who stuck to their regimens also perceived themselves as having the necessary abilities to complete the programs as required.

Should athletes fail to see any improvement in performance despite sticking to training schedules, then they may question the training's efficacy, the wisdom of their coach, or their own capabilities. In such circumstances, adherence is unlikely.

Further reading

Ajzen, I. (1991) 'The theory of planned behavior,' *Organizational Behavior and Human Decision Processes* vol. 50, pp. 179–211.

Mummery, W.K. and Wankel, L.M. (1999) 'Training adherence in adolescent competitive swimmers: an application of the theory of planned behavior,' *Journal of Sport & Exercise Psychology* vol. 21, pp. 313–28.

ADRENALINE RUSH

The sudden sensation of excitement and power that often occurs in stressful situations is described as an adrenaline rush, adrenaline (sometimes called *epinephrine*) being one of the two main hormones released by the medulla of the adrenal gland which covers part of the kidney – the word 'adrenaline' derives from the Latin for toward the kidney, *ad* meaning to and *renal* kidney. In sports **competition**, the rush of adrenaline into the system can act as a spur to athletes, often at unexpected moments. The reason is that adrenaline causes profound change in all parts of the body.

The release of the hormone effectively mobilizes the whole body for either *fight or flight* by stimulating the release of glycogen (which serves to store carbohydrates in tissues) from the liver, the expansion of blood vessels in the heart, brain and limbs, and the contraction of vessels in the abdomen. It diminishes fatigue, speeds blood coagulation and causes the spleen to release its store of blood. The eyes' pupils dilate. Sweat increases to cool the body and sugar is released into the bloodstream to provide more energy for vigorous muscular activity. The value of adrenaline release to the sports performer is obvious, which is why many often reflect on good performances as happening when 'the adrenaline was pumping' or try to break a **slump** during a competition by 'getting some adrenaline going.' The effects are similar to the stimulation of the sympathetic division of the autonomic **nervous system**: an advantageous state of **arousal**.

Under certain, usually dangerous, conditions, the skeletal muscles might receive up to 70 per cent of the cardiac output: that is, the blood pumped from the heart. More blood is fed to muscles that need it at the expense of the viscera, especially the abdomen, where the needs are not urgent. Feelings of pain and tiredness are minimized and the body is prepared for extraordinary feats.

The whole process is mobilized by the sympathetic division of the autonomic nervous system (ANS), which regulates heartbeat, breathing, digestion and other internal processes. The sympathetic division stimulates the body and causes it to expend energy. Once the adrenaline rush subsides, the parasympathetic division of the ANS kicks in to bring the body's function back into balance; for example, breathing and heart rate slow down and digestion increases.

While competitors consciously hope for an adrenaline rush at some point during a flaccid performance, the surge typically occurs in the context of events that use natural conditions rather than synthetic environments, such as a stadium or an indoor arena. Long-distance swimming, orienteering, car rallying and rock climbing are examples of sports in which the performers' lives may occasionally be in jeopardy. **Risk** creates perfect conditions for an adrenaline rush. The sense of exhilaration and might is difficult to reproduce artificially, of course, though part of the summer Olympics triathlon course in 2000 was held in Sydney harbor and it was speculated that the sharks that habitually lurk in the waters might hasten triathletes to personal bests. One wonders what distances long jumpers could cover if 100-foot drops replaced sandpits!

Some coaches have preached the benefits of **fear** to sporting performance. For example, Cus D'Amato, who trained world heavyweight champions Floyd Patterson and Mike Tyson among others, gave every boxer the same illustration of a deer crossing an open field. 'Suddenly, **instinct** tells him danger is there,' D'Amato related to writer Peter Heller, in his 1990 book *Tyson*, 'and nature begins the survival process, which involves the body releasing adrenaline into the bloodstream, causing the heart to beat faster and enabling the deer to perform extraordinary feats of agility and strength.'

D'Amato might have added the example of Maxwell Rogers, a Florida mother weighing 123lb (8st 11lb or 65.9kg), who lifted a 3,600lb (almost 2 tons or 1,633kg) station wagon under which her son was trapped. In normal circumstances, the task would have been impossible, perhaps even for weightlifters twice her weight. Yet the life-threatening nature of the predicament precipitated a number of physiological changes that allowed her body to perform extraordinarily.

One of the properties of the drug pseudoephedrine, which is found in many cold remedies and decongestants, is that it mimics the adrenaline rush. It is on most sports' list of banned substances. Five different types of the stimulant were found in the urine of Argentina's soccer player Diego Maradona when he was tested at (and subsequently banned from) the 1994 World Cup championships.

Further reading

Cashmore, E. (2000) 'Adrenaline rush,' pp. 5–6 in Cashmore, E. (ed.) *Sports Culture: An A–Z guide* London: Routledge.

Dunn, S. (1996) 'Thrills and chills: taking on a risky sport is not just an adrenaline rush – it's a glimpse into your soul as well,' *Shape* vol. 15, no. 6, pp. 116–19.

Sandford, B. (1987) 'The "adrenaline rush,"' *Physician and Sportsmedicine* vol. 15, no. 12, p. 184.

AGGRESSION

While 'aggression' has been used as an inclusive term to capture diverse behavior containing hostility, harm and violation, there is so little common ground among scholars that we might profitably start by establishing what it is *not*: 'An attitude, emotion or motive … Wanting to hurt someone is not aggression. Anger and thoughts might play a role in aggressive behavior, but they are not necessary or defining characteristics … Accidental harm is not aggression … kicking a bench is not … sadomasochistic and suicidal acts [are not],' according to Diane Gill.

Yet Barry Husman and John Silva contend that aggression is 'an overt verbal or physical act that can psychologically or physically injure another person or oneself,' meaning that sadomasochistic and suicidal acts would be, contrary to Gill, instances of aggression. In this definition, abusive email that can 'psychologically' injure its recipient counts as aggression. But Richard Cox emphasizes that the aggressive 'behavior must be aimed at another human being with the goal of inflicting physical harm ... there must be a reasonable expectation that the attempt to inflict bodily harm will be successful.'

Even the consistent feature of *intention* does not elicit complete agreement among scholars. Leif Isberg exchanges this for 'the concept of *awareness* that an act will or could injure someone.' Even if a person did not intend to harm another, the fact that he or she was aware that they might makes their behavior aggressive. Isberg deviates from most definitions when he suggests that aggression is not behavior, but rather 'an unobservable starting point for potentially aggressive behavior.'

There are other, deeper disagreements, but for present purposes we might propose that *aggression is behavior, or a propensity to behave in a way, that is either intended or carries with it a recognizable possibility that a living being will be harmed, physically or psychologically.* In this sense, aggression is quite different from what nowadays we call **aggressiveness**, or assertiveness. Both are from *aggressio*, Latin for attack.

Conventionally, two types of aggression are specified: *hostile* and *instrumental.* The primary **goal** of hostile aggression is to cause harm to another: a soccer player might believe he or she has been unfairly tackled and retaliate by chasing and striking feet-first at the opponent's ankles with no intention of retrieving the ball. With instrumental aggression, there is a specific purpose beyond the aggression itself and the intention to harm or awareness that the action might cause harm to another is incidental: the same soccer player, later in the game, might jump to head the ball, at the same time deliberately elbowing an opponent in the face – the goal is to head the ball and the aggression is a way of deterring another player who might otherwise obstruct the path to the goal. In both cases, aggressive behavior inflicts harm and is quite different from aggressiveness, or assertiveness, which involves legitimate goal-directed action though no necessary intention to hurt an opponent.

The distinction between hostile and instrumental aggression is not always clear-cut: in sports, all aggression has a point, a purpose – in short, a goal. Even an enraged athlete who intentionally bites an opponent's ear *à la* Tyson does so in the context of a **competition** in which he or she has the overarching aim of victory. Tyson's action in 1997 was widely interpreted by the media as the escape of 'the beast within,' his aggressive instincts breaking through his civilized façade.

Some schools of thought support this type of view, maintaining that aggression is a natural **drive**.

Ethologists (who study humans in the same way as they would any other animal) contend that we are born with an aggressive instinct that has been quite serviceable in our survival as a species. So we defend our 'natural' territory when it is under threat. Konrad Lorenz wrote that human aggression is like other forms of animal aggression, only we have learned to route it into safe outlets, sports being an obvious one.

Sigmund Freud too viewed sport as a way of discharging aggression. In his theory, we all have a *death* instinct that builds up inside us to the point where it must be discharged, either inwardly (self-destructive acts) or outwardly. Because we do not always have socially acceptable opportunities for turning our aggression outward, we *displace* it into acceptable channels. Sports are perfect: we can get all our aggression out of our system either by participating or by just watching; either way, we rid ourselves of the aggression.

Without denying that aggression had its source in a biological drive, other accounts **focused** on the context in which aggression manifests, noticing that some environments seem to have more potential for eliciting aggressive behavior than others. The competitive environment of sport often provides plenty of cues for aggression. Sports, of course, are crucibles of frustration: individuals pursue aims while others try to stop them. Several theorists have argued that frustration creates a readiness for aggressive behavior.

The frustration–aggression hypothesis, as it is called, states that, when goal-oriented behavior is blocked, an aggressive drive is induced. Further frustrations increase the drive. On this account, all aggressive behavior is produced by frustration. The hypothesis was introduced as an alternative to theories of aggression based on innate characteristics. Scholars such as John Dollard rejected the notion of human behavior as programmed by nature and argued instead that the way we act is the product of **stimuli** in the world about us – frustration being the stimulus that produces aggressive behavior. Unlike Lorenz, Freud and others who portrayed sports competition as **catharsis**, allowing all the aggressive energies to flow out, frustration–aggression theorists interpreted sports as heightening the possibility of aggression. Frustration of some order is inevitable in any competition. But while this might help explain why aggression of some kind is likely to appear in sports, it leaves the issue of spectator aggression unresolved.

A 1987 study by Robert Arms *et al.*, 'Effects on the hostility of spectators of viewing aggressive sports,' concluded that 'the observation of aggression on the field of play leads to an increase in hostility on the part of the spectators.' Why? If we are exposed to models who are rewarded for aggressive behavior as opposed to models who are punished, we are likely to imitate them. Research in the 1960s, much of it by Albert Bandura, revealed the powerful part played by imitation in shaping our behavior. Simply observing aggressive behavior can affect our own behavior, if that aggression was positively sanctioned in some way or, we should add, if the person interpreted the aggression as being positively sanctioned.

Bandura's famous **modeling** experiment with Bobo dolls involved asking groups of children to watch an aggressive model beating up a toy Bobo doll or treating it kindly. The tendency of the children was to copy the model they observed, especially when they witnessed the aggressive model being rewarded for the assault. Bandura concluded from this and other studies that we *learn* aggression and in this sense it is a social rather than natural phenomenon. Clearly, this finding is totally at odds with the view of many coaches and players who believe (presumably with Lorenz) that sports are a good way of letting off steam or getting our aggression out of our system. The aggression has never been in there, according to social learning theorists: we acquire it during our interactions with others. (Crudely summarized, sport is an outlet for aggression in biologically based approaches, a mediating factor in the frustration–aggression hypothesis and an environment in which aggression is acquired in social learning theory.)

This does not exclude frustration from the account: in social learning theory, frustration is one of several experiences that lead to an **emotional** arousal. But there may be others, including physical discomfort or even pleasant circumstances, such as dancing in a club. Aroused by the physical exertion of dancing and a feeling of well-being, a person may be aggressive toward someone who accidentally bumps into them and makes them spill a drink. It may well be that the aggressor has learned this response through observing others at the same club, whose behavior was rewarded. Even if the person had been thrown out, his or her peers may have been suitably impressed. Several studies indicate that emotional **arousal**, regardless of the source, can increase aggression when the requisite stimuli are present. The consequences of or the reaction to the aggression can have decisive effects in shaping future behavior.

But consequences are not always clear-cut. For example, Latrell Sprewell's attack on his coach in 1997 and Tyson's ear-biting in the same year both drew swift and sharp retribution in the forms of fines and suspensions. On the other hand, Dr Dre's public beating of a female rapper and TV host, while his bodyguards kept onlookers at bay, was condemned by many, though not necessarily other male devotees of rap for whom aggressive behavior in defense of one's status is an appropriately macho response. In one context, aggression is vilified; in the other, it is often endorsed. Governing federations or clubs frequently censure aggressive sports performers. This can serve to boost athletes' statuses with fans and establish them as models whose behavior is likely to be respected, if not imitated.

As noted before, most aggression in sport is instrumental, or goal-directed, with perhaps a modest amount of **fear** induced aggression (when a normally meek athlete is threatened by an aggressive opponent, experiences an **adrenaline rush** and fights rather than flees). Whether one understands its source as lying in natural or social realms, the importance of context is undeniable: aggression typically arises in the pursuit of objectives. Two athletes clashing aggressively during a contest may pass each other by or exchange banter when they meet in a shopping mall or a bar. This also applies to fans. However aggression in sport is conceived, the significance of the context in which it is expressed should not be underplayed.

Further reading

Gill, D.L (2000) *Psychological Dynamics of Sport and Exercise*, 2nd edition, Champaign IL: Human Kinetics.

Husman, B.F. and Silva, J.M. (1984) 'Aggression in sport: definitional and theoretical considerations,' pp. 246–60 in Silva, J.M. and Weinberg, R.S. (eds) *Psychological Foundations of Sport*, Champaign IL; Human Kinetics.

Isberg, L. (2000) 'Anger, aggressive behavior, and athletic performance,' pp. 113–33 in Hanin, Y.L. (ed.) *Emotions in Sport*, Champaign IL: Human Kinetics.

AGGRESSIVENESS

Expressing assertive, forceful, offensive, dominant tendencies, a person with aggressiveness relentlessly pursues goals but without necessarily engaging in intentional harmful behavior. The root is *aggressio*, Latin for attack. In sport, aggressiveness is typically applauded and carries a positive connotation, unlike actual **aggression**, which is directed toward damaging others.

While Burris Husman and John Silva, in 1984, disapproved of the term 'aggressiveness' as a 'popularized' attempt 'to legitimize behaviors that are illegal and injurious to opponents,' their favored term 'assertiveness' seems close, if not synonymous: 'This goal-directed behavior may, and often does, involve the use of legitimate verbal or physical force ... requires unusual energy and effort, which in most other social settings would appear to be aggressive behavior.' According to the authors, assertive behavior 'must be exhibited with no intent to harm or injure another person, nor may they violate the constitutively agreed upon rules of the sport.'

In the sports vernacular, 'aggressiveness' is now used interchangeably with 'assertiveness'. Athletes who show a ruthless disposition in their play are often praised for their desire to win at all costs. On the other hand, competitors who habitually make illegal challenges on opponents, frequently hurting and injuring them, are scolded and sometimes decried as 'dirty.'

Aggressiveness in sports is instrumental, in the sense that it is directed toward clear objectives; the *goals* may be specific (such as scoring in specific situations) or general (such as overall dominance in a **competition**). Tackling hard but fairly, without flinching and without obvious regard for one's own safety, would be an example of the former. Staring down, or **psyching** out an opponent by some other means, would be an instance of the latter. In neither case is any physical harm intended: the aggressiveness is intended to procure an advantage within the rules of the game. Whatever the context, aggressiveness to be effective must be *displayed*: the competitor must make visible to opponents and spectators at the outset that he or she is intent on reaching the desired goals. Aggressiveness should be pre-emptive. As a pre-emptive strike is designed to prevent an attack by disabling a threatening enemy, so aggressiveness – at its most potent – inhibits opponents, making them indecisive and wary.

Further reading

Husman, B.F. and Silva, J.M. (1984) 'Aggression in sport: definitional and theoretical considerations,' pp. 246–60 in Silva, J.M. and Weinberg, R.S. (eds) *Psychological Foundations of Sport* Champaign IL; Human Kinetics.

Widmeyer, W.N., Dorsch, K.D., Bray, S.R. and McGuire, E.J. (2002) 'The nature, prevalence, and consequences of aggression in sport,' pp. 328–51 in Silva, J.M. and Stevens, D.E. (eds) *Psychological Foundations of Sport* Boston MA: Allyn & Bacon.

AGING

The process of progressive, irreversible change in the body that occurs during the passage of time, aging (or 'ageing'), after a certain stage, results in a decline in task performance abilities and in mental agility –

though the latter may be offset by increased knowledge and experience. While it is often assumed to be an independent biochemical process, many believe aging is the product of an interaction with the social and physical environment and, as such, may vary across cultures and stages in history. In sports, aging defines a kind of parabola in which the competitor rises to **peak performance**, usually somewhere between late teens and early thirties, then proceeds on a downward curve to the point where he or she can no longer perform at a competitive level. Degenerative changes guarantee that a sports performer cannot endure past a certain age: aging increases the probability that a competitor will lose with more frequency and more emphatically as his or her **skill** degrades and types of body cells die. There are huge variations between individuals and sports.

Examples of the variability of aging abound. Fu Mingxia was 12 years old when she won the world diving championship in 1991. Nadia Comenici was 14 when she was awarded six perfect scores of 10 for her winning performance on the asymmetric bars at the 1976 Olympics. The other famed gymnast of the period, Olga Korbut, was considered old when she won Olympic gold at the age of 17; by 21, she was finished. Björn Borg, Stefan Edberg and John McEnroe were all dominant tennis champions, but none won a Grand Slam title after the age of 25. Wilfred Benitez had his first professional fight two months after his fifteenth birthday, won the first of three world titles at the age of 17, lost to Thomas Hearns when aged 23 and slid into obscurity thereafter.

In contrast to athletes such as these who hit their peak early and, in sporting terms, aged early, there are others who peaked much later. Archie Moore was a professional boxer for twenty-eight uninterrupted years and did not win a world title until he was 39; he was almost 50 when he had his last fight (which he won by a third round knockout). Miruts Yifter won two gold medals on the track at the 1980 summer Olympics at the age of 43. Forty-two-year-old Yekaterina Podko-payeva was the world's number one ranked female 1,500 meters runner in 1994. Linford Christie was an indifferent sprinter up to the age of 25: from then until he was 35, he won eleven major championship golds, and in the process became the oldest man (33) to win an Olympic 100 meters title. George Foreman turned professional in 1969 at the age of 20, won a world title at 23, another (after a ten-year retirement) at the age of 45 and fought his final fight at the age of 49.

It has been estimated that an adult human being produces 3–4 million cells per second; these replace a similar number of cells that have died. Some cells, such as muscle and nerve cells, do not undergo cell division at all in the adult being, while others, such as the cells in bone marrow that produce red blood cells, may divide twice in each 24-hour period. Obviously, the muscle and nerve-ending cells that are not replaced will cause an athlete to decline physically, which makes Foreman's experience all the more remarkable. Never a mobile fighter, Foreman was virtually stationary in his forties; his reactions were also relatively slow – no amount of training can improve reactions. But he had compensating attributes, including punch power and a vast experience that enabled him to use timing, balance and leverage to good effect. (There is also evidence that some loss of sensitivity to **pain** comes with age, so Foreman may not have felt some of the body shots that would make younger men wince!) Nevertheless, a sporting **life course** of almost 30 years is exceptional for boxing, as it is for most other sports, save those that are relatively sedate and carry little **risk** of serious injury. This is why Jack Nicklaus could tie for sixth place in the 1998 US Masters – ahead of favorite Tiger Woods – when he was 58.

Golf, like chess, bowls, snooker and several other sports, requires only limited physical prowess, a degree of 'mental agility,' but most importantly a great deal of judgement, anticipation and tactical awareness. These are values that are acquired through experience. While 'mental agility' as measured by **intelligence** tests, declines, experience increases, making the age of peak performance in these sports between 30 and 50.

In other sports, speed is a factor; and peaks typically arrive much earlier. John Elway's Super Bowl XXXIII win with Denver Broncos, at the age of 38, is a vivid exception, especially in a sport where the risk of **injury** is constant. Elway exhibited no evident slowdown in simple aimed movements or sensory motor tasks – i.e. making decisions about whether to pass, handoff, scramble, etc. (cognitive and intellectual rather than motor functions). Yet research has shown that, while there is a loss of 10 per cent in aimed movements between the ages of 20 and 70, there is a loss of up to 25 per cent in sensory motor tasks, and this may increase to 50 per cent on more complex tasks. While there are no definitive answers to why, the reason appears to be that the signals from the sense organs to the brain and from one part of the brain to another become weaker, while random neural activity in the brain tends to increase. The latter interferes with the former.

This is why, in some sports in which speed is not a factor, older players have no obvious disadvantage. The darts player usually takes time to settle, aim and perfect the throw so it is accurate. A subtle, experienced player refuses to be rushed; there are no points to be gained for speed. Despite this, some loss of sensibility to the detection of fine movements of various joints will eventually hamper a darts player, as will a reduction of sensitivity to touch and vibration.

Aging brings with it a loss of **memory**, the reason being that the transfer of data from short- to long-term storage is more troublesome and an amount of material is lost in the process. But material that has been safely stored is not forgotten more easily in later life: so well-learned motor skills, including driving, playing bridge or shooting, may be retained. New motor skills take longer to acquire. But Formula One drivers do not usually drive into their forties. This is because, while they remain proficient in motor skill and judgement, their reactions may slow and their visual acuity may be reduced. There are other reasons, of course: most have earned so much money by the time they reach their mid-thirties that they have no material need to continue in a sport where the risk of death is high.

Barring fatal injury, **retirement** is inevitable and this poses problems for some athletes: faced with more time and opportunities to pursue interests, but perhaps restricted by changing capacities and delayed-onset injuries (such as osteoarthritis), ex-athletes sometimes become disoriented and go through profound **personality** changes. Such changes are probably compounded by contemporary cultural values: youth, vigor and athleticism are idealized and individuals who once embodied all these but have since lost them all may suffer. On the surface, this may appear to be more poignant for women than men, though female athletes often maintain training and dietary regimens to stay in shape. No doubt several join the hundreds of thousands of women who attempt to counteract the visible signs of aging with face-lifts (rhytidectomy) and other forms of cosmetic surgery. There is some research indicating that continuing sports activity and other forms of exercise in middle and old age has the potential to promote **self-efficacy**, though no causal relationship between the two has been demonstrated. A **comeback** is always an option for an athlete who cannot cope without actual **competition**.

Aging certainly has many features of a universal process, though cultural variations alert us to the probability that types of diet and nutrition, standards of health care and sanitation and other environ-mental conditions can affect the pace at which aging proceeds. There are other cultural factors to consider, including the growth of an industry devoted to the postponement of aging (health clubs, health foods, surgery, etc.). In cultures that venerate the aged, such factors may not be present; but in those that elevate youth, the idea of aging is unlikely to be welcomed and there will be strenuous efforts at counteracting it – the evidence surrounds us.

Further reading

Austed, S.N. (1997) *Why We Age: What science is discovering about the body's journey through life*, New York: Wiley.

Brown, D.R. (1992) 'Physical activity, ageing and psychological well-being: an overview of the research,' *Canadian Journal of Sports Sciences* vol. 17, no. 3, pp. 185–92.

ANDROGYNY

From the Greek *androgunos*, a combination of *andros*, for man and *gune*, woman, androgyny is the condition of having certain male and female attributes. Androgen is the male hormone capable of developing and maintaining some male sexual characteristics. An androgyne is a human, or other kind of animal, possessing features of both males and females but which can usually be assigned to one biological **sex** or another – as distinct from a hermaphrodite (from the name of the son of the Greek mythological figure who was the son of Hermes and Aphrodite and who was joined in one body with the nymph Salmacis), which cannot be so assigned. In sports, female athletes who exhibit attributes typically associated with men as well as those associated with women have been called psychological androgynes.

Psychological androgyny is a term introduced in the 1970s when the feminist movement was in its ascendancy. It disputed the deterministic notion that one's biology determines capability, competence and aptitude; or, as a feminist slogan of the time expressed it, 'biology is not destiny.' Research indicated that female athletes, far from being limited by their biological sex, had a great many of the attributes traditionally assigned only to men.

The term came from the Bem Sex Role Inventory (BSRI), a sixty-item questionnaire designed in the early 1970s to test subjects' **personality** and relate this to biological sex. Twenty of the attributes on the scale reflected features popularly associated with masculinity in contemporary culture: independence, athleticism, assertiveness and so on. Another twenty included affection, gentleness, nurturance and other qualities often identified with popular conceptions of femininity. A further twenty were neither masculine nor feminine. Subjects who scored high on both masculine and feminine items were designated androgynous, while those who registered high scores on only one dimension or another were sex typed as masculine or feminine (those who scored low on both were undifferentiated). The test concluded that androgynous athletes were more flexible and better able to adapt to changing circumstances than their sex-typed colleagues.

The concept of psychological androgyny indicated that humans could possess proportions of both types of characteristics traditionally associated with one sex or the other and sex-typing was meaningless. Later research on female athletes built on the BSRI conclusions, further undermining the notion that females have particular types of personalities and dispositions which do not equip them for competitive sports.

Further reading

Bem, S.L. (1974) 'The measurement of psychological androgyny,' *Journal of Consulting and Clinical Psychology* vol. 42, pp. 155–62.

Del Rey, P. and Sheppard, S. (1981) 'Relationship of psychological androgyny in female athletes to self-esteem,' *International Journal of Sport Psychology* vol. 12, pp. 165–75.

ANDROSTENEDIONE

While 'andro,' as it is frequently abbreviated, is known principally as a training supplement, it is actually a natural androgen (a **sex** hormone responsible for the development of male sex characteristics) found in both males and females, produced mainly by adrenal cortices and, to a lesser extent, gonads.

Androstenedione is a precursor of testosterone, which is, of course, the most powerful androgen of all. A commercial synthesis of andro is legally available as a training supplement, and it was this substance that leapt into the public consciousness in 1998 when baseball hitter Mark McGwire revealed that he was a regular user. McGwire made the announcement when in the midst of his home run record-breaking season.

Major League Baseball did not include androstenedione on its list of banned substances, though Randy Barnes, the Olympic shot putter, was suspended for two years after andro was found in his sample. Taking andro was tantamount to illegal **doping** in many sports other than MLB.

Further reading

Yesalis, C. and Cowart, V. (1998) *The Steroids Game: An expert's look at anabolic steroid use in sports* Champaign IL: Human Kinetics.

ANGER

The **emotion** of anger is typically a reaction to offense, outrage, displeasure or acute frustration; it manifests in facial expressions, **body language**, an **arousal** of the sympathetic division of the autonomic **nervous system** and, at times, outright **aggression**. The word itself is probably drawn from Old Norse *angr*, grief, which in turn may derive from the Latin for choke, *angere*. While coaches typically warn that anger is an enemy of **composure** and militates against **control**, some athletes use it to their advantage. 'There's nothing wrong with getting a little angry as long as you use it positively,' former tennis pro Virginia Wade once reflected, adding that John McEnroe could 'orchestrate' so as to bring himself to his mettle. A study published in 1989 by McGowan and Schultz indicated that many athletes do likewise, although prior to a game rather than during it.

In his essay, 'Anger, aggressive behavior, and athletic performance,' Leif Isberg breaks anger into four components.

1 *Cognitive and motivational*: anger can enhance or impair **cognition** and hence judgement; it can also affect **achievement motive**. The social context in which the emotion arises may reinforce or inhibit the expression of anger.
2 *Bodily-somatic*: angry subjects have been shown to have an in-creased pulse rate and significantly high blood pressure (even sup-pressing anger may result in elevated blood pressure); there is contradictory evidence about the role of anger in the **risk** of cardiovascular disease, some studies suggesting that the opportu-nity to release anger facilitates heart recovery – but only in men.
3 *Behavioral*: anger is typically expressed in the form of aggression, though, of course, **aggressiveness** in sports is not always ac-companied by anger.
4 *Affective*: there are situational determinants that affect whether or not anger will be expressed, i.e. a 'person may let all anger out in one situation but keep a tight lid on it in another.'

According to Isberg, the intensity and content of anger is determined by the environment in which it occurs.

Like other emotions, anger has effects on athletic performance. 'Anger focuses the athlete's attention on the past,' write Heather Deaner and John Silva, 'but sport demands a present and future orientation to respond quickly and anticipate play.' On this account, anger distracts an athlete away from 'task-relevant variables (components of the game)' and toward 'outside variables.' Yet is this true for all sports?

McGowan and Schultz's research concluded that college football players performing relatively simple tasks used anger as a pre **competition** motivating strategy: a way of getting **psyched** up. Anger, in common with other strong emotions, often displaces reason, and in sports, no less than any other sphere of activity, it can seriously interfere with the rational prudence that is necessary to all but the most basic of tasks. So a weight lifter, whose sole task is to raise a bar, may find anger beneficial in executing a basic lift. Similarly, a shot putter might put anger to good use. In these and some other events, technique has already been mastered and success depends on a brief, explosive response. One of the purported effects of **doping** with anabolic steroids is the tendency for the user to undergo bouts of 'roid rage,' which may enhance performance. On the other hand, fencers, rhythmic gymnasts, archers and myriad other athletes who rely on **skill**, fineness of judgement and a degree of composure, would be disadvantaged by experiencing anger prior to or during competition.

Several scholars, including Carol Tavris, have written of how subjects who are particularly prone to habitual bouts of anger develop a **dependence** on the feelings associated with it. The physiological processes that accompany anger are not dissimilar to those accompanying sexual arousal and, when supplemented with the empowerment reported by some angry subjects, this produces an agreeable **emotional** state – though not one with necessarily agreeable consequences, of course.

One of the most explosive fits of anger in the heat of competition came at the 1993 world track and field championships. Leading the 10,000 meters at the bell, Moses Tanui became irritated by the near proximity of second-placed Haile Gebrselassie, who actually ran so close that he trod on the leader's heel, causing his shoe to come loose. Tanui erupted in rage, clapping his hands against his head before wildly kicking off the loose shoe and sprinting for home. His race plan abandoned and badly fatigued, Tanui was vulnerable to the patient Gebrselassie who reeled him in on the home bend and won the race.

Had Tanui managed his anger and stuck to his tactics, he may still have lost; he did, after all, have only one shoe properly fastened and his rival's finishing burst was deadly. Still, Tanui's failure to control his rage did not help him. Nor does it help other athletes. Containing emotion is one of the assignments of the many athletes who make use of finesse and artfulness. This is a strenuous activity in a context abounding with potential for anger. In 1989, Leonard Berkowitz argued convincingly that feelings of frustration lead to anger and, ultimately, aggression. Sports, by definition, involve frustration: while one party strives to achieve a **goal** of some sort, another aims to prevent that happening – and vice versa. In the absence of a complete blowout, the competitive activity continually generates frustration. As person or team A pursues their clearly defined ambition – to win – person or team B does their best to frustrate that ambition. If ambitions were not frustrated, there would be no competition. Anger is most likely to occur when the source of the frustration is seen as illegitimate: for instance, if foul play persistently impedes an athlete, he or she is more likely to experience anger, an anger which may either be diffuse or directed at the offenders. This is commonplace in contact and collision sports where physical impact is germane to the competition.

Anger is by no means confined to such sports. Witness, for example, tennis matches in which one player becomes frustrated at his or her own inability to execute shots. The anger is directed not at the opponent, but inwards; it manifests in truculent screaming and, occasionally, smashing rackets. Penalties accrue to players who express their anger in this way, so it is in their own interests to contain or manage their emotions as far as possible. The case of tennis is instructive in another sense: prior to the 1980s, racket smashing was unheard of. Yet it became so prevalent that tennis authorities actually designated it racket abuse and introduced penalties to restrain it. The diffusion of angry histrionics culminating in racket breaking may well have owed something to **modeling**.

Inspired perhaps by the previously mentioned McEnroe, tennis players contrived theatrical performances, exaggerating their anger with displays of showmanship. It was almost as if a new script had been written for the expression of anger.

Further reading

Deaner, H. and Silva, J.M. (2002) 'Personality and sport performance,' pp. 48–65 in Silva, J.M. and Stevens, D.E. (eds) *Psychological Foundations of Sport* Boston MA: Allyn & Bacon.

Isberg, L. (2000) 'Anger, aggressive behavior, and athletic performance,' pp. 113–33 in Hanin, Y.L. (ed.) *Emotions in Sport* Champaign IL: Human Kinetics.

McGowan, R.W. and Schultz, B.B. (1989) 'Task complexity and affect in collegiate football,' *Perceptual and Motor Skills* vol. 69, no. 2, pp. 671–4.

ANOREXIA NERVOSA *see* eating disorders

ANXIETY

There are several forms of anxiety, all related by a general **emotional** and cognitive reaction to a stimulus in which apprehension and trepidation are present. The term is from the Latin *anxius*, from *angere*, to choke. While anxiety often involves the **perception** of a threat, it should be distinguished from **fear**, which always assumes a person, event or object, **arousal**, which is usually understood as a physiological response to a stimulus, and **stress**, which is also a physiological response either to stimuli or to the absence of a stimulus (known as *hypostress*).

The unpleasant sensations and physical changes result from a stimulus. But, as John Raglin and Yuri Hanin point out, the same stimulus 'may be perceived as a beneficial challenge to one individual, threatening to another, and neutral to a third.' So, in **competition**, anxiety, as Mark Anshel expresses it, 'reflects the performer's feelings that something may go wrong, that the outcome may not be successful, or that performance failure may be experienced.' To a different performer, the same competition may be an opportunity to demonstrate his or her mettle, or **character**. Perhaps the most effective antidote to anxiety is **confidence**.

Trait anxiety is a relatively fixed behavioral disposition: some athletes are disposed toward some anxiety regardless of the quality or level of the challenge: many top athletes confess to vomiting and other nauseous manifestations before a competition. These are known as high A-trait individuals and their tendency is to appraise situations as threatening. *State anxiety* is a less permanent condition and affects competitors intermittently, depending on their perception of the particular situation: it may subside or increase during the actual competition.

At least one study (of top cricketers, by Jones and Swain in 1995) found that highly skilled performers interpret their anxiety as helpful to their performance. Less skilled athletes did not. Presumably the absence of anxiety would in itself be troublesome to top players: complacency can set in. The type of anxiety that can actually enhance performance is known as *somatic* state (pertaining to the body: increase in heart rate, sweating, muscle tension, etc.) and this ebbs and flows during a contest.

Cognitive state anxiety (the mental dimension), on the other hand, usually has a negative effect on athletic performance. It can take the form of 'pre-competition nerves' and may continue to affect performance throughout a competition, particularly at crucial moments. Athletes whose performances wither in critical situations are said to **choke**.

Anxiety typically results from the perception of some kind of threat, either to the physical self or to the reputation; it can also be precipitated by uncertainty or even a disruption of routine. While some athletes simply never suffer from trait anxiety, it would be unusual if they did not experience some sort of state anxiety. Even athletes known for their **composure** are likely to approach a big contest or a **comeback** after **injury** with some anxiety. The 'secret' of those who are able to overcome this is that they interpret their symptoms as propitious: they actually use it to their advantage, probably feeling anxiety and the physiological effects associated with it but interpreting this as normal in the circumstances. **Reversal theory**, as promoted by John Kerr, suggests that, while the symptoms may be interpreted positively or negatively, competitors sometimes transfer from one to another during a competition – a reversal. What matters is not so much the objective level of anxiety, but how the athlete interprets and responds to the situation.

The Competitive State Anxiety Inventory–2, devised by Rainer Martens and colleagues, was one of several instruments designed to identify and measure anxiety levels in changing situations, though it yielded few definitive conclusions. There are few reliable indicators of when cognitive or somatic anxiety will take hold, nor when or how anxiety will impact athletic performance. Raglin and Hanin believe the **IZOF (individual zones of optimal functioning)** model offers promise: this attempts to isolate an ideal range of anxiety in which an athlete can reach **peak performance**. They recognize the significance of **emotion**, meaning that athletes' optimal anxiety zones are highly individual. On this account, general interventionist strategies to reduce – or induce – anxieties in athletes are unlikely to be successful; approaches should be sensitive to individuals and contexts.

Further reading

Anshel, M.H. (1997) *Sport Psychology: From theory to practice*, 3rd edition, Scottsdale AZ: Gorsuch Scarisbrick.

Kerr, J.H. (ed.) (1999) *Experiencing Sport: Reversal theory* New York: Wiley.

Raglin, J.S. and Hanin, Y.L. (2000) 'Competitive anxiety,' pp. 93–111 in Hanin, Y.L. (ed.) *Emotions in Sport* Champaign IL: Human Kinetics.

Smith, R.E. and Smoll, F.L. (1990) 'Measurement and correlates of sport-specific cognitive and somatic trait anxiety: the sport anxiety scale,' *Anxiety Research* vol. 2, pp. 263–80.

APPLIED SPORT PSYCHOLOGY

In contrast to theoretical or pure sport psychology, applied sport psychology is devoted to employing or making use of discoveries, insights and knowledge. In a way, the description is implicit in the term: 'applied' (from the Latin *applicare*, fasten to) means putting one thing to another; and 'psychology' is, of course, formed from 'psych' (*psukhe* is Greek for soul, or life) and 'logy', denoting a subject of study (*logos* is Greek for word).

Ralph Vernacchia reasons that: 'One of the accepted tenets of applied sport psychology is the belief that thought precedes and influences athletic performance.' A science, however imperfect, of sport must be based on a body of existing and developing knowledge derived from rational research, judicious argument and informed discussion. Its applied branch should properly extend these principles into practical settings, advocating the use of strategies and interventions that are themselves based on reason rather than, for example, **superstition**, custom or groundless beliefs.

Sport psychology's practical purpose lies in, as J.M. Williams and W.F. Straub usefully describe it, 'identifying and understanding psychological theories and techniques that can be applied to sport and exercise to enhance the performance and personal growth of athletes.' In fact, sport psychology was created in this spirit, the work of Bruce Ogilvie and Thomas Tutko in 1966 imparting this in its title *Problem Athletes and How to Handle Them*. Arnold Beisser's *The Madness in Sport* showed the virtues of the individual case study approach – an approach that is still pursued today.

In his preface to the volume edited by Mark Thompson *et al.*, *Case Studies in Applied Sport Psychology: An educational approach*, David Cook writes: 'We believe that sport psychology is an art and that case studies provide a powerful tool.' It is an unusual but revealing reading of applied sport psychology: not as a science, but as an art. While he does not elaborate, we might take Cook's point to mean that, while sport psychology itself may aspire to producing scientifically verifiable knowledge, employing that knowledge is more akin to an art. It requires imagination, interpretation, design and skillful execution if it is to have practical utility.

The burgeoning of sport psychology in competitive sports settings has led to what might be regarded as a pre-eminence of the applied division. Sport psychologists are retained as consultants by sports clubs, Olympic squads and even in commerce and industry. This has not always been the case. David Wiggins traces the roots of discipline back to the nineteenth century, showing how much of the early research was not guided by practical imperatives. Wiggins identifies George Fitz's experiments on **reaction time** in 1895 as the first significant academic study to have 'ramifications for sport psychology.'

While in recent years applications have become crucial, sport psychology, like any other mature discipline, has developed a **nomothetic** tradition dedicated to discovering 'laws' or generalizations. This received a boost through the research and theorizing of Rainer Martens, who distinguished between applied knowledge and applied research, the former 'sifting through all the research available on a problem, using one's tacit knowledge regarding the problem, and developing creative programs for how to solve it' (in his 1987 article 'Science, knowledge, and sport psychology'). In other words, while the separation between applied and academic sport psychology may appear distinct, the former cannot exist without the output of the latter.

Further reading

Martens, R. (1987) 'Science, knowledge, and sport psychology,' *The Sport Psychologist* vol. 1, pp. 29–55.

Thompson, M.A., Vernacchia, R.A. and Moore, W.E. (eds) (1998) *Case Studies in Applied Sport Psychology: An educational approach* Dubuque IA: Kendall/Hunt.

Wiggins, D.K. (1984) 'The history of sport psychology in North America,' pp. 9–22 in Silva, J.M. and Weinberg, R.S. (eds) *Psychological Foundations of Sport* Champaign IL: Human Kinetics.

Williams, J.M. and Straub, W.F. (1998) 'Sport psychology: Past, present and future', pp. 1–10 in Williams, J.M. (ed.) *Applied Sport Psychology: Personal growth to peak performance*, 3rd edition, Mountain View CA: Mayfield.

AROUSAL

When stirred to activity, we experience a state of alertness, anticipation and all-round readiness described as arousal. It is a diffuse pattern of activities, both physiological and cognitive, that prepares us for a task. The word itself is formed from *a*, meaning on, up, or out, and *rouse*, for startle or become active. Typically, a high level of arousal involves the sympathetic autonomic **nervous system**: metabolic rates increase, as does respiratory volume; blood vessels constrict, pupils dilate and sweat glands open. **Attention** narrows and focus sharpens as we approach the task. Whether a person experiences such changes as a desirable part of **psyching** up for a task or a source of **anxiety**, apprehension or downright **fear**, depends both on the individual and the context, as well as the moment-to-moment changes in circumstances.

Some activation is needed for any task, whether watching a game of baseball on television or playing in the field. The fielder will be alert and prepared to respond as the pitcher settles on the mound; but if the hitter strikes the ball in his direction he will experience an increase in arousal as he runs to catch the ball.

Arousal might increase during any sports **competition** when a sudden, unexpected event occurs, no matter how minor: a plane passing overhead might arouse a tennis player preparing to serve, or a particularly rowdy fan may raise the arousal level of a football player; more seriously, a boxer leading comfortably on points might be knocked down by a speculative shot, causing a sharp arousal. All tasks have an optimal level of arousal: the aim of athletes is to calibrate that level to the vagaries of competition while maintaining **composure**. Björn Borg was famous for his ability to sustain the appropriate level of arousal throughout any game of tennis, never becoming so over-aroused that he tightened up and made errors, yet never drifting into the complacency that sometimes accompanies under-arousal.

The precise relationship between arousal and sports performance has occupied psychologists since the 1950s, when **drive** theory's equation *performance = arousal + skill level* held sway. A high level of arousal will assist a performance if the athlete has a high degree of **skill**; but it will hurt a performance by an athlete without skills. The formula was crude and unreliable and was superseded by others, one of the most influential being the inverted-U theory.

If levels of arousal are imagined as the horizontal axis of a graph with 'low' plotted to the left of 'high' and performance plotted along the vertical axis, then we may think of arousal as defining an inverted U-shape. Performance is optimal between low and high and tapers off if arousal is either too low or too high. Borg, along with several other imperturbable athletes, consistently operated with arousal levels inside the arc at the top of the inverted U. Other athletes seem to reach that state only occasionally or, in the case of James 'Buster' Douglas, just once: in 1990, he produced one of the upsets of the twentieth century when he stopped the hitherto unbeaten Mike Tyson; yet in previous and subsequent fights, Douglas seemed restrained and distracted, never approaching the levels of arousal he experienced in that one fight.

Boxing, like football and sprinting, is a sport in which powerful gross motor behavior is crucial, but optimum performance in other sports relies more on fine motor skills. So, darts and pool players will probably reach **peak performance** when their arousal levels are at lower levels. Imagine this as the arches of the McDonald's 'M,' with the left arch describing the arousal curve of darts, pool and other sport performers who need low arousal levels to hit peaks. Still others need to switch: the precision and fineness of judgement Tiger Woods used when putting probably required only a modest level of arousal, but a drive involved cognitive activity plus muscular activity and almost certainly required a much higher level of arousal.

While inverted-U theory looked good on paper, actual competition tended to expose its limitations. How, for instance, can it explain Jana Novotna's extraordinary collapse in the 1993 Wimbledon final? Leading 4–1 in games and 40–0 up with serve in the final set, Novotna, who had exuded **confidence** up to this point, seemed stricken with anxiety and disintegrated in the face of her opponent Steffi Graf's consistency. Novotna's reputation for choking was boosted two years later in the French Open when she allowed Chanda Rubin to survive nine match points and crashed to defeat. Richard Cox gives a comparable example from the 1996 Masters when Greg Norman surrendered a six-shot lead with one round to go and lost to Nick Faldo. In these instances, results suggest the onset of a catastrophe: performance did not decline smoothly as the athletes, sensing victory, became too aroused, but suffered an abrupt descent – graphically resembling an inverted-$\sqrt{}$.

To explain this, Fazey and Hardy argued that, if a competitor is highly physiologically aroused and experiences cognitive state anxiety, then a sudden and often dramatic deterioration will occur: in other words, a catastrophe. High levels of physiological arousal do not in themselves cause downfalls: it is when they are combined with increases in cognitive state anxiety. The prospect of closing in on a victory can precipitate this kind of anxiety and, once the catastrophe has occurred, small reductions in arousal will do nothing to get the performance back to its former level. As most catastrophes happen toward the end of a competition, it is often too late for the aroused athlete to rescue the situation.

The effort of many athletes, including distance runners, is to combine an optimum level of arousal with a degree of **relaxation** – the two are not at all incompatible, as Yuri Hanin's **IZOF (individual zones of optimal functioning)** model shows. The IZOF model strays from theories that suggest general principles and stresses that each performer has individual levels of optimal intensity. Hanin used a self-report method, asking athletes to identify which types of positive and negative emotions they experience prior to and during competition. Some level of anxiety is desirable. While arousal has physiological dimensions, Hanin is more interested in investigating its **emotional** side. The model might help explain improbable upsets, such as Douglas' win or the wild-card Goran Ivanisevich's 2001 Wimbledon triumph. Presuming they have modest opposition, the favored individuals remain outside their ZOFs and fail to get sufficiently aroused, while the underdogs function effectively within their own zones.

Like the other theories discussed, IZOF works best when focusing on individuals. But many sports involve more complex, collective forms of arousal that may transmit throughout a team. Returning to catastrophes, we might mention the 1992 collapse of the Houston Oilers in the 1992 NFL play-offs. Aroused to what appeared to be an optimal level, the Oilers ran up a seemingly unassailable 32-point third-quarter lead against the Buffalo Bills. Confronted with an almost certain win, the whole Houston team seemed to tense up visibly, each player becoming affected by a contagion of negative anxiety. Houston contrived to lose 38–41.

The concept of **social facilitation** is another factor that complicates studies of arousal. Operating at an optimal level of arousal in relatively mundane competitions is a different proposition from performing in front of large crowds in crucial games: some performers can rise to the occasion, reaching appropriate levels of arousal without becoming anxious; others become too aroused and fail to perform when the situation demands, often fearing the evaluations of others.

While arousal is clearly a vital concept in understanding the psychology of sports performance, generalizations about it are vitiated by mediating variables, including the individual, the task variables and the context in which the arousal takes place. Equally, generalizations about how best to manage arousal or harness it most effectively are notoriously difficult to formulate.

Further reading

Cox, R.H. (1998) *Sport Psychology: Concepts and applications*, 4th edition, Boston MA: McGraw-Hill.

Fazey, J. and Hardy, L. (1988) *The Inverted-U Hypothesis: A catastrophe for sport psychology?* British Association of Sports Sciences, Monograph No. 1, Leeds: National Coaching Foundation.

Hanin, Y.L. (ed.) (2000) *Emotions in Sport* Champaign IL: Human Kinetics.

Hill, K.L. (2001) *Frameworks for Sport Psychologists* Champaign IL: Human Kinetics, chapters 2 and 3.

ASSERTIVENESS *see* **aggressiveness**

ATTENTION

The faculty of **perception** that allows us to select and bring into focus some features of our environment while screening out others, attention, as its root word *attentio* (Latin for take notice of) suggests, is directed: we *attend to* characteristics that lie outside us or to aspects of ourselves, often consciously but sometimes without being explicitly aware of the process. Effective sports performance demands that an athlete's attention be directed as selectively as possible at relevant persons, circumstances and other factors, at the same time excluding irrelevancies.

Cricket captains must attend to a complex of factors, including weather, state of pitch, opponents and opponents' strengths, weaknesses and anticipated strategies as well as their own team's qualities and the likely changes in physical environment over the period of the game (which can last five days). Hundred meter freestyle swimmers, by contrast, must attend to their sport in a way that shuts out a great many environmental factors and focuses more narrowly on the execution of their own singular performance.

One way is to think of attention as a series of pools or spaces, each with separate resources for different senses, sight, hearing and tactility. At times in a **competition**, an athlete might need to watch very carefully and listen, but without needing to touch, still less smell. At other times the sense of touch may be paramount, as might sound and vision, so the athlete deploys all three to attend to the tasks. Just after the snap, a quarterback will need breadth of vision to pick his receiver, touch to ensure the pass or handoff is just right and sound to be able to listen for defense players from behind. Obviously, we do not have limitless attentional capacities. The same quarterback could not attend to all these and wave to his wife in the crowd – at least not without getting sacked. His particular job at that moment will require his entire attentional capacity.

So every sports performer must become adept at **gating**, the ability to attend selectively to relevant information while screening out irrelevancies.

Because of the complexity of our powers of **concentration**, we can attend either to an extremely restricted range of sensory material or to innumerable **stimuli** in the environment simultaneously, while we also remain aware of our own thoughts, feelings and behavior. So attention can be broad or narrow, external and internal. This is the scheme of Robert Nideffer. Our quarterback will probably be using *broad* attention, taking in a wide range of cues when finding his receiver, his attention also directed *externally* on objects and circumstances outside himself. A diver peering from a board over an Olympic pool will be attending very *narrowly*, probably only to his or her posture and balance, and *internally*, probably listening to the cadence of his or her breathing.

Further reading

Eysenck, M.W. (1996) 'Attention,' pp. 302–18 in Colman, A.M. (ed.) (1996) *Companion Encyclopedia of Psychology*, vol. 1, London: Routledge.

Janelle, C.M., Singer, R.N. and Williams, M.A. (1999) 'External distribution and attentional narrowing: visual search evidence,' *Journal of Sport & Exercise Psychology* vol. 21, pp. 70–91.

Nideffer, R.M. (1976) 'Test of attentional and interpersonal style,' *Journal of Personality and Social Psychology* vol. 34, pp. 394–404.

ATTRIBUTION

The act of assigning or imputing a characteristic or motive to oneself or others is known as attribution; this is the exact meaning of its root term, the Latin *attributum*. In sports, the attribution of causality is of special interest: when athletes explain the outcome of a competitive performance, they attribute the causes either to personal factors, or to the actions of other people or aspects of the physical environment, or to a combination of these.

Wherever athletes believe the responsibility for their performance lies is the *locus of causality*, or locus of **control**. This means that if they believe they should accept blame or praise as the architect of their own destiny, the locus is *internal*. On the other hand, if they believe they are at the mercy of forces beyond their control, the locus is *external*. Attribution research built on the early work of Fritz Heider, who in 1958 argued that everyone craves order in their lives and is constantly searching for ways of predicting and controlling the seemingly unpredictable and uncontrollable flow of life.

Bernard Weiner argued that we attempt to understand success and failure in terms of ability, effort, task difficulty and **luck**, the latter two being out of our control, of course. Ability and task difficulty are stable in that they remain relatively consistent, while effort and luck are variable and, in the case of luck, random. **Emotion** and **expectancy** also factor into the equation, the result of which determines future behavior. While we do not know how Taiwan's weight lifter Feng-

Ying Li attributed her silver medal in the 53kg class at the 2000 Olympics, let us imagine it was to an internal locus: that she had not worked hard enough in training on her clean and jerk, for example. This was within her control and something she could change in the future. Alternatively, she might have believed it was due to a *force majeure*, an unforeseeable course of events: the gold medallist, Yang Xia of China, broke the world record in her winning performance and that 225kg was simply beyond Li's capability. Thus, nothing in her power could have altered the medal positions. Li's future performance would be based on how she made her attributions.

Research had been done on how attribution patterns differ between men and women: the work is inconclusive, though women are found to locate causes externally more than men. Among the reasons offered for this difference are a 'fear of success' that is more prevalent among women, and the higher expectations of men. Neither is convincing.

More certain is the finding that more skilled athletes, who have experienced success, attribute failure to unstable, external factors (incompetent officiating; bad luck) because they realize failure is temporary. Combined with a willingness to attribute success (whether individual or as part of a team) to effort or other internal variables suggests a tendency to protect their self – which is obviously important in sustaining **self-efficacy** and, ultimately, **confidence**. Less skilled athletes who have tasted defeat more often are likely to attribute failure to their own deficiencies; this leads to low future expectations, the likelihood of further defeats and a probable withdrawal from **competition**. Sometimes this group might experience a condition known as **learned helplessness**.

Further reading

McAuley, E. and Duncan, T.E. (1990) 'Cognitive appraisal and affective reactions following physical achievement outcomes,' *Journal of Sport & Exercise Psychology* vol. 11, pp. 187–200.

Metzler, J. (2002) 'Applying motivational principles to individual athletes,' pp. 80–106 in Silva, J.M. and Stevens, D.E. (eds) *Psychological Foundations of Sport* Boston MA: Allyn & Bacon.

AUTOGENIC

Formed from *autos*, Greek for self, and *gen*, for produced, autogenic is often used synonymously with 'autogenous' to describe actions that are self-initiated. In sports, autogenic **relaxation** techniques are practiced as part of training regimes. They were first introduced in the 1950s by Johannes Schultz, who, when working with patients under **hypnosis**, discovered that his subjects reported a heaviness of limbs and a sensation of warmth. His version of autogenic training was designed to reproduce the two states.

Typically, autogenic relaxation involves self-initiated procedures in which the subject experiences progressive relaxation through sensations of weight and heat. **Imagery** is also used, as is **self-talk**. Athletes have been known to use autogenic training as a form of self **reinforcement**. The technique has been commercialized in the form of audio and videotapes which contain instructions and suggested self-statements.

Further reading

Liggett, D.R. (2000) *Sport Hypnosis* Champaign IL: Human Kinetics.
Williams, J.M. and Harris, D.V. (1998) 'Relaxation and energizing techniques for regulation of arousal,' pp. 324–37 in Williams, J.M. (ed.) *Applied Sport Psychology: Personal growth to peak performance*, 3rd edition, Mountain View CA: Mayfield.

AUTOMATICITY

True to its root *automatos* (Greek for acting of itself) automaticity refers to the property of a process that operates independently of conscious **control** and **attention**. In sports, athletes, having mastered a basic **skill**, can often execute it without **concentration**, focusing instead on other aspects of their performance such as tactics or their opponent's intentions. Aspiring golfers are discouraged from thinking about their swing: once the basic technique is practiced, they should emulate proficient golfers and allow the swing to be automatic. The same injunction applies to all sports **skill acquisition**.

In classic sports examples, the arduous, conscious process of learning how to tee off, serve, parry, pass, etc. are eventually replaced by automatic operations: skilled performers can surrender the information on how to consign the skill to **memory** and think not about what they are doing but why they are doing it, for what overall purpose and what they will do if it does not work. Too much reflection on the mechanical elements of a skill will actually interfere with its smooth functioning.

This stage in the skill acquisition process is often called the *autonomous* stage, though it should be stressed that not every athlete can attain it: pitchers, for example, sometimes need to make conscious adjustments to their style to accommodate either particular conditions or different batters or perhaps a loss of form. The same applies across the spectrum of sports performers. When skills erode, automaticity gradually disappears, and retiring athletes often rue that they have to think about what they once did automatically.

There is no single process that leads to automaticity. Coaches often use schedules of **reinforcement** designed to reward the appropriate behavioral skill. Approaches based on changing an athlete's **cognition** of situations and persons (including him or herself) have also been shown to be effective, as has **cognitive–behavioral modification** which ushers athletes toward a position from which they can see the demonstrable effects of their skilled behavior and change their thinking about that behavior accordingly. The ultimate aim is to preclude any conscious thought about the skill at all.

Further reading

Fitts, P.M. and Posner, M.I. (1967) *Human Performance* Belmont CA: Brooks/ Cole.

AUTONOMIC NERVOUS SYSTEM *see* biofeedback and nervous system

AUTOTELIC

As its name suggests, an autotelic experience is engaged in for its own sake, without any instrumental purpose. *Auto* is Greek for self and *telos* means **goal**. Behavior may be described as autotelic when, as Karen Lee Hill puts it: 'The activity itself is intrinsically motivated, and external rewards are reduced to a position of secondary motivators.' Sometimes people's characteristics are described as autotelic, meaning that they are primarily oriented to their own aims and purposes, including self-protection.

References are made to autotelic experiences in various accounts of sport. For example, the concept of **flow** has nine elements, one of which is autotelic. **Reversal theory** involves a **telic state** and paratelic state, which bears close resemblance to autotelic experience. The **IZOF (individual zones of optimal functioning)** model includes several performance-related states in which autotelic experience may occur. Athletes who report that they have been either training or competing in the **zone** sometimes describe a near-autotelic state.

Further reading

Hanin, Y.L. (ed.) (2000) *Emotions in Sport* Champaign IL: Human Kinetics.
Hill, K.L. (2001) *Frameworks for Sport Psychologists* Champaign IL: Human Kinetics.

BEM SEX ROLE INVENTORY *see* **androgyny**

BIOFEEDBACK

The technique that enables the manipulation or modification of a process or organism by returning information about results, effects or outputs is known as biofeedback – from *bios*, Greek for human life. Its basic principle is that humans cannot sense the current state of, for example, heart rate and blood pressure, and so cannot alter them. By feeding back information about them, especially about the difference between desired and actual somatic functions, we can minimize that difference. Athletes have used biofeedback to align their bodies with desired states.

Mathematician Norbert Wiener, who subscribed to the philosophy that humans are complex machines, introduced the term 'biofeedback' (and 'cybernetics,' according to Pesi Masani in *Norbert Wiener, 1894–1964*). For Wiener, biofeedback is a method of controlling a system by 'reinserting back into it the results of its past performance.' Humans, as machines, can be controlled in the same way. In fact, some degree of biofeedback is essential to our survival and we use biofeedback habitually. For example, when we walk into a dark room and grope forward until we feel something, kinesthetic feedback (i.e. sensations of muscles, tendons and joints) tells us our arm's position so that we can make the next move. In other words, we use the information we receive through our bodies to adjust and regulate our behavior. This is made possible by our autonomic **nervous system** (ANS).

The ANS is a secondary system of nerves, many cell bodies of which lie outside the brain and spinal cord and receive information from receptors in the various organs of the body. After receiving the information, the bunches of cell bodies – known as ganglia – send out appropriate instructions to muscles such as the heart and glands such as salivary glands. As its name implies, the ANS is independent and self-regulated, whereas in fact the centers that **control** ANS activity are in the lower areas of the brain and usually below the threshold of conscious control. Devotees of yoga try to bring the functions of the ANS under conscious control: yogis have been able to slow heartbeat quite voluntarily, without corresponding changes in the rest of the body.

The appeal of such control in sport is obvious. Many competitors try to banish feelings of **negativity** and establish feelings of inner calm or **relaxation** which release tension and enable them to align body and mind on the proximate assignment. Some accounts suggest that the state of having this kind of focus involves neural functions, principally the assembly of alpha brainwaves. These are measurements of electrical activity in the brain and their graphic presentations as recorded on an **electroencephalogram (EEG)** show multiple patterns reacting to sensory information which is fed through our senses. When the various brainwaves emit synchronously, an alpha rhythm or alpha state is said to occur. On the other hand, when beta waves predominate, the subject is over-excited and aroused. There are two other types of brainwaves: theta, when drowsiness occurs, and delta, during deep sleep.

By using the EEG the subject can learn how to control his or her ANS under laboratory conditions and perhaps transfer the responses to competitive situations. Other instruments that have been used to similar effect are electromyography, which enables subjects to control muscular tension, and the galvanometer, which measures galvanic skin response (perspiration is often an indicator of anxiety).

While biofeedback is mostly associated with attempting to reduce anxiety, the most popular instrument for obtaining feedback and responding accordingly is the heart rate monitor, which athletes use principally in training (though certain cyclists have been known to use them in **competition**). The device, comprising a chestband transmitter and a wrist-worn receiver, indicates how fast the heart is beating. The principle of exercising within a certain percentage of maximum heart rate is not new, but the monitor enables athletes to train within precise limits.

Further reading

Boutcher, S.H. and Zinsser, N.W. (1990) 'Cardiac deceleration of elite and beginning golfers during putting,' *Journal of Sport & Exercise Psychology* vol. 12, pp. 37–47.

Humphrey, J.H., Yow, D.A. and Bowden, W.W. (2000) 'Reducing stress through biofeedback,' pp. 141–5 in, Humphrey, J.H. (ed.) *Stress in College Athletics: Causes, consequences, coping* Binghamton NY: Haworth Half-Court Press.

Petruzzello, S.J., Landers, D.M. and Slazar, W. (1991) 'Biofeedback and sport/
exercise performance: applications and limitations,' *Behavior Therapy* vol. 22,
pp. 379–449.

BODY IMAGE

The conceptions and evaluations we have of our own bodies,
particularly our assessments of how others see us, are known
collectively as body image. While Cash and Pruzinsky define body
image as the 'internal, subjective representations of physical appearance and bodily experience,' we should recognize that these
representations are filtered through cultural portrayals of bodies,
media depictions and peer group expectations. In other words, the
way in which we see our physical selves is not a 'natural' process, but a
culturally mediated one.

We learn how to recognize fatness, thinness, attractiveness and
ugliness and so on. We also learn how to associate these: *thinness* =
attractiveness; *fatness* = *ugliness*, etc. Rewards are available to those
whose bodies measure up to cultural expectations; these include job
opportunities and preferential treatment at school. Women and, to a
lesser degree, men struggle to live up to cultural expectations and as a
result become discontented with their own bodies. Cash and Henry
reported 48 per cent of women evaluated their physical appearance
negatively, suggesting a widespread dissatisfaction. This alludes to
another dimension of body image: the adjustment we make based on
our conceptions.

Among the options available are: lifestyle changes, such as working
out at a gym or training for competition; behavioral changes, like
dieting and other forms of **weight control**; protective changes,
including wearing heavy makeup and clothes that hide one's body; or
changes in **cognition**, which means simply rearranging thoughts and
attitudes about our own body – 'learning to live with ourselves.'

Young women are prone to body dissatisfaction: this typically
begins in puberty when rapid, though normal, weight gain provokes
stress. Males, by contrast, have less concern with changes in physical
appearance that arrive with the onset of maturity. Culturally, there is a
different meaning for physical attractiveness in women than in men:
women are encouraged to assent to what Naomi Wolf called *The
Beauty Myth*. The myth holds that there is an ideal type of body
women should either have or aspire to; but it is one that is physically
not attainable for the vast majority of women. Striving for it often

results in physically and emotionally debilitating conditions, including **eating disorders**.

Further reading

Cash, T.C. and Henry, P.E. (1995) 'Women's body images: the results of a national survey in the USA,' *Sex Roles* vol. 33, pp. 19–28.
Cash, T.C. and Pruzinsky, T. (1990) *Body Images: Development, deviance and change* New York: Guilford.
Wolf, N. (1991) *The Beauty Myth: How images of beauty are used against women* New York: Morrow.

BODY LANGUAGE

Of the several forms of nonverbal communication, body language is perhaps the most obvious means through which humans express thoughts and emotions and so make representations of their experience visible to others. It involves gestures, facial expressions, eye movements, breathing patterns, skin color changes, muscle tone, interpersonal distance and, perhaps most interestingly for analysts of sports, posture. Some analysts, such as Susan Quilliam, in her *Body Language Secrets* series of publications, argue that the total impact of any message is as much as 55 per cent nonverbal (1996).

A football player may traipse languidly across the field, shoulders drooping, head inclined downwards. The body language signals an acceptance of defeat. A tennis player may stride impatiently to her baseline ahead of her opponent, repeatedly tapping her racket head against her leg and staring intently ahead. She is alert, enthusiastic and eager to compete; her **arousal** level is high. A baseball hitter fidgets, his eyes darting, as he waits for the pitcher to settle. His actions betray his lack of **composure**. During a **competition**, every athlete expresses aspects of him or herself, sometimes intentionally but more usually unintentionally: body language often reveals a representation at odds with the athlete's express intentions. No competitor wishes to communicate **anxiety**, resignation, **fear** or any other form of **negativity**; yet they are frequently incapable of suppressing the nonverbal cues that communicate exactly these.

Body language, like other nonverbal communication, involves coding and decoding. Subjects may consciously encode their body movements and gestures in anticipation that teammates, opponents and spectators alike all decode in accordance with their intentions. Or they may be unaware that their actions are disclosing more than they wish. Worse still, they may encode significant information about themselves only for others to decode a completely different message.

In sports, most of the communicating is done via the body. Pre-competition body language has become very much part of the spectacle. Boxer Naseem Hamed's outlandish backflip over the top rope into the ring was a theatrical demonstration of his supreme **confidence**, designed to entertain the crowd but also to daunt his opponents. Sprinter Maurice Greene's rivals may have once mistakenly decoded his jerky, agitated movements before a race as a sign of nervousness; but they eventually realized it was simply his way of **psyching** up. Players of virtually any contact sport will try to convey an impression of **aggressiveness** during the preliminaries of a game, maintaining a stern facial expression, keeping muscles flexed and striding assertively.

During a competition, body language has several functions. At the most explicit level, a handshake, a thumbs-up sign or a clenched fist may function as emblems communicating widely acknowledged meanings. There may also be nonverbal cues that **control**, guide or regulate the flow of a competition. For example, a basketball or soccer player may extend arms downwards and turn palms outwards to indicate to a colleague that he or she should take possession of the ball. Body language may amplify speech: coaches often grimace and point arms or punch the air as they issue instructions; team players frequently gesture flamboyantly as they encourage each other.

In each of these instances, the content of the message could have been communicated by speech. But Kendon argues that gesture has different characteristics and functions from speech. As a silent but visible mode of communication, it can be useful in sports: for instance, by attracting the **attention** of a teammate but not a rival who may be looking in a different direction, or by transmitting a deliberately vague piece of information regarding tactics – this may be useful in making opponents wary that something is going to happen and may possibly induce tension.

Seeing evidence of an opponent's uncovered competitiveness may also make athletes wary. 'Players like [Lleyton] Hewitt and [Michael] Chang are obviously very competitive because they pump their fists,' Pete Sampras once reflected on his tennis contemporaries, adding that his own body language reveals the same competitiveness, though in 'a much more subtle way.' 'People who know me know when I'm fighting. You can see it in my eyes and my expression. I just do it in a more introverted way' (quoted in the *Independent on Sunday*, 'Sports-week', 17 June 2001, p. 3).

But perhaps the most interesting features of body language are the gestures, facial expressions and body postures that change in the context of a competition and occur without conscious awareness. Unlike most areas of life, in which speech and body movement complement each other in communication, sports harbor the potential for contradiction. Nonverbal cues rarely conflict with speech: one person may assure another, 'I'm perfectly relaxed,' while dilated pupils might suggest otherwise. 'Honestly, it's the truth,' may be accompanied by what Ekman and Friesen called 'non-verbal leakage' in which information about a deception is transmitted through body movements (people try to control facial movements when trying to deceive others and are more likely to give themselves away with arm and torso movements). A sports competitor will never intend to affirm to a rival that he or she has lost composure and is resigned to defeat, yet their body language may do precisely that. One of the characteristics of elite competitors is a **skill** in successfully communicating a 'never-say-die' approach even in the most overawing circumstances.

Confidence in sport is often conveyed through eye contact. **Eyeballing** in particular is a strategy popularly employed not only to suggest confidence but also to intimidate rivals. This is largely nullified if one of the eyeballers rubs or scratches body parts, guards the mouth or touches jewelry. These may be taken as signs of nervousness by an astute opponent.

Further reading

Bull, P. and Frederikson, L. (1996) 'Non-verbal communication,' pp. 852–72 in Colman, A.M. (ed.) *Companion Encyclopedia of Psychology*, vol. 2, London: Routledge.

Ekman, P. and Friesen, W.V. (1969) 'Non-verbal leakage and clues to deception,' *Psychiatry* vol. 32, pp. 88–106.

Kendon, A. (1985) 'Some uses of gesture,' pp. 215–34 in Tannen, O. and Saville-Troika, M. (eds) *Perspectives on Silence* Norwood NJ: Ablex.

BRAINWAVES *see* electroencephalogram (EEG)

BULIMIA NERVOSA *see* eating disorders

BURNOUT

Burnout is 'a psychological, **emotional**, and physical withdrawal from a formerly pursued and enjoyable sport as a result of excessive **stress** which acts on the athlete over time.' This is the definition favored by Daniel Gould *et al*. 'It is the manifestation or consequence of the situational, cognitive, physiologic, and behavioral components of excessive stress.'

The condition typically affects teenage sports performers whose rise is sudden, if not meteoric, but whose decline is premature and abrupt. Young tennis prodigies such as Tracy Austin and Andrea Jaeger were exemplars of burnout, both being top class pros in their teens and seeming to be destined for long reigns at the top. Both were prolific achievers on the professional circuit, but neither fulfilled their early promise, recurring back and neck problems curtailing Austin's career when she was 21, a chronic shoulder **injury** ending Jaeger's prospects before she was 20.

Austin and Jaeger were well-publicized prodigies. There are countless others who burn out before even approaching their potential. At the time of the 1996 summer Olympics at Atlanta, a report was published that claimed that the rigors of competitive gymnastics amounted to child abuse. According to the 1996 report's authors, over-ambitious parents were pushing their children to succeed in sports out of selfish reasons. 'Achievement by proxy' is how Tofler *et al*. described the manner in which parents drove their offspring toward an almost certain burnout.

Joan Ryan reached similar conclusions in her book *Little Girls in Pretty Boxes*. She chronicles the short-lived careers of Betty Okikino, practicing and competing with a broken neck, wearing a brace when resting; Kelly Garrison, pounding her ankle while waiting her turn until the pain of the stress fracture was numbed; Julissa Gomez, fatally snapping her neck in Tokyo; Chrysty Henrich, who should have made the 1992 Olympics, but died instead two years later, weighing less than 50lb. A combination of parental pressure and coaching tyranny contrived to bring a premature halt to many promising sporting careers.

There are several theories that purport to account for burnout. In 1986, Ronald E. Smith argued that there is a progression to burnout, with the child being placed under pressure to train and develop competitive approaches by significant others, including parents and coaches. The young athlete then begins to see the demands placed on her or him differently, some finding the situation threatening, others not so. If the demand is perceived as threatening, the youth enters a third stage in which there is a physiological response, such as fatigue or insomnia. Finally, in a fourth state, the physiological response leads to **coping strategies**: these might manifest in decreased levels of competitive performance, interpersonal problems or complete with-drawal from the sport. For Smith, **personality** and motivational factors influence the four stages of the burnout process. The player's senses of **self-esteem**, ambition and personal **anxiety** are all factors, so it is difficult to generalize from his theory. Some young sports performers might react positively, whereas others will feel the pressure.

In 1990, John M. Silva identified 'training stress' as the determinant in the burnout process. This is a physical characteristic: sometimes the body becomes overloaded with the burden of training and **competition**, but at other times the young body becomes stronger and adapts to the rigors associated with higher levels of competition. The young competitors who are prone to burnout will experience a 'psycho-physiological malfunction' after their body's failure to respond positively to training. Their mental orientation is then affected and they become incapable of meeting the demands placed on their bodies. Again, emphasis on how individuals respond limits the applicability of the theory.

Lindsey MacDonald was a 16-year-old schoolgirl from Scotland when she reached the final of the 400 meters at the Moscow summer Olympics of 1980. Although she was well beaten, she recovered three days later and helped the British team to bronze in the relay. The surprise performance spurred her to great ambitions and she set herself a challenging and draining training schedule. Injury and illness beset the rest of her career and the promise shown in her teens was never fulfilled. She competed only until the age of 25.

The importance of 'perfectionism' in the burnout process should not be overlooked. Frequent worry about others' evaluations, uncertainty regarding one's own abilities and competitive state anxiety are all factors affecting young athletes striving and being encouraged to reach an ever-improving level of performance. 'Some youngsters have an "at-risk" perfectionist personality that may predispose them to burnout,' Gould and his co-researchers concluded. They also believed that many of those mistakenly identified as burnout cases in fact drop out not because of any stress but simply because their interests and ambitions change.

Jay Coakley argues that the **intensity** of competitive professional sports and the time-demands it places on promising young players denies the young person the opportunity to develop a normal multifaceted **personality**. The youth is encouraged to focus totally on success in their sport and to exclude other experiences in their social life. The Jennifer Capriati case would fit perfectly with this model. A young girl from Florida urged to play tennis at a very early age and provided with every manner of top-class coaching and facility, Capriati had endorsement contracts estimated to be worth $5 million before she hit a ball as a professional. She reached the final of her first tournament on the women's professional tour when she was only 13. Two months later, in her first Grand Slam event, she progressed to the semi-finals of the French Open. The youngest ever semi-finalist at Wimbledon in 1991 (at 15 years old) and the youngest US Open semi-finalist since Jaeger in 1980, Capriati won a gold medal at the 1992 Olympics, beating Steffi Graf in the women's final. By this time, Capriati, though sound physically, was in the throes of psychological burnout caused by a conflict between public and parental expectations of her and her own desire to indulge herself as an 'ordinary' teenager. She dropped out of the WTA tour and went back to school. Arrested for shoplifting and caught in possession of drugs in Florida, Capriati underwent drugs **rehabilitation** and made an abortive **comeback** in November 1994. Then she disappeared for two years, seemingly finished.

Coakley contends that a young prodigy's ability to make decisions that affect her or his life are taken away, or minimized to the point where they feel powerless to influence the direction of their own lives. It is this sense of inability or disempowerment that creates the burnout. This gives rise to a further question: is burnout reversible? The tentative answer is: yes. In 1994, Capriati seemed certain to be linked with Austin and Jaeger as a brilliant tennis prospect who had too much, too soon. At the age of 24, Capriati resurfaced dramatically, beating world number one Martina Hingis 6–4, 6–3, to win the 2001 Australian Open. In fact, Capriati had been steadily climbing the rankings in previous years, though seldom looking a world-beater.

Burnout is a far from inevitable experience for precocious sports performers. Steve Cauthen, for example, was already the US champion jockey and rider of the Kentucky Derby winner of 1978 by the time he was 18. Cauthen moved to England and enjoyed a laurel-strewn career until 1993. A shorter but equally successful career was that of Puerto Rico's Wilfred Benitez, who had his first professional fight two months after his fifteenth birthday and won the first of three world titles at the age of 17. Benitez's six years as a world champion ended in 1982. Still only 23, he lost to Thomas Hearns and his star waned thereafter.

Perhaps the most overlooked group of burnout sufferers are coaches, who are often subject to **stress** and anxiety comparable to that of their charges, a fact evidenced by Betty Kelley et al. in 1999.

Further reading

Coakley, J.J. (1992) 'Burnout among adolescent athletes: a personal failure or social problem?' *Sociology of Sport Journal* vol. 9, pp. 271–85.

Gould, D., Udry, E., Tuffey, S. and Loehr, J. (1996) 'Burnout in competitive junior tennis players: I. A quantitative psychological assessment' and 'Burnout in competitive junior tennis players: II. Qualitative psychological assessment,' *The Sport Psychologist* vol. 10, pp. 322–40.

Kelley, B.C., Eklund, R.C. and Titter-Taylor, M. (1999) 'Stress and burnout among collegiate tennis coaches,' *Journal of Sport & Exercise Psychology* vol. 22, pp. 113–30.

Tofler, I., Styer, B., Micheli, L. and Herman, L. (1996) 'Physical and emotional problems of elite female gymnasts,' *New England Journal of Medicine* vol. 335, pp. 281–3.

CATHARSIS

Katharsis is Greek for cleanse, purify or purge. Psychoanalysts use the term 'catharsis' to suggest how 'reliving' or recalling experiences that have prompted **anxiety**, but which have been repressed, can effect a cleansing discharge of tension. Some theorists have argued that playing or even watching sports functions as a catharsis, enabling participants and spectators to eliminate natural **aggression** that might otherwise build up and become destructive.

One of the proponents of this view was Konrad Lorenz, who regarded sport as a kind of safety valve: a controlled mechanism for releasing innate behavioral tendencies – an **instinct**. Because aggressive instincts were natural, nothing could be done about them. Human society had to devise ways to accommodate them, or face continual **violence** and devastation. Unlike other animals, humans had sufficient ingenuity to design measures that would allow the behavioral expression of aggressive instincts. Sport was the principal among them. It was a formalized, rule-bound order that licensed combative, violent, even warlike conduct but within a relatively secure framework. Competing in sports, either actually or vicariously (through watching others) allowed humans to rid themselves of aggressive instincts, usually without incurring, or doing, too much damage.

The theory of sport-as-catharsis was based on a model of the human being as a sophisticated animal, but an animal nevertheless and so, to a large degree, at the mercy of instincts. While this may have intuitive appeal, research on the topic yielded mixed results. For example, the work of, among others, Martin, published in 1976, lent some support to the concept of catharsis, concluding that athletes were less aggressive after competition. On the other hand, a succession of research projects, including those of Ryan in 1970 and Zillman *et al.* in 1972, revealed that athletes were *more* aggressive after **competition**. Other research on the effects of watching sports indicated that the vicariously experienced catharsis does not occur either. In a 1987 paper on 'Effects on the hostility of spectators of viewing aggressive sports,' Robert Arms *et al.* concluded that 'the observation of aggression on the field of play leads to an increase in hostility on the part of spectators.' Even viewing a hockey game on television can arouse aggressive tendencies. While none of the studies that found aggression to be triggered by watching sports explicitly acknowledged it, there was an implicit recognition of the role of **reinforcement** in shaping behavior.

Further reading

Arms, R., Russell, G. and Sandilands, M. (1987) 'Effects on the hostility of spectators of viewing aggressive sports,' pp. 259–64 in Yiannakis, A., McIntyre, T., Melnick. M. and Hart, D. (eds) *Sport Sociology*, 3rd edition, Dubuque IA: Kendall/Hunt.
Lorenz, K. (1966) *On Aggression* New York: Harcourt, Brace & World.
Ryan, E. (1970) 'The cathartic effect of vigorous motor activity on aggressive behavior,' *Research Quarterly* vol. 41, pp. 542–51.

CELEBRITY

From the French *célébrité*, which derives from *celebrare*, Latin for renown. Celebrity, as it is understood today, is a status conferred on subjects who are widely recognized. The actualization of that status is achieved through the mass and multimedia's dissemination of images, stories and, generally, narratives about persons or caricatures and their consumption by a receptive population. This is a definition that avoids conceiving of the contemporary sports celebrity as a person and interprets him/her as a constructed position of exaltedness. Celebrity describes the end product of a manufacturing process rather than the raw material involved in the production.

'Celebrities are well-known (through the media) for nothing in particular, whereas the truly famous are in some way *deserving* of individual recognition,' writes David Giles in his *Illusions of Immortality: A psychology of fame and celebrity*. For Giles, the 'truly famous' are acknowledged for their accomplishments, while celebrities become widely known, though not necessarily for great deeds and often not for very long. So celebrity status is fragile and ephemeral. Consider

Eric Moussambani, of Equatorial Guinea, who was instantly celebrated around the world, following his failure in the heats of the 100 meters freestyle swimming at the 2000 Olympics. Competing in slack trunks, 'Eric the Eel,' as he was dubbed by the world's media, was inundated with sponsorship offers, in the same way as other failures like 'Eddie the Eagle' Edwards, who finished last in the 1988 winter Olympics ski jump. The celebrity they enjoyed contrasts with the earned approval of the likes of Joe DiMaggio, Muhammad Ali or any number of other athletes whose triumphant feats formed the nucleus of their public recognition.

This does not rule out the possibility that contemporary celebrity athletes may also boast considerable achievements nor that they would have been famous in any age. Yet the global reputation of many athletes, often in parts of the world where their sports are not played, suggests that the media *celebration* process has enhanced, if not fabricated, their status. Britain's David Beckham was elevated to a position usually reserved for rock or movie stars following his marriage to Spice Girl Victoria Adams. Dennis Rodman's off-court revelries ensured his rep in places where basketball is not played. These and many other athletes were known for their sporting deeds, but became celebrities because the media and a fascinated **fandom** were absorbed in other facets of their lives.

Of course, celebrity is not actualized unless there is a broad interest in the kinds of narratives disseminated by the media. The celebrity is an animal whose natural habitat is as much *Hello!* and *The National Enquirer* as it is the football field or the basketball court and who is often seen prowling the savannas of movie premières and nightclub launches. Fans enthusiastically consume stories about extra-curricular activities, suggesting a form of *identification*. Giles cites several studies dating from the 1940s, when the Hollywood 'star' was in its ascendancy. He concludes that fans idealize, are inspired by and model themselves on their favorites, so that they form 'parasocial relationships' in which they 'know' a persona. They do not know Beckham, or Rodman, or indeed any other athlete: but they know a figure that exists independently of time and space and resides in their imaginations. It is a figure with which they believe they have a close, perhaps deep relationship. While there is obviously a delusion, the fans' relationship is no more a *folie à deux* than the countless other relationships that television viewers have with soap characters – not the actors, but they characters they play.

Perhaps the orientation of fans toward celebrities is rather like that of avid readers of horoscopes: they know that the forecasts have no scientific validity, yet remain comfortable with the fallacy that the predictions of good fortune will somehow materialize.

The proliferation of celebrities – not only athletes but chefs, lawyers, TV presenters, etc. – has been made possible by a combination of devoted fans, many perhaps in parasocial relationships but many others simply intrigued by the pursuits of others. A voracious media ready to devour the minutest details of a person's life abets them. Dramatizing this is the confessional television show in which 'ordinary' people are prepared to disclose the most intimate details of their lives, while an audience of millions looks on with voyeuristic relish. In these shows, transitory, minor celebs are created, then quickly superseded by others. Any number of celebrities are created, then erased from **memory**.

Up to the final decade of the twentieth century, outstanding individuals in sport were known as superstars; almost by definition there were very few of them and they were usually outstanding performers. Today, there are at any one time hundreds, perhaps thousands, of celebrity athletes, some more enduring than others. Most are not outstanding athletes, but perhaps have other properties that the media publicize and consumers find engaging.

Further reading

Andrews, D.L. and Jackson, S.J. (2001) *Sports Stars: The cultural politics of sporting celebrity* London: Routledge.

Giles, D. (2000) *Illusions of Immortality: A psychology of fame and celebrity* New York: St Martin's Press.

Rojek, C. (2001) *Celebrity* London: Reaktion.

CENTERING

Although there are several senses in which the term 'centering' is used, in sports it usually refers either to: (1) directing thoughts inwards before **competition**, introspectively checking whether **attention** is **focused** and **arousal** is at the appropriate level; or (2) focusing on a particular aspect or detail of a stimulus, to the exclusion of other properties, prior to or during competition.

In (1), athletes strive to become consciously aware of their entire bodies, trying to locate a center of gravity, while they gate out thoughts of their immediate environment. Many athletes in all manner of sport can be seen to do this prior to competition: they close their eyes and remain motionless, sometimes for only a few seconds, sometimes longer. An athlete who is experienced at centering can execute the whole process in a few seconds, monitoring focal auditory and visual attention, and arousal, before seeming to snap out and attend to a task-relevant cue in readiness for competition. Sprinters can often be seen seconds before they are called to the start line, their eyes closed, lying or standing perfectly still and breathing deeply, while they center. As soon as they hear the call, they leap to action, looking only at the track ahead of them to minimize distractions. Centering is one of the four techniques prescribed by Robert Nideffer for facilitating entry into the **zone**, the others being self **hypnosis**, improving **concentration** and developing faith.

In (2), an athlete or team plays a dangerous game, centering activity around one detail of an opponent. A boxer may be wary of a rival's especially potent left hook and circle to his left to avoid it. The **risk** is that he or she may run into a right. A football or soccer team may have earmarked a key player on the opponent's team and delegate two players to patrol that player, i.e. double-mark or double-cover. A San Francisco Giants–Houston Astros matchup in 2001 highlighted the dangers of centering, in this case on the Giants' Barry Bonds, then in the middle of one of his best **streaks** and going for a record-equaling seventy home runs. The Astros studiously pitched him four balls, allowing Bonds to walk to first base. Having centered on Bonds, the Astros were then hammered by the next man in, who promptly batted in two runners for a 6–3 lead and an eventual 11–8 victory.

While its significance is quite different, Jean Piaget used the similar concept of *centration* in his *The Origins of Intelligence in Children*, when describing the tendency of children in the pre-operational stage of development (about 18 months to 7 years old) to concentrate on only one aspect of a problem at a time. As a result, they could not solve problems that demanded attention to the whole, particularly involving conservation; for example, children did not comprehend that pouring liquid from a tall bottle into a flat tray does not decrease its volume. The similarity is that, in both the competitive situation and that of the child's problem-solving, centering on one feature necessarily means losing sight of the *mise en scène*, the other properties surrounding that feature.

To avoid misunderstanding, mention should be made of *decentering*, which is not commonly used in sports, save for when an individual exhibits an unwavering belief that he or she is the focus of everyone else's attention and this leads to **anxiety**. Decentering is the process of counseling designed to change this **perception**. Like centering, the term is associated with Piaget, and in his theories refers to a stage when children are able to see themselves in objective relationships with other persons and events in their environment.

Further reading

Nideffer, R.M. (1992) *Psyched to Win* Champaign IL: Human Kinetics.
Nideffer, R.M. and Sagal, M.-S. (1998) 'Concentration and attention control training,' pp. 296–315 in Williams, J. (ed.) *Applied Sport Psychology: Personal growth to peak performance*, 3rd edition, Mountain View CA: Mayfield.

CHARACTER

Sometimes referred to as 'the right stuff,' character suggests **mental toughness** or strength, moral fortitude or resilience and all-round determination to win fair and square. The root of the term is the Greek *kharakter*, stamp or impress. Sport is popularly regarded as a builder of character.

Character can be reduced to four constituents: (1) the capacity to overcome adversity and ultimately triumph; (2) the competence to lead others; (3) the ability to resist the temptation to transgress, i.e. break rules; and (4) altruism, the regard for others' interests and welfare above one's own. Does participation in sport instill these in a competitor?

1 Studies, particularly those of Susan Harter, have drawn on White's concept of competence **motivation**. According to Harter, we are all innately motivated to be competent: athletes whose perceptions of their own competence and self-control are high will exert more effort and persist at tasks in achievement situations. Success promotes feelings of **self-efficacy** and the athlete is encouraged to establish greater challenges and strive even harder. But if an athlete's efforts result in failure, even perceived failure, then low competence motivation will result and the athlete will probably drop out. Almost by definition, the athletes we watch and read about are in the first group: they have had to overthrow failure at some stage of their sports career and have redoubled their efforts to progress. Those who have not will have dropped out and disappeared. In this sense, sport does imbue in its participants the capacity to shrug off failure. But there remains an unknowable mass of other once-aspiring but now absent competitors for whom sport worked only to discourage and demoralize.

2 **Leadership** is integral to sports: some figure or figures must exert authority and influence over others, either through inspiration or

by example, or both. Early psychological studies treated leadership as a **personality** trait or a combination of features possessed by individuals. More sophisticated treatments have accentuated to contingencies that are specific to situations and facilitate leadership skills. What is clear from the research is that effective leadership in sports needs flexibility: leaders need to adapt to or from, for instance, autocratic styles to more democratic approaches, depending on the circumstances and people involved. But does involvement in sports equip athletes with the qualities and skills necessary for leadership? The answer is: yes and no. Obviously, the fact that there are managers and coaches or trainers who delegate leadership duties to captains who can respond to situational demands means that sports must equip some athletes with leadership qualities. Yet for every captain there is a team of players who either conform or else **risk** undermining team **cohesion**. In individual sports, the athlete is typically the one following instructions, not giving them. So while it is reasonable to suggest that leadership skills are an inherent part of the sports experience for some, for others – probably the majority – the capacity to follow directions unquestioningly is a more useful **skill**.

3   Perhaps the most contentious part of the assertion that sport builds character concerns fair play and cheating: playing fair and square and accepting defeat without grumbling are popularly regarded as qualities of good character. The values of fair play and abiding by rules were once central in sports, especially when the amateur ethos prevailed and reward of winning was subordinated to the joy of competing for its own sake. Professionalism introduced a more instrumental orientation, and qualities such as prudence and calculation have seeped into sport. According to some writers, such as William Morgan, rules have become little more than technical directives and professional athletes will break every rule they can get away with and comply with every rule they cannot. In other words, pros follow rules not out of a moral **commitment** to their intrinsic rightness, but because their calculations tell them that breaking them will lead to penalties. This approach does not seem confined to competitors. Administrators, managers, coaches, officials and even presidents of major sports federations have all been guilty of fraud, corruption or mendacity of one kind or another. Sport may once have been an institution that encouraged and infused a sense of fairness and obligation to obey rules. Now, the availability of extrinsic rewards

has probably nourished a more instrumental mentality in which rules are not seen as inherently good or bad, but merely devices.

4　Intuitively, we might think that competing in sports, whether individually or as part of a team, compels us to act altruistically and to distribute credit for success among a variety of teammates or aides. On the other hand, we often hear athletes attributing their success to their own determination and hard work. There is a body of literature on **attribution** in sports. Various studies have shown that after success in a **competition** athletes claim credit for themselves, while after defeat they cite external causes for their failure as a way of protecting their **self-esteem**. Other research indicates that athletes often blame internal factors for defeats too, not wishing to be seen as making excuses for their failure. Ambiguous outcomes, however, are attributed to external factors. So a tennis player on the wrong end of a tight call might interpret this as a 'moral win' and blame inept judges for the ultimate defeat; the winner is likely to take credit.

There is little straightforward logic in blame/credit attribution: some athletes prefer never to invoke self-serving strategies and take responsibility for their own fortunes, good and bad, while others spurn personal responsibility for failure. This does not exactly tell us much about athletes' altruism, but it tells us something about their **egocentrism**, which is, in many senses, its opposite. Rarely do athletes simply concede that a better opponent beat them. The opponent might be said to have been better 'on the day' or have prevailed because of uncontrollable external factors ('our team was depleted by injuries'); these are unstable factors and susceptible to change. The reason is that, in sport, the locus of causality must be understood as an internal state. For example, it would be ludicrous if coaches told athletes that their progress was determined by all manner of uncontrollable external factors, such as weather conditions, injuries, referees, judges, fate or even pure **luck**. Athletes are taught that they hold the keys to their own success (or failure). If sports performers feel little or no **control** over competitive outcomes, they may veer toward **learned helplessness** – and probable withdrawal. As if to underline their narrow ego orientation, athletes sometimes describe themselves in the third person, providing a phony objective perspective from which they presumably think they can escape the accusation of conceit: 'Lennox Lewis fought a beautiful fight tonight; his jab was working to perfection and . . .' Lewis might tell a ringside interviewer. The ego protection/enhancement that is so central to progress in sports is hardly likely to lead to altruism – more likely a narrower, selfish approach that prioritizes personal success to the complete disregard of others.

Sport's capacity to engender character in its participants is not as self-evident as it appears. More likely, sport advocates the kinds of qualities and attributes that are, in many ways, inimical to character, as it is popularly defined.

Further reading

Harter. S. (1981) 'The development of competence motivation in the mastery of cognitive and physical skills: is there still a place for joy?' pp. 3–29 in Roberts, G.C. and Landers, D.M. (eds) *Psychology of motor behavior and sport – 1980* Champaign IL: Human Kinetics.

Lee, M.J., Whitehead, J. and Balchin, N. (2000) 'The measurement of values in youth sport: development of the youth sport values questionnaire,' *Journal of Sport & Exercise Psychology* vol. 22, pp. 307–26.

Morgan, W. (1994) *Leftist Theories of Sport* Urbana IL: University of Illinois Press.

CHOKE

A choke is a sudden occurrence of severe **anxiety** at a critical stage of a **competition**. It is typically experienced by an athlete who is approaching victory but becomes tense and apprehensive at the prospect and loses form. The term is, of course, taken from the original sense of the word 'choke,' which describes temporary or permanent suffocation, loss of breathing or even paralysis due to a blockage of the throat. In sports terms, the choke is rarely temporary: the competitor suffers an acute attack and seldom has chance to recover **composure** before his or her rival capitalizes.

Historically, the event that became known as The Choke involved Jana Novotna, who led Steffi Graf 4–1 in games and 40–0 with serve in the third set of the 1993 Wimbledon women's singles final. Novotna, who had looked confidently in **control** of the game, crumbled and lost. A technically able player, Novotna choked again, this time in the French Open when leading 5–0 and 40–30 with serve against Chanda Rubin, in 1995. Her opponent survived nine match points. The question raised about Novotna was whether or not she was a 'choker' – a player whose **personality** disposed her to become temporarily inept because of **emotion**. This raised the wider question of whether there are mechanically proficient athletes who block up in certain types of situations.

As a specific form of anxiety that happens only at critical junctures of a competition, choking has unique features that are not shared with many other types of sports anxiety. For example, the choke may occur whenever athletes encounter a situation that seems beyond their control: an unfamiliar circumstance that has not been organized and integrated into their view of themselves. Novotna eventually assimilated the concept of her being a Grand Slam winner and later became a Wimbledon champion. Underdogs, especially inexperienced underdogs, frequently maneuver themselves into winning situations but eventually lose because they had not taken seriously the concept of upsetting the odds. In other words, they did not really believe they could win.

When winning becomes an active possibility, **arousal** levels may increase to the point where physiological functions interfere with performance. All athletes are told to guard against thinking too far ahead as this detracts from focusing; but with victory in sight there may be a tendency to imagine the prospect of winning. This thought in itself may prompt an increase in, for instance, metabolic rate and respiratory volume, a constriction of blood vessels and perhaps an abundant perspiration. Once these exceed optimum levels for athletic performance, they can lead to sharp decrements. As form deteriorates, the **relaxation** that would allow them to return to optimum performance becomes difficult if not impossible to attain.

Psychologists have contributed various other factors. Using archival baseball data as the basis for their 1989 article 'The "championship choke" revisited,' A.W. Heaton and H. Sigall analyzed the 'fear of failing' as a factor in 'performance decrements under pressure.' Interestingly, the study undermines the purported value of a **home advantage** because the fear of failing is experienced more severely in front of a supportive home audience. The research concluded that home teams' frequency of fielding errors increased and contributed to their inability to maintain leads in decisive situations. This was a reflection of their choking, especially in decisive games of playoff series. But in contrast to explanations that rest on situational factors, R.W. Grant in his *The Psychology of Sport: Facing one's true opponent* believes that upbringing, athletic history, personal experiences and interactions with coaches and others come together to affect a competitor's propensity to choke, as well as his or her unique way of handling **stress**.

'Are we our own worst enemies?' asked L.M. Leith in the subtitle of his 1988 research article which concluded that just talking about the possibility of choking before a competition may contribute to the probability of its happening. Research conducted with a basketball team revealed that talking about the choke works as an independent variable, the dependent variable in this study being free throws: groups that did not discuss choking performed significantly better than groups that did.

Complicating the issue is the fact that choking is evident in some sports yet not others. Tennis is a game that has to be won: leads cannot simply be protected. In other sports, they can: a boxer might begin to choke two-thirds of the way through a fight and still emerge a winner by decision, despite having lost the final four rounds. An entire basketball team can choke in the fourth quarter and see its points lead shrink but not disappear. The point is that only in certain sports does choking lead almost certainly to defeat. Golfers sensing victory, for instance, often report a spell of the 'yips' when they become un-characteristically tentative and inaccurate as their form deserts them. They may complete their final hole gracelessly, but have enough of a lead to secure success. The sources of a choke are diverse, as are the conditions under which it occurs, the type of performer it is likely to affect and the type of sports in which it becomes visible. (In complete contrast, so-called 'clutch' players actually become more **focused** and raise their performance to unprecedented levels when faced with daunting situations.)

Further reading

Baumeister, R.F. and Showers, C.J. (1986) 'A review of paradoxical performance effects: choking under pressure in sports and mental tests,' *European Journal of Social Psychology* vol. 16, pp. 361–83.
Leith, L.M. (1988) 'Choking in sports: are we our own worst enemies?,' *International Journal of Sport Psychology* vol. 19, pp. 59–64.

COGNITION

The faculty for or action of knowing is cognition, a term formed from the prefix *co*, meaning with other subjects or jointly, and *gnoscere gnit*, the Latin for attend or apprehend. Cognition includes conceiving, perceiving and reasoning, as well as planning, remembering and **decision making**; it also embraces processes of an abstract **character**, such as anticipation, problem-solving, complex rule use and the construction of images and symbols. In sum, cognition defines the way humans use, process and manage information in order to make sense of the world.

Cognition is a uniquely human capacity: for example, while horses or dogs running around a track may behaviorally resemble human athletes, the horses run out of a combination of **instinct**, training and command, while humans are cognizant – they have cognition of objectives, tactics, anticipated outcomes and an entire range of knowledge that contributes to the athletic performance. The concept of triumph is unknown to a horse, which simply runs without comprehension of rules or any concept of the meaning of a race.

Cognitive psychology, as its name suggests, focuses on how knowledge-processing is organized and how it functions. It provides an alternative to psychological approaches which explain human conduct in terms of stimulus input and behavioral output. By accentuating cognition, this branch of study explores how knowledge, both general and situational, is put to use in practical encounters. Underlying this is an assumption. As Karen Lee Hill puts it, 'the cognitive model views the individual as an active participant in creating reality through information processing.' Hill's chapter 'The cognitive model' is a serviceable introduction to cognition's role in sport psychology. Hill begins by outlining the difference between bottom-up and top-down **information processing**. From the moment we are born, we are involved in gathering, storing, sorting and assigning importance to data from the outside world. The data that we take in via the peripheral **nervous system** (the senses) and the central nervous system (spinal cord and brain) is processed via the bottom-up route. Top-down processing, by contrast, starts with us: we organize and relate pieces of data together, shaping knowledge that we can then use to guide future actions. This is how we make sense of the data and the world from which it came.

The patterns of processing are *heuristics*: these are essentially quickfire methods for finding elements of data, or for solving problems – techniques that enable reducing a huge range of possibilities to a manageable number of probabilities. Heuristics may be provisional formulations that allow for testing, evaluation and improvement of ideas or theories. They enable us to process information quickly and with less effort as we mature. As such, they are important in the **skill performance** when rapid assessments of situations and the selection of appropriate responses are critical.

Thoughts that are processed on a regular basis are arranged into packets of three kinds, all of which have bearing on sports. Recent, accessible thought is *voluntary* and amenable to change, while *automatic* thought is more entrenched, though not as deeply entrenched as *schema* (from the Greek *skhêma*, for form, or figure), which is an architecture of knowledge, beliefs and expectations relating to a particular subject. It enables us to integrate new data into an existing structure of thoughts. The cognitive schema is what provides us with a sense of stability with relatively fixed conceptions of the world and our self. Yet this does not suggest that cognitive content is completely unalterable: quite the opposite – thinking processes and existing knowledge are open to challenge.

Cognition affects every component of sports preparation and performance: the knowledge we have and how we use it guide conduct in and out of the competitive arena. Often, athletes have performance-related problems that have no rational basis. Hill gives the example of choking when athletes are unable to perform to their maximum when the stakes are high. The **choke** approaches as an athlete's confidence drains and apprehension not so much creeps but rushes in, precipitating **anxiety**. The source of the problem lies in the athlete's cognition: how he or she sees and thinks about the predicament. According to Hill, this could be connected to the athlete's schema, which is difficult though not impossible to change. Substandard athletic performance is a consequence of cognitive processes and can be addressed by examining those processes rather than the performance. Cognition is often contrasted with **emotion** or *conation*, which is concerned with willful action.

Further reading

Fiske, S.T. and Taylor, S.E. (1991) *Social Cognition* New York: McGraw-Hill.
Hill, K.L. (2001) *Frameworks for Sport Psychologists* Champaign IL: Human Kinetics.
Lazarus, R.S. (1991) *Emotion and Adaptation* New York: Oxford University Press, chapter 4.

COGNITIVE RESTRUCTURING *see* **cognitive–behavioral modification**

COGNITIVE–BEHAVIORAL MODIFICATION

Combining techniques designed to restructure **cognition** with physical **relaxation** procedures is known as cognitive–behavioral modification, or intervention, and it is used to modify the manner in which subjects apprehend, interpret and respond to situations or specific **stimuli**.

Cognitive restructuring is intended to use intellectual and perceptual **skill** to alter the way subjects view situations or stimuli in the environment. It is based on the premise that stimuli do not automatically imprint themselves on human senses: they are subject to interpretation. Responses to stimuli are the result of interpretations of them rather than the stimuli themselves. The properties we infer or conjecture rather than the objective properties of the stimuli are crucial to the way we think and act toward them.

For example, the impressive home records of the Denver Broncos and Manchester United typically awe teams that travel to Mile High Stadium or Old Trafford, respectively. Other teams and fans alike believe, with some justification, that **home advantage** is a big factor. Yet, objectively, opponents of the Broncos and United play by the same rules, on the same size field and get no breaks from officials (technically, at least), suggesting that the **anxiety** raised by the prospect of playing there is irrational. Because the awe inspired by both stadia has sources in beliefs and apprehensions, it may be advantageous to change cognition about the visits to the stadia. Athletes visiting Denver and Manchester would benefit from cognitive restructuring before their games.

Other examples of cognitive restructuring include **coping strategies**, **self-talk** and **centering**; all of which are aimed at changing the athlete's response to stimuli rather than the stimuli themselves. Like all types of cognitive restructuring, they assist in managing an athlete's interpretation of what might otherwise be perceived as threatening situations.

Allying such restructuring with interventions to stabilize physio-logical **arousal** may involve the use of **reinforcement**, applying the techniques of operant conditioning to reduce or eliminate problematic behavior or to encourage new behavior. While the approaches seem theoretically incompatible, in practice they are less unsuited: desired behavior is rewarded and unwelcome behavior punished. The basic principle encourages preferred responses to pertinent stimuli, and once the consequences are observed a change in cognition may follow. Conversely, cognitive restructuring may be first: John Silva's study describes a hockey player who retaliated against opponents as a way of regaining **self-efficacy** when dispossessed of the puck and who was persuaded that this was ineffective. He modified his behavior and witnessed a corresponding, and ultimately reinforcing, improvement in form.

Modeling is another related strategy, inviting subjects to imagine they are someone else or to behave as they believe another would behave in a particular type of situation. Breaking the association between an **emotion** and the presence of a certain stimulus can modify **emotional** behavior. For instance, a basketball player might freeze with anxiety when approaching free shots, or a soccer player may **fear** taking penalties. Separating the emotion from the stimuli is known as *desensitization*. Other behavioral techniques rely less on reinforcement and include relaxation training and skill rehearsal, though the upshot is similar – to instigate actual behavioral change to precede or follow and complement cognitive restructuring.

Further reading

Cornelius, A. (2002) 'Introduction of sport psychology interventions,' pp. 177–96 in Silva, J.M. and Stevens, D.E. (eds) *Psychological Foundations of Sport* Boston MA: Allyn & Bacon.

Silva, J.M. (1982) 'Competitive sport environments: performance enhancement through cognitive intervention,' *Behavior Modification* vol. 6, pp. 443–63.

COHESION

When a team, squad or a roster of players has cohesion, or co-hesiveness, its members are united in a common purpose. If they tend to stick together outside sport because similar tastes and interests attract them to each other, there may be total harmony, or *social cohesion*. But even if the members do not like each other they may join together in the pursuit of shared goals and produce *task cohesion*. The two forms of cohesion operate independently of each other, and while social cohesion may be desirable it is by no means as critical to success as task cohesion. The word is a compound of the prefix *co*, for jointly or mutually, and the Latin *haerere*, meaning stick.

Cohesion is something of a Holy Grail for coaches and team managers: it is hard to find but almost magical in its effects, transforming an aggregation of individuals into a collective unit. Teams comprising outstanding individual athletes often underachieve, while teams of modest players exceed all expectations. The difference is that the latter team is usually cohesive: its members selflessly work toward the aims of the team rather than their own personal ambitions. The Wimbledon soccer team of the 1980s is an example: none of the players were headliners but they collectively overachieved, frequently beating star-laden rivals. Many other expensively assembled teams have failed to win anything.

It is possible to have both star players *and* cohesion: the Chicago Bulls team that won six NBA titles, 1991–3 and 1996–8, was full of stars, some of them – like Dennis Rodman – supreme individualists.

Becoming a **team player** did not mean losing one's individuality or suppressing one's personality: coach Phil Jackson convinced his players that only within the framework of the team could their talents fully blossom. Jackson believed in what he called 'the power of one-ness instead of the power of one man.' Jackson's accomplishment was in 'making players connect with something larger than themselves.'

Like Jackson, every coach strives to produce a *sui generis* entity, something that has unique properties over and above those of individual competitors. To do so requires subordinating the interests of individuals to that of the team. Even when this is achieved, cohesion can disappear quite suddenly. The reason for this is, as Albert Carron pointed out: '[Cohesion is] a dynamic process, which is reflected in the tendency for a group to stick together and remain united in the pursuit of its goals and objectives.' As a *process*, it cannot be presumed simply to be *there*; it has to be initiated and sustained. The question is: how?

Carron offered some answers in his 1982 article 'Cohesiveness in sport groups: interpretations and considerations,' in which he wrote of 'determinants of team cohesion.' *Situational factors*, such as living near each other, or rooming together on road trips, assist bonding, according to Carron. So does distinctiveness from other groups; dressing in a particular uniform or possessing a unique ritual contributes toward cohesion. The New Zealand rugby team's pre-game *haka* ritual would be a fine example of this. *Personal* factors such as **commitment** and satisfaction also play a part, as do *leadership* factors, democratic styles of **leadership** working more effectively than autocratic approaches. Carron also cited *team* factors, such as the clarity with which each member of the team understands his or her role and the manner in which he or she accepts it. Success in **competition** predictably increases cohesion. Carron later discovered that cohesion decreases as group size increases; so it would be harder to keep a football team cohesive than it would a volleyball team (especially a beach volleyball team).

Various scholars have emphasized the importance of developing unspoken standards or codes that are accepted by and adhered to by all members, a process known as *norming*. Members who challenge the norms challenge the cohesion of the whole group, so methods must be found to exact conformity, but without using coercion or duress. Even if a player does not believe in the norms, he or she should still conform, if only out of a sense of obligation. Norms may relate to performance: for example, observing curfews and eating habits before a competition. Or they may have little direct bearing on performance;

the Wimbledon team had a well-established practice of burning the clothes of every new player while the beginner was away from the locker room, blissfully unaware that his designer threads were on fire.

Successful cohesive teams are likely to comprise players high on **confidence** who do not blame themselves when their team loses and share in the credit following victory. Players who engage in behaviors that sabotage their own ability to function provide a convenient ready-made excuse for failure ('I felt the flu coming on before the game'; 'I never play well in cold weather'), but accept personal credit for success. This behavior is known as **self-handicapping**. Studies show that high levels of self-handicapping are associated with low task cohesion, and low self-handicapping is related to high social cohesion. The problem is that, while a self-handicapper might fit into a task-cohesive team quite well, the expectations of the team may be quite moderate.

While it seems obvious that a task-cohesive team will be more effective, the effects of social cohesion on team performance are not clear. 'For years coaches have assumed that positive feelings among team members result in better sport performance,' writes Mark Anshel. 'While this outcome is intuitively appealing, researchers aren't certain that it is true.' He cites the example of teammates passing only to friends. We might add that high achieving teams, such as the New York Yankees of the late 1970s or Manchester United of the 1990s, had several players who refused to speak to each other. Despite the lack of social cohesion, both teams had sufficient task cohesion for success.

Further reading

Anshel, M.H. (1997) *Sport Psychology: From theory to practice*, 3rd edition, Scottsdale AZ: Gorsuch Scarisbrick, pp. 293–308.

Carron, A.V. and Dennis, P.W. (1998) 'The sport team as an effective group,' pp. 127–41 in Williams, J.M. (ed.) *Applied Sport Psychology: Personal growth to peak performance*, 3rd edition, Mountain View CA.: Mayfield.

Lazenby, R. (2000) *Mind Games: Phil Jackson's long, strange journey* New York: McGraw-Hill.

COHESIVENESS *see* **cohesion**

COMEBACK

The return of a once-retired athlete aiming to recapture his or her former position and status is, of course, a comeback. Recovery from long periods of incapacity caused by illness or **injury** sometimes warrant the term 'comeback,' though it is usually reserved for the resumption of a sports career that was considered over. Comebacks are legion in sports and, while the aphorism 'they never come back' suggests that **aging** competitors' attempts inevitably conclude in failure, several comebacks have been conspicuously successful.

Mario Lemieux came out of **retirement** in 2000 and, at the age of 35, resumed his garlanded career with Pittsburgh Penguins and played hockey with the same kind of brilliance as he had in the first phase of his career. George Foreman returned to the ring in the 1990s at 45, after a ten-year break, and enjoyed considerable success until retiring for good at 49. By contrast, Björn Borg dropped out of tennis at 26, when still a top five ranked player, only to come back ten years later. He suffered a series of ignominious defeats by modest players. George Best also retired in his twenties; this was the first of several 'retirements,' each followed by a comeback; the progressive decay of his once-formidable **skill** was evident in his every return to the soccer field. When he left soccer entirely, his progressive **dependence** on alcohol became life-threatening.

Clearly every athlete takes risks when deciding to come back; the more prestigious the athlete, the greater the **risk**. For them, the possibility of a humbling is accentuated: witness the embarrassment suffered by multiple gold medalist Mark Spitz, his gray hair colored to conceal his age, but his physical decline painfully revealed in a sequence of defeats in the pool. Spitz won seven gold medals at the 1972 Munich Olympics and worked as a television analyst at the 1984 Los Angeles Olympics. The experience of watching others compete frustrated him so much that he made his unfortunate comeback several years later.

The **motivation** behind some comebacks may be obvious. Borg, for example, had become involved in disastrous business ventures and needed money. Best too was lured by the temptation of riches. The majority of retirees need to work and are poorly prepared to do so, having spent fifteen or so years in competitive sports. Lacking preparation for any occupation outside sports, many return simply to make a living. But in the case of successful athletes who clearly have wealth enough to sustain them through several lifetimes, the motivation is less certain.

Journalist Blake Morrison suggested an interesting possibility in speculating on the much-discussed comeback of Michael Jordan in 2001: 'The obvious explanation is that he misses the buzz, the adrenaline and applause ... when a man's **celebrity** is based on something he no longer does, he can feel very strange about it – exiled from himself and unentitled [sic].' Jordan was 38 at the time of the conjecture about his return, older than most comebacking athletes. Morrison argued that many men (he did not mention women) venture toward some way of 'confirming and vindicating' themselves as they approach 40. Harley Davidson motorcycles have a large market comprising males of that age group.

The 'midlife crisis' supposedly accounts for many fortyish men embarking on unexpected and often dangerous pursuits, presumably as a way of endorsing their credentials as active and dynamic agents rather than listless, middle-aged residues of people whose vitality and youth have long gone. For athletes, the predicament is arguably more acute: for a substantial part of their maturity they are engaged in pursuits that demand vitality and youth, as well as many other physical attributes. Their sense of self as well as their public persona is based not so much on wisdom, sagacity, insight or soundness of judgement, but on performance. When they are no longer able to perform to appropriate levels, managers, coaches, critical fans and the media rudely remind them of this. There is no room for self-delusion in sports. Retirement may be the result of conscious decision, but that decision is usually affected by the judgement of others or, in some cases, serious injuries. Once the echoes of others' criticisms have faded and the injuries have healed, fresh perspectives appear and the athlete may sense the chance of proving him or herself all over again.

Ray Leonard's comeback seem to fit into this model. Regarded as a suitable inheritor of Sugar Ray Robinson's mantle, Leonard led a triumphant amateur and professional career, establishing himself as one of the finest pound-for-pound boxers in history. A detached retina forced him out of the sport. Surgery repaired the injury and Leonard plotted an outrageous comeback, moving up a weight class to middleweight to challenge – and beat – Marvelous Marvin Hagler (who promptly retired himself and refused several lucrative offers to come back). Leonard's critics were silenced as he regained his finest form, making several successful defenses, at one point stepping up a further weight class. The present writer interviewed Leonard at his camp while he prepared for what was to be his penultimate fight (a defeat to Terry Norris) and sought the sources of Leonard's attachment with his sport. 'This is the only place I feel who I really am,' said Leonard. (Leonard actually made four comebacks, the first – prior to the Hagler fight – lasting only one fight.)

Sport was the context for establishing Leonard's **self-efficacy**, for validating himself, both through public approval and intrinsic grati-fication: in short, he regarded himself as quintessentially a fighter – all other aspects of his **character** were secondary. Deprived of his ability to fight, Leonard believed he could no longer be who he truly was. Like Lemieux, Foreman and several other athletes who came back after long, prosperous careers (Leonard had already earned an estimated $30 million when he first 'retired'), Leonard returned to sport because he felt *deprived*. Stripped of opportunities to perform to an audience, to demonstrate their worth and to draw acclaim, athletes lose a facility that has been with them for the majority of their adult lives and which actually forms part of their lives.

Other factors contributing toward the comeback derive from the sports **socialization** – the learning process through which athletes acquire particular values, ambitions and designs. Athletes are usually immersed in sports culture by the time they reach 11; in many sports (such as gymnastics and tennis), competitors are training hard and cultivating ambitions from about the age of 6 (Chris Evert was one such athlete who did not come back and famously declared 'there *is* life after tennis'). By the time any sports performer is 13, he or she will have started to formulate plans. As ambitions in sports take priority, so athletes discard other career aims and involve themselves in an environment in which significant influences include coaches, managers, scouts and, perhaps, agents. These form a type of protective enclosure, shielding the athlete from the travail and irritation that affect most people – like procuring a mortgage, paying bills, investing for the future. Unless the athlete prolongs his or her involvement in sport after retirement (as a manager, or TV commentator, for instance), he or she is likely to lose the enclosure and become part of a different environment. Coming back may be a way of re-entering what was once a comfortable environment.

Those who populate the enclosure continually dispense advice, and one of the first caveats a prospective athlete hears is that a career in sport is relatively short. As Billie-Jean King once said: 'When athletes reach their thirties ... everybody keeps telling them they should quit. They start to think they are slowing down because everybody asks "are you slowing down?" ' (King made a money-motivated comeback at 40 and made it to the Wimbledon singles semi-finals.) In other words, athletes often retire prematurely because of mere convention and, when they sense that other, perhaps older athletes have resumed their careers, they are inspired to follow suit. Comebacking athletes who approach or even surpass their previous form provide living proof that the comeback trail is not always a dead end.

Competitiveness also comes, or is at least heightened, through socialization in sports, and once an active career is over challenges disappear. Sometimes they are replaced by new challenges; but what greater challenge is there than to relaunch a sports career?

Socialized into rising to meet challenges, no matter how awesome, a retired athlete may construe the comeback as the ultimate challenge. This seems to account for the comeback of rower Steve Redgrave, who in 1996, after winning his fourth Olympic gold, ordered the media: 'Shoot me if I go near a boat again.' Four years later, he returned to win a fifth gold medal.

Finally, we should also acknowledge the explanation of Matt Biondi, who retired from competitive swimming after the 1988 Olympics, having amassed six gold medals. 'I realized that it was ridiculous to give it up because I still enjoyed it' (he won two more golds and a silver in his comeback). Competitive sports are a way of earning a living for professional athletes, but the initial interest in the activity was intrinsic **autotelic**. It is at least possible that, despite the years of arduous training interspersed by injury, the joy of competition lingers long enough to motivate a comeback.

Further reading

Lainson, S. and Sportstrust (1997) 'Comebacks,' *The Creative Athlete*, Issue 18, pp. 1–2, www.onlinesports.com/sportstrust/creative18.html.
Morrison, B. (2001) 'Jordan, me, and the lure of the comeback,' *Independent on Sunday*, 'Focus,' 20 April, p. 15.

COMMITMENT

Any engagement or involvement that restricts freedom of action is a commitment. The sense in which the term is used in sports is actually not so different from its other meanings: to deliver someone officially to custody (of, for example, a psychiatric treatment program), or the pledge to obligate oneself to another person. All, in some way, implicate subjects in a course of action from which there are limited escape routes. The word is a compound from the Latin *com*, for together, and *mittere*, entrust.

Clearly, progress in sports requires some level of commitment, whether it is in terms of times dedicated to training or abstinence from other fulfilling endeavors. One conception of commitment to sports suggests that an aspirant athlete should remain narrowly **focused** on specific goals and exclude other, perhaps distracting, interests. This understanding contrasts with that of Mark Thompson, who, in his essay, 'A charge,' maintains that a sport psychologist can only achieve results if his or her charge or charges are committed: 'Unless the athlete or team is truly willing to commit themselves to mental skills training and are competitive enough to transfer what is learned in counseling sessions or through educational workshops into practice or onto playing, I philosophically question how effective we really are in terms of performance enhancement training.'

Yet Thompson also endorses the view that 'sport is not and should not be the only avenue in which they [athletes] derive a sense of self-worth.'

While the author does not develop this argument, its implication seems to be: (1) any ancillary aid to an athlete(s), whether it be coaching or **applied sport psychology**, has severe limitations imposed on it by the athlete – if he or she lacks commitment, then the aid's effectiveness is compromised; (2) commitment is not the same as monomania (an inflexible fixation on one thing), but an adaptable orientation which allows the athlete to pursue task-related objectives, although not to the exclusion of other potentially fulfilling pursuits.

Enlightened as this conception of commitment appears to be, it is not one recognizable in the behavior of several top athletes. Gabriela Szabo, the pre-eminent middle-distance athlete of the early twenty-first century, spent her entire waking day training and needed between 12 and 14 hours sleep because of the physical demands of her sport. Steve Redgrave, who won five gold medals at successive Olympic games, dedicated himself to a grueling training program almost every day for over twenty-four years. Buddy Lazier postponed surgery on a broken back to allow him to train seven days a week in preparation for his successful shot at the Indianapolis 500 in 1996. A legion of topflight boxers, including Muhammad Ali and Rocky Marciano, were known to hide themselves away at training camp and lead an austere Spartan existence for months approaching a fight. Andrea Jaeger, a casualty of **burnout** after an immensely promising start to her tennis career, reflected how, in her teen years, she would 'dread' training and competing, though there was little else in her life.

Sports may not be the only avenue from which many athletes can 'derive a sense of self-worth,' but, for the minority who succeed consistently at the highest possible levels, it seems to be precisely that. Commitment is a variable concept: its meaning for those seeking pleasure, **self-efficacy** and perhaps some measure of **confidence** is more flexible than for those driven by a high **achievement motive** and for whom alternatives are not readily available.

Motivation affects the degree of commitment an athlete is prepared to make, and while there are few irrefutable indicators as to what determines an athlete's motives and orientations, deprivation may be one of them. As the sports writer Bob Waters noted when writing about why African American athletes seem to have a resolve lacking in some of their white counterparts: 'Desire and dedication are easier to come by when the alternative is a one-way ticket back to the ghetto' (quoted in my own book *Black Sportsmen*).

Further reading

Olsen, J. (1968) *The Black Athlete* New York: Time Life.

Thompson, M.A. (1998) 'A charge,' pp. 257–60 in Thompson, M.A., Vernacchia, R.A. and Moore, W.E. (eds) *Case Studies in Applied Sport Psychology: An educational approach* Dubuque IA: Kendall/Hunt.

COMPETITION

Although competition invariably suggests a contest against others, the concept's original meaning is wider: from the Latin *com*, meaning for, and *petere*, seek, it defined a search or endeavor for superiority in some quality or qualities, either *with* or against others. The term shares a common source with *competence*.

Competition is, of course, the 'essence' of sports, though it carries no necessary connotation of opposition or rivalry. This property has been added by cultures that encouraged contest as part of the struggle to demonstrate competence. In 1976, Rainer Marten defined competition as 'a process in which comparison of an individual's performance is made with some standard in the presence of at least one other person who is aware of the criterion for comparison and can evaluate the comparison process' (quoted in Gill, 2000). The 'comparison' is typically understood as a contest.

The question germane to competition is: does there have to be a necessary bifurcation of winners and losers, victors and vanquished? Karen Lee Hill, in examining the 'humanistic model' of sports, offers a conception that is close to the original meaning of the term: 'Rather than conceptualizing competition as a "war" with one's adversary, it is looked upon as a cooperative venture in which "associates" ... agree to provide each other with the necessary resistance to catalyze development of each other's potential.'

In other words, opponents in a competition are not trying to eliminate or destroy their opponents, but are providing legitimate resistance sufficient that their opponents can develop potential and demonstrate capabilities. There is, of course, only one winner, though both parties profit from the encounter in the sense that they have both exercised **skill** and demonstrated **self-efficacy**. This conception of competition seems at odds with commonsense interpretations which stress winning as the end point. While this may seem to be the case, competitors are actually helping each other reach individual goals by forcing them to produce their best effort and perhaps improve their performance. Without stern opposition, this may not be possible. The rules of any competition define the conditions under which human excellence may be realized and advanced. In this conception, final scores, results, standings and other measures of success are linear and misleading. All parties, winners and losers, are beneficiaries of the competitive experience.

Hill's humanistic interpretation of competition contradicts conventional notions of competition, most of which are predicated on 'winning is the only thing,' or similar slogans. Interestingly, it is compatible with the orientation of many sports performers. Research by Diane Gill and her associates indicates that highly skilled athletes gauged success not by the outcome of a contest but by their evaluation of their personal performances. Obviously, they strove toward victory in competition, but competitive orientation, defined as 'desire to strive for success in competition,' was only one element of their overall **motivation**: the quality of their own accomplishment was integral to the sports experience.

While competition, as conceived today, involves an interaction between two or more parties in pursuit of the same **goal** and the ultimate failure of one or more of the parties to attain it, the term should properly be understood in its original form. Even in contemporary competition, it seems, defeat is not a synonym for failure: it is one of several criteria used to evaluate the competitive experience.

Further reading

Gill, D.L., Dowd, D.A., Williams, J., Beaudoin, C.M. and Martin, J.J. (1996) 'Competitive orientation and motives of adult sport and exercise participants,' *Journal of Sport Behavior* vol. 19, pp. 307–18.
Hill, K.L. (2001) *Frameworks for Sport Psychologists* Champaign IL: Human Kinetics.

COMPETITIVENESS *see* **competition**

COMPOSURE

Composure is the quality of calmness possessed by athletes who can arrange their thoughts, behavior and even expression for a specified purpose and refuse to be fazed (disconcerted, perturbed) by activities around them. It derives from the Latin *com*, together, and *ponere*, put, and its meaning in sports stays true to its origins: a composed athlete remains organized and together regardless of changing circumstances.

Achieving and retaining composure is a function of arousal **control**. Every athlete needs a level of **arousal** to execute a sporting performance; those who are able to master the level required remain composed, or *poised* – a related term that describes an athlete's sense of balance (for example, weighing up the urgency of trailing with only five minutes left of a football game with the need to avoid panicking). Composure invariably facilitates effective performance in the face of pressure.

While some athletes are said to be gifted with 'natural poise,' the composure exhibited during **competition** is more likely to be the result of learned technique. Richard Gordin relates the findings of case studies in which various interventions were tested for effectiveness. The 'treatments' for performance **anxiety** included: learning *coping skills* – keeping control over how the performer reacts to the changing circumstances of a competition; **self-talk** – maintaining an *inner dialogue* throughout the competition; **concentration** training – focusing on the process of performing not the outcome of the performance; *simulation* (or model) training – facing **fear** and doubt as a way of strengthening oneself.

By employing techniques such as these, Gordin was able to demonstrate that, far from being a natural trait, composure can be acquired. In one interesting case, a swimmer practiced techniques that actually impeded his performance rather than inducing composure. A perfectionist, the swimmer **focused** externally: that is, on a wide range of cues outside himself – a technique more appropriate to **team players**. He also engaged in self-talk which was 'virtually all negative' because of the high expectations he had of himself. The swimmer effectively sabotaged his performance. He was recommended **coping strategies**, which involved recognizing the destructive effects of his perfectionism; he was also advised to remove himself mentally from the pool environment before a race. Gordin believed that, by using these and other techniques, the swimmer would control anxiety and build composure before and during races.

Further reading

Gordin, R.D. (1998) 'Composure: arousal and anxiety dynamics,' pp. 37–62 in Thompson, M.A., Vernacchia, R.A. and Moore, W.E. (eds) *Case Studies in Applied Sport Psychology: An educational approach* Dubuque IA: Kendall/Hunt.

CONCENTRATION

Concentration is the means through which **attention** is engaged and managed, 'attention' referring to the mental process that allows us to focus on some features of our environment, at the same time excluding, at least partially, several others. In short, concentration employs, directs and controls all of one's attention, usually in the pursuit of a definite **goal** or assignment. In sports, as in other aspects of life, the distinction between concentration and attention is not always clear: being urged to 'pay attention,' for example, means, for all intents and purposes, to concentrate by bringing together all attentional capacities to converge on a central image or task. In this sense, its application in sports is not so different in meaning from its Latin foundations, *cum* for with or together, and *centrum* for center.

A tennis player preparing to serve must use concentration to focus his or her attention narrowly on executing the task, ignoring or **gating** out irrelevant sensory data in the environment, such as murmurs in the crowd or planes passing overhead. The position of his or her opponent is, of course, relevant and must be attended to. By contrast, opponents are irrelevant to a sprinter, who needs to concentrate attention even more narrowly, selecting only cues that are essential to the immediate assignment.

Usually, the more adept athletes become at their sport, the more able they are to concentrate efficiently. For example, a beginning judo player will need a great amount of conscious thought in accomplishing a shoulder throw, as would a novice fencer in mastering a thrust. They need to be aware of their own body movements as well as their opponents', processing input and output information and responding to perceptual and motor demands. More experienced athletes perform these skills seemingly without thinking, or even much effort, the reason being that input and output information is so quickly processed that it has become reflexive, or automatic. Learning new skills requires attending to a great many features and, correspondingly, needing strenuous mental effort. Having gained the skills, the athlete can lessen the mental effort and concentrate on other aspects of the environment relating, for example, to tactics and changes in circumstances; this is a form of *attentional narrowing*, often known as getting **focused**.

Imagine attention as a light beam with concentration being the flash lamp that controls it. Early in an athlete's development, the beam will be broad, illuminating a range of materials that need attention. Later, when the basic and even more complex skills are acquired, the beam narrows so that it sheds light only on more analytical matters, such as planning moves and reading situations as they develop. The experienced athlete need not concentrate on the more elementary tasks that once demanded so much effort. They can accomplish several different tasks at the same time, as easily as an experienced driver can drive, listen to the CD player and have phone conversations while concentrating on the route ahead. Similarly, players of team sports need to concentrate on several contingencies of the game so they are ready to respond to a wide range of situations.

Yet even experienced athletes can have their concentration shattered. As the motorist's might be broken by a fellow motorist running a red light and causing a near-miss, the athlete's concentration can be disrupted by a bad decision from an official or foul play from an opponent – which is why trailing players often foul their opponents, attempting to break their concentration and divert their attention away from the competition. Elite athletes who know the importance of concentration will sometimes make special efforts to interrupt their opponents'. Consider Martina Hingis' attempts at the 1999 French Open final against Steffi Graf: Hingis demanded that the umpire inspect a mark on the clay surface after her forehand landed adjacent to the baseline, took a five-and-a-half minute restroom break and even served underarm when facing match point on two occasions. Graf's concentration remained unperturbed and she went on to win.

So-called 'powers of concentration' may appear to be 'givens' – taken-for-granted abilities – but sport psychology regards them as acquired through practice and has developed procedures for removing the enemies of concentration, the principal ones being distractions, **anxiety** and inappropriate focus, according to Jeff Simons.

Further reading

Moran, A.P. (1996) *The Psychology of Concentration in Sport Performers: A cognitive analysis* East Sussex: Psychology Press.

Simons, J. (1998) 'Concentration,' pp. 89–114 in Thompson, M.A., Vernacchia, R.A. and Moore, W.E. (eds) *Case Studies in Applied Sport Psychology: An educational approach* Dubuque IA: Kendall/Hunt.

CONDITIONING *see* reinforcement

CONFIDENCE

From the Latin *con*, meaning for, and *fidere*, trust, confidence is typically understood as an attribute possessed by subjects who trust their own abilities and judgement, are self-reliant and assured and perhaps, on occasion, bold. Confident athletes enter **competition** certain in the knowledge that they will achieve their **goal**. Resolute and secure, confident competitors approach contests with 'the belief or degree of certainty,' as Robin Vealey puts it, 'about their ability to be successful in sport.' Accurate as this statement is, it does not convey the unstable feature of confidence: it can be built, damaged and sometimes destroyed by events and personalities.

William Moore argues that confidence enables an athlete to move from conscious **control** to **automaticity** – the automatic execution of tasks needed for **peak performance**. In other words, the confident performer does not think about the job at hand: he or she just does it. Persuading an athlete to surrender conscious effort to motor control involves trust, and this involves a belief in one's own capacities, or what Albert Bandura called **self-efficacy**. Repeated successes enhance self-efficacy to the point where occasional defeats are insignificant and have little impact on a performer's confidence. Vealey's research suggested that 'sport-confidence' may be transferable, so confidence in one discipline may carry over to others if the athlete has a particular kind of personality trait. (Manzo criticized Vealey's concept of sport confidence, arguing that it is too close to self-efficacy and unclear how to measure athletic 'success.')

Skill without confidence can damage performance, especially in pressure situations such as penalty shoot-outs in soccer. In a 2000 European championships game, host nation Holland missed a total of five penalties and lost the semi-final shoot-out to Italy. The calamity was presumably not the result of lack of practice or proficiency, but of a betrayal of players' confidence at critical moments. Each penalty miss would have raised **anxiety** levels, inducing soccer's equivalent of **choking**. The effects of an infusion of confidence can also be spectacular. Going into her 100 meters semi-final at the 2001 world track and field championships, Zhanna Puntusevich-Block faced the forbidding prospect of Marion Jones, who was undefeated in fifty-four straight races. Unexpectedly, the Ukrainian ran a 10.93 to squeeze Jones into second place. Both qualified for the final, and while observers may have dismissed Jones' loss as irrelevant, Puntusevich-Block used it as evidence of Jones' vulnerability and her own prowess.

In the final, she repeated her win over Jones, recording 10.82 to take the gold medal. 'The semi gave me a lot of psychological confidence,' she said after the final. 'I realised that I could beat Marion' (quoted in *Athletics Weekly* vol. 55, no. 34, 22 August 2001).

Instilling confidence in an athlete can involve affirmations, 'strong, positive statements about something that is believable and has a realistic potential for becoming true,' as Moore defines them. It may also involve the athlete in **imagery**: to visualize a favorable scenario prior to competition. But the 'as if' approach is one of the most effective ways: encouraging athletes to put themselves in the shoes of another whom they wish to emulate. What begins as a fake display, or perhaps an attempt at **modeling**, may develop into confidence.

For instance, Muhammad Ali, in his early career, modeled himself on Gorgeous George, a brash and boastful wrestler in the 1960s. Ali later confessed that he was so apprehensive about his first title fight with Sonny Liston that he needed an act to hide it. His success in this and subsequent title fights increased his confidence to the point where he genuinely believed he could never lose. On occasion, Ali, like many other athletes, allowed his confidence to become insolent pride, or presumption; in other words, *over-confidence*. On one notable occasion, Leon Spinks was nemesis to Ali's hubris.

Other dangers to confidence include *pressing*, or trying too hard, which leads to tension, and *controlling*, in which athletes concentrate on the mechanics of what they are doing. Confidence allows the competitor to let go of conscious **control** and trust his or her skill, so that their performance feels 'instinctive.' Arrogant or bombastic athletes are not necessarily confident: it is possible that their bold appearance is manufactured to mask *self-abatement*, which develops from excessively critical self-evaluation and the debasement of their own abilities.

Effective **leadership** in sport often depends on the confidence athletes have in another, for example a coach or manager: if they trust that figure and believe in his or her ability to guide them, they will accept decisions, follow instructions and respect that person's judgement. Once a leader-figure loses the confidence of players, leadership breaks down and resignation or dismissal usually follows.

Further reading

Manzo, L. (2002) 'Enhancing sport performance: the role of confidence and concentration,' pp. 247–71 in Silva, J.M. and Stevens, D.E. (eds) *Psychological Foundations of Sport* Boston MA: Allyn & Bacon.
Moore, W. (1998) 'Confidence,' pp. 63–88 in Thompson, M.A., Vernacchia, R.A.

and Moore, W.E. (eds) *Case Studies in Applied Sport Psychology: An educational approach* Dubuque IA: Kendall/Hunt.

Vealey, R.S. (1986) 'Conceptualization of sport-confidence and competitive orientation: preliminary investigation and instrument development,' *Journal of Sport Psychology* vol. 8, pp. 221–46.

CONTROL

The power to guide, command, restrain, regulate or manage is control (from the Latin *contra*, against, and *rotulus*, roll). In a sense, sport psychology aims to control by modifying or changing thought and behavior in a way that is conducive to improved athletic performance and enriched sporting experience. It does so by assuming charge of a situation or, more often, enabling a subject to assume charge of his or her own experiences; this typically involves changes to both behavior and **cognition**. In the latter sense, the purpose of control in sports is about, to use the title of David Kauss's book, *Mastering Your Inner Game*: arming athletes with the tools to manage the 'factors that often determine who's an all-star and who's an also-ran.'

Control is most popularly associated with branches of psychology that systematically use **reinforcement** to reward desired responses to **stimuli** and punish unwanted behavior. Yet control is implicit in all sport psychology interventions, even those that aspire to 'unlocking potential,' or 'liberating' subjects through **catharsis** and analogous expedients. To achieve a successful outcome, some measure of control must be attained, whether over a subject(s) or a situation.

Most strategies available to the sport psychologist are predicated on control: **cognitive–behavioral modification**, **coping strategies**, **stress management training** and **stress inoculation training** all address the regulation of either behavior or **emotion**. Indeed, facilitating **emotional** control **skill** is one of the most valuable contributions to improved **skill performance**, as well as enriched competitive experience.

Physical techniques designed to facilitate self-control include **biofeedback**, progressive **relaxation** and breathing control, while cognitive operations consist of **autogenic** procedures, **hypnosis**, **imagery** and meditation. In practice, many of these are combined. Cognitive restructuring and **self-talk** are thought modification techniques designed to allow athletes to appraise themselves and situations differently so as to create a capacity to guide action with authority rather than let situations slip away. Perhaps the most abundant form of control practiced by athletes, especially elite athletes, is intended to restore some measure of command over the near-ubiquitous **stress** that affects competitors.

Further reading

Dawson, K.A., Brawley, L.R. and Maddux, J.E. (2000) 'Examining the relationships among concepts of control and exercise attendance,' *Journal of Sport & Exercise Psychology* vol. 22, pp. 131–44.
Kauss, D.R. (2001) *Mastering Your Inner Game: A self-guided approach to finding your unique sports performance keys* Champaign IL: Human Kinetics.

COPING STRATEGIES

To cope is, of course, to deal successfully with a person, a predicament or some other kind of unwelcome situation. A coping strategy is a deliberate, rationally planned program for contending with persons or circumstances that might otherwise produce **anxiety** and **stress**. Usually, the coping strategy is aimed at the source of the anxiety, unlike *defensive* strategies, which are directed at the anxiety itself. Interestingly, the term comes from the Greek word *kolaphos*, later anglicized to *cop*, meaning a strike with the fist or a punch.

Some athletes use coping strategies in preparation for a particular event, while others employ them on a continuing basis; still others have no need for planned strategies. Whatever strategy is used, it must be **focused**, whether on the upcoming affair, an ongoing condition or a personal state. Problem-solving strategies, for instance, are directed at trying to change the conditions under which anxieties or stresses occur. Enhanced planning, more information, greater effort or new **skill acquisition** may be in the repertoire of strategies that will enable a subject to contend with a situation or an opponent more effectively and thus reduce anxiety.

By contrast, emotion-focused coping implicates the athlete in trying to identify the specific **emotion** or set of emotions that lie at the source of his or her anxiety. **Emotional control** begins way before an event, when athletes start to turn thoughts inwards, scrutinizing their own case histories to recognize specific persons, events and situations where a sudden emotion has been experienced before. They can then rehearse appropriate responses.

Controlling an emotion means being sensitive to cues, so that an emotion like **anger** can be recognized before it displaces rational thought and leads to unreasonable responses, such as **aggression** and perhaps **violence**. Athletes with reputations for being **temperamental** use emotion-focused strategies, such as **self-talk**, to suppress the tendency to react violently to certain episodes (such as when a soccer player is continually fouled, or a hockey player body checked). In this way, they can better cope with situations that might otherwise produce too much **arousal** and subsequent anxiety.

Further reading

Lazarus, R.S. and Lazarus, B. (1994) *Passion and Reason: Making sense of our emotions* New York: Oxford University Press.

Smith, R.E. (2000) 'Generalization in coping skills training,' *Journal of Sport & Exercise Psychology* vol. 20, pp. 358–78.

DEATH WISH

While the popular use of the term 'death wish' owes much to the five Charles Bronson movies between 1974 and 1994, it is accepted in some psychological circles as representing the motivational state of persons who habitually seek out hazardous situations. Freudians prefer to interpret the behavior of such persons in terms of Thanatos, or the death **instinct**, which inclines individuals away from gratification and toward denial, restraint and expiation (Thanatos was the Greek god of death). Some athletes, especially those in sports in which there is a considerable **risk** of harm, are often thought to be possessed of a death wish.

Every sport involves the risk of death or serious **injury**. Boxing draws the wrath of American and British medical associations because of the physical punishment incurred in virtually every fight by virtually every boxer. Statistically, however, motor racing and air sports have far more victims than other sports, with accidents claiming the lives of competitors in what are clearly high-risk endeavors involving elaborate pieces of technology. Research by R.C. Cantu and F.O. Mueller indicated that American football, ice hockey, gymnastics and wrestling (not WWF) were sports in which competitors were at greatest **risk**. Less obviously, dangerous sports include running and cycling: in these, athletes are typically killed in road accidents while training, or by **overtraining** when in middle age. Even sedentary competitions, such as chess or bridge, harbor unseen perils (such as the onset of deep vein thrombosis after remaining stationary for long periods!).

While the notion of a death wish has a superficial plausibility, it remains in the realms of hypothesis: there is no empirical research to consolidate its status as anything but a popular phrase. Further, there are no known athletes who resemble Bronson's death-dealing urban vigilante who hurtles into treacherous situations at every opportunity. Even Formula One drivers, whose professional *raison d'être* is to travel at unsafe speeds, are motivated by more tangible incentives than the chance to cheat death – like the prospect of earnings of twenty-something million dollars per year.

Xtreme sports devotees are also considered to be driven by a death wish: they readily acknowledge nurturing a **dependence** on the **adrenaline rush** that typically accompanies high-risk activities. Technically, it is possible to become dependent on an activity that elicits a particular type of sensation, though the term 'adrenaline junkies' may not be completely appropriate.

Further reading

Cantu, R.C. and Mueller, F.O. (1999) 'Fatalities and catastrophic injuries in high school and college sports, 1982–1997: lessons for improving safety,' *Physician and Sports Medicine* vol. 27, pp. 35–48.

Cashmore, E. (2000) 'Death,' pp. 80–2 in Cashmore, E. (ed.) *Sports Culture: An A–Z guide* London: Routledge.

DECISION MAKING

The process of making a choice between alternatives when the outcome cannot be known in advance is decision making. It involves often complex deliberations, such as predicting probable consequences, balancing moral and technical considerations and attending to the likely impact of the decision on others. Decision making is an intrinsic part of sports. Decisions are made about which sports to enter, whether or not to pursue them fulltime, when to retire and, possibly, when to make a **comeback**. In **competition**, decisions are constantly made from an array of options, many of them tactical in nature and others based on the employment of **skill**.

Decision making is performed in conditions of uncertainty. Those making the decisions will try to maximize expected utility, utility being the subjective value of the outcome. Every decision involves a degree of **commitment**: a choice leads to some outcomes and closes out others. Choices are made in anticipation that the consequences of them will be more valuable than the ones that would have resulted from the options eschewed. But the choice has to be ranked in some order of probability. A cricket batsman facing a spin bowler has about 0.2 of a second to make a choice whether to attack the ball and try for a boundary or to defend. He must rapidly rate his chances of achieving a boundary against those of only snicking the ball and getting caught in the slips. Baseball batters face similar decisions: go for a big run-earning slug, but one that carries with it a chance of total failure, or perhaps just bunt.

No athlete (indeed, no human being) makes the appropriate choice every time. Good athletes make them more consistently than average athletes. Experienced athletes, in particular, use their **memory** as a resource in decision making. Of course, making decisions and having the ability to execute them are not the same and, while **aging** athletes frequently know the right choice, they also know that their chances of executing them exactly as they wish grow slimmer through the years.

Reliable and consistent decision makers are often credited with **leadership** roles. Sound decision making contributes to team **cohesion** and individual **confidence**. Yet there is no single blueprint adopted by all dependable decision makers. There are several types of decision-making styles: at one extreme, the autocratic type makes decisions on his or her own, without seeking input from other team members; at the other, the democratic decision maker solicits the views of all other members. Research by Vroom and Jago in 1988 concluded that each style required different skills. The autocrat needs to appraise various options before deciding on the best course, while the democratic decision maker needs to be participative, involving others in discussion and negotiation. The latter may take longer but produces more innovative decisions.

In the heat of competitive action, of course, time is a valuable resource and a democratic style may not be practicable. Members of a football team must place their faith in the decisions of a leader, such as the quarterback. A boxer must listen to the advice of his or her corner. Rally drivers simply react to the decisions called by their navigator. Rowers attend to every instruction of their cox. In each case, the decisions must not only be made quickly, but they must be communicated lucidly with no room at all for misunderstanding.

Further reading

Baron, J. (1988) *Thinking and Deciding* Cambridge: Cambridge University Press.
Vroom, V.H. and Jago, A.G. (1988) *The New Leadership: Managing participation in organizations* Englewood Cliffs NJ: Prentice-Hall.

DEPENDENCE

When individuals have a strong, compelling desire continually to use a drug or other substance excessively, they are said to have dependence.

The term 'dependence' is favored over *addiction*, which was originally used only for dependence deriving from physiological changes (themselves resulting from repeated administrations of the drug or substance). But the line between purely physiological addiction and dependence, which may be psychological, is not clear. Dependence can be the result of a craving for a substance that provides relief or euphoria to the user but does not produce fundamental biophysical changes such that further intake of the substance is needed for normal functioning (the term stems from the Latin *pendere*, meaning to hang).

Few substances that are widely used have genuinely addictive properties: prolonged use of heroin induces physiological changes in the user, which is why addicts need to be weaned off it or given the substitute analgesic methadone. Long-term use of alcohol is capable of affecting the functions of the central **nervous system** and the sudden cessation of its use can cause withdrawal symptoms; further ingestion of alcohol alleviates these temporarily. But studies have shown that most heavy drinkers drink to experience the positive effects of alcohol rather than escape the aversive experiences produced by its absence. Some scholars, such as Geoffrey Lowe, argue that the concept of addiction can be expanded to encompass the 'total experience involving physiological changes in individuals (some of whom may be genetically and/or psychologically predisposed). These changes are interpreted and given meaning by the individual within the sociolocultural context in which the addictive behaviour occurs.'

It also possible to acquire a dependence on a substance that has no tolerance potential, meaning something that does not lead the body to adapt in such a way that ever larger doses are needed to get the same effect. So while 'addiction' is still used popularly to describe, for instance, cravings for chocolate or caffeine habits, 'dependence' more accurately describes the psychological dynamic behind continued use of these substances. Serena Williams acknowledged a dependence on on-line shopping, sometimes spending up to three hours before a game surfing the net with her credit card at the ready.

Reports of athletes with dependence, or addictions, particularly on alcohol and narcotic drugs, are legion. Mickey Mantle and Daryl Strawberry had two of the best-known dependences in sports history, Mantle's on alcohol, Strawberry's on crack cocaine. Paul Merson and Tony Adams, both members of the successful Arsenal soccer team of the 1990s, admitted to having alcohol dependence (Merson was also a habitual cocaine user). Nicotine dependence is less prevalent, though not totally absent from sports: in 1997, New York Mets pitcher Pete Harnisch was placed on the disabled list while he tried to overcome his dependence; he was the first player to be incapacitated by withdrawal symptoms resulting from his attempts to quit tobacco.

Before systematic drug-testing (the IOC introduced its first fullscale tests in 1972), amphetamines were popular among many athletes. Dave Meggyesy's *Out of Their League* exposed his predilection for pills to get pumped for games. It is entirely possible that many players developed dependence on such stimulants. Ted Kotcheff's 1979 movie of the Pete Gent memoir *North Dallas Forty* depicted pro football players jogging on to the field like near-zombies after taking copious amounts of sundry stimulants augmented by analgesic painkillers. Analgesics are commonly used in sports, especially collision sports such as football and soccer, where painful injuries are customary but often not serious enough to prevent an athlete's performing. Painkillers are administered regularly, and have been for decades. Brett Favre's well-publicized dependence on painkillers in the late 1990s may be but one of an unknown number of similar conditions among athletes or ex-athletes who carry injuries beyond their playing careers.

Given the demands of particularly professional sports and the pressure under which athletes perform, it would be unusual if many did not seek relief through antidepressants or other psychoactive drugs. Benzodiazepines, such as diazepam (e.g. Valium) and nitrazepam (Mogadon) were reported to have been popular in the 1970s, Paul Hoch reporting that athletes were 'tranquilized to get their eyeballs back in their head – to even get a night's sleep,' in his *Rip Off the Big Game.*

It is also likely that there is a high incidence of antidepressant dependency among sports performers. Prozac alone has been taken by an estimated 38 million people since it was introduced in 1988. Whether or not antidepressants can lead to addiction is open to debate: some argue that long-term use of Prozac and similar drugs may pose a significant **risk** of neurological side effects, while others dismiss such claims. Clearly though, the risk of dependence is palpable; the greater the dose and duration of consumption, the greater the risk. This rule holds good for any type of dependence, though cocaine taken in the form of crack, or freebase, is known to have high 'addiction potential' and can accelerate its occasional users to compulsives or addicts rapidly.

There is no unequivocal answer to the question: why do people become dependent on a substance? While some approaches prefer to treat each form of dependence uniquely, others view dependence and addiction more inclusively. Genetic arguments center on the hereditarian principle that we are born with the potential to become dependent on substances and that culture merely supplies triggers. There is some support for this, especially in the area of 'alcoholism' (a rather crude term to describe all kinds of chronic or heavy drinking). But there is less support for the related view that dependence is a consequence of an 'addictive **personality**.' Both approaches focus on individuals rather than social contexts.

Social learning models, by contrast, accentuate the role of learning in the 'sociocultural context,' as Lowe calls it. This includes **modeling** behavior on that of others, or responding to the pressures of a cultural milieu that values indulgence in alcohol, drugs or other substances and responding positively to the temporary sensation of empowerment supplied by the substance (for example, avoiding responsibility, or avoiding the feeling of **stress**). This approach holds more promise for understanding dependence in sports. Typically, athletes have long intervals in their weeks or months when training is over but **competition** not yet begun; they also spend periods traveling, staying in hotels away from their family and close friends. This may be an ideal context for developing habits that develop into dependence. The situation is often accentuated when athletes retire from competition and find an even greater amount of free time available to them. Countless sports performers have developed sometimes chronic dependence in their retirements.

Further reading

Lowe, G. (1996) 'Alcohol and drug addiction,' pp. 950–68 in Colman, A.M. (ed.) *Companion Encyclopedia of Psychology*, vol. 2, London: Routledge.
Stainback, R.D. (1997) *Alcohol and Sport* Champaign IL: Human Kinetics.

DEPRESSION

Depression is a **mood** typified by a sense of insufficiency, dejection, sadness, hopelessness, fatigue or acute lack of **motivation**. It may arise in response to a specific incident or set of circumstances, or it may be part of a complex or syndrome of related symptoms. Gloria Balague and James Reardon's case study of an athlete whose mother had died illustrates how depression can affect form rapidly. The athlete reported 'lack of energy, low motivation to perform and several recurring injuries' which were later revealed to be symptomatic of depression. The athlete grew irritable with peers and isolated himself from them. The term stems from the Latin for press, *pressio*, prefixed with *de* for down, or from.

Severe depression is often treated with antidepressant drugs, though in the above case the athlete used a **cognition** based **intervention** that included new **goal setting** procedures and a pre-**competition** ritual. Research by, among others, LaFontaine found that there is a relationship between aerobic exercise and the relief of depression as well as other forms of **negativity**. Reasons for depressions are varied and change with changing contexts. **Eating disorders** are often a manifestation of some forms of depression and reflect dissatisfaction with **body image**.

Further reading

Balague, G. and Reardon, J.P. (1998) 'Case studies of a clinical nature,' pp. 227–44 in Thompson, M.A., Vernacchia, R.A. and Moore, W.E. (eds) *Case Studies in Applied Sport Psychology: An educational approach* Dubuque IA: Kendall/Hunt.

LaFontaine, T.P., DiLorenzo, T.M., Frensch, P.A., Stucky-Ropp, R.C., Bargman, E.P. and McDonald, D.G. (1992) 'Aerobic exercise and mood: a brief review, 1985–1990,' *Sports Medicine* vol. 13, pp. 160–70.

DEVIANCE

Formed from the Latin *de*, from, and *via*, way, 'deviance' describes the manner in which society responds to behavior that has been defined, usually in some official way, as unusual, irregular and, in some extreme cases, threatening. Deviance, it should be emphasized, does not describe behavior, nor any properties of it; nor does it characterize particular individuals or groups. It refers to the process in which a label is stuck on to people designated as rule-breakers and their actions nominated as transgressions. So deviance is a relative concept: what constitutes rule-breaking in one culture at a certain stage in history may not in another culture or at a different time. In other words, deviance is context-sensitive: the reaction of society to behavior determines whether or not behavior will be designated *deviant*.

For instance, **doping** designed to enhance athletic performance was practiced systematically in many countries, both in and out of the Soviet sphere of influence, particularly from the late 1950s, when the utility of anabolic steroids became well known. A great many athletes took drugs with impunity. The introduction of rules prohibiting doping (from 1972) officially changed the status of this behavior and of the athletes engaging in it. So the enactment and enforcement of the rules created the conditions under which this piece of deviance came into being. Progressively strict testing procedures and punishment for violators aided by an occasionally hysterical media were all features of a reaction that defined doping as deviance and those discovered taking drugs as deviants.

Even once the rules are introduced, it is perfectly possible to break them habitually and not be caught. Only after the behavior is known publicly can what many call the 'labeling process' click into motion. The classic example in sport is Ben Johnson: once hailed as the fastest man in the world, he was labeled 'the world's greatest cheat' following his expulsion from the 1988 summer Olympics.

Drug taking is an example of how a behavior defined as a serious violation of rules in one context may be permissible in another. The types of substances typically taken by athletes are often legally available either on prescription or over the counter of any pharmacy. The reverse is also true: behavior tolerated and, in some cases, approved of in sport would be harshly punished outside the context of sport. Imagine what would happen if a violent incident from a typical NHL game took place in a shopping mall. In some circumstances, perpetrators of violent behavior in, for example, hockey, rugby and soccer, have been held accountable through civil and criminal courts.

The **motivation** to break rules lies in the desire to win at any cost, a desire that has been nurtured by the copious amount of money available in professional sports. This may not be the only factor, but it combines with, for example, **personality** characteristics, **achievement motivation** and a cluster of situational variables to produce a propensity to transgress.

Various theories have been advanced to explain why people become deviant. Earlier models based on genes, crania and other individual endowments have given way to theories that accentuate the role of social processes, including the background of the rule-breakers, their investment in society and their peer groups associations on the one hand and enforcement agencies, the courts and the entire criminal justice system on the other. In other words, accounts of deviance need to take account of the whole context in which rule violation is defined and processed as well as produced.

Some theories hold that a certain amount of deviance is *functional*, its punishment serving to remind society where the boundaries between right and wrong lie. Others insist that deviance is about a relationship between groups who have economic and political power and the ability to write the rules (law) and groups who have no power nor access to resources. The incessant *conflict* between them brings about deviance, with the powerful framing law in a way that reflects their best interests and penalizing the powerless for breaking it. And still other theories maintain that deviance is a question of interaction between rule-breakers and the *social reaction* to them, which is essentially the framework used in this entry. Studies using this frame of reference tend to focus on agents of **control** (police, courts, etc.) rather than the rule-breakers.

Much play has been made about the impact of sports participation on young people's tendencies toward deviant behavior. The '*Angels with Dirty Faces* effect' (from the classic 1938 movie) refers to the rehabilitative consequences of sports for young offenders and potential offenders. A fusillade of research on this subject since the 1930s has failed to make a direct hit. Some studies found that sports curbed rule-breaking tendencies, or perhaps subordinated them to the greater **goal** of succeeding athletically. Others unearthed a bonding subculture among athletes, which promoted the kinds of attitudes and values that commissioned rule-breaking. Some studies have found that a disproportionate number of athletes are accused of sexually related offences, yet only a tiny minority are convicted, suggesting that the status associated with being a sports performer may be a valuable resource in escaping conviction.

Further reading

Benedict, J. and Klein, A. (1997) 'Arrest and conviction rates for athletes accused of sexual assault,' *Sociology of Sport Journal* vol. 14, pp. 86–94.

Cashmore, E. (2000) 'The *Angels with Dirty Faces* effect,' pp. 20–5 in Cashmore, E. (ed.) *Sports Culture: An A–Z guide* London: Routledge.

Coakley, J.J. (2001) *Sport in Society: Issues and controversies*, 7th edition, New York: McGraw-Hill, ch. 6.

DISCIPLINE

The maintenance of ordered conduct in the pursuit or preservation of a standard is discipline, a term derived from the Latin for learn, *discipulus*. Its connotations with learning still hold: discipline is usually practiced with the intention of cultivating a **skill**, proficiency, competence or qualification for entry to a higher realm. In sports, as in other areas, discipline is of two kinds: (1) exercised by an authority over subordinates; or (2) exercised by oneself – self-discipline. Success in sports involves both.

Discipline is often enforced by the use of *punishment*, a term with which it is sometimes confused. For example, order is maintained over schoolchildren, prisoners or soldiers who operate within a framework of rules and norms, deviation from which is punishable. **Control** of behavior is facilitated by a transparent system known to all: if the rules or norms are transgressed, then transgressors are liable to punishment and **deviance** occurs. Although this is effective in the structured environments of institutions, it is less effective in more permissive milieus where the rules are not so clear and punishments are not always enforceable. In such circumstances, desirable conduct can be rewarded: this type of **reinforcement** serves to maintain discipline without resort to castigation.

To be effective, punishment must also function as what Michel Foucault, in his *Discipline and Punish: The birth of the prison* called a 'fable': it conveys a moral message, explaining and justifying itself. Punishment contains a 'lesson' not just to recipients but to all others in the institution. Football, baseball, basketball and other kinds of sports clubs are institutions, and athletes as well as other staff are subject to rules. Violators are punished with fines and suspensions. Discipline is not maintained through surveillance, but by athletes' awareness that surveillance is possible without knowing whether it is actual. This principle is based on the late eighteenth/early nineteenth-century philosopher Jeremy Bentham's concept of the Panopticon, his ideal prison where cells were arranged around a central watchtower in which a concealed authority figure could inspect without being inspected. (Bentham would have approved of speed cameras on highways: drivers can see them, but do not know whether they have film in them.)

Many other sports lack the formal structure of club-based team sports. Cyclists and motor racing drivers, for example, compete for a team, but not within the structure of a club. Surveillance by the media is always possible, of course. Players are often exposed gambling, partying or indulging in other types of disreputable pleasures. The punishment typically entails embarrassment or humiliation. This may work as a negative reinforcer (life without embarrassment is less painful), though more effective is **incentive**: rewards for virtuous behavior.

Other athletes operate outside any formal structure of control. Boxers, tennis players and the majority of Olympic athletes may, on occasion, compete as part of a team, but operate for the most part outside any formal structure. **Commitment** requires that the individual arranges his or her conduct according to a regimen (i.e. a prescribed course of exercise and diet) involving a degree of abstinence. Recall the scene from the first *Rocky* movie when Balboa rises before daylight, swallows raw eggs and grinds out his miles through the streets of Philadelphia in subzero temperatures. There is no one to punish Rocky if he skips a day or eases up on his pace: his discipline is imposed and sustained by himself, his behavior reinforced by the prospect of the title fight.

Robert Rinehart's engaging study of a swim school includes the observation: 'The swimming body has discipline imposed from both outside and inside: it is inscribed by others, including coaches and parents, and it is inscribed by itself.' Rinehart describes how, working as a coach at the school, he was urged to train according to a prescribed method and all disciples (he does not use this word, but it seems appropriate) were inculcated accordingly. Young swimmers, who were initially attracted to the sport because of the 'love of water' or the sheer joy of swimming, had soon surrendered any notion of enjoyment and accepted that competitive success would only come through regular, predictable systematic training. There was, writes Rinehart, 'an ironically abnegating yet self-absorbed discipline' that pervaded the school.

Drawing on Foucault, Rinehart argues that punishment convinces potential transgressors why they should stick to the regimen. The 'relative freedoms of swimming,' as Rinehart calls them, are gradually eroded 'to be replaced by a disciplinary system both insidious and tenacious.' Movements are broken down into minute fragments, each analyzed and subject to electronic surveillance; attendance is checked, progress is monitored, goals are set – 'a form of panopticism within swimming,' Rinehart calls it. The study illustrates how the denial that is so important to discipline in competitive sports is not simply imposed: it is internalized.

Further reading

Foucault, M. (1977) *Discipline and Punish: The birth of the prison* New York: Pantheon.

Rinehart, R. (1998) 'Born-again sport: ethics in biographical research,' pp. 33–46 in Rail, G. (ed.) *Sport and Postmodern Times* Albany NY: State University of New York Press.

DOPING

Taking or administering substances intended to assist or enhance performance is known as doping. In sport, the substances usually refer to drugs, though foodstuffs and other materials, such as enriched or even artificial blood, may also qualify as 'dope' (the word itself deriving from the Dutch *doop* for sauce). The purpose in taking dope is invariably to improve athletic performance, though in horse racing doping may be intended to slow down an animal, making it easier for less-favored horses to win – and thus help knowing punters make a killing.

Human beings take dope or are provided with dope in order to: (1) gain a competitive advantage over opponents; or (2) deny opponents suspected of doping from gaining an advantage. With only rare exceptions, sports forbid doping and penalize infractions with suspensions and fines, citing the possible harmful consequences on the health of the athlete and the violation of fair play as reasons for the ban. Yet athletes disregard such bans. 'Despite the many dangers associated with performance-enhancing chemicals, their use continues and even increases,' writes D. Stanley Eitzen in his *Fair and Foul: Beyond the myths and paradoxes of sport*, adding that: 'The motive is obvious – an extreme desire to excel.'

This may be a simple but accurate summary of the **motivation** behind doping in sport, though it prompts a further question: why should competitors transgress rules, **risk** long-term suspensions, jeopardize their careers and possibly endanger their health not only to excel but to surpass all others in their pursuit of a **goal**? To uncover this motive, we need to understand changes in the meaning of competitive sport and in the culture of which it is part.

The need to achieve is a cognitive factor related to **attribution**: the **achievement motivation**, as it is called, refers to a subject's propensity either to approach success or to avoid failure. Those who have a need to succeed are usually high achievers while those who try to avoid failure are not. It follows that an athlete prepared to engage in doping will be driven by a motivation to achieve. Typically, such a person relishes a challenge, even when the odds are stacked against him or her. The most highly motivated achiever will also be inclined to take chances, perhaps even encourage situations when risk-taking is necessary. This type of 'win-at-all-costs' mentality has been fostered by an environment in which winning has been afforded a pre-eminent value and merely competing or even excelling have been assigned lesser values.

The value of winning in sports has always been recognized, though not accentuated in the way it has been since the 1960s. The period saw the onset of professionalization in all major sports, including tennis and track and field, both old traditional sports that had embodied the amateur ethos. Both spurned professionalism for decades, maintaining that the essence of sporting competition lay in participating, not winning. While the conception of athletics as paid work goes way back to the 1860s – when the Cincinnati Red Stockings became the first salaried baseball club and the English instituted the 'gentlemen *v.* players' distinction to ensure that the working-class players who were paid were not genuine sportsmen – professionalism in sports picked up **momentum** from the 1960s. By the end of the century, no mainstream sport was still completely amateur. Amateurism crumbled under the weight of the money heaped on sport in the last few decades of the twentieth century.

As the **achievement ethic** permeated practically all sports, competitors became more task-oriented: instead of understanding their ability as a stable personal feature, they saw it as dynamic, changeable and responsive to their own efforts. The very concept of having a coach to supervise or assist in training and other forms of preparation is evidence of an orientation that places onus on achievements wrought from work and perseverance rather than God-given 'gifts' or natural **talent**. (Training itself was regarded as tantamount to cheating by English gentlemen cricketers of the nineteenth century.) Athletes developed in a sports culture that encouraged them to take **control** of their own destiny and not to look outside themselves in their **attribution** of success and failure.

The use of substances to improve performance is as old as sport itself: there is evidence of competitors in ancient Greek games and Roman **competition** either side of the Christian era ingesting animal parts, especially testicles, in the belief that they could acquire characteristics of, for example, bulls (strength) or dogs (ferocity). Research in the first half of the twentieth century disclosed the potential of certain types of pharmaceutically produced materials as aids to athletic performance. In particular, an anabolic steroid Dianobol, first manufactured by the Ciba company in 1958, aroused interest among strength-based sports performers in both the USA and the Soviet Union.

In 1960, the former East Germany (then a communist state) introduced Program 1425, which provided for the induction of about 10,000 young people into sports academies where they were trained, conditioned and supplied with performance-enhancing drugs.

Far from being the restorative **discipline** it is today, sports medicine was originally conceived to advise on appropriate substances to improve athletic performance. As Ivan Waddington writes in his 1996 article 'The development of sports medicine': 'It is not possible to separate out the development and use of performance-enhancing drugs from the development of sports medicine.' Drug testing was not introduced until 1968 and even then it was designed as for research purposes rather than to root out 'cheats.'

At the Munich Olympics of 1972, a more systematic approach to drug testing was taken, though there was no reliable way of differentiating anabolic steroids from oral contraceptive steroids. A way had been found by 1976, though a test for testosterone proved elusive until 1982, by which time a protein hormone that confused results was available. Every four years, it seemed the International Olympic Committee introduced new tests designed to identify new drugs.

Signpost events indicated that anabolic steroids, amphetamines and other substances were progressively becoming part of sports: the death of Tommy Simpson during the 1967 Tour de France, the disqualification of Ben Johnson from the 1988 summer Olympics, the expulsion of Diego Maradona from soccer's World Cup of 1994. The insistence of coaches that athletes were responsible for their own accomplishments or downfall appeared less plausible amid a culture in which doping was prevalent. Even the most task-oriented athletes must have entertained the suspicion that their defeats were attributable not entirely to their lack of preparation, exertion or desire, but to the fact that their rivals were on dope of some sort. One way of rescuing the internal locus of causality – that is, the sense of agency for controlling one's own fortunes – was to improve one's own performance by similar means.

It is possible that much of the doping that grew out of the post-1988 (i.e. Johnson) period was a product of a 'if you can't beat 'em, join 'em' resignation, rather than a willful attempt to gain an unfair advantage; though there is scant evidence to support this, and even then the evidence is inferential. For example, surveys of young athletes suggest that, given the opportunity to take a banned substance that would guarantee success, almost 98.5 per cent of young athletes surveyed said they would take it; even if the substance would mean certain death within a couple of decades, over half would still take it (reported in 1997 by Bamberger and Yaeger). The willingness to sacrifice long-term health in the pursuit of victory seems perfectly consistent with the achievement ethic of contemporary sports, but why would healthy achievement-oriented athletes be prepared to risk disqualification, shame and the stigma that typically attaches to athletes found to be using dope? The tentative answer is that they are aware or at least suspect that a great many of their rivals are using dope and that 'the minority of athletes who are natural are at a *disadvantage*,' as the Olympian discus thrower Werner Reiterer put it in his autobiography

Positive (2000). He reflected on his own reluctant decision to take dope: 'You must adapt to an environment as it is, not as you think it should be.' If this view is taken, athletes who have been suspended for dope violations and who are labeled 'cheats' probably have powerful achievement orientations and devotion to retaining an internal locus of causality; they may also feel compelled to abandon any ideals as they 'adapt to an environment' in which drug taking is common. This may sound a charitable interpretation, but the role of the sports scholar is to examine and comprehend rather than make pronouncements.

Further reading

Reiterer, W. (2000) *Positive: An Australian Olympian reveals the inside story of drugs and sport* Sydney: Pan Macmillan Australia.
Waddington, I. (2000) *Sport, Health and Drugs: A critical sociological perspective* London: Spon.
Yesalis, C. and Cowart, V. (1998) *The Steroids Game: An expert's look at anabolic steroid use in sports* Champaign IL: Human Kinetics.

DRIVE

A motive force, whether instinctual or learned, that impels a subject in a certain direction (usually toward a **goal**) is a drive. There are two main kinds of drive: *primary* and *acquired*. The first arises from deviations from a state of homeostasis, meaning the body's tendency to maintain a constant internal environment: excessive temperature or prolonged deprivation of a needed substance can activate a drive to restore homeostasis, as can the need to avoid **pain** or loud noise. The second type of drive is learned through **socialization** and is usually associated with a primary drive: money is an example, and while this may function as an acquired drive in sports there are others, such as winning titles, breaking records and setting new standards of excellence. The adjective 'driven' is often applied to athletes who exhibit especially high levels of **commitment**. An Old Norse word *drífan*, meaning chase or urge in a direction, is the probable source.

Drive theory is associated with Clark Hull, who in the 1940s and 1950s formulated an influential equation: $B = HS \times D$, with B standing for behavior, HS habit strength and D drive. There are primary and secondary elements: how subjects behave is a consequence of primary drive and how they have learned best to reduce it. The higher the drive, the more likely they are to behave in a certain way, what Hull called the 'dominant response,' or the behavioral response that has the greatest habit strength. Habit strength is learned through conditioning, a process in which repeated **reinforcement** plays a central role.

The dominant response is not always the most appropriate one and this is glaringly obvious to sports fans who have witnessed dramatic switches in style during **competition**. A boxer who is a decent brawler, may, in preparation for a particular fight, work assiduously at perfecting long-range tactics. For most of the fight he may execute the plan, but with two rounds remaining and the fight poised, drive may rise and he will switch to the dominant response, which is to brawl. A tennis player's greatest habit strength may be to run around her weaker backhand to return with her stronger forehand (HS), but she may practice returning with backhand when playing a left-handed opponent. At tie-break in the second and trailing 1–0 in sets, a high drive is evoked (D) and she may start running around the serve (B) again. In line with the prediction of Hull's theory, **arousal** increases the dominant response, even though it may not be the preferred or even correct one in the circumstances.

In a different context, the concept of drive has been used to explain **aggression**, the hypothesis being that, when goal-directed behavior is obstructed in some way, an aggressive drive is induced, which then manifests aggressive behavior. In this view, all aggression is the result of frustration, with drive as the motivating force. As with Hull's theory, this was seminal in producing research and related theories, but both accounts are now dated.

Further reading

Dollard, J., Doob, J., Miller, N., Mowrer, O. and Sears, R. (1939) *Frustration and Aggression* New Haven CT: Yale University Press.
Hull, C.L. (1943) *Principles of Behavior* New York: Appleton-Century-Crofts.

DROPOUTS

Ex-athletes who have abandoned their participation in sport after disagreeable experiences are known, in the often cruel vernacular of sports, as dropouts. Often they are fatigued, dejected, resentful, sometimes tormented and wounded, and occasionally mortified. Some leave sports sorrowful if not downright heartbroken.

Glorious as triumph in sports undoubtedly is, the statistical chance of success even at modest levels is inhibiting. An example is given in the 1994 film *Hoop Dreams* in which a basketball coach confronts his protégés with some sobering statistics: each year, 500,000 boys play high school basketball, 14,000 progress to intercollegiate levels and less than 25 per cent of that group ever play for one season in the NBA. The majority of aspiring professional athletes are destined to be dropouts at some stage in their development.

Studies in the 1970s reported that young dropouts left sports because they disliked the competitive emphasis, or they did not have enough time, or they just hated their coach. Some jumped from one sport to another, while others were remitting – in other words, taking time out. Only a minority of dropouts were victims of negative experiences, though it strains credulity to think that young people would leave a sport in which they have favorable or positive experiences. If experience in some activity is rewarded – if not by winning – by camaraderie, valuable interaction and some semblance of learning, then a person does not willingly leave. Dropping out, almost by definition, implies an unpleasant encounter, like a spate of disappointing defeats, a series of injuries, or a total loss of **motivation**. Jennifer Capriati recalled that, despite her early career success (in 1990, she reached the semi-final of the French Open at the age of 14 and had made her first million), she was exhausted even in her teens: 'Mentally, I'd lost it. I wasn't happy with myself, my tennis, my life, my coaches, my friends,' she told Brian Viner of the *Independent* (Review section, 22 June 2001, p. 7).

Capriati, like other dropouts, returned to her sport renewed and restored. Jay Coakley concludes that many others who appear to leave sports actually stay involved, usually not in actual **competition**. He also regards dropping out as transitional: young people get married, or start a new job, or have children, and prioritize these over sports; this is backed up by Konstantinos Koukouris's research on 'disengagement' from sport. In Coakley's view, dropping out may actually be a sensible decision. Sticking with sports brings with it all manner of problems, especially for 'those who have no **identity** apart from sports or who lack the social and material resources they need to make transitions into other careers.'

Despite this slant on dropouts, it is hard to escape the conclusion that **reinforcement** in competitive sports comes primarily, though not exclusively, through success, and the very nature of sports means that only a minority will achieve success, apart from the intrinsic sensation of **self-efficacy** and boost in **confidence** that involvement may deliver. Yet even these are often contingent on at least a degree of success.

Further reading

Coakley, J.J. (2001) *Sport in Society: Issues and controversies*, 7th edition, New York: McGraw-Hill.

Koukouris, K. (1994) 'Constructed case studies: athletes' perspectives of disengaging from organized competitive sport,' *Sociology of Sport Journal* vol. 18, pp. 114–39.

DRUGS *see* doping

EATING DISORDERS

When unusual eating habits become health-threatening, they are known as eating disorders, the two most common being *anorexia nervosa*, a condition characterized by an obsessive avoidance of food, and *bulimia nervosa*, a syndrome that involves binge eating followed by self-induced vomiting or use of laxatives and diuretics (a less common condition is *pica*, eating material not considered nutritious). Both are typically driven by dissatisfaction with one's own **body image** and are attempts to correct imagined defects in appearance. Eating disorders are more prevalent in certain sports than in the general population. Competitors in sports that emphasize the importance of physical appearance, such as gymnastics, ice dancing and synchronized swimming, are especially inclined to eating disorders. Estimates of the prevalence of eating disorders in the sporting population vary between 4 and 22 per cent. The term *anorexia athletica* was introduced to describe set of symptoms affecting this group. The term 'anorexia' is from the Greek *an*, for not, and *orexis*, meaning appetite; the Greek *bous* is for ox and *limos*, hunger.

Anorexia nervosa, often shortened to just anorexia, was first documented medically in 1874, though bulimia nervosa is a twentieth-century term, both entering the popular vocabulary from the 1980s onward when cultural evaluations of fatness changed significantly. The value placed on being slim was promoted and maintained in popular culture, particularly by a fashion industry that projected images of waif-like models as ideals. It was thought that an exaggerated sense of being fat impelled between 1 and 4 per cent of the female population toward one of the two main eating disorders (with an increase in anorexia occurring primarily in white females between the ages of 15 and 24 years). Only a small minority of men had eating disorders – an estimated 10 per cent of the total reported cases.

Research has revealed no hereditary basis for eating disorders and there appears to be no pattern in family background. Subjects with eating disorders commonly have disturbances of **mood** or **emotional** tone to the point where **depression** or inappropriate elation occurs; but no causal link between the two has been found, only an association. The disproportionately high number of women affected has invited an interpretation of eating disorders as a striving for empowerment: women with such disorders are not usually high-achieving and financially independent professionals and, as such, have few resources apart from the ability to **control** their own bodies. But in this respect they have total sovereignty.

Explanations of eating disorders in sports rely on the same cultural factors, but include additional sports-specific constituents. Monitoring weight is normal in most sports: in some, leanness is considered of paramount importance. Sports that are subject to judges' evaluation, like gymnastics, diving and figure skating, encourage participants to take care of all aspects of their appearance. About 35 per cent of competitors have eating disorders and half practice what researchers term 'pathogenic **weight control**.'

In some sports, looking young and slender is considered such an advantage that competitors actively try to stave off the onset of menstruation and the development of secondary sexual characteristics, or to counterbalance the weight gain that typically accompanies puberty. Menstrual dysfunction, such as amenorrhoea (absence of menstruation) and oligomenorrhoea (few and irregular periods), frequently results from anorexia. In endurance events, excess weight is generally believed to impair performance. Athletes reduce body fat to increase strength, speed and endurance, though they risk bone mineral deficiencies, dehydration and a decrease in maximum oxygen uptake (VO_2max). The biologist Jorunn Sundgot-Borgen suggests that the training load typically carried by endurance athletes may induce a calorific deprivation which, in turn, elicits 'certain biological and social **reinforcement** leading to the development of eating disorders' (in 'Eating disorders in female athletes'). But the prevalence of bulimia is more difficult to explain.

A further finding of Sundgot-Borgen and several other scholars is that coaches actually recommend the use of pathogenic control methods, including vomiting, laxatives and diuretics. Coaches and trainers in weight-sensitive sports need to keep an eye on their charges' eating habits in preparation for competitions. For example, lightweight rowers and jockeys must meet weight restrictions before competition. In their 1992 study, Diane Taub and Rose Benson found that: 'Excess body fat and body weight in both males and females are widely considered by coaches, parents and participants to hinder performance.'

Sundgot-Borgen also reports that a change of coach can trigger an eating disorder, as can an **injury** that prevents the athlete training at usual levels. Perhaps the most ironic conclusion from Sundgot-Borgen's research is that the competitors most at risk tend to be characterized by 'high self-expectation, perfectionism, persistence and independence.' In other words, the very qualities that enable them to achieve in sports make them vulnerable to eating disorders.

While it is not a recognized medical term, 'orthorexia nervosa' was used in Stephen Bratman and David Knight's popular 2001 book *Health Food Junkies – Orthorexia Nervosa: Overcoming the obsession of healthy eating*, which, as the title suggests, warned against the compulsions of fastidiously healthy eating. Orthorexia bears similarities to other eating disorders: sufferers fixate on their food. The emphasis on ostensibly healthy food, including fresh, high-quality produce and the avoidance of all food considered 'bad' (fast food, pizzas, ice cream, etc.) leads to a pathology in its own right, according to Bratman and Knight: a compulsion to eat pure and superior ingredients – the 'right' food.

One of the most notable athletes to fall prey to an eating disorder was Ellen Hart Peña, a former marathon runner who was bulimic and later became a renowned speaker on eating disorders. Her story is told in Jan Egleson's 1996 movie *Dying to Be Perfect: The Ellen Hart Peña story*.

Further reading

Cooper, P.J. (1996) 'Eating disorders,' pp. 930–49 in Colman, A.M. (ed.) *Companion Encyclopedia of Psychology*, vol. 1, London: Routledge.

Hepworth, J. (1999) *The Social Construction of Anorexia Nervosa* London: Sage.

Sundgot-Borgen, J. (1994) 'Risk and trigger factors: the development of eating disorders in female elite athletes,' *Medicine and Science in Sports and Exercise* vol. 26, pp. 414–19.

EFFECTS *see* **home advantage, Ringelmann effect** and **social facilitation**

EGOCENTRISM

Ego is Latin for I and, as the term suggests, egocentrism or egocentricity (as it is sometimes known) refers to a preoccupation with the self and insensitivity to others. This should not be confused with *egotism*, which is usually equated with conceitedness and selfishness, nor with *egoism*, which is an ethical theory based on the conception of self- interest as the central **motivation** of humans. But it does share a great many features with what sports psychologists call *ego orientation*, which is used to describe the state of athletes who define success according to exceeding the performance of others.

An ego-oriented runner may record a poor time in a 1,500 meter race, but as long as she finished in front of the field it counts as more of a success than if she had run a personal best but finished second. A football player may have a nightmare game, but if his team won it will be evaluated as a far greater triumph than if he had played the game of his life but ended up on the losing side. Their counterparts who focus on the process of competing are called task-oriented. Both subjects have ample motivation but have starkly different goals.

In achieving a ferocious victory at the Nürburgring Grand Prix of Europe, in 2001, Michael Schumacher all but squeezed his younger brother Ralf into the pit wall to defend his pole position. While technically permissible, it was a potentially perilous maneuver and one that accented the self-absorption so integral to Schumacher's quest for success. It could be argued that some degree of egocentrism is required of all athletes with the ambition to succeed at elite professional levels. At some stage in any sport, an athlete must be ruthless (which, incidentally, is from the Old English word *hreow,* for compassion, and '-less'). Leniency, sympathy and sensitivity to others may be in evidence during the formative years of an athletic career, but athletes who progress to the higher echelons typically become relentless. The adage 'nice guys finish last' has a resonance that extends beyond any one particular sport.

There is some debate over whether egocentrism is an integral part of an athlete's **personality** or a quality that is acquired progressively as the subject moves into the higher realms of **competition**. In other words, are successful athletes the ones who actually learn to be egocentric, or did they simply have the right kind of personality for sports?

In developmental psychology, egocentrism refers not to selfishness or arrogance but to a child's tendency to perceive, understand and interpret the world in terms of the self. It is characterized by a inability to take the role of another person.

Further reading

Duda, J.L. (1993) 'Goals: a social-cognitive approach to the study of achievement motivation in sport,' pp. 421–36 in Singer, R.N., Murphey, M. and Tennant, L.K. (eds) *Handbook of Research on Sport Psychology* New York: Macmillan.

Miller, P.H. (1983) *Theories of Developmental Psychology* San Francisco CA: W.H. Freeman.

ELECTROENCEPHALOGRAM (EEG)

From the Greek *en*, for in, *kephale*, head, and *gramme*, line, the EEG (which is used almost interchangeably with electroencephalograph, or EEC) is an instrument for visually recording the changes in the electrical discharges of the brain. The graphic presentations of the discharges as recorded by the EEG are called brainwaves.

Brainwaves are of several types. Alpha waves are high amplitude waves with frequencies of 8–12 Hz and are characteristic of relaxed subjects, whose **attention** is directed toward a relevant task and have shut out other distracting **stimuli**. These are perfect conditions for an athlete to get **focused**. When a subject is under some kind of **stress** or in a state of high **arousal**, the EEG will usually record a predominance of beta waves. Drowsiness is typified by theta waves and delta waves are very low frequencies of 1–3 Hz, high amplitude, that occur during deep, dreamless sleep.

EEGs have applications in sports, especially in what is known as brainwave training. This entails attaching electrodes to the scalp and observing one's own brainwaves, the purpose being to set up a **biofeedback** loop in which the subject can monitor his or her own output with a view to aligning it with a desired state, for instance an alpha wave rhythm.

Further reading

Cox, R.H. (1998) *Sport Psychology: Concepts and applications*, 4th edition, Boston MA: McGraw-Hill.

Kandel, E.R. (1991) 'Brain and behavior,' pp. 5–17 in Kandel, E.R., Schwartz, J.H. and Jessell, T.M. (eds) *Principles of Neural Science*, 3rd edition, New York: Elsevier.

EMOTION

An emotion is a subjective state or sensation that momentarily interrupts otherwise steady functioning with sudden and unexpected physiological, experiential and behavioral changes. Derived from the French *émotion* (from *émouvoir*, to excite, after *mouvoir* to move), the term is used loosely and frequently conflated with *affect*, which is a broader, less focused concept that covers both emotion and *feeling*, itself a more diffuse sensory impression, and *sentiment*, a more permanent disposition. All lead to particular courses of action.

Emotion is integral to sports. Spectators are excited to **emotional** extremes such as euphoria and despondency when watching **competition**. Athletes deliberately try to induce emotions in rivals: they may try **psyching** them into experiencing dread or outright **fear**; or they may try to make them angry enough to lose **composure** and perhaps become violent. In these and other ways emotion affects performance. Competitive sports are emotional: without emotion, sports would lose their *raison d'être*.

More precisely, we should identify distinguishing features. An emotion is:

1 ephemeral – it is always a short-lived transitory state;
2 intentional – it is always directed at a person, event or object, so that there is a relationship between the state and whatever it is intended toward or about (embarrassed by ...; proud of ...);
3 evaluative – it is always good, bad or a mixture of the two, never neutral;
4 disturbing – it interrupts and agitates mental states;
5 unexpected – its arrival and impact can rarely, if ever, be anticipated;
6 irrational – it often displaces reason and rational thought, leading to erratic action;
7 subjective and objective – it is experienced subjectively, but involves bodily changes that are observable.

Love, hate, horror, relief, happiness, sadness, **anger**, serenity: these are labels we apply to the complex, kaleidoscopic expanse of emotions experienced in sport. The behaviors they instigate are referred to collectively as emotionality and these can be measured by, for example, heart rate and galvanic skin response, or observed by emotional responses, such as crying, trembling, shouting or **aggression**.

The attempt to explain emotion dates back to the 1880s when two independent publications advanced a similar proposition: that when events or persons in our environment produce sudden bodily responses, particularly in the autonomic **nervous system**, we feel these changes and *that* is the emotion. In other words, the bodily changes that come about as a result of something unexpected or shocking act as a signal which we pick up, and our **perception** of them is the emotion. This was the answer to the question William

James posed himself in his 1884 article, 'What is an emotion?' and his answers were approved by Carl Georg Lange. Hence the title 'the James–Lange theory of emotion.' One implication of the theory was that every particular emotion is originated by a unique set of bodily and visceral (relating to abdominal cavity and organs) responses.

The theory was challenged in the late 1920s by Walter B. Cannon who found, among other things, that all the major emotional states, such as anger and fear, were accompanied by the same general emergency response that prepares the body for activity. The response was sympathetic **arousal** and was based on the sympathetic system of the autonomic nervous system (ANS), leading to an increase in metabolic rate and energy mobilization (the centers that **control** ANS activity are in the lower parts of the brain and usually below the threshold of conscious control). Increase in heart rate and blood pressure, heightened respiratory volume, constriction of blood vessels in the skin and sweating were among the characteristic responses. Whereas James and Lange argued that we experience emotion because we feel our bodies in a particular way, Cannon held that there were common emotional patterns that respond to occurrences in the environment and then trigger bodily and visceral expressions. For James and Lange, we feel embarrassed because we experience a hot flush; for Cannon we flush because we feel embarrassment.

Neither theory recognized the part played by cultural factors in initiating and shaping the experience of emotion. In an effort to do so, Stanley Schachter, in 1964, drew on James' idea that emotion depends on feedback from changes in the body, but also accepted that different emotions share the same bodily response, as Cannon had insisted. Schachter affixed the positions with his own view that information from the surrounding context in which the experience takes place modifies the way an emotion is appraised or interpreted. A single physiological arousal state can result in dozens of different, possibly conflicting, emotions, depending on how the individual interprets the situation – whether pleasant/unpleasant, benign/dangerous, joyful/scary, glad/sad, and so on.

Research by Schachter and Singer, published 1971, supported this approach. They concluded that situational factors played a part not only in modifying the expression of an emotion, but in actually constituting that emotion. In this view, **cognition** was vital: the precise manner in which we interpret a state of arousal affected both the quality and the effect of the emotion. 'If you believe your state of arousal is caused by a wild animal that is chasing you, then you are likely to experience the state as fear,' suggests Bryan Parkinson to illustrate the point, adding, 'if you think that your arousal is triggered by the close presence of somebody attractive, you might well come to feel your reaction as love, or at least as lust, for that person.' Emotion, in Schachter and Singer's view, hinges on the **attribution** of arousal to the events, persons or other factors in the immediate context.

Of course, attributions do not *cause* emotions, but they explain a limited amount of variance. For example, a team wins an important game, but an individual player feels he or she played poorly, so the success is attributable to others. If the team had lost, the player might feel shame, the defeat being attributable in large part to his or her performance. In success, the player experiences elation, though perhaps not as much pride as teammates, and may even have guilt. This configuration of emotions results from a *reflective appraisal*. After a heavy defeat, an athlete might decide the competition was not important, whereas if the same player had won, he or she might have viewed it as important. The appraisal will alter the **intensity**, type and possibly duration of the emotions experienced.

Readiness for action is obviously vital to any successful athletic performance and active emotions, such as fear and fury, facilitate this. By contrast more passive emotions like anguish and gloom will not. Research supports the link between action readiness and involuntary and sometimes impulsive emotions. In 1986, N.H. Frijda used the term *control precedence* to indicate that the urge to behave, or refrain from behaving, in a certain way is often not willful: it just comes over people, like the well-known red mist that descends in moments of rage.

Interpreting a situation in one way might arouse one to an optimal state in which sensations of anger, if not outright rage, will facilitate a determined and vigorous athletic performance; interpreting the same situation another way may result in awe, in which case the performance may be tentative and irresolute. Trying to identify the optimal emotional state for competitive performance is the task of much research deriving from the **IZOF (individual zones of optimal functioning)** model.

Either side of the optimum, there are problems for athletes because emotion and cognition can become disordered. Competing in front of a roaring crowd may appear to confer **home advantage** on players, but when the fans start encouraging attacking play, the players begin to swell with **confidence** and see offensive opportunities where, objectively, there are none. In other words, emotion can momentarily blind athletes to important cognitive clues. Equally negative for athletes are situations when emotion displaces reason. Emotion is often contrasted with rationality, of course. Every sport has instances of competitors 'losing it': tennis rackets are smashed, opponents are punched, officials are abused – all involve transgressions that, ultimately, prove detrimental to athletic performance.

Straying momentarily from sports: there is a story of the rear admiral from the British Royal Navy who was introduced to Diana, Princess of Wales, shortly after her wedding. Overwhelmed by elation bordering on rapture, the officer lost all track of appropriate greeting and, instead of saluting, bowing or shaking hands, dropped a curtsey, which is a strictly female salutation. There are no comparably bizarre examples of emotion's overpowering of reason in sport, though Mike Tyson's biting Evander Holyfield's ear is close.

Clearly, emotions issue from circumstances that have relevance to individuals' immediate and long-term aspirations, whether they be meeting an iconic member of the royal family or trying to win back a world title. Where those aspirations, or goals, are thwarted, then emotions are likely. Emotions, in this instance, would be associated with failure, frustration or disappointment. Once experienced, unpleasant emotions such as these may act as a motivation for future action. For instance, the Bolton Wanderers soccer club that triumphed in the 2001 first division playoffs had in the previous season been beaten in the semi-finals of the playoffs and two other competitions. This prompted great resolve, as the manager Sam Allardyce reflected: 'There was a lot of determination from the players who realized how disappointed they were last season. Those players weren't going to have those feelings again. They wanted to feel the other side of it.'

Further reading

Cannon, W.B. (1927) 'The James–Lange theory of emotions: a critical examination and an alternative theory,' *American Journal of Psychology* vol. 39, pp. 106–24.

Lazarus, R.S. (1991) *Emotion and Adaptation* New York: Oxford University Press.

Parkinson, B. (1996) 'Emotion,' pp. 485–505 in Colman, A.M. (ed.) *Companion Encyclopedia of Psychology*, 2 volumes, London: Routledge.

EMOTIONAL

Designating a state or reaction 'emotional' indicates that it is in some measure affected by an underlying **emotion**. In sports, there is a class of expressions prefixed by emotional, perhaps the most significant being emotional **control**.

Jack Lesyk uses the term 'emotional control' to characterize situations in which: 'The sudden, powerful emotion compels **attention** away from appropriate stimuli, and **concentration** is lost.' This may be the case when an official's call goes against expectations or after a provocation by an opponent. Lesyk's prescription is to maintain focus on the task at hand and on immediate matters that can be controlled; this may include **self-talk**, articulating statements such as 'Just let it go; plan your next action.'

Emotional control begins before **competition**: athletes examine their own case histories to identify specific hot spots, including persons, events and situations where a sudden emotion has been experienced. They can then rehearse appropriate responses. Controlling an emotion means being sensitive to cues, so that an emotion can be recognized before it displaces rational thought and leads to unreasonable behavior. When athletes persistently fail to control emotion, they are said to have emotional *instability*, meaning that they exhibit inappropriate behavior in and, possibly, away from a competitive context. Their behavior is variable and possibly unpredictable. Often emotional instability threatens an athlete's competitive career: the intrusion of intense subjective experiences interferes with their ability to perform complex tasks competently. The inability is sometimes known as emotional *blocking*, where emotions overwhelm all other states.

This is but one of several conditions in which emotions induce behavioral reactions that are inappropriate to the immediate task; they are known collectively as emotional or affective *disorders* and include the oft-quoted emotional *immaturity* – which is used to describe athletes who regularly throw temper tantrums or challenge officials *à la* John McEnroe. At the other extreme, there are athletes who never display emotion during competition. While it is unlikely that such athletes have a disorder, there is actually a condition known as emotional *anesthesia*. As the name indicates, there is an unusual amount of insensitivity or numbness related to this condition: subjects react indifferently to circumstances and persons who might be expected to arouse them.

Further reading

Biddle, S. (2000) 'Exercise, emotions and mental health,' pp. 267–92 in Hanin, Y.L. (ed.) *Emotions in Sport* Champaign IL: Human Kinetics..

Lesyk, J.L. (1998) *Developing Sport Psychology Within Your Clinical Practice: A practical guide for mental health professionals* San Francisco CA: Jossey-Bass.

ENDORPHINS

The body manufactures its own natural painkillers, known as endorphins. These are neurotransmitter chemicals that bind with a certain kind of neuron called an opiate receptor and have a powerful effect on sensation, mood and behavior. The 'natural high' often reported by athletes exhilarated by a hard workout has been popularly attributed to secretion of endorphins – the name being a compound of *end*, from endogenous, meaning originating within, and *orphins*, from morphine, the **pain** suppressing derivative from opium.

The effects of plant extracts containing opiates are well-documented, though it was not until the 1970s that it was discovered that the body produced its own compounds that worked on receptors in response to pain or **stress**. Opiate receptors work to reduce pain sensations, and many pain reducing drugs, especially derivatives of opium (including morphine, of course), are administered to stimulate these opiate receptors.

The exact mechanisms of the endorphin production process are not clear. Studies of animals have shown that the application of continuous stress or pain activates the process. In humans, it has been speculated that endorphins inhibit the release of excitatory substances for neurons carrying information about pain. But evidence for a direct relationship between intense exercise and the secretion of endorphins is scant. Attributing the sensation of wellbeing or even euphoria during or after a workout or **competition** to endorphins is appealing, though far too reductive. Endorphins represent only one of many neurotransmitters involved in pain modulation. There is also the cluster of social and cultural influences that bear on the experience of pain, how it is interpreted and expressed.

Further reading

Hoffmann, P. (1997) 'The endorphin hypothesis,' pp. 163–77 in Morgan, W.P. (ed.) *Physical Activity and Mental Health* Washington DC: Taylor & Francis.

Kraemer, R.R., Dzewaltowskj, D.A., Blair, M.S., Rinehardt, K.F. and Castracane, V.D. (1990) 'Mood alteration from treadmill running and its relationship to betaendorphine, corticotrophine, and growth hormone,' *Journal of Sports Medicine and Physical Fitness* vol. 30, no. 3, pp. 241–6.

EQUALITY

From the Old French *equalité*, which in turn derives from Latin *æqualis*, meaning even, equality describes a condition of sameness in value, degree, rank, status, standing or position between two or more subjects. It is sometimes confused with *equity*, which refers to fairness and principles of justice, something quite different. It is possible to have a **competition** that upholds principles of equity but which is also unequal. All entrants compete under a system of rules and conditions that apply indiscriminately, yet the competition is designed to ensure, or at least maximize the chances of, inequality of outcomes. Ties, draws and deadheats notwithstanding, there will be winners and losers. In this sense, the whole point of sporting competition is to establish and verify inequality.

Some sports deliberately prevent equal outcomes by supplementing competitions with overtime, golden **goal** extra time and penalty shootouts, the principle being that, even when competitors are even in all respects covered by the framework of a regulation game, there will be always be one respect in which they will be unequal. Without this, many sports would be meaningless, or at least lose their spectator appeal.

Gestalt psychology has a second meaning for equality: as more than one **stimuli** in a perceptual field become similar, they will tend to be perceived as a single unit. This is known as the *law of equality.*

Further reading

Morgan, W.J. (2000) 'The philosophy of sport: a historical and conceptual overview and a conjecture regarding its future,' pp. 204–12 in Coakley, J. and Dunning, E. (eds) *Handbook of Sports Studies* London: Sage.

EUSTRESS

The delight, elation or blissfulness experienced after an especially satisfying event is known as eustress, *eu* being Greek for good or pleasant (as in *eu*phoria, *eu*thanasia and *Eu*reka!). While the term **stress** has negative connotations, this is not always the case and the state of **arousal** that is elicited by eustress is agreeable.

Eustress is one of four variants of the more generic concept of stress, the others being distress, which is the kind misleadingly regarded as the only type, hyperstress, which occurs when our body cannot adapt to demands made on it, and hypostress, which is a lack of the appropriate amount of stress – such as when we are bored or physically incapacitated through injury.

Further reading

Kremer, J. and Scully, D. (1994) *Psychology in Sport* London: Routledge.

EXPECTANCY

The state of anticipating the probability of an outcome is expectancy. It is formed from *ex*, meaning out, and *specatare*, Latin for look. Expectancy bears heavily on how athletes evaluate the significance and consequences of a **competition** and how they respond in an **emotional** sense to situations arising once that contest is underway.

An example of how this works in practice is given by Peter Crocker *et al.*, who hypothesize a basketball player who has been injured during a game: 'Initially she is very angry if she believes that the other person was responsible.' The **anger** subsides as she realizes that she may be out for the rest of the season, paving the way for 'unhappiness' to set in. Then she examines the **injury**, only to discover it is not so serious and realizes that she will receive top medical treatment. 'Her expectancies are that the situation will get better.' As the extent of the injury becomes clear, she anticipates that she will still be able to pursue her goal after all. 'This will change the emotional state of unhappiness into a different emotional state, such as relief.'

In this example, expectancies change as appraisals of immediate situations change and the athlete modifies her anticipation of the future. Expectancy is part of a general appraisal process. The precise way in which expectancy is understood depends on theoretical approach. For instance, a behaviorist interested in the **reinforcement** value of contingencies will study expectancy through such objective features as muscular tension, eye dilation and, perhaps, other indicators of **arousal**, while a researcher **focused** on **cognition** will wish to study expectancy through the **perception**, states of awareness and general subjective apprehension of the subject.

Expectancy is one of three different types of belief that contribute to **motivation**, according to a 1964 book by Vroom, the others being instrumentality (the belief that a performance will be rewarded) and valence (the perceived value of the reward to the individual). An athlete who never receives reinforcement when practicing a **skill** may have a low expectancy level that, no matter how hard they try, they will not achieve a higher level, and may not try too hard. Even if they do work hard and still receive little or no reward, motivation is likely to recede. If and when the rewards do arrive, they have to be appropriate (there is no point in rewarding a child learning a new skill with a new computer game if they were longing for a mountain bike).

Further reading

Crocker, P.E., Kowalski, K.C., Graham, T.R. and Kowalski, N.P. (2002) 'Emotion in sport,' pp. 107–31 in Silva, J.M. and Stevens, D.E. (eds) *Psychological Foundations of Sport* Boston MA: Allyn & Bacon.
Vroom, V.H. (1964) *Work and Motivation* New York: John Wiley.

EYE MOVEMENTS *see* eyeballing

EYEBALLING

Perhaps the most interesting eye movement in sports is the mutual *fixation*, better known as 'eyeball-to-eyeball,' or just 'eyeballing,' the latter sometimes meaning a one-way stare. This involves two rivals simultaneously orienting their eyeballs so that the projection of the viewed object – in this case, the other's pupils – falls on the fovea (the tiny depression at the back of the eye) and stays in focus. If we could draw lines from both subjects' pupils to the objects of their gaze, there would in theory be just two lines rather than four, as the fixation point for each would be the other's pupils.

Mutual fixations, or 'mutual gazes,' occur during everyday conversation, though rarely for more than 30 per cent of the interaction and hardly ever for more than five seconds. More typically, eyes dart over the other's facial features, dwelling for about 0.3 seconds on each, perhaps longer on the mouth; this jerky screening movement is known as a *saccade*. Eyeball-to-eyeball contact for several seconds demonstrates interest and an increase in **arousal**, suggesting that an important message is being communicated. In sports, by contrast, the fixation is a barely coded social signal: a threat designed to elicit agitation, **fear** and alarm in the opponent. A rival who does not or cannot respond by fixing eyes will be 'stared down' and forced to concede a perhaps small but symbolic defeat either prior to or during a contest. In boxing, it became a popular **psyching** technique.

There is no empirical evidence that dominance in the eyeballing encounter necessarily translates into competitive dominance, and its value may be concomitant rather than direct. For example, the opponent who breaks off the fixation and looks at a rival's shoulders or away completely may do so because of an unwillingness to break **concentration** on the actual **competition** and not because of intimidation. The dominant eyeballer, on the other hand, may interpret this as a significant victory in the psychological battle that accompanies the actual competition; that interpretation will enhance his or her **confidence**. Today, when eyeball-to-eyeball fixations are so commonplace as to be ritualistic, some athletes refuse to engage in them and instead grin mockingly, sending out another signal: 'I'm not getting involved in this nonsense; I just want to get on with business.'

The question remains: why should eye contact carry the potential to evoke such powerful behavioral and **emotional** reactions? Human infants respond to fixed eye contact as young as four weeks, allowing the parents to employ a gaze or stare as a simple yet effective form of **control** and **discipline**. Through maturity, the child learns to decode other meanings for fixed eye contact. He or she learns that paying **attention** is accompanied by mutual gazing: 'Look at me when I'm talking to you!' Later, the value of mutual fixations in demonstration of affection may appear: 'They stared deeply into each other's eyes.' The stimulus properties of eyes in signaling sexual attraction are, of course, great. Winking, staring and even self-consciously averting one's gaze are all strategies of courting rituals, though they are used in different ways in different cultures – as are eye movements generally.

Because the **perception** of others' intentions and behavior is so crucial in sports, eye movements are important, both to communicate visual information and to deliver/receive social signals. So much of sport is conducted in the absence of speech that alternative means of communication are employed. Eye movement is one element of a whole repertoire of **body language** that comes to the fore in any contest. The pattern of glances in everyday life is closely coordinated with speech, whereas in sports it is often coordinated with nonverbal gestures. A tennis player may raise an arm in apology for a winning let cord shot, but the import is lost unless it is accompanied by eye contact for a few seconds. Teammates in many sports use glances to collect information from each other and to make affiliative contact through the course of a contest. In any sport, a glance followed by an exaggerated blink and a turn away signals contempt or ridicule.

Referees also look for eye movements in athletes. In boxing, referees famously look into a fighter's eyes to ascertain his (or her) condition. This is a spurious technique: there are no reliable ocular indicators for determining the boxer's overall physical condition. Referees rarely disclose what they are looking for, though they sometimes report a 'glazed look.' A boxer under pressure is likely to fix his sights on the opponent rather than the referee, perhaps misleading the official to conclude that he or she cannot focus. In soccer, players can be cautioned for 'dissent' if a referee interprets a look as signaling disagreement with a decision. Baseball umpires are less sensitive and habitually engage in mutual fixations with managers.

Further reading

Bull, P. and Frederikson, L. (1996) 'Non-verbal communication,' pp. 852–72 in Colman, A.M. (ed.) (1996) *Companion Encyclopedia of Psychology*, vol. 2, London: Routledge.
Rakos, R.F. (1991) *Assertive Behavior* London: Routledge.

FANDOM

Formed from 'fan' or fanatic and 'dom,' meaning a collective domain in which subjects share common practices, manners and elements of lifestyle (like king*dom*, official*dom* or free*dom*) fandom refers to the condition in which whole congregations of people devote parts of their life to following or just admiring a rock star, a sports team or virtually anything. Sports attract followings that support teams and athletes with a near-worshipful devotion and zeal that justifies the root word of fan – the Latin *fanum*, meaning a temple. *Fanaticus* means being part of a temple; a fanatic is, of course, someone who is excessively and unreasonably enthusiastic. The alternative version of the origin of the word 'fan' is that it is a shortened version of 'fancy,' a term used to describe patrons of boxing in nineteenth-century England and which is itself probably a contraction of 'fantasy'; the English still use phrases such as rose-fancier, pigeon-fancier and dog-fancier.

'The history of fandom is full of parallels with the history of **religion**,' writes David Giles in his *Illusions of Immortality: A psychology of fame and celebrity.* He describes fans' relationships with the objects of their devotion as 'parasocial interaction.' Meaningful as they are for the fans, 'they can never be more than unilateral.' In other words, the club, the **celebrity** or the show cannot enter the relationship, which is always destined to be one way. This is clear when we recognize that fandoms are not restricted to sports: pop music, soaps and other shows, like *Star Trek* and *The X-Files*, develop followings of devotees, who occasionally exhibit **obsession** with their chosen genres or icons. The behavior of fans has been interpreted variously as escapism, compensation, wish fulfillment and fantasy.

Another interpretation is that fandom signals a powerlessness that is in some way negated by following the exploits of others and perhaps displacing one's own inadequacies in the process. In her 1998 essay, 'A sociology of television fandom,' Cheryl Harris argues that being a fan confers a power: she writes of fandom 'as a phenomenon in which members of subordinated groups try to align themselves with meanings embodied in stars or other texts [i.e. things that have meaning to the fan] that best express their own sense of social **identity**.' In this view, fans try to align themselves with others as a way of expressing some part of their self. This is experienced as empowering, especially for subjects who have little material power.

In his 1992 book *Textual Poachers: Television fans and participatory culture*, Henry Jenkins argues that while fans are often treated as having immoderate tastes and abnormal likings, they are actually reappropriating elements of cultural material. Fans are unjustifiably depicted as 'others' unlike 'us' in their beliefs and activities; they are also seen as dangerous. Jenkins is critical of this pathological conception of fans, though there have been instances when fans have been predators.

Unresponsive objects of desire have on occasion become targets of attacks or unwelcome **attention**, as in Tony Scott's movie *The Fan*, in which Robert De Niro plays a knife salesman with a grudge against the baseball star he once idolized. The story has some basis in fact. For example, in 1949, a fan shot Philadelphia Phillies player Eddie Waitkus. In the 1990s, tormented admirers harassed Katarina Witt and Steffi Graf. Graf's rival Monica Seles was stabbed in an attempt to prevent her from ousting Graf from the number one spot in women's tennis. Her attacker kept a shrine to Graf in his aunt's attic.

Up to the late 1970s, the celebrities themselves were remote, glamorous figures and fandom was based on mystery and ignorance. In recent decades, the media have demystified the stars: secrets are shared with magazines, close-up interviews are featured on television, and biographies spare no detail of personal lives. Videos have made it possible for fans to capture moments of an individual's or a team's life for their own delectation. There is now an entire industry geared to selling proximity to celebrities. This has occasionally created the illusion of intimacy, fans gaining such an expertise in the personal lives of subjects that they experience feelings of closeness that are at once real yet artificially induced.

While fandoms were in evidence in the 1940s and perhaps even before the Hollywood star system existed, the advent of global mass and multimedia has taken parasocial interaction to a new level. In fact, in 1997, Steve Redhead argued that the term 'fandom' was no longer adequate to describe the types of relationships that have been engendered by commercial sports culture. He suggests there is now *post-fandom*, in which fans may never leave their home or their local bar but can still experience intense **emotion** and a sense of empowerment.

Further reading

Giles, D. (2000) *Illusions of Immortality: A psychology of fame and celebrity* New York: St Martin's Press.

Harris, C. (1998) 'A sociology of television fandom,' pp. 41–54 in Harris, C. and Alexander, A. (eds) *Theorizing Fandom: Fans, subculture and identity* Cresskill, NJ: Hampton Press.

Wann, D.L, Melnick, M.J., Russell, G.W. and Pease, D.G. (2001) *Sports Fans: The psychology and social impact of spectators* London: Routledge.

FEAR

Unlike **anxiety**, which is usually regarded as an apprehension or anticipation of something unwelcome, or phobia, which is a persistent, irrational aversion to something, fear is an **emotion** associated with an actual impending danger or evil. It is often characterized by the subjective experience of discomfort and **arousal** and sometimes by sympathetic physiological responses, such as those accompanying an **adrenaline rush**. The relevance of fear to sports is equivocal: fear can induce a kind of paralysis in some competitors so that they 'freeze' in the face of a forbidding rival. It can also act as what Mike Tyson's first trainer Cus D'Amato called 'a friend,' causing an exhilaration that facilitates optimum performance.

In both types of situation, fear may be experienced similarly, the analogous physiological changes may be close and the outward expressions of fear will almost certainly be disguised (most athletes are trained not to show fear). The behavioral responses, on the other hand, are different: the first is a type of avoidance, while the second encourages an **aggressiveness** if not outright **aggression**. Repeated exposure to formidable opposition and fear-inducing situations will benefit competitors with a tendency to freeze, though athletes who thrive on fear and eventually become desensitized to it may experience difficulty in 'getting up' for opponents. The former's fearlessness will almost surely result in greater **confidence**, while the latter's will lead to insensibility. Either way, fear is an emotion that has to be confronted and assimilated by many competitors.

Some sports by their very nature are bound to bring about the experience of fear in all but the most desensitized competitors. Formula One racing, for example, carries the ever-present **risk** of death, as do air sports, skiing, surfing and Xtreme sports. All forms of motor racing, including Nascar, are dangerous, but the financial incentives are very high and one presumes these persuade competitors of the need to live with their fear. Yet the other high-risk sports are not so rewarding financially and require some explanation.

In his book *Culture of Fear*, Frank Furedi argues that we actually seek out fearful situations because we find them agreeable. Furedi's argument is that the apparent lust for danger is a product of a safety-first culture in which personal security, public protection and environmental management have become priorities. As the search for safety gains **momentum**, the ways to escape it become more ingenious. Established practices like mountain climbing, stunt cycling and potholing continue as newer adaptations flourish. Zorbing, bungee jumping and whitewater rafting contain ersatz dangers: they offer thrills, though under controlled conditions. Other responses, such as hang gliding, kayaking off waterfalls or Xtreme sports, are less amenable to **control** and so have genuine life-threatening potential.

While we avoid risks that lie outside our control, we are quite prepared to take voluntary risks. The so-called 'lifestyle risks' such as smoking, drinking and driving are examples of this. But sports present us with something quite different: manufactured risks that are actually designed in such a way as to preserve natural dangers or build in new ones and so elicit fear in us. Michael Bane, author of *Over the Edge: A regular guy's odyssey in extreme sports*, agrees that: 'In our personal lives, we accept the government's (and the legal system's) position that life should be free of risks.' For Bane, fear-inducing sports are a response to an increasingly safe environment.

Fear has been used in another sense to clarify uncertainties in sports. Athletes who are overwhelming favorites to win a **competition** are sometimes disabled by a *fear of failing*: stricken by the high expectations of others, they fail to perform to their best. Fear of failing is often conquered by a combination of an **achievement motivation** (to reach goals) and an intrinsic motivation (to engage in the activity). Some athletes seem disposed to **choke** at crucial stages in competitions they are poised to win. This may be because of fear, in this case a *fear of* *success*, a term coined by Matina Horner to describe the horror some people experience at the prospect of actually accomplishing their goals or of succeeding in other people's eyes. Horner's much-criticized 1972 work argued that women are more afflicted by this, not only in sports but in society generally. Women fear that if they succeed in a domain traditionally dominated by men, others will deduce a lack of femininity. As a consequence, they perform modestly at a level below their optimum. Research has not supported Horner's argument.

There is another application of fear, this time in the context of audiences. Time and again in sports, athletes emerge who can perform exceptionally well in certain competitive environments, but cannot reproduce their form in front of large audiences, especially away from home where the crowds are hostile. Whether a crowd can intimidate some players and thus confer a **home advantage** on the team it supports is open to question. There is also debate on the issue of **social facilitation**: whether an audience will improve or inhibit performances. Impressions gleaned across the spectrum of sports appear to confirm that some athletes perform better away from the limelight. If this is because of some form of fear, it must be a fear of embarrassment, or some other predicament that causes acute discomfort in the competitor.

Further reading

Bane, M. (1997) *Over the Edge: A regular guy's odyssey in extreme sports* London: Gollancz.

Furedi, F. (1997) *Culture of Fear* London: Cassell.

Horner, M.S. (1972) 'Toward an understanding of achievement-related conflicts in women,' *Journal of Social Issues* vol. 28, pp. 157–76.

FEEDBACK

The modification or **control** of a process or system by returning information about its results, output or effects is known as feedback. Originally an electrical term (referring to the return of a faction of an output signal from one stage of a circuit), feedback in sports describes the process of trying to minimize the difference between desired and actual results by relaying data about the results of performers' actions back to the performers. In this way, a **skill** is honed and perfected.

As a thermostat monitors temperature and feeds this information back into the heating system it regulates, so information about the outcome of skilled action feeds back to the performer and provides the basis for modification or stability. *Extrinsic* feedback is the observation of the results of an action (possibly by others, including coaches), while *intrinsic* feedback is the subjective feelings the performer gets. For example, boxers sometimes say they know when they have scored a knockout by the sensation they get at the point of impact of their punch; baseball sluggers claim they know they have hit a home run as soon as they make contact with the ball. The term used to cover the sensory systems involved in providing information about position, location, orientation and movement of the body is *proprioception*. The information received operates as a basis for future action. The nature of the event dictates what type of feedback is available. For example, show jumpers or motor racers can instantly see the results of their actions and have both forms of feedback available to them, whereas divers rely on proprioceptive information, at least until they have the chance to view a video or talk to their coaches.

Feedback is part of the mechanics of **skill acquisition**. For example, an unskilled person may be able to produce what appears to be a skilled piece of behavior on a one-off or even occasional basis: a football fan might kick a 30-yard field **goal**; a tennis fan might serve an ace; an archer might score a bullseye. The possessor of a skill, on the other hand, can produce the behavior time and again. In other words, skilled behavior has a consistent outcome. An NFL kicker will make the field goal eight times out of ten; a tennis pro will serve a quota of aces in every game; an Olympic archer can find the bullseye regularly. This does not mean that the skilled athlete uses exactly the same combination of muscle contractions and skeletal movements on every occasion; the results, however, are very similar. Knowledge of the results, or KR as it is sometimes abbreviated, provides the performer with information about the outcomes of his or her actions. The novice kicker will adapt his movements as a result of the flight of the ball. Coupled with this is the advice of coaches and teammates who will proffer further information that aid the performer in refining the kicking skill; this is known as knowledge of performance, or just KP.

Feedback operates in different ways at different levels of an athlete's development. A beginner might rely heavily on what is known as closed loop control: concentrating on the feedback he or she receives during the execution of a particular skill and consciously attending to as many features as possible. At more advanced stages, when skills have been mastered, feedback is less important, though serves the purpose in adapting skills to particular environments (as a golfer might toss grass in the air to assess the direction and force of the wind). In some situations, no feedback is necessary at all: this is known as open loop control and athletes can complete a skill without paying **attention** to information, either intrinsic or extrinsic. The expression 'as easy as riding a bike' applies perfectly to skills subject to open loop control.

A less familiar control system is known as *feedforward*. If the thermostat is the exemplar for feedback, then the washing machine is feedforward's equivalent: as a wash sequence is controlled by a program, so muscular activity is controlled by a particular set of instructions or advice from the brain though the ultimate output is influenced by local conditions. Whereas feedback monitors the divergence between actual and desired output, feedforward anticipates the relation between the environment and the organism (or system) to determine a course of action.

Further reading

Adams, J.A. (1971) 'A closed loop theory of motor learning,' *Journal of Motor Behavior* vol. 3, pp. 111–50.
Annett, J. (1969) *Feedback and Human Behavior* Harmondsworth: Penguin.

FIGHT OR FLIGHT *see* **adrenaline rush**

FLOW

Coined originally in 1990 by Mihaly Csikszentmihalyi to describe the state many call the 'natural high,' flow has been studied systematically over the years with a view to identifying its characteristics and the conditions under which it can be achieved. The term's origin is the Germanic *Flo*, meaning flood.

In everyday parlance, of course, flow refers to a smooth procession or movement, a yielding, stream-like pouring, or a gushing, abundant supply of something, such as blood, money or electric current. Essentially, this is its meaning in sport: a mental state in which an athletic performance seems to move by itself without any undue effort from the individual, who experiences a number of sensations, all of which combine to produce a flow. In many senses, the experience closely resembles what athletes call the **zone**.

Csikszentmihalyi later collaborated with Susan Jackson to formalize the concept in *Flow in Sports: The keys to optimal experiences and performances*. As the title suggests, there is a relationship with experience and performance: if one is optimal, the other should correspond. Jackson and Csikszentmihalyi delineated nine features of flow. These are:

1 A balance between an athlete's **perception** of challenge of a situation and the athlete's skills (the c–s balance): the task must extend the athlete without being impossibly difficult.

2 Merging of action and awareness: consciousness of one's own body results in a sense of totality or union of body and mind.

3 Clear goals: the immediate ambition is so explicit that the athlete can visualize him or herself accomplishing it throughout the whole athletic performance.

4 Unambiguous **feedback**: kinesthetic feedback from the athlete's own body and outcome feedback from the performance itself (and perhaps coaches and spectators) enables the athlete to monitor progress.

5 **Concentration** on the immediate task: alertness to the here-and-now is crucial and the athlete must be able to pick up clues from the environment.

6 Sense of **control**: there is no forcing from athletes, who should experience utter **confidence** and sense an effortless **momentum** carrying them along.

7 Loss of self-consciousness: doubts, criticism and judgements do not concern the athlete, who does not entertain negative thoughts at all.

8 Transformation of time: perceptual distortions often accompany flow states, runners experiencing long races as gone in 'a flash,' or tennis players seeing the tennis ball as big as a beachball.

9 **Autotelic** experience: the flow experience is totally agreeable in its own right, so that it is intrinsically valuable to the athlete.

The ninth feature is interesting because sports are, by definition, competitive and as such have aims or goals to which all endeavor is directed. It is possible to watch tapes of Michael Jordan in the 1990s and understand his often exquisite performances as completely autotelic, as if he were involved in a display of **skill** rather than a contest. Of course, the point about Jordan's apparently flow-like states is that they were made possible precisely because they were organized around achieving a prescribed objective. It is the concept of challenge that elicits the flow – as Jackson and Csikszentmihalyi recognize in (1) the c–s balance. Even allowing for this apparent contradiction, the model provides empirical as well as conceptual information, much of it gleaned from Jackson's 1996 research with elite athletes on the constitution of flow. Subsequent research published in 1999 by Jackson and another team concluded that 'it does appear that cognitive, rather than physiological processes may be related to the flow experience.'

The problem with flow is how to replicate it. For example, in 1982, David Moorcroft unexpectedly broke the world's 5,000 meter record in 13.00.41. There was nothing in Moorcroft's form to indicate he was capable of such a time: he had never approached the mark before and, indeed, never approached it again. It was strictly a once-only performance, on which Moorcroft reflected that once he took the lead in the race he seemed to be carried along almost independently of his own efforts – **automaticity**. His description squared almost perfectly with the Jackson–Csikszentmihalyi schema.

Similarly, Bob Beamon offered no explanation for his logic-defying, record-shattering long jump of 29 feet 2 inches (8.90 meters) at the 1968 Olympics in Mexico. He reported a sensation of unprecedented power as he soared through the air for a barely believable record – and collapsed, probably in disbelief, shortly afterward.

By contrast, the previously mentioned Jordan seemed to be able to produce flow-like states at will, as were some other outstanding athletes. The cricketer Brian Lara appeared effortlessly graceful at the crease, where he would remain unbeatable for hours at a time. Andre Agassi was on many occasions unsurpassable, such was his uncanny anticipation and unconstrained returns on both forehand and backhand sides. Once into his rhythm, Agassi was impossible to beat. The reputation of the likes of Jordan and Lara was built on their ability to function at optimal levels and, presumably, operate in flow-like states regularly, while many others can produce flow but cannot predict exactly when.

Further reading

Csikszentmihalyi, M. (1990) *Flow: The psychology of optimal experience* New York: Harper & Row.

Jackson, S.A. and Csikszentmihalyi, M. (1999) *Flow in Sports: The keys to optimal experiences and performances* Champaign IL: Human Kinetics.

Jackson, S.A., Ford, S.K., Kimiecik, J.C. and Marsh, H.W. (1999) 'Psychological correlates of flow in sport,' *Journal of Sport & Exercise Psychology* vol. 20, pp. 358–78.

FOCUSED

Although athletes and sports writers use the term 'focused' to describe a state of **arousal** in which **concentration** is unwavering, psychologists prefer the more accurate term *focused auditory/visual attention*, or *focal attention*, to describe the selective aspects of **perception** athletes employ when they are in **competition** (or, sometimes, in training). Being focused means operating at the highest possible level of **attention**, screening out all irrelevant **stimuli** in the environment and selecting only auditory and visual information that is pertinent to the immediate task. The word *focus* was originally Latin for fireplace, or hearth.

Being focused in the lead-up to an event is actually a different process to being focused during the event itself. For instance, a high-jumper may claim to be focused for up to four years, insisting that he or she is focused on winning an Olympic gold medal and that all endeavor over that period is a form of preparation for a single, ultimate competition. The athlete means that intervening competitions, like the IAAF world championships or the Pan American games, will be subordinate challenges and that training schedules will be designed to ensure he or she peaks for the Olympics. In this sense, 'focused' describes a pattern of activities organized around a grand plan. The athlete may be preoccupied with the Olympics to the point where she pays less attention to what she regards as less important affairs, but is unlikely to wreck her car or burn down the house because attentional focus was so narrow. Yet, in the actual Olympic competition, focused attention will be strictly on a single task and a process of sensory **gating** will have begun; extraneous stimuli, both external (in the environment) and internal (thoughts), will be shut out.

Being focused during competition means that attention is undivided. In some sports, like high jumping, swimming or boxing, visual attention is sharply focused: visual stimuli falling in the central area of vision are processed much more thoroughly than those further away from the central area. A well-focused athlete will extract little information from the peripheral areas of the visual attentional spotlight – visual perception resembles a car headlight with everything at the center of the beam visible with clarity, but objects lying at the edge or outside the beam only imperfectly, if at all. Auditory information, from the crowd for example, will be ignored as far as possible. Formula One places unusual attentional demands on drivers: while their visual focus falls on the track ahead, they are constantly receiving instructions through their helmets from their pit crew and must respond alertly and accurately; focusing for them is a matter of dividing visual and auditory attention.

Competitors in team sports, on the other hand, must focus in a different way. Both visual and auditory foci must be broader to take

117

account of movement and sounds. Athletes must be able to integrate information, including instructions from teammates and the actions of opponents in peripheral vision. So the scope of both attentional channels must be wider. Van Schoyck and Grasha suggest that allocating attentional focus in this way is 'scanning.' This does not mean the player of team sports is any less focused than a high jumper: to be an effective **team player**, the athlete must learn to divide his or her focal attention. Maintaining a high level of performance in team sports depends on combining often complex tasks, and this demands the development of **automaticity** which makes little or no demand on attentional resources. So, for example, the high jumper can attend to the run-up, the take-off position and the height of the bar (external) and the manner in which he will make his approach and execute his flight (internal); the mechanics of the jump itself will be so well practiced that he will not need to attend to them.

The different styles of focal attention have been formalized by Robert Nideffer, who argued that there are two dimensions: width (broad to narrow) and direction (internal to external). A team member, say a midfield soccer player, needs a broad focus when appraising attacking options, but may need to narrow focus when passing or involved in a tackle. The direction of the focus will be external, spotting cues from other players and, of course, the movement of the ball. A weight lifter, by contrast, will maintain a narrow focus and internal direction, attending the cues from his or her own body. A boxer's focus will be narrow because there is only a single opponent and the direction of the focus will be mainly external, though, of course, internal cues such as tiredness and **injury** will also become part of the focus as the fight progresses.

Factors that inhibit focusing include distractions and the arrival of multiple stimuli. Athletes frequently introduce distractions, appealing to umpires or referees or behaving theatrically to direct opponents' attention to a new stimulus. Returning focused attention to the target stimulus then becomes difficult. Multiple stimuli can include virtually any auditory or visual information not absolutely relevant to the immediate task. So a football player in a team engaged in a crucial game that determines whether that team makes the playoffs may be interested in the score of another game featuring a rival team that kicked off at the same time. But the player's focus will be inhibited if the score comes through to the bench during the game. Crowds are often thought to confer a **home advantage**, though players who heed the crowd do so to the detriment of their focus and, probably, their performance. Being focused should not be confused with related but distinct experiences, such as achieving **peak performance**, being in a **flow** state or entering the **zone**.

Further reading

Janelle, C.M., Singer, R.N. and Williams, A.M. (1999) 'External distribution and attentional narrowing: visual search evidence,' *Journal of Sport & Exercise Psychology* vol. 21, pp. 70–91.

Nideffer, R.M. (1976) 'Test of attentional and interpersonal style,' *Journal of Personality and Social Psychology* vol. 34, pp. 394–404.

Van Schoyck, S. and Grasha, A. (1981) 'Attentional style variations and athletic ability: the advantages of a sports-specific test,' *Medicine and Science in Sport and Exercise* vol. 26, pp. 495–502.

GATING

Gating, sensory gating or gating-out means excluding, disregarding or filtering features of the environment that are not relevant to the immediate task. Athletes at any level must be adept at inhibiting extraneous pieces of sensory information as they prepare for and while they perform their activities; without this faculty, they could not attend effectively to their task, making **concentration** impossible.

Think of a gate: the athlete must allow it to open only just wide enough to let in the sensory input he or she needs, shutting out the other, possibly distracting, pieces of information. At the same time, a spectator watching the athlete is probably also gating: keeping out the potentially diverting influences of cold weather, an uncomfortable seat and a growing hunger for decent food, while remaining enthralled with the contest.

In both instances, the individual is paying selective **attention** to relevant materials. Were the spectator watching the sport on television from home, he or she may not be gating in such a restrictive way: he or she may pay attention to, for example, a ringing phone, a thirst for a drink or the need to go to the bathroom, all of which might elicit a response. These are distractions, but not necessarily pernicious ones – they will not ruin enjoyment of the game. If the athlete is unable to gate out inessential data, he or she may be in trouble. Any kind of distraction can prove costly. These can range from a jeering crowd to the lingering **memory** of an error, even one from several years before.

Depending on the sport, performers often need to open and shut the gate to suit circumstances: a soccer goalkeeper will open the gate only a sliver when facing a penalty kick, but he or she may push it wider during open play and, if trailing 0–1 with seconds remaining and needing to play upfield, may thrust the gate open to take in a broad range of situational factors.

Further reading

Cox, R.H. (1998) *Sport Psychology: Concepts and applications*, 4th edition, Boston MA: McGraw-Hill, ch. 3.

GAY

The brief and, in many ways, ironic adjective-cum-noun 'gay' describes people with homosexual proclivities and the lifestyle practices associated with them. The irony, at least when the term was introduced in the 1970s, was that being gay was anything but cheerful. Men and women with homosexual inclinations were marginalized, socially, legally and, indeed, economically. (Some accounts of the origins of 'gay' suggest it was originally an acronym for 'good as you.') While homophobia (antipathy toward or fear of gay people) still exists, it has abated to the point where many prominent figures, including some elite athletes, have voluntarily come out (disclosed their sexual orientations) or been outed by others, without significant harm to their professional careers.

In his *The Arena of Masculinity: Sports, homosexuality and the meaning of sex*, Brian Pronger argues that sports constitute a 'covert world of homoeroticism,' where members of the same **sex** are licensed to touch, kiss and openly hug each other quite openly, as well as sharing showers, locker rooms and, in some sports, even bathtubs. This is given some support by the various essays in the collection *Making Men: Rugby and the masculine identity*, edited by John Nauright and Timothy Chandler, in which rugby is analyzed as a sport in which heterosexual 'maleness' is used as a protective shield to cover a sport in which sustained physical contact is inevitable. The same point applies to varying extents to other predominantly male sports.

Female athletes were for long regarded suspiciously as 'mannish.' Labeled as tomboys or hoydens, they were thought to lack 'femininity' and even represent a moral degeneracy in the early twentieth century. One of the many warnings issued by medical authorities to women either in sport or thinking about entering it, concerned *virilism*: this was a process supposedly brought on by exercise and had the effect of turning women into men!

For these historical and related contemporary reasons, both male and female sports have been guarded about homosexuality. The slurs about Mildred 'Babe' Didrikson in the 1920s and 1930s were presumably sufficient to prevent females from coming out, though in 1981 the tennis player Billie-Jean King was taken to court by her former secretary and later acknowledged that she had a lesbian relationship with her. King lost her portfolio of endorsement contracts and was, for a while, forsaken, only to be rehabilitated by the media in later years. While King's experience may have chastened many, it also emboldened others to declare their homosexuality, though Pat Griffin, in *Strong Women, Deep Closets*, suspects that the 'demonizing' of lesbians in sport continued into the late 1990s – and probably beyond.

One of the first male athletes to come out died with AIDS in 1987: Tom Waddell, the Olympic decathlete from the 1968 Mexico games, was one of the founders of the Gay Games in 1982. He became involved in a legal case with the US Olympic Committee, which refused to let him use the word 'Olympic' to describe the tournament. After Waddell, there were sporadic declarations or involuntary outings of athletes, including that of Olympic diver Greg Louganis and Justin Fashanu, who played pro soccer in Britain and the USA and committed suicide in 1988.

Sports performers have been slow to follow the example of entertainers like George Michael or Ellen Degeneres, whose careers have not suffered since their homosexuality became known. Cultural prohibitions on revealing one's homosexuality receded after the 1980s, but many athletes who take part of their income from endorsements remain hesitant about disclosing their orientation. There are at least two other related reasons. First, a homophobia permeates many male-dominated sports that remain obstinate about their macho nature. Also, the spread of popular misconceptions about the infectious properties of AIDS, particularly in the 1990s, had the effect of daunting gay men who might otherwise have come out but did not for fear of ostracism by heterosexual friends.

Further reading

Griffin, P. (1998) *Strong Women, Deep Closets: Lesbians and homophobia in sport* Champaign IL: Human Kinetics.

Nauright, J. and Chandler, T.J.L. (eds) (1996) *Making Men: Rugby and the masculine identity* London: Frank Cass.

Pronger, B. (1990) *The Arena of Masculinity: Sports, homosexuality and the meaning of sex*, New York: St Martin's Press.

GENDER

In contrast to **sex**, which describes the binary classification of animals according to biological criteria, 'gender' refers to the manner in which a society responds to those biological differences. In this sense, the way societies designate roles, styles and institutional arrangements determines the boundaries of gender differences. These in turn are accepted and internalized by subjects so that we may speak of gender identities – the ways in which people think about themselves and, indeed, about others. Sports, like the rest of society, are organized around gender differentiation: few sports are 'mixed,' or co-ed, while most are organized into male and female competitions. The reasons for this are historical and cultural, based on prevailing beliefs, practices and codes that mirror assumptions about the fundamental differences between men and women. The term is from the French *gendre*, which derives from the Latin *genus*, meaning class or kind (of animals or plants).

It has been argued that the entire institution of sports is established on a gender division. Established by men for men, organized sport was intended to validate masculinity at a stage in history (late nineteenth century) when the factory system was superseding human labor, making men's physical input less important than at earlier stages in industrialization. Competitive sport was an arena in which men could exhibit and develop their physical prowess. Women's roles were confined to that of spectators: the only sports they were permitted to participate in were 'ladylike' pastimes, such as croquet or a gentle game of tennis, a game that had no resemblance to the explosive type of activity witnessed today. Gender was inscribed in sport from its inception. Women were excluded from the first Olympic games, though four years later, in 1900, they were allowed to compete in a restricted number of events. So the Victorian era saw the start of what is often called the 'gendering of modern sport.'

Medical opinion solidified the gendering, cautioning that vigorous physical activity, while acceptable for men, was actually dangerous for women, who were too frail to participate in competitive sports and risked all manner of side effects (including the loss of reproductive functions and the transformation of sexual characteristics) if they did so. Helen Lenskyj's study pays particular **attention** to the ways women's achievements in sports were discredited, typically by accusations of impropriety or unnatural status.

It should not be assumed that sports were merely repositories of society's prejudices against women. Nancy Therberge argues that gendered sports advanced a particular type of gender arrangement: 'What is critical about the contribution of sport to the construction of gender is that sport provides an image of idealized, or "culturally exalted" ... masculinity.' In other words, the dominance of men, material and cultural, has been reproduced in some part by sports. *Hegemonic masculinity* is the phrase used to describe the manner in which a whole range of women's attributes and activities, including sports, are devalued, while men's equivalents are elevated.

While Victorian ideals of masculinity and femininity have been considerably modified and women's accomplishments in sport have assisted this, challenges are often thwarted. The denigration of **gay** female as well as gay male athletes has served as a bulwark for traditional gender arrangements. Women's exposé of the myth of frailty through their achievements has not persuaded everyone: marathons are still split into separate races; women tennis players are often ridiculed as incapable of beating a man ranked in the 200s.

The media-assisted accentuation of the physical appearance of women as opposed to the athletic performance of men persists. Female athletes, especially tennis players, are 'sexualized' – that is, turned into objects of the male gaze.

Further reading

Lenskyj, H. (1986) *Out of Bounds: Women, sport and sexuality* Toronto: Women's Press.
Therberge, N. (2000) 'Gender and sport,' pp. 322–33 in Coakley, J. and Dunning, E. (eds) *Handbook of Sports Studies* London: Sage.

GOAL

An aim, objective or end result that a person plans for, or intends to achieve is, of course, a goal (a word whose origins are obscure, but which may be a version of *gol*, a Middle English term for boundary). The concept should not be confused with a *dream*, which is a mental image or fantasy that carries no necessary assumption that action will follow, or a *purpose*, which is a purely internal target that guides behavior. A goal is external to the subject (though goals cannot, in practice, exist without an internal purpose). An aspiring athlete may say her dream is to win the US Open, yet fail to practice enough to make necessary improvements. Another athlete may have a purpose that motivates her to train hard to improve, but may have no clear specific goal that will strengthen her **commitment** and narrow her **attention**. But an athlete with a **goal orientation** will have a practical program designed to enable the attainment of tangible objectives.

To be effective, goals have to have two parts: (1) direction (for behavior); and (2) quality of product (or minimum standard of performance required). They allow an athlete to devote full attention to implementing intentions, and once they are achieved supply the **confidence** to make key decisions.

It is impossible to entertain the idea of an athletic career without goals. **Competition** demands that proficiencies, standards and accomplishments are achieved, and achieving them is inconceivable without goals to orient the athlete. A common strategy to direct athletes is **goal setting**, in which each specific objective reached works as **reinforcement**, conferring **self-efficacy** and encouraging further progress.

Further reading

Burton, D. (1992) 'The Jekyll/Hyde nature of goals: reconceptualizing goal setting in sport,' pp. 267–97 in Horn, T.S. (ed.) *Advances in Sport Psychology* Champaign IL: Human Kinetics.

Harwood, C., Hardy, L. and Swain A. (2000) 'Achievement goals in sport: a critique of conceptual and measurement issues,' *Journal of Sport & Exercise Psychology* vol. 22, pp. 235–55.

Zinsser, N., Bunker, L. and Williams, J.M. (1998) 'Cognitive techniques for building confidence and enhancing performance,' pp. 270–95 in Williams, J.M. (ed.) (1998) *Applied Sport Psychology: Personal growth to peak performance*, 3rd edition, Mountain View CA: Mayfield.

GOAL ORIENTATION

The stable tendency to position oneself in the direction of a **goal** is known as a goal orientation. It is an underlying long-term inclination that guides a subject and so exerts a significant influence on the subject's **motivation**, not only in sports, but in any enterprise that requires task **mastery**, or **skill acquisition**.

There are two types of goal orientation: (1) performance goal orientation: an athlete's perceived mastery of new tasks, or all-round improvement in **skill**; (2) outcome goal orientation: objective, measurable confirmation of improvements, such as winning and beating others. Mastery of skills is a means to the end of winning, not an end in itself, though the goals to be set typically concern performance rather than outcome.

In (1), athletes tend to gear their thoughts and efforts to quality of performance and the satisfaction they derive for this: the actual outcome of a **competition** is of secondary importance. By contrast, in (2) athletes would prefer to perform badly as long as they win: the result is what matters. Sometimes one can be mistaken for the other. For example, during Jennifer Capriati's remarkable **comeback** year, 2001, it was widely assumed that she harbored an outcome goal orientation, having won the Australian and French Opens. The outcome in question was the Grand Slam. Only after her defeat at Wimbledon did she reveal that: 'Everybody was making a big deal out of the Grand Slam except me. I'm pretty happy the way the year has gone so far.' Even allowing for a degree of rationalization in her verdict, it seems fair to assume that, after her troubled career interval, her goal orientation was geared to holding her own on the circuit rather than winning titles.

The fact that she won two (which must have seemed like a bonus) supports the findings of Burton, who in 1989 concluded that performance goals have a greater effect on enhancing performance than outcome goals. Outcome-oriented athletes are more susceptible to **anxiety** and other forms of **stress** than athletes who are oriented to their own performance goals. This makes sense, especially when we raise the possibility that, after Capriati's two Open wins, it is at least possible that the performance orientation she acknowledged was displaced by an outcome orientation and that the tightening-up in her Wimbledon semi-final against Justine Henin (after leading by a set) may have been a symptom of anxiety.

Further reading

Burton, D. (1989) 'Winning isn't everything: examining the impact of performance goals on collegiate swimmer's cognitions and performance,' *The Sport Psychologist* vol. 2, pp. 105–32.

Nicholls, J.G. (1984) 'Achievement motivation: conceptions of ability, subjective experience, task choice and performance,' *Psychological Review* vol. 91, pp. 328–46.

GOAL SETTING

The process in which long- and short-term goals are established is goal setting. An athlete may set goals intuitively at the outset of a career, for example to throw a decent spiral, sustain a rally or just finish a race. As a career progresses, athletes typically clarify specific goals, sometimes establishing a long-term **goal** that can be broken into less ambitious short-term goals, setting up a kind of hierarchy of goals to be achieved one by one.

In other words, effective goal setting involves the prescribing of limited, realistic objectives which once met lead to further objectives – which again should be small. Former Olympic hurdler David Hemery reflected in his *Sporting Excellence* how he used hundredths of a second as goals, rather than aiming at lopping significant chunks off his personal best. Tiny, gradual improvements work most rationally as goals, though the element of challenge must be present or there will be little intrinsic value to the athlete. There is also only limited value in goals that are imposed, for example by a coach or manager: the objectives must be negotiated and ultimately accepted by the subject trying to reach them. The goals should also be made 'public': harboring 'private' goals secretly may be satisfying, but it is not nearly as effective as making known the goals at which athletes are aiming.

Mark Anshel reports on a strategy of grouping goal setting so that a single poor performance does not invalidate the goal: this is known as interval goal setting and may take an average time from a cluster of five time trials, not every single one. The average times may themselves be intervals in a more ambitious long-term goal, such as an end-of-season personal best or a placing at a major championship. This approach emphasizes the second type of goal orientation, not the subject's interpretation of progress, the effort he or she sinks into pursuing the goal or, indeed, the athlete's own experience of personal success or failure. In other words, it lacks a subjective dimension which would allow an athlete's **anxiety, confidence, goal orientation** and, in general, **cognition** a role in the process.

Commitment is one of four 'moderator variables,' as Locke and Latham called them in their *A Theory of Goal Setting and Task Performance*. Highly committed athletes reach their goals regardless of whether they are hard or easy; so only tough goals work for this type of subject. The other moderators are the athlete's ability, feedback from others (monitoring) and task complexity. The effectiveness of goal setting depends on all these variables.

While goal setting seems an eminently sensible and effectual method, its results are equivocal. Reviews of research on goal setting by, among others, Burton in 1993 and Kyllo and Landers in 1995, concluded that, although goal setting is a superior technique to a 'go out there and do your best' approach, much of its effectiveness depends on individual differences. Athletes who have **self-efficacy**, for example, prosper in a self-fulfilling manner: if they believe they will achieve a great deal from goal setting, they generally create conditions under which they will.

Further reading

Anshel, M.H. (1997) *Sport Psychology: From theory to practice*, 3rd edition, Scottsdale AZ: Gorsuch Scarisbrick.

Kyllo, L.B. and Landers, D.M. (1995) 'Goal setting in sport and exercise: a research synthesis to resolve the controversy,' *Journal of Sport & Exercise Psychology* vol. 17, pp. 117–37.

Weinberg, R.S. (1992) 'Goal setting and motor performance: A review and critique,' pp. 177–97 in Roberts, G.C. (ed.) *Motivation in Sport and Exercise* Champaign IL: Human Kinetics.

GROUP DYNAMICS

Processes that generate change in groups are known as group dynamics, a concept that insinuates that, as the maxim goes, 'the whole is more than the sum of the parts.' The word 'dynamic,' from the Greek *dunamikos*, for power, refers to energizing or motive force; and the dynamism's source lies in the emergent properties of the group. Rather being a mere aggregation of individuals, the group generates properties over and above those of the individual members: they *emerge* during the interactions of the individuals. This is especially important in sports: not only team sports, in which factors such as **cohesion** and **leadership** are pivotal, but in individual sports when the right kind of 'chemistry' between an athlete and his or her coaching staff can yield significant changes in performance.

The concept of group dynamics is often associated with Kurt Lewin, who was influenced by early twentieth-century Gestalt psychology (*Gestalt* is German for structure, or configuration) which examined the dynamism of the **personality** holistically (i.e. as a structured whole). Groups are approached as entities in their own right rather than compositions of individuals: once a group is formed, it generates characteristics of its own quite independently of its members. The term used to describe this independent **character** is *sui generis*.

Group dynamics are evident in practically any situation in which individuals interact on a meaningful basis: when they have awareness of each other's presence, an insight into others' **motivation** and an expectation of what the outcome of their interaction with others might be. In sports, groups – whether teams, squads, rosters or even partnerships – come together with a **goal** to succeed at some level. That unity of purpose introduces dynamic processes that affect **decision making** roles, the collective **motivation** of the group, the methods of communication and other features that cannot exist at an individual level. Like the brushes and pails of the sorcerer's apprentice, the group takes on a life of its own.

Conflicts, tension and especially power struggles frequently characterize group dynamics, as viewers of such television series as *Survivor* and *Big Brother* will appreciate. Often, the context of the group allows a blossoming of personality styles or other characteristics that are not evident outside the group.

Examples of teams overachieving are legion. Individual athletes who look ordinary on paper can sometimes produce exceptional performances when the group dynamics are 'right.' The 1979 World Series-winning Pittsburgh Pirates team, with its adopted anthem 'We are family,' is an illustration, as is the self-styled 'Crazy Gang' Wimbledon team that won the FA Cup in 1988. Even great individual athletes benefit from group dynamics. Michael Jordan clearly flourished in the context of a unified Chicago Bulls team. Deeper into history, Pelé earned his status as the greatest ever soccer player within the solidarity of the Brazilian national team. Proficient as individuals, each was also a **team player**.

The bridge between group dynamics and sport psychology was **social facilitation** research, according to Partridge and Stevens; we should also highlight the importance of the **Ringelmann effect** and **social loafing**, both of which suggest the pre-eminence of collective processes over those of individuals in certain settings. Julie Partridge and Diane Stevens emphasize the emergence and maintenance of group norms in encouraging predictability, highlighting central values and minimizing **deviance**. As group norms (i.e. informal rules that govern the manner in which the group is organized) are created, formal rules are needed less and less and **obedience** becomes un-problematic.

Further reading

Lewin, K. (1948) *Resolving Social Conflicts* New York: Harper.

Partridge, J. and Stevens, D.E. (2002) 'Group dynamics: the influence of the team in sport,' pp. 272–90 in Silva, J.M. and Stevens, D.E. (eds) *Psychological Foundations of Sport* Boston MA: Allyn & Bacon.

HALO EFFECT

Basing overall judgement of a person on a single outstanding characteristic and glorifying that person on this misleading basis is known as the halo effect. A halo is, of course, a luminous circle of light surrounding the head of a saint or an idealized person; it comes from the Greek *halõs*, disc. Sports history is full of individuals who have been assessed enthusiastically or become widely known because of one feature. There is a tendency to see positive characteristics going with other characteristics which, objectively, may not be so positive.

It is very much a matter of argument whether one conspicuous and perhaps remarkable attribute is enough to qualify an athlete as a 'great.' Some might contend that, if the attribute is influential enough to turn entire games, then the individual who has it is genuinely worthy. Others would counter that great athletes who have one exceptional quality often learn to integrate others into their over makeup to become complete athletes, and those who do not should not deserve to be considered as greats.

David Beckham, for instance, was renowned as an exponent of crosses: he could find targets from unusual and unexpected angles and put so much 'bend' on his crosses that defenders were often deceived. Other aspects of his game were adequate; his crossing alone elevated him. Whether the all-round assessment of him was a result of inferring positive general characteristics from only one is a matter of contention. Similar arguments could be held over an athlete such as Pat Rafter: did his highly effective groundstroke play make him an excellent player or just a good volleyer? Did people regard Marion Jones as one of the best pound-for-pound athletes of her time just because she was an extraordinary 100 meters sprinter? Over 200 meters she was good, and her long jump was decent. In an athlete with few weaknesses, it is often easy to be misguided by one outstanding strength.

Further reading

Nisbett, R.E. and Wilson, T.D. (1977) 'The halo effect: evidence for unconscious alteration of judgements,' *Journal of Personality and Social Psychology* vol. 35, pp. 250–6.

HOME ADVANTAGE

Competing in front of a home crowd is popularly thought to confer benefits on a team or an individual, those benefits being known as home advantage, or sometimes home field or court advantage. Intuitively, it might be thought that the advantage derives from the comfort of competing in a familiar environment, the freshness of not having to travel or the boost of a partisan crowd; all these have been investigated.

Some teams would seem to have an obvious edge by virtue of familiarity. For example, playing in Buffalo in mid-winter would appear to present the Bills with a distinct advantage, especially against teams such as Tampa Bay Buccaneers, who practice and play in warm climates (and for long had a reputation for never winning games when the temperature was 40°F/4.4°C or lower) – and vice versa, of course. Travel is another factor: a long, draining flight across time zones from Miami to Seattle would seem to leave the Mariners with competitive leverage over the Marlins. But a review by Courneya and Carron concluded that, in themselves, these could not account for the tendency for teams playing at home to win (over 50 per cent of the time across several sports, according to the review).

Research on the role of the crowd is also inconclusive, though there is a substantial body of literature dating back to the early twentieth century on the effects on performing in front of others, whether spectators or other competitors, as against performing in isolation. While research revealed measurable changes in performance when conducted in the presence of others, the link between the two remained the subject of debate. Zajonc's **social facilitation** theory suggested that the mere presence of others was enough to arouse competitors or increase the motivational state known as **drive**. This works well for skilled performers who respond appropriately; but not so well for less skilled performers for whom more **arousal** can prove inhibiting. So the crowd does not facilitate good performances for everyone. Subsequent research revealed the limitations of this theory, the most serious one of which was its failure to take into account how athletes perceive and interpret the crowd, whether hostile or friendly. **Cognition**, it was argued, mediated between crowd presence and actual performance. For example, athletes performing in front of a crowd that is judging them in some way may experience **anxiety**, distraction and other manifestations of what is called *evaluation apprehension*.

But even in front of judgemental crowds, other research concluded, athletes competed with zeal. Varca's 1980 investigations showed that basketball players on both sides played more assertively in front of fans: interestingly, while home players produced a higher performance, visitors typically committed more fouls. A vocal crowd made both teams more assertive, though only the home team converted that assertiveness – or what we would now call **aggressiveness** – into superiority. The away players' persistent fouling was what Varca called dysfunctional assertive behavior.

This alerts us to the fact that the counterpart to home advantage is away disadvantage; at least one project concluded that home teams did not necessarily raise their game when playing at home, but visitors' standards of performance declined so markedly that it *appears* the home teams play better. Statistical research using historical data disclosed a pattern of underachievement by road teams, while home teams' statistics remained constant. Of course, statistical analyses reveal more about some sports than others (the study used basketball), but the overall point about traveling teams suffering in front of unfriendly crowds may be a universal one.

Sometimes, crowds themselves capitalize on this. 'Welcome to Hell' was emblazoned across banners that usually greeted visitors to the home stadium of the soccer club Galatasaray in Istanbul. The 100,000 fans who regularly watched Barcelona play in the Nou Camp stadium were famously antagonistic to visiting teams, chanting, banging drums and blowing horns to create a deafening cacophony. (Crowd size is not the only factor: small, densely packed crowds in more intimate stadia can serve a similar purpose.) This can have the effect of inhibiting road teams, but it can also work to disadvantage home players – by making them more self-attentive or aware of the expectations resting on their shoulders, especially on big occasions.

Fans often talk of 'hometown referees' and 'hometown decisions,' highlighting misgivings about the neutrality of officials in the face of partisan crowds. A research letter in *The Lancet* (24 April 1999, p. 1,416) reported a small study involving eleven referees, coaches and players who were split into two groups and asked to make calls on fifty-two incidents as they watched a video of a game of soccer. One group watched the tape with background noise, the other with the 'mute' button on. 'Observers had a greater tendency to award a foul when viewing challenges by away players in the presence of the crowd noise,' related Nevill *et al.*, whose conclusion was that observers did not adjudicate objectively 'but referred to the crowd for guidance.' (The letter did not state whether the refs, coaches or players were more or less influenced, or whether there was any pattern.) The same research team (this time as Balmer *et al.*) studied the winter Olympic games over ninety years and unearthed 'significant evidence of home advantage,' most of it explicable in terms of 'subjective assessment by officials.' The findings reflected 'the way judges respond to the reactions of the crowd.'

While this research did not address Varca's earlier findings, it implicitly cast doubt on them: do away players commit more fouls, or are they simply penalized more by referees who are 'guided' by crowd noise? It is likely that home advantage is as much to do with the crowd's effect on the officials as it is on the competitors.

A further line of research was pursued by Bray and Widmeyer in their 'Athletes' **perception** of home advantage: an investigation of perceived causal factors.' As the article's title suggests, the interest lay in whether or not athletes themselves believe in home advantage. The results of the research indicated that they do, the most common reasons being that playing in familiar surroundings is helpful and a home environment gives players **confidence**. While Bray and Widmeyer do not mention it, their research throws up the possibility of a self-fulfilling element: if, when on the road, players believe they will be at a disadvantage, their decrements in confidence may contribute to their performance, which in turn affects their performance and facilitates a defeat, thus confirming the players' original suspicions.

Further reading

Balmer, N.J., Nevill, A.M. and Williams, A.M. (2001) 'Home advantage in the Winter Olympics (1908–1998),' *Journal of Sports Sciences* vol. 19, pp. 129–39.
Bray, S.R. and Widmeyer, W.N. (2000) 'Athletes' perception of home advantage: an investigation of perceived causal factors,' *Journal of Sport Behavior* vol. 23, pp. 1–10.
Courneya, K.S. and Carron, A. (1992) 'The home advantage in sport competitions: a literature review,' *Journal of Sports Exercise Psychology* vol. 14, pp. 13–27.

HYPNOSIS

From the Greek *hupnos*, for sleep, and the suffix *osis*, denoting an action or condition, hypnosis describes a process of inducing extreme suggestibility in human subjects. The precise mechanism through which this is achieved is not clear, some theorists believing that a different state of consciousness is attained, while others argue that the peculiar interaction between subject and hypnotist facilitates changes in **perception** and awareness. The uses of hypnosis in sports are various: by suggesting specific modes of thought and behavior to a hypnotized athlete, desired posthypnotic responses may be evoked. Athletes have sought hypnotherapy as an aid to ridding themselves of one or several forms of **dependence**. Recovery from **injury** can also be accelerated through hypnotism.

The first well-known use of hypnotism in sport was that of Ken Norton who fought three tough fights with Muhammad Ali in the 1970s. A rank underdog in the first of the series, Norton sought hypnotic help to convince him that he could upset the odds and beat Ali – which he did. Former middleweight champion Nigel Benn also employed a hypnotist to help him prepare for fights. But the danger is apparent: hypnotically induced sense deceptions can render an athlete less sensitive to **pain** and so more open to serious punishment. Yet favorable applications of hypnosis in sports are available: **nervous** athletes who may be proficient in training yet suffer **anxiety** in **competition** have benefited from newfound **confidence** or perhaps just an ability to relax. Other sports performers have acquired a hitherto elusive ability to concentrate in clutch situations.

The origins of therapeutic hypnosis lie in the practices of eighteenth-century medic Franz Anton Mesmer, from whose name the term 'mesmerism' derives, though its first systematic application came with Manchester physician James Braid. Braid's ideas were developed by the French neurologist and later the American psychologist Ernest Hilgard, who in 1986 argued that there are several systems of cognitive **control**, all monitored and governed by the executive ego of a central structure. When a subject is hypnotized, the hypnotist removes much of the normal monitoring and control functions, so much so that the subject experiences motor movements as involuntary, memory and perceptions as hazy and hallucinations as real. Hilgard introduced the term 'hidden observer' to describe a part of the mind that is not within awareness yet seems to be watching the subject's whole experience: that is, a mental structure that monitors everything that happens, including events that the hypnotized subject is not consciously aware of perceiving at the time. Hilgard's experiments in the relief of pain revealed how hypnotized subjects were able to describe the pain felt, at the same time responding to the hypnotist's suggestions that they should be relieved of the pain. This process is called 'dissociation' and has been influential. Hypnotized subjects have allegedly been able to undergo operations without anaesthetic, regress to childhood memories, temporarily lose sensory functions and experience imaginary phenomena as 'real.'

But others have doubted whether hypnotized subjects are transported to another type of consciousness, the altered state suggested by this line of work. In contrast, they insist that, although hypnosis exists, it is best understood not as a special state but as a label for a context. The work of Graham Wagstaff in 1981 and N.P. Spanos in 1991 suggests that the involuntary behavior of hypnotized subjects is not automatic at all, but may be retrospectively interpreted by subjects as non-volitional. In other words, the relationship between the subject and the hypnotist creates a context ripe for compliance, or even faking. This is not to deny that subjects have a heightened susceptibility: they are certainly susceptible to the influence of the hypnotist. But, according to this view, they do not enter a separate state of consciousness.

While explanations of hypnosis differ, there is no dispute about its effects, some of which are measurable in terms of physiological response. Changes in the electrical potential of the brain, respiration rate, skin temperature and blood pressures have been recorded, though there is not a unique correlate of the hypnotic state; many of the quantifiable changes resemble those achieved through progressive **relaxation**. This is complicated by the fact that hypnotized subjects may engage in vigorous physical activity. Some writers argue that such subjects may remain relaxed in a cognitive sense even while exerting themselves physically. But even if the physiological profiles of subjects under hypnosis and progressive relaxation are very similar, there remain interesting differences in the experiences of subjects. For example, accounts of hallucinations and amnesia seem to suggest that hypnotized subjects become involved in what has been called 'trance logic' in which normal expectations of consistencies in time and space are nullified. There are also claims that subjects are able to perform feats quite beyond normal expectations.

Hypnotic analgesia has obvious application in sports, though, again claims are disputed: subjects reporting relief from painful injuries when hypnotized have been interpreted by followers of Hilgard as surrendering the actual pain to a separate cognitive subsystem. Detractors argue that humans have a capacity to control and tolerate pain without chemical analgesics, but we learn thresholds of tolerance and how to express pain according to cultural imperatives.

Whatever the interpretation of hypnotic experiences, the results are undeniable. Hypnotized subjects' **attention** is extremely selective and they receive instructions without challenging them from one source. Posthypnotic responses are sometimes strong and subjects frequently observe suggestions about behavioral or cognitive habits – sometimes without knowing why (hypnotic amnesia occurs where a subject cannot recall what he or she has been told). It is open to doubt whether this is the product of an altered state or merely an extreme state of suggestibility in subjects who are susceptible to influences anyway.

Further reading

Le Unes, A. and Nation, J. (1996) *Sport Psychology* Chicago, IL: Nelson Hall.
Liggett, D.R. (2000) *Sport Hypnosis* Champaign IL: Human Kinetics.
Wagstaff, G.F. (1996) 'Hypnosis,' pp. 991–1,006 in Colman, A.M. (ed.) *Companion Encyclopedia of Psychology*, vol. 2, London: Routledge.

IDENTITY

The stable conception a subject has of him or herself as an individual is an identity. There are two major components. Personal identity is the continuous awareness of distinctness and uniqueness, while social identity is a conception reflected from the images others have of a person. In practice there is a close relationship, if not convergence, between the two: the conception we have of ourselves is, in large part, a mirror of how others see us (the word itself is taken from the Latin *identitas*, meaning same). This is especially interesting in terms of athletes' identities. A great many professional athletes think of themselves as, in essence, athletes. When this is no longer so (after a career-ending **injury** or voluntary retirement), fans, peers and significant others, who have for years supported and sustained that conception, stop seeing them as such. The resulting lack of congruence may trigger what some call an identity crisis – a mismatch between how the individual regards him or herself and how others see him or her, leading to a loss of continuity.

A similar crisis of identity may occur when athletes who think of themselves as proficient or exceptional experience a loss of form and are forced to confront the uncomfortable actuality that they may not be as accomplished as they thought. One of the identity-protecting mechanisms often used by athletes is to rationalize a poor performance with 'that wasn't the *real me* out there, tonight.' In the middle of his 2001 **slump**, during which his batting average dropped to 0.183, home run record-breaker Mark McGwire claimed: 'It's not *me*. And I'm tired of not being *me*.'

Wolf-Dietrich Brettschneider and Rüdiger Heim believe that: 'Individuals can only regard themselves as unmistakable, distinct, or unique (identity) when they are able to sufficiently describe themselves (self-concept).' In their view self-concept is multidimensional, composed of aspects of ourselves, including **gender**, political ideology, personal philosophy, leisure activities, etc. 'Identity, on the other hand, represents the complete integration of different self-perceptions and values and their reflexive processing.' The reflexive processing refers to the way we interpret others' perceptions of us. So identity is a coherent totality of particles of knowledge about ourselves.

Because the development of a subject's identity involves not only being different from others but a sense of coherence and an apprehension of how one appears to others, the body is central. 'Physical self-concept' is a constituent of the self-concept and hence identity, according to Brettschneider and Heim, who studied young athletes involved in sports with a view to understanding how the body impacts on identity formation. In all sports, **body image** and body maintenance activities are crucial factors in athletes' self-concepts. Sports provide arenas for the development of positive physical self-concepts.

Understanding identity as stable does not necessarily mean that it is fixed or permanent. Indeed, many contemporary theorists contend that our sense of who we are has become increasingly fluid in postmodernity, as the present condition of society is often described. The thrust of this argument is that there are no essences of identity: we think of ourselves in terms of multiple frames of reference, including our ethnicity, gender, sexuality, class and physical location, and all these are flowing and potentially transformable. In this conception, identity is less a personal property and much more a junction between how a culture defines us and how we imagine ourselves. In other words, identities exist only in relation to everything else in the surrounding environment.

Further reading

Brettschneider, W.-D. and Heim, R. (1997) 'Identity, sport and youth development,' pp. 205–27 in Fox, K.R. (ed.) *The Physical Self: From motivation to well-being* Champaign IL: Human Kinetics.
McGuigan, J. (1999) *Modernity and Postmodern Culture* Philadelphia: Open University Press.

IDIOGRAPHIC

Idiographic study is based on the uniqueness or individuality of phenomena and its findings resist generalization. The name is taken from the Greek *idios*, meaning own, the idea being that the results of a piece of research relate only to that phenomenon – they are its own. The **IZOF (individual zones of optimal functioning)** theoretical model is an example of an idiographic approach. Formulated as a response to the **nomothetic** inverted-U theories of **arousal**, the model aimed, as Yuri Hanin expresses it, 'to provide an idiographic (individual-oriented) sport-specific approach to performance-related emotions.'

Further reading

Bullock, A., Stallybrass, O. and Trombley, S. (eds) (2000) *New Fontana Dictionary of Modern Thought* London: Fontana.
Hanin, Y.L. (2000) 'Introduction: an individualized approach to emotion in sport,' pp. ix–xii in Hanin, Y.L. (ed.) *Emotions in Sport* Champaign IL: Human Kinetics.

ILLNESS *see* injury

IMAGERY

From the Latin *imago* (imitate), imaging involves mentally picturing an event as vividly as possible with the intention of duplicating that event in actuality. As a technique used prior to **competition**, it is predicated on the idea that mentally rehearsing a desired outcome enhances the probability that the desired outcome will materialize.

The subject needs to be able to construct clear and real images, controlling their content and action. There are two possible perspectives: subjects can either try to simulate experience of, for example, traveling over the high-jump bar or executing a perfect dive, or imagine they are viewing themselves from the vantage point of an outsider, like a photographer. For example, an athlete might recall a previous performance with which he or she was satisfied and imagine him or herself repeating the exact movements involved in the **skill**. The 'insider' perspective is slightly more effective, according to Hinshaw.

The evidence about whether this actually results in performance improvements is equivocal. In reviewing several studies, Karen Lee Hill concludes that there have been 'mixed findings,' though the weight of evidence favors the view that imaging does contribute to improved performance, especially in basketball, darts, golf, gymnastics and tennis. These are, mostly, sports that require an element of

decision making: imagery enables athletes to think through possible scenarios. Elite athletes are more accomplished at imagery, if only because they are more likely to visualize technically correct procedures. Hill also points out that imagining a negative outcome in sport leads to deterioration in **skill performance**. But imagery can also aid novices in **skill acquisition**, for example, by **modeling** their performance on that of an experienced athlete.

This begs an important question: how does imagery work? Allen Cornelius pulls together four groups of explanation.

1 Psychoneuromuscular or 'muscle memory': imaginary movements produce muscle enervation similar to those used in actual movement. For example, a swimmer visualizes performing the backstroke, these images produce a low-level activation of the nerves and muscles involved in swimming and these are sufficient to affect the motor pattern in the motor cortex responsible for the execution of the movement. There is only weak support for this theory.

2 Symbolic learning: imagery works like a mental blueprint that we can use later, i.e. a symbolic coding of information. Again, only weak support.

3 Informational processing: an image is an organized set of propositions in the brain and, when imaging, we activate stimulus propositions that describe the content of the image as well as response propositions. Cornelius gives the example of a basketball player who 'may imagine the crowd noise, sweaty palms, and nervousness prior to stepping to the foul line with 0.5 seconds left and the score tied (stimulus proposition).' He also imagines shooting and watching the ball fall clean through the net, which is the response proposition.

4 Triple-code: this has three components: (a) the imagery which facilitates; (b) somatic responses (such as optimal **attention** and/or **arousal**; and (c) the meaning of the image to the subject. The meaning component is crucial because one athlete's image of a situation may evoke **anxiety** and **stress**, while another's image of the same situation evokes **confidence**.

While imagery is popularly thought to work at the level of **cognition**, research by Martin and Hall in 1995 indicated that it can also operate at the levels of **motivation**. Through imagining competitive situations, subjects can become energized in a way that readies them for the fray. Even though the mechanisms through which imagery works are not clear and there are doubts about whether it does in fact affect performance, there is no evidence that it damages performance (unless negative outcomes are imagined).

Further reading

Cornelius, A. (2002) 'Intervention techniques in sport psychology,' pp. 197–223 in Silva, J.M. and Stevens, D.E. (eds) *Psychological Foundations of Sport* Boston MA: Allyn & Bacon.

Hill, K.L. (2001) *Frameworks for Sport Psychologists* Champaign IL: Human Kinetics.

Hinshaw, K. (1991) 'The effects of mental practice on motor skill performance: critical evaluation and meta-analysis,' *Imagination, Cognition and Personality* vol. 11, pp. 3–35.

Martin, K.A. and Hall, C.R. (1995) 'Using mental imagery to enhance intrinsic motivation,' *Journal of Sport & Exercise Psychology* vol. 13, pp. 149–59.

INCENTIVE

Any incitement or provocation that motivates behavior is an incentive, from the Latin *incentivus*, meaning setting the tune. Incentives in sport are varied, ranging from trophies with little extrinsic worth to substantial cash inducements. Underlying them all is the supposition that incentives are objects or conditions that are perceived as fulfillers of needs.

Incentive has links with the concept of **drive** in the sense that the level of the drive state determines its utility and effectiveness. Water has incentive value for a dehydrated castaway; a million dollars may have no incentive value for a basketball player who already owns two Lear jets.

Establishing incentives that motivate workers to greater output by offering supplemental rewards (i.e. 'incentivizing') is common in a culture that rewards the reaching of targets. Many industries adopt a practice used in sports perhaps since before the Christian era: inducing desired behavior rather than trying to force it – carrot rather than stick. A combination of the two was favored by Livia, the wife of Augustus, in Robert Graves' *I, Claudius*: disgusted by the lack of effort of some of the gladiators, she decides: 'These Games are degraded by more and more professional tricks to stay alive ... I won't have it. So put on a good show and there'll be plenty of money for the living and a decent burial for the dead. If you let me down, I'll break this guild and I'll send the lot of you to the mines.'

Further reading

Roberts, G.C. (ed.) (1992) *Motivation in Sport and Exercise* Champaign IL: Human Kinetics.

Smith, R.E. (1998) 'A positive approach to sport performance enhancement: principles of reinforcement and performance feedback,' pp. 28–40 in Williams, J.M. (ed.) *Applied Sport Psychology: Personal growth to peak performance*, 3rd edition, Mountain View CA: Mayfield.

INFORMATION PROCESSING

In the 1950s, a series of papers by Nobel Prize winner Herbert A. Simon suggested that psychological phenomena could be simulated using the computer and that traditional psychological problems could be envisioned in terms of information processing. In this model, the human being was a processor of information, the senses providing an input channel for information and the **memory** operating as a mental repository for the transformed input that would, in turn, generate responses. The *information*, in this sense, refers to any knowledge that is capable of being received, and *processing* is organizing, interpreting and responding to incoming stimulation (i.e. information).

Richard Cox provides the example of a quarterback who 'stores thousands of pieces of information about offenses and defenses.' Just prior to the snap, he notices a late change in the opposition's defense, decides on a new play and calls an audible. Cox explains what has happened in information processing terms: 'Previously stored information about the opposing team was retrieved from memory and used to initiate a different but appropriate response.' In any sport, information processing like this is going on constantly.

In information processing, the same rules that govern how the quarterback encodes, stores and recalls information about defenses apply to all other situations. While people and physical **stimuli**, whether rival football players, motorcycles, people who work on the supermarket checkout, etc., have strikingly different features that attract **attention**, once one pays attention to the player, the machine or the sales assistant, processing is likely to be the same. So information processing offers a general, or **nomothetic**, model that holds good regardless of individual or context.

Information processing has been used to explain how **imagery** works, the idea being that an image is an organized cluster of propositions or plans in the brain that comprises stimulus propositions and response propositions. The basic processes of encoding, storing and recalling apply. Similarly, information processing has been applied to **anxiety** and **arousal** in sports, the conclusions supporting the predictions of the **Yerkes–Dodson law**: at a particular level of arousal, the information processing capacity of the system is at its maximum and performance will be optimal.

Further reading

Cox, R.H. (1998) *Sport Psychology: Concepts and applications*, 4th edition, Boston MA: McGraw-Hill.

Strean, W.B. and Roberts, G.C. (1992) 'Future directions in applied sport psychology research,' *The Sports Psychologist* vol. 6, pp. 55–65.

INJURY

Any involuntary, physically disruptive experience constitutes an injury. At its mildest, an injury interrupts or restricts, while, more seriously it can harm, damage and sometimes terminate a sports career. Like other forms of illness, an injury has both physical and psychological consequences and, according to some research, it may have psychological causes too. From the Latin *in*, or un, and *juria* for right.

Athletes experience loss after an injury: not only do they lose a physical capability, they also lose a salient part of their self. 'The integrity of the self is assaulted and threatened,' writes Andrew Sparkes: 'Earlier taken-for-granted assumptions about possessing a smoothly functioning body are shaken, previous assumptions about the relationships between body and self are disturbed, and the sense of wholeness of body and self is disrupted.' Because many athletes shape their lives around the performance of their body in sports, an injury has manifold effects: studies have shown that depression, **anxiety** and low **self-esteem** frequently accompany an injury.

The impact of knee injury on, say, someone who serves coffee at Starbucks may not appear to be profound; a similar injury for a pro squash player may be traumatic. Anyone is affected by an injury to a limb, and in many instances this may result in a loss of work. The player may experience an added sense of failure, followed by a fragmentation of self. Athletes rely on a unity of body and self to accomplish their deeds; the **discipline** they practice is designed to subordinate their bodies to conscious **control**. When their bodies no longer responds to their commands, the unity is broken. The proficient squash player, whose speed of reaction is aligned to anticipation, may experience his or her injured body as alien, as something that stands in opposition to his or her wishes.

Sparkes and other researchers have applied the idea of a narrative, or storyline, to make sense of how athletes respond to injury. This is a framing device that shapes athletes' understanding of their progress in sport. Injury ruptures the narrative, forcing the athletes to recognize the limitations of their bodies. As well as constraining the competitors' mode of expression, the injury, according to Heil, 'raises uncertainty about return to **competition**.' Of course, some athletes never do return, while others are forced to make adjustments to their style in order to do so. Like patients with terminal illnesses, athletes can go through 'denial,' refusing to accept the extent of their injury. Problematic as denial is, it can on occasion be functional when it 'protects the athlete from being overwhelmed by negative emotions.' Consider Sugar Ray Leonard: a detached retina is generally a career-ending injury for a boxer, but, after surgery, Leonard staged a **comeback** and won further world titles.

Leonard experienced a self-restoring return to competition: he re-unified his body and **identity** as a world champion. Other injured athletes fail to restore themselves fully and settle for a contingent personal identity: never quite the competitor they once were, but still adept. Patrick Ewing might fit into this category: a wrist injury in 1997 forced him to miss most of the following NBA season. He was 36 when he returned and never quite recaptured his best form. Those who accept they have no chance of resuming their former selves try to salvage some part of their previous identities. How athletes respond to injury psychologically is as crucial to their rehabilitation as their physical response, though in a practical sense the two are not separable.

Athletes may respond to injuries rather differently from others. Research by H.L. Nixon concluded that, because they are inculcated into a culture in which **risk**, **pain** and injuries are regarded as commonplace, athletes tend to interpret these as features of their working lives. The sports media convey messages that affirm this, inclining athletes toward the view that they should accept injuries most would understand as serious as quite normal.

While injury and, indeed, other kinds of illness are often attributed to accidents, some research indicates that athletes' perceptions of situations are contributory factors. For example, if competitors respond to what they regard as threatening situations with muscle tension and a narrowing of visual fields, then they will become vulnerable. This is what is known as a **stress** response and together with other factors, such as previous injuries or general life stress, can enhance the athlete's chances of getting injured. This may help explain why some athletes, most famously Michael Jordan, led an almost injury-free career, while others gain reputations for being 'injury-prone.' The problem with this is that it bases too much expectation on the personal qualities of individual performers; a more satisfactory account would require more detail on, for example, the state of fatigue, the difficulty of the **skill** being attempted at the time of the injury, the importance of the occasion and other circumstantial factors.

On the other hand, research into the recurrently injured athlete may show a clear antecedent history and suggest that the behavior leading to the injury is quite predictable. Paul Gascoigne, the former soccer star, for example, typically played with a combative recklessness that added to his effectiveness as a player but ensured that his career was punctuated with injuries. On some accounts, this would be because of his particular **personality**. Various kinds of **personality assessment** tests have concluded that certain psychological types of player can be matched with different types of injury, though Silva and Hardy's research in 1991 concluded that there is not nearly enough knowledge to be able to predict injury risk from personality **profile** information.

Further reading

Heil, J. (2000) 'The injured athlete,' pp. 245–65 in Hanin, Y.L. (ed.) *Emotions in Sport* Champaign IL: Human Kinetics.

Nixon, H.L. (1993) 'Accepting the risks of pain and injury in sport: mediated cultural influences on playing hurt,' *Sociology of Sport Journal* vol. 10, no. 2 (June), pp. 183–96.

Sparkes, A.C. (2000) 'Illness, premature career-termination, and the loss of self: a biographical study of an elite athlete,' pp. 14–32 in Jones, R.L. and Armour, K.M. (eds) *Sociology of Sport: Theory and practice* Harlow, Essex: Longman.

INSTINCT

An inborn propensity to behave without conscious intention, but with apparent rationality under appropriate conditions, is an instinct – a word that derives from the Latin *instinctus*, meaning incite, instigate or impel. Being innate, instincts are biological and cannot be learned: they are patterns of behavior fixed from birth by hereditary factors and usually responses to simple **stimuli**. Sports are full of athletes described as 'instinctive players' or, those who, on occasion, 'play by instinct alone.'

Prior to the publication of Charles Darwin's *On the Origin of the Species by Means of Natural Selection* in 1859, and indeed for long after, nonhuman animal behavior was attributed to instincts. Devoid of intellect and the power to reason, animals were considered fundamentally different from humans. Darwin, in revealing continuity in evolutionary adaptations, cast serious doubt on the assumed distinction between humans and other primates, a point made by, among others, Jeff Wallace in his introduction to the 1998 edition of Darwin's influential volume. This suggested to some, particularly the British-born American psychologist William McDougall who died in 1938, that humans, like other animals, were guided by instinct rather than rational thought. While McDougall believed that inherited instincts were susceptible to modification through experience and social learning, the sources of behavior were biological. He even went so far as to identify the compelling instincts; these included 'acquisition,' 'flight,' 'pugnacity' and 'self-assertion.' His model left no room for **decision making** and reasoned interpretation or indeed for the role of **cognition** or **reinforcement**: the **motivation** behind behavior was instinctive. As such, the human being was at the mercy of innate forces (the philosophical implications of this are explored in Janet Radcliffe Richard's *Human Nature after Darwin*).

Darwin himself had regarded instincts as complex reflexes that were made up of inherited units and were subject to change through evolutionary adaptations to the environment. His work influenced, among many others, the ethologist Konrad Lorenz who maintained that animal behavior included a number of fixed-action patterns that were characteristic of species and largely genetically determined. Each instinct was a fixed-action pattern.

In a different way, Freud believed that inner forces determined human conduct by two opposing instincts, Eros, which enhances life, and Thanatos, the **death wish**.

The energy of Eros is libido which revolves primarily around sexual activities. Thanatos can be directed inward in the form of suicide or other self-destructive behavior or outward in the form of **aggression** toward others. Freud believed that **sex** and aggression were two basic motives of human behavior. During the 1920s, instinct theory was replaced by the concept of **drive** – a state of **arousal** that results from a biological need, for example for water, sex or the avoidance of **pain**. Freud's debt to Darwin is analyzed in chapter 7 of Frank Sulloway's *Freud, Biologist of the Mind*.

Few contemporary theorists cling to instinct theories and, though many allow that there is a biological predisposition behind many behaviors, few consider genetic factors solely responsible for human conduct. Discredited as instinct theory is, it is tempting to interpret sports in instinctual terms. Much of the aggression and **violence** in sports appears to be a manifestation of destructive instincts, or Lorenz's fixed-action patterns. The instinctive 'play' of certain types of animals bears resemblance to human forms of sports and leisure activities. Even the bonding, particularly of males, in team sports has counterparts among other animals. From this perspective, sports constitute a healthy and socially acceptable outlet for instinctive behavior. Despite this, the perspective is not a current one. Most contemporary analysts of sport focus on the institution of sport as a cultural construction and the **motivation** of athletes as the product more of the interaction between circumstances and individuals than of immanent forces.

Further reading

Atkinson, R.L., Atkinson, R.C., Smith, E.E., Bem, D.J. and Hilgard, E.R. (1990) *Introduction to Psychology*, 10th edition, New York: Harcourt, Brace, Jovanovich.
MacFarland, D.J. (1987) 'Instinct,' pp. 374–5 in Gregory, R.L. *The Oxford Companion to the Mind* Oxford: Oxford University Press.

INTELLIGENCE

Intelligence may be described as the capacity to comprehend, understand and reason in a way that enables successful adaptations to changing environments. This is a distillation of several, often widely differing definitions offered over the decades of a term that stems from the Latin *intellectus*, for **perception**. In a famous project in 1921 the editors of the *Journal of Educational Psychology* solicited definitions from fourteen eminent psychologists. The responses ranged from the crisp 'ability to carry on abstract thinking' (Lewis S. Terman) through the pragmatic 'capacity to learn or to profit from experience' (W.F. Dearborn) to the rather cryptic 'capacity to acquire capacity' (H. Woodrow). Common to many offerings was the capacity to learn and abstract from actual experiences and to adapt to the environment. Contemporary psychologist Robert Sternberg brings these together in his 'the ability to make sense of and function adaptively in the environments in which one finds oneself.'

Sternberg's definition is well suited to sports, in which there is often thought to be a specific form of intelligence. Journalists often praise 'intelligent play' and compare intelligent athletes to their cruder counterparts who trade on raw power. The athlete who has the ability to make sense of and to play effectively and/or adaptively under competitive conditions (environments) has intelligence that is specific to sports.

Adaptively also has a variety of meanings. A rookie learning a certain type of play in a football team, a boxer modifying his or her style to accommodate a cut that opens up during a fight, a basketball player traded from another club who tailors his or her game to fit in with new colleagues, a baseball pitcher who alters every pitch to inconvenience different batters, a cricket captain who changes the field to discomfort batsmen: these are examples of adaptive play that occur regularly in **competition**. The responses are instances of sporting intelligence.

Many of the colossal disputes over intelligence, and particularly attempts to measure it with IQ tests, revolve around how conceptions of intelligence differ from culture to culture. Whether or not the capacity we call intelligence actually is the same across or even within cultures, we should acknowledge that it is not universally regarded in precisely the same way. What is intelligence in one culture may not be in another. So, while sport carries 'jock' connotations and criticisms of its anti-intellectual leanings, it should not be dismissed as unintelligent. A particular type and quality of intelligence operates in sport, and though it has not been measured by conventional tests evidence of it is abundant in any competition where tactics and good sense are required.

Further reading

Sternberg, Robert J. (1987) 'Intelligence,' pp. 375–9 in Gregory, R.L. *The Oxford Companion to the Mind* Oxford: Oxford University Press.

Sternberg, Robert J. (1996) 'Intelligence and cognitive styles,' pp. 583–601 in Colman, A.M. (ed.) *Companion Encyclopedia of Psychology*, vol. 2, London: Routledge.

INTENSITY

The amount or quality of eagerness, ardency, effort or sheer passion a subject either inputs or experiences is 'intensity,' a word that has evolved from *intendere*, Latin for strain, stretch or direct. Arthur Reber advises that the term is borrowed from physics: 'Hence, physical **stimuli** will be characterized in terms of intensity, e.g. of a light, a tone, an electric current, etc.' In accounts of **motivation**, intensity is frequently, though simplistically, identified as one of the two major dimensions, the other being direction: *motivation = direction + intensity of behavior*. Both applications *quantify* the strength or the ardor of a behavior.

In a *qualitative* sense, intensity is experienced when a sensation of, for example, pleasure or **pain**, is reported, though technically this too may be rendered measurable via self-reporting. The degree to which an **emotion** is felt, a **commitment** adhered to, a belief held might be recorded on a scale of intensity. In all instances, intensity is a single dimension along which some effort or experience can be expressed.

In her essay 'Understanding individual motivation in sport,' Laura Finch defines intensity as 'how much effort an athlete puts forth in particular situations.' She points out that, if an athlete is attracted toward a sport, he or she is likely to exhibit high intensity in pursuing it. But this is not always the case, and a competent soccer player may appear listless and unmotivated. Changing coaches, switching to a different club or league, or new types of **goal setting** can increase the player's intensity. So intensity of both experience and effort is not constant and can be changed by altering environments. The player would not only intensify input, but he or she would presumably feel more intensity from playing in a more challenging environment.

Finch acknowledges that, while using intensity in this way helps practitioners identify the components of motivation, it cannot be separated from cultural factors, such as an emphasis on winning, coaching philosophies or even the particular environment in which the athlete performs. All these will affect the intensity of effort and of experience.

Further reading

Finch, L. (2001) 'Understanding individual motivation in sport,' pp. 66–79 in Silva, J.M. and Stevens, D.E. (eds) *Psychological Foundations of Sport* Boston MA: Allyn & Bacon.
Reber, A.S. (1995) *Dictionary of Psychology*, 2nd edition, Harmondsworth: Penguin, pp. 380–1.

INTERVENTION

An intervention is the action of coming between so as to interrupt, prevent or modify a result (from the Latin *inter*, between, and *venire*, come). The intervening agent is extraneous – that is, having origins external to whatever process is being changed. Intervention techniques are systematic procedures aimed at changing existing processes. They are used in surgery, for example, to stop **pain**; in psychotherapy they are typically designed to arrest behavior patterns; in education they are intended to enhance learning competencies. While there are many types of psychological interventions designed to assist athletes with their performance, they all share basic features: they involve detailed evaluation or assessment, some element of education or re-training, and practical attempts to modify both **cognition** and behavior.

According to Allen Cornelius, all sport psychology interventions progress through four phases.

1 Assessment phase: this involves accumulating detailed knowledge of an athlete's **skill**, resources, past experience and problems. The assessment typically takes the form of an examination with structured interviews, objective tests and performance **profile**, yielding the data needed to inform the intervention. Structured and semistructured interviews are valuable in gathering information about an athlete's experiences and his or her **goal** or goals. Objective tests are also used, one of the best-known being the Psychological Skills Inventory for Sport, which measures six cognitive abilities. A related test is the Test of Performance Strategies (TOPS), which measures the frequency of behaviors of athletes in training and in **competition**. Sixty-four items are used to assess eight strategies: **goal setting**; **imagery**; **self-imagery**; **self-talk**; **relaxation**; **emotional** control; attentional **control**; self-confidence; and **automaticity**.

2 Education phase: this involves **skill acquisition** or perhaps more accurately *new* skill acquisition – athletes who already possess skill are re-tooled to equip them more fully. In this phase techniques such as **biofeedback** are employed to enable an athlete to gain more control and self-discipline. Relaxation techniques are also used to engineer appropriate levels of **arousal** in the athlete. Alternative educative techniques are based on **reinforcement** and involve rewards as incentives for desired and punishment for unwanted responses. **Cognitive–behavioral modification** is predicated on the assumption of the athlete's specific interpretation of **stimuli** in the environment, i.e. rather than the stimuli *per se*.

3 Practice phase: proficiency is never immediate and, once new skills are acquired, a period of systematic practice follows with monitoring of progress *in situ* being vital. For example, a newly acquired ability to relax may serve an athlete well in many practice situations, but will he or she be able to replicate this in the middle of competition, or will **anxiety** creep in? Interventions usually take place away from the competitive arena, but to be effective they must translate into practical action when they are needed.

4 Evaluation and modification phase: the question that informs this

phase is simply whether or not the intervention has worked/is working. The evaluation may be subjective, soliciting the perspectives and opinions of athletes involved. Or it may be objective, scanning the performance of an athlete to assess the quantifiable improvements, if any. This is a crucial phase, as interventions must work: they should be geared to the enhancement of athletic performance. While enriching the subjective experience of participation in sports is valued, the effectiveness of interventions is graded on the actual competitive performance of the subjects. It is assumed that there is a close relationship between the two.

Kenneth Fox writes of the *skill enhancement hypothesis*. 'The assumption is becoming popular that involvement in physical activities and improvement in skill, knowledge, fitness, or health will enhance self-perceptions.' Fox points to the reflexivity of **skill performance** and mental wellbeing, holistic health – in general, self-enhancement. Being able to display physical competencies is linked to conceptions of **self-efficacy** and how positively we feel about ourselves, Fox concludes: 'Programs designed for skill and fitness improvement can have a positive impact on **self-esteem**.'

Further reading

Cornelius, A. (2002) 'Introduction of sport psychology interventions,' pp. 177–96 in Silva, J.M. and Stevens, D.E. (eds) *Psychological Foundations of Sport* Boston MA: Allyn & Bacon.

Fox, K.R. (1997) 'Introduction – let's get physical!', pp. vii–xiii in Fox, K.R. (ed.) *The Physical Self: From motivation to well-being* Champaign IL: Human Kinetics.

Thompson, M.A., Vernacchia, R.A. and Moore, W.E. (eds) (1998) *Case Studies in Applied Sport Psychology: An educational approach* Dubuque IA: Kendall/Hunt.

INVENTORY

From *inventorium*, Latin for things discovered, which comes from *invenir*, for find, an inventory is a detailed, ordered list or catalog of items designed to assess or measure a stock of goods. **Psychological skills inventories** are used to take stock of aptitudes, attitudes, beliefs, coping **skill**, opinions, **personality** traits or other psychological attributes. They are usually administered via questionnaire.

In sports, one of the best-known inventories is the *Psychological Skills Inventory for Sports*, a 45-item register that measures **anxiety**,

control, **concentration**, **confidence**, mental preparation, **motivation** and team orientation. The *Athletic Coping Skills Inventory* extrapolates from information on coping skills to predict athletic performance.

Further reading

Ostrow, A.E. (1996) *Dictionary of Psychological Tests in the Sport and Exercise Sciences* Morgantown WV: Fitness Information.

IZOF (INDIVIDUAL ZONES OF OPTIMAL FUNCTIONING)

The theoretical model, or approach to study, known as IZOF is based on the view that, as its originator Yuri Hanin puts it, 'to understand why and how outstanding performers achieve consistent excellency, one needs to focus primarily on their unique experiences.' In contrast to **nomothetic** theories, which seek abstract or general principles, Hanin favored an **idiographic** approach that treats individuals singularly.

Devised in part to challenge the popular inverted-U theory of **arousal**, itself nomothetic, IZOF is based on the view that the optimal performance occurs when individually meaningful **emotional** states are in specific zones. Both the state and the **zone** differ from athlete to athlete. So empirical testing is the only way to ascertain the precise zone an athlete should be aiming for. Athletes describe their own emotional states: positive – such as 'happy,' 'vigorous' or 'daring' – and negative – such as 'angry,' 'worried' or 'afraid.' For each of these there is a zone of optimal **intensity** that is associated with **peak performance**. The emotions are rated in terms of their intensity. Poor performances are also associated with emotions, positive or negative, and their intensity: dysfunctional states are identified. Athletes who rate their **competition** performances as successful are more likely to be closer to their optimal facilitating zones and outside their dysfunctional states.

For every facilitating **emotion** there is a zone of optimal intensity. Given the idiographic emphasis, each individual has a different zone. So it is possible for one athlete to produce peak performances when he or she experiences, say, very intense eagerness, while another athlete experiencing the same emotion with the same intensity may not. The latter might perform optimally when feeling eager, but only mildly eager; too much intensity may hinder the performer ('over-eagerness'). The IZOF model holds that emotions have both facilitating and debilitating effects on performances, depending on the athlete's individual optimal zone.

While devotees of IZOF believe that it is a pathbreaking and enlightening theory full of potential applications, critics are not so sure. Its resistance to generalizations obviously limits its utility as a theory. There are also several key questions left not only unanswered but unasked, according to Peter Crocker *et al*. For example: how are specific emotions produced in athletes? Why would the same emotional state produce individual differences in performance (i.e. what are the mechanisms)? As the model has only been tested on elite athletes, does it have validity for younger, less experienced athletes?

Further reading

Crocker, P.E., Kowalski, K.C., Graham, T.R. and Kowalski, N.P. (2002) 'Emotion in sport,' pp. 107–31 in Silva, J.M. and Stevens, D.E. (eds) *Psychological Foundations of Sport* Boston MA: Allyn & Bacon.

Hanin, Y.L. (ed.) (2000) *Emotions in Sport* Champaign IL: Human Kinetics.

Woodman, T., Albinson, J.G. and Hardy, L. (1997) 'An investigation of the zones of optimal functioning hypothesis within a multidimensional framework,' *Journal of Sport & Exercise Psychology* vol. 19, pp. 131–40.

KNOWLEDGE OF RESULTS

Often shortened to KR, knowledge of results is a form of **feedback** used by the learner to adapt responses to the model specified by a trainer or coach. While the term applies across a variety of settings in which learning takes place, it has particular relevance to **skill acquisition** in sports. KR is usually measurable in terms of, for instance, lap times, number of shots on target, speed of serve, etc. This information should form the basis of future responses to similar situations and thus contribute toward **mastery** of skills.

A novice will typically receive advice and tuition in the form of information about the appropriateness of his or her response to a given situation. This is known as knowledge of performance, or KP, and is issued directly by a coach, trainer or manager, in the form of advice and tuition.

Both forms of feedback are extrinsic in the sense that they are transmitted by sources external to the individual. Intrinsic feedback refers to the sensations received by the individuals as they execute actions. Athletes use both forms to modify their movements and develop skills. Feeding back knowledge of results typically yields the most rapid mastery of **skill**.

Further reading

Salmoni, A.W., Schmidt, R.A. and Walter, C.B. (1984) 'Knowledge of results and motor learning: a review and critical appraisal,' *Psychological Bulletin* vol. 95, pp. 355–86.

LEADERSHIP

The deployment of power, authority or influence to guide others' thought and/or behavior and induce them to follow, willingly or not, is leadership, a word that, interestingly, evolved from *lædere*, an Old English word for someone or something that takes the load. Leadership describes not so much the quality of a person as a process of a social group in which power relations are asymmetrical or levels of influence are hierarchical.

In sports, occupants of leadership positions – managers, coaches, captains – lack authority over how others think, feel and relate to one another. Managers and coaches, in particular, influence – or at least try to influence – others' behavior, the assumption being that good performances will yield positive relations between themselves and their charges or between members of a team. Effective leadership inspires or directs competitors, though in some situations coercion and **control** can yield beneficial results.

Attempts to understand leadership by distilling the qualities of great leaders were known as *trait models*, the traits, or characteristics, being a checklist of attributes possessed by leaders. More sophisticated approaches emphasized how situations factor into the equation. For example, an authoritarian **personality** might be an effective leader in highly structured situations where rules are clear and rigid, but the same person may be laughed at and disrespected in other contexts. Identifying which combination of traits is effective in which situations was the task of the *contingency model*. Its chief proponent, F.E. Fiedler, concluded that 'situational favorableness' affects leadership, so that a task-oriented leader (who concentrates strictly on performance) will work best in situations that are either favorable or unfavorable, i.e. where the leader has very little or lots of control and influence. In situations of only moderate favorableness, a relationship-oriented leader, who stresses good interpersonal relationships with athletes, is likely to be more effective. In other words, the fit between the type of leader and the context is crucial.

Other approaches to leadership moved even further away from leaders themselves and **focused** on followers. *Life cycle theory* suggested that the maturity level of the subjects determined the effectiveness of the style of leader. Young and immature subjects have low levels of ability to set and achieve goals, accept responsibility and experience; a more task-oriented leader who brings structure would find them responsive. According to this theory, a more relationship-oriented leader who builds trust and fosters mutual respect will reap rewards among more mature subjects who have experience and knowledge and do not need so much structure. Hersey and Blanchard's 1977 research using this approach found that neither group at each end of the continuum – very young/immature and vastly experienced – responded well to leaders who emphasized task structure.

Path-goal theory conceived of leaders as figures who illuminate, guide and assist followers in the pursuit of their goals. Leadership is less to do with any qualities the leader might possess, more to do with the aspirations and preferences of the subjects. The leader merely facilitates (or retards) progress. Leadership lies not with either party but in the changing relationships between them. This has some similarity to the *charismatic leader*, someone to whom special qualities are attributed regardless of whether the leader actually possesses them; again the stress is on the relationship.

P. Chelladurai and colleagues tried to formalize the leadership relationship in a *multidimensional model*, comprising three interacting components: (1) stable factors that precede leader behavior – characteristics of the situation, leader and members; (2) leader behavior – required, actual and preferred (by members); (3) consequences of combining (1) and (2) on team members' satisfaction and performance. Coaches who are autocratic or domineering are effective in some sports, such as basketball, because team members prefer this and the sport is compatible with a bossy approach; this would be the case with football, rugby and combat sports. Would it work with other sports? Maybe not tennis, certainly not golf and probably not in several other sports that demand individual judgement and initiative.

An interesting feature of this model is its inclusion of cultural preferences. Leadership styles that are effective in one culture may backfire badly in another, even in the same sport. The point is brought out in Fred Schepisi's 1992 film *Mr Baseball*, in which experienced Major League Baseball pro Tom Selleck opts to play out his career in the Japanese league, where he finds his new coach a martinet, completely unlike his former coaches. Inevitably, clashes follow.

Succession of leadership is a problem that faces any sport: replacing a successful manager or coach. Drafting in a successor with an outstanding track record with other teams or clubs is never a guarantee of continuity because player preferences and expectations as well as other situational contingencies change. It is possible that the 'Rebecca Myth' may take effect: as in the Daphne du Maurier book *Rebecca* (in which the housekeeper idolizes her late mistress and refuses to accept her employer's new wife), team members may fail to show their new manager/coach proper deference or respect; they resist the newcomer as a 'legitimate heir' to the position once held by someone they knew and trusted. In sport there are countless examples of coaches with solid credentials transferring to new clubs and failing. Leaders may move, but leadership is not always portable.

Further reading

Chelladurai, P. (1993) 'Leadership,' pp. 647–71 in Singer, R.N., Murphey, M. and Tennant, L.K. (eds) *Handbook of Research in Sport Psychology* New York: Macmillan.

Fiedler, F.E. *A Theory of Leadership Effectiveness* New York: McGraw-Hill.

LEARNED HELPLESSNESS

Learned helplessness describes a state produced by repeated exposure to unpleasant, negative situations from which there seems to be no escape; persons experience helplessness as an unavoidable condition, their failure to reach goals seen as the result of inevitable, uncontrollable forces.

The term was originally used by Martin E.P. Seligman in his 1975 book *Helplessness: On depression, development and death*, but was adapted by Carol Dweck who argued that 'learned helpless' children attributed failure under competitive conditions to such things as lack of ability or **luck** – factors over which they have no **control**. They show a tendency to concede defeat and opt out of sports after initial failures because they see no prospect of improvement. They avoid challenges, believing that they can do nothing to influence the course of events. Failure is certain, in their eyes.

Early experiments were conducted with dogs which were systematically subjected to unpleasant treatment: even when the dogs were presented with the opportunity to escape the painful treatment, they did not take it; thus their helplessness was a learned, not natural, state. The painful experience of sequential early career defeats has a similar effect on young aspiring athletes: they are unable to avoid failing.

Failure in itself matters far less than how young athletes interpret that failure. For example, if they believe it is because of their inability to improve or continually poor refereeing, they are likely to learn helplessness and drop out. But if they assign the causes of their defeats to lack of practice, experience or adequate coaching, they may well persist. Those who see success as a matter of personal performance improvement, rather than sheer win-or-lose results, are likely to sink more effort into their preparation, believing that their fate is in their own hands. So learned helplessness is linked closely to patterns of **attribution**: how athletes explain outcomes or results.

People whom the competitor respects can have an influence on attribution patterns: a gymnast consoled in defeat by a former Olympic champion who assures her that she was judged too harshly may not be deterred. A young pentathlete whose coach assures him that a slight modification in pole vault technique will yield positive results will probably try strenuously to change his technique. An absence of this kind of input or, worse, negative responses ('you didn't deserve to win,' 'you're useless with that pole') is likely to promote learned helplessness.

Attributional retraining is designed to empower subjects with the feeling that they can control performance outcomes: success or failure is not predetermined but in their own hands. Success or failure does not always equate to wins and losses: participation in itself may be viewed as success. Steering athletes clear of learned helplessness involves convincing them that outcomes are not inevitable and that they can assume a degree of **self-efficacy**, influencing the course of future events in a way they desire.

Further reading

Dweck, C.S. (1980) 'Learned helplessness in sport,' pp. 1–11 in Nadeau, C.H., Halliwell, W.R., Newell, K.M. and Roberts, G.C. (eds) *Psychology of Motor Behavior and Sport – 1979* Champaign IL: Human Kinetics.

Seligman, M.E.P. (1975) *Helplessness: On depression, development and death* San Francisco CA: W.H. Freeman.

LEFT-HANDED

People whose left hands are more serviceable than their right are known, of course, as left-handed, though the more formal term is *sinistral,* deriving from the Latin for left, *sinister,* which also means an evil omen (e.g. sinister-looking person) or something malignant (sinister motive). Historically, there was little difference: left-handed people were associated with malevolence. As the belief receded, it was replaced by more enlightened empirical research. One piece of research by Michel Raymond *et al.* found that, compared to their representation in the total population (about 10 per cent of men and 8 per cent of women), left-handers are over-represented in particular sports: those in which opponents are confronted directly, such as baseball, boxing and fencing. This applies at all levels of **competition**. The closer the interaction between competitors, the greater the prevalence of left-handers. Raymond *et al.'s* conclusions strongly favored the view that left-handed athletes enjoy an advantage in confrontational sports.

The reasons for handedness are not clear. It is a distinctly human trait: other animals show no bias or preference in claws, paws, hoofs, fins, etc. Human populations have a predominance of right-handedness, or dextrality, that has remained stable for centuries. Most theories are based on the lateralization of the brain, that is the degree to which the right and left cerebral hemispheres of the brain differ in specific functions. The human brain is divided into two hemispheres, the left side often being described as the dominant half because that is where the centers of language and speech and of spatial **perception** are located in most people. Nerves on the two sides of the body cross each other as they enter the brain, so that the left hemisphere is associated with the right-hand side of the body. In most right-handed people the left hemisphere directs speech, reading and writing, while the right half is responsible for **emotion**.

It was thought that left-handedness was the result of a reversal of the more usual pattern, with the main functions of the brain being on the right. But in the 1970s research showed that, in fact, most left-handers are still left-brain dominant and have their centers of language, speech and spatial perception in the same place as right-handers. In only a minority of left-handers is the pattern reversed.

Cerebral Lateralization by Geschwind and Galaburda proposed that there was an association between left-handedness and immune or immune-related disorders, and that this stemmed from birth-related problems. Left-handedness was also related to disabilities such as stammering and dyslexia. In a widely reported article in *Psychological Bulletin* Coren and Halpern claimed that left-handers die sooner than right-handers. The mean age of death for lefties was 66 compared with 75 for dextrals. Coren and Halpern gave two explanations for this.

First, environment: we live in a world that has been designed and built with right-handed people in mind. Door handles, telephones, cars: the construction of these and countless other technological features reflect right-handedness. So when left-handed people perform even the simplest of functions, they find it slightly more awkward and so have a higher **risk** of accidents (and accident-related injuries). Several subsequent studies confirmed that lefties were more prone to accidents.

Second, birth problems: referring back to Geschwind and Galaburda's studies, Coren and Halpern hypothesized that exposure to high fetal testosterone at birth may lead to developmental problems for left-handed people. This particular aspect, and indeed the whole early-death theory, did not go unchallenged, and other studies by, among many others, Harris, Hicks *et al.* and Muris *et al.* questioned the findings and uncovered others. For instance, Warren Eaton *et al.* took one strand of Coren and Halpern's research and argued that: 'Indirect evidence for an association between sinistrality [left-handedness] and maturational lag can be found from the fact that males, who are more likely to be left-handed, are less advanced in language and skeletal development than are females.'

This corpus of research raises a question: if, as most of the evidence suggests, left-handers are disadvantaged in some way, why do so many excel in sports? Every sport has at least one exceptional left-handed athlete: Babe Ruth, Rod Laver, Marvin Hagler and co. Raymond *et al.'s* research found that, over a six-year period, about 16 per cent of top tennis players were left-handed and between 15 and 27 per cent of bowlers in international cricket and pitchers in Major League Baseball. For close-quarter sports, the difference is more pronounced: 33 per cent of competitors in the men's world foils championships, increasing to 50 per cent by the quarterfinal stage of the competition. Remember: this is a group that represents about 10 per cent of the total male population. The pattern was less marked for women, though there was still over-representation at the fencing championships.

One tempting thought is that, if left-handed people are disadvantaged in several areas of development and functionality, they may be overcompensated when it comes to sports skills, like hand-to-eye coordination, quick reflexes, astute judgement, tactical awareness or just raw strength. Or it could simply mean that the sheer fact of favoring one's left arm in a context geared to right-hand biases lends the southpaw a strategic advantage. Because of the frequency of right-handers in any given population, sports performers are habituated in training and in competition to facing other dextrals. So left-handers, because of their relative scarcity, have an edge of sorts: they hit, run and move in unexpected ways.

Certainly, sports are full of stories of orthodox (left leg forward) boxers who detest fighting southpaws because of the special problems they pose. These include having to jab along the same path as the opponent's jab and constantly having one's front foot trodden on. Baseball hitters swing at the ball in such a way that their **momentum** carries their bodies in the direction they want to move to get to first base; saving fractions of a second can be vital in a game where fielding is crisp and accurate. Pitchers, like cricket bowlers, can deliver at unfamiliar angles. Returning serve against left-handers is known to be difficult for a right-hander, especially defending the advantage court; lefties are known for their ability to cut the ball diagonally across the body of the receiver. In basketball, a portsider typically tries to pass opponents on the side they least expect; there is barely time to determine whether the opponent is left-handed or not.

The strategic advantage of playing against opponents who are used to a different pattern of play seems to be the answer to the preponderance of them in some sports. In others, where being left-handed counts for little, their prevalence is about the same as in the general population. According to Raymond et al., 9.6 per cent of goalkeepers in soccer are lefties; and left-handed field-eventers account for 10.7 per cent of all competitors. At the top levels of darts, snooker, bowling and gymnastics, southpaws are actually under-represented. Somehow they gravitate toward the sports in which they possess a natural advantage.

An anonymous journalist with *The Economist* magazine adds an evolutionary level to this argument: over the years, the strategic advantage enjoyed by lefties outweighed the other possible disadvantages uncovered by the previously mentioned research. Natural selection, of course, favors the best physically equipped (fittest) species, which survived and were able to pass on their genes to their children. This would account, albeit in a crude way, for the persistence of left-handed people in an environment built largely by and for right-handers and in which social pressures (such as associating sinistrality with wrong-doing) might reasonably have expected to pressure lefties to change their biases.

Further reading

Anonymous (1997) 'Sinister origins,' *The Economist* (15 February) vol. 342, pp. 80–1.

Coren, S. and Halpern, D.F. (1991) 'Left-handedness: a marker for decreased survival fitness,' *Psychological Bulletin* vol. 109, pp. 90–106.

Eaton. W.O., Chipperfield, J.G., Ritchot, F.M. and Kostiuk, J.H. (1996) 'Is a maturational lag associated with left-handedness? A research note,' *Journal of Child Psychology and Psychiatry and Allied Disciplines* vol. 37, pp. 613–17.

Geschwind, N. and Galaburda, A.M. (1987) *Cerebral Lateralization* Cambridge MA: MIT Press.

LIFE COURSE

In contrast to life cycle, which describes the pattern of phases every living organism passes through from birth to death, a life *course* is the process of change brought about as a result of the interaction between an organism and the environment. The term 'course' (as in onward movement, or direction, from the Roman *cursa*, run) suggests that, unlike many other living forms, humans do not experience their lives according to a strict chronological sequence of stages. For example, an **aging** athlete may be said to be approaching the end of a professional career life cycle. While this may appear to be a completely natural process, it is affected perhaps by a deterioration of body parts hastened by participation in a sport, conflicting demands that multiply as the athlete grows older and a cluster of cultural expectations that athletic careers typically end in the early thirties.

An athlete's life course does not conform to stages of growth and degeneration in the fixed pattern of, say, a plant. Examples of athletes who peak young and decline while still in their youth abound, as do late developers who reach the zenith of form late in their careers. Many an athlete has defied critics by mounting a successful **comeback** at an age when many others have retired. In other words, the only inevitability about a sporting life cycle is that it will eventually end, through either **retirement**, **injury** or death.

In Erik Erikson's model, development does not end with physical maturity but proceeds through eight *psychosocial* stages from cradle to grave. Each stage has its own particular problems or crises that need to be confronted and its own significant social relationships. So, for example, in adolescence, or stage five, the psychosocial crisis involves confusion over **identity** and the significant social relationships are with peer groups and outgroups. At stage seven, middle adulthood, Erikson writes of *generativity*, which is a concern with guiding and providing for the next generation, and the feeling of despair that the **goal** or goals that were set earlier in life will not be achieved. Erikson's *Childhood and Society* is extensively quoted as a key study in identity formation, our conceptions of who we are mutating as our psychosocial development progresses. Critical moments in an athlete's life course, brought on by, for example, serious injury or retirement, often have major effects on an athlete's **self-efficacy** and even **personality** as well as his or her identity.

Further reading

Baillie, P.H.F. and Danish, S.J. (1992) 'Understanding the career transition of athletes,' *The Sport Psychologist* vol. 6, pp. 77–98.
Erikson, E. (1963) *Childhood and Society* New York: Norton.

LUCK

Luck is from the Middle High German *gelücke*, modernized to *Glück*, which translates as happiness or good fortune. There is, however, a difference between luck and fortune: if something agreeable happens to a person in the normal course of events, then he or she is fortunate; luck intervenes when something agreeable happens despite the odds against its happening. Luck is ubiquitous in sports; it is this that preserves sports from the domesticating influences of rational management, at the same time maintaining fans' fascination with the unpredictability that **competition** always creates. No matter how well prepared an athlete or team may be, the best-laid plans are often at the mercy of circumstances beyond the **control** of anyone or anything. As Nicholas Rescher observes: 'Competence alone is not enough to secure success in a chancy world.'

For Rescher, luck involves three elements: (1) a beneficiary or maleficiary (recipient of harm); (2) a development that is benign (positive) or malign (negative) from the standpoint of the interests of the affected individual; (3) unforeseeability, i.e. it must not be expected. The first two elements have clear relevance in sports. A soccer team that is leading 3–0 when the floodlights fail and then loses the replayed game is clearly the maleficiary of luck, while the opponents get lucky. The third element is absolutely crucial to the enduring appeal of sports competition. Much of sports is founded on the concept of merit. Yet the fascination of sports lies in the very fact that, if: *talent* + *work* = *merit*, merit is not always rewarded. Otherwise, all of sports competition would be calculable.

In 1929, A.A. Brill constructed a timeless argument about the attraction of sports in which he offered an insight into the drabness and formality of modernity and the security it holds for most people. 'The restrictions of modern life,' as Brill called them, meant that life was governed by predictable patterns. 'Life organized too well becomes monotonous; too much peace and security breed boredom.' Sports reintroduced unpredictability and uncertainty into people's lives, according to Brill. Similar arguments have been advanced to explain why humans actively seek out situations that involve **risk**.

While coaches remind athletes of the perils of relying on good luck, they are just as aware that it is a part of any contest. For this reason, **superstition** is rife in sports: typically, athletes stumble across a particular piece of behavior that precedes an exceptionally good performance and then repeat the behavior before every contest. No matter how elaborate the ritual or how fastidiously it is followed, its benefit is always subjective: performing it imbues competitors with **confidence**. If, as competitors suggest, the aim is to bring good luck, it must fail. Luck can never be invoked – if it could be, it would not be luck.

Further reading

Brill, A.A. (1929) 'The why of a fan,' *North American Review* part 228, pp. 428–35.
Rescher, N. (1995) *Luck: The brilliant randomness of everyday life* New York: Farrar Straus Giroux.

MASTERY

The accomplishment or application of a **skill** is known as mastery, a term taken from the Old French word *maistre*, in turn from the Latin *magister*, a commanding superior. The derivations of the term are clear: for example, magistrate, maestro, master bedroom, etc. While its use in sports is common, particularly in the context of skill ('she demonstrated complete mastery of the crosscourt backhand'), it is a contestable concept: is it a **gender** neutral term or does it carry sexist connotations?

Certainly, historical uses of 'master' and 'mastery' suggest male dominion. A ship's master was invariably male, as was the master of a house, a master-at-arms and Master of the Lodge. The masters of a house or school masters were contrasted to the female mistresses. These and myriad other uses of 'master' intimate an equivalency of maleness and superiority and femaleness and subjection. The historical reasons for this have been removed, to a large degree, and in some cases the word has been replaced with more neutral appellations, like 'head teacher.' On the other hand, there are still Master's degrees, Old Master works of art and master craftsmen.

The extensive use of the term 'mastery' in sports suggests the term has been 'neutralized,' uncoupled from its sexist origins or perhaps used in the same way as master key, master switch or masterstroke. Its cognate adjectives, 'masterful' and 'masterly' – highly skilful – have lost much of their gender specificity, though perhaps not quite all. Arthur Reber, in his *Dictionary of Psychology*, has no qualms in defining mastery as simply: 'The achieving of some pre-set (and usually high) level of functioning on some task.' And in the fourth edition of his *Sport Psychology: Concepts and applications*, published in 1998, Richard Cox defines a mastery environment as 'a motivational climate conducive to the development of independence, self **confidence**, and **self-esteem**.' Cox equates the concept with the less disputable 'task environment' and reminds readers that 'mastery orientation' and 'task orientation' are 'identical.' Note: task orientation, in Nicholls' 1984 formulation, is the tendency to perceive ability based on personal improvement rather than how others perform, the concept being part of the model of **goal orientation**.

As recently as 2002, Allen Cornelius uncritically used the term 'mastery imagery' to describe the method of 'imagining executing the proper technique and movement of a free throw [and potentially any other skill].' **Imagery** is a much-favored technique used in the **skill acquisition** process.

While reservations about the unqualified use of 'mastery' remain, it has yet to be replaced in sport psychology's lexicon, and it seems safe to assume that its continued use will further sever its links with its patriarchal and **sex** specific meanings. Of the possible alternatives, 'grasp' seems somehow insufficient and 'command,' while technically adequate, fails to convey the innovation, creativity or 'flair' that excellence in a skill performance often elicits. 'Apprehension,' like 'grasp,' indicates a subject's hold over a skill, but without communicating the high level of functioning included in Reber's definition.

Further reading

Cornelius, A. (2002) 'Intervention techniques in sport psychology,' pp. 197–223 in Silva, J.M. and Stevens, D.E. (eds) *Psychological Foundations of Sport* Boston MA: Allyn & Bacon

Cox, R.H. (1998) *Sport Psychology: Concepts and applications*, 4th edition, Boston MA: McGraw-Hill.

Reber, A.S. (1995) *Dictionary of Psychology*, 2nd edition, Harmondsworth: Penguin.

MEMORY

While memory is often regarded as a single entity, it is actually a portfolio which contains several different but related mental processes through which we retain or encode information, store it and, later, retrieve it. In some situations, we need to store material for only the briefest of moments. To take a simple example from rugby, a player may glimpse and hear one of his teammates running to his right. He makes use of this memory seconds later when he makes a lateral pass to that teammate. Once the pass has been completed, he has no further need of the memory. But to make the pass he needs to have a vast bank of knowledge of how to play rugby at all, so that he can draw on aspects of that store at any time.

In making the pass, the athlete makes use of a series of *sensory* memory systems, including a brief visual image, or iconic memory as it is known, and a momentary sound, or *echoic* memory. The sounds and images may last for only up to two seconds before they are discarded. *Short-term memory* describes the functions at work during these moments. Rita Atkinson *et al.* once used the metaphor of a 'mental box with seven slots' to describe short-term memory: 'So long as the number of items does not exceed the number of slots, we can recall the items perfectly,' they wrote in 1983. In practice, we are always introducing new items into the box, so existing ones have to make way or, if they are important enough, are dispatched to the *long-term memory* for storage.

The way information is filed away in the long-term memory is often through chunking, which means clustering information together in familiar forms that can be readily retrieved. If a person was asked to remember thirteen letters HAOCDAIEMLNRJ, it would prove difficult; unless they chunked them into two words, Michael Jordan, in which case it would be easy. Athletes do similarly during **skill acquisition**, rendering complex instructions more accessible by re-framing them in sequences that can be retrieved more easily.

The long-term memory itself involves material that may have been retained for intervals of only a few minutes or as long as a lifetime. Specific pieces of information are usually encoded in terms of meaning rather than content. Someone might vividly recount the plot of Nick Hornby's *High Fidelity*, but they will not be able to recite the text line by line. No one recalls every instruction given to them by their first coach, but most athletes will be able to recollect the meaning. The more information we organize in terms of its meaning, the greater our chances of a successful retrieval.

Long-term memory is much more than a vast repository of meanings. It is a convenient term for several types of information and the processes by which they are stored and recovered. Altering an example from Endel Tulving, there are differences between a memory of watching a particular football game on television and remembering how many players there are in a football team. Both require memory, but while Tulving argued that they reflect the operation of distinct and separate systems in the brain, others, such as Alan Baddeley, suggest it may be the same system operating under different conditions. For Tulving, *episodic* memory refers to the conscious recollection of personally experienced events, while *semantic* memory involves factual knowledge. I might remember that Zinedine Zidane headed the first goal of the 1998 World Cup Final for France against Brazil (semantic), but I have no memory of how it felt to score that goal – that episodic memory is exclusively Zidane's.

Retrieval of information from long-term memory is affected by the way in which we originally encoded the material. The obvious analogy is that of a library: trying to locate a certain book is a huge task unless you understand the cataloging system, or the ways in which the books are organized, either in terms of subject or author's surname etc. The task is simplified and retrieval is possible. The more information we organize in terms of its category, or class, the greater our chances of a successful retrieval.

The context in which we originally encode information also affects retrieval. A context may be a physical environment, such as a place or a certain type of situation or even someone's face, or it may be a subjective state, such as an **emotion** felt at the moment the information was first encountered. That same **emotional** state facilitates subsequent retrieval of the information from the long-term memory. Even induced states, such as those experienced under the influence of alcohol or drugs, can affect retrieval. Research has shown that a drunk person may, for example, hide something, then completely forget where it is once they are sober. The next time they are drunk, they remember! The memory, in this case, is *state dependent*.

Emotions are important in several ways. The term 'flashbulb memory' was coined to describe memories that are sharp, moving and frequently evoke details of the context in which the information was encoded. 'Where were you when you heard about the attack on the World Trade Center?' is a question that typically draws a comprehensive answer from people who can recount accurately where they were, with whom, doing what, etc. New and startling information that excite a high level of emotional **arousal** can be expected to become the material of flashbulb memories.

The ultimate retrieval failure is also influenced by emotion, in this case elicited by a traumatic experience that functions to block access to target memories. Women who have been raped, for example, may not be able to recollect the specifics of the rape nor indeed the rapist. There are various views on the mechanism behind this repression. Some believe that the **anxiety** brought about by the experience does not cause the memory failure: it is associated with other incidental thoughts that are not germane to the rape itself, but which serve to interfere with retrieval.

Further reading

Baddeley, A. (1996) 'Memory,' pp. 281–301 in Colman, A.M. (ed.) (1996) *Companion Encyclopedia of Psychology*, vol. 1, London: Routledge.
Tulving, E. (1972) 'Episodic and semantic memory,' pp. 381–403 in Tulving, E. and Donaldson, W. (eds) *Organization of Memory* New York: Academic Press.

MENTAL PRACTICE

When thought processes are used as part of the **skill acquisition** process, the term 'mental practice,' or sometimes 'mental preparation,' describes the collection of techniques available. These frequently involve **imagery** (not usually pre-**competition** imagery), though, as Richard Cox points out in his *Sport Psychology: Concepts and applications*: 'Mental practice implies that an individual is practicing a physical task in some covert way, although actual images of the task may or may not be present.' It is equally possible that athletes use imagery without visualizing a **skill performance** (they may imagine themselves on the victory rostrum, for example). In other words, mental practice, while often used synonymously with imagery, is actually distinct.

The term itself is not entirely unproblematic. 'Mental,' which is from the Latin *mentalis*, for mind, is not a word that elicits universal approval: the age-old debate over the status, or even existence, of the mind is unlikely ever to reach a conclusion and this has implications for the way in which the adjective 'mental' is used. In popular use, 'mental' refers to functions that reflect **intelligence** or the lack thereof. In another sense, mental processes are those that mediate between physical **stimuli** and the observable responses of a human subject. 'Mental' may also be said to be a general rubric under which elements of **cognition** are drawn together. In mental practice, mental is contrasted with physical: the athlete is not hurdling or shooting hoops, but he or she is thinking about performing those tasks.

Mental practice is typically done when in repose, possibly, though not necessarily, at an advanced state of **relaxation**. As such it can be done when far away from the athletics field: at home, on a plane, virtually anywhere an athlete can establish a degree of solace. Practiced athletes are sometimes able to gate out distractions and mentally practice even in crowded, noisy places.

Intuitively, the idea of mentally practicing a technical skill or some facet of a **skill performance** or even an entire sequence of tasks has appeal. But, does it work? The balance of research results tend toward a tepid 'yes.' Robert Weinberg in 1981 and Feltz and Landers in 1983 agreed that there is a beneficial effect on performance, but it is not nearly as effective in **skill acquisition** as physical practice, though it is better than no practice at all. In 1994, Murphy confirmed what common sense suggests: that a combination of mental and actual practice is most effective, one complementing the other. Hird *et al.* concluded that mental practice is not uniformly effective across the board: it works best with tasks, and hence sports, that lay the accent on cognitive skills as well as purely physical ones. Also, sequence is important: mental practice before physical practice is more effective than after, according to a 1996 study by Etnier and Landers. More experience and skilled athletes will extract more benefit from mental practicing than novices. Despite the reservations and qualifications, mental practice is accepted as an accessible **intervention** and one that is used almost universally by contemporary athletes.

Further reading

Etnier, J.L. and Landers, D.M. (1996) 'The influence of procedural variables on the efficacy of mental practice,' *The Sport Psychologist* vol. 10, pp. 48–57.

Hird, J.S., Landers, D.M., Thomas, J.R. and Horan, J.J. (1991) 'Physical practice is superior to mental practice in enhancing cognitive and motor task performance,' *Journal of Sport and Exercise Performance* vol. 13, pp. 281–93.

Murphy, S.M. (1994) 'Imagery interventions in sport,' *Medicine and Science in Sports and Exercise* vol. 26, pp. 486–94.

MENTAL TOUGHNESS

Mental toughness describes a bundle of qualities that include an unusually high level of resolution, a refusal to be intimidated, an ability to stay **focused** in high-pressure situations, a capacity for retaining an optimum level of **arousal** throughout a **competition**, an unflagging eagerness to compete when injured, an unyielding attitude when being beaten, a propensity to take risks when rivals show caution and an inflexible, perhaps obstinate insistence on finishing a contest rather than conceding defeat.

In contrast to *physical* toughness – which is durability, an exceptionally high threshold of **pain** or a rugged-style approach to competition – mental toughness suggests qualities of mind or intellect (*mentalis* being Latin for mind, toughness from the Old English *tōh*, strong or hard to break).

This is a ubiquitous noun, used generously by sports journalists and scholars, yet usually without explication. An exception is Jean Côté who writes: 'Mentally tough athletes are able to keep their emotions in control and are calm and relaxed under pressure situations.' This is a serviceable definition, though narrower than the one drafted here.

Côté's review of research on 'Coach and peer influence on children's development through sport' draws on 1996 work by Smith and Smoll, who describe mental toughness for children as 'the ability to keep physical arousal within manageable limits.' Again, this is a more limited interpretation, though of course it applies specifically to children. The relevance of this work is that it challenges popular notions that mental toughness is simply an innate quality that some athletes have and others do not.

Côté discusses four procedures designed to 'enhance children's mental toughness.'

1 Changing aspects of situations that place unnecessary **stress** on young athletes: this might include practicing away from spectators or even changing rules to suit the **skill** level of the athlete.
2 Increasing resources for dealing with pressure situations: this involves working on technical **skill acquisition** so that the young athlete acquires the **confidence** to be able to execute the skills in competitive situations.
3 Helping children develop a positive attitude toward competition: at the outset, young athletes should be taught that **anxiety** is 'not produced solely by a situation but rather by the way one interprets that situation' and that **cognition** is the key to responding appropriately to even the most taxing situations.
4 Rehearsing **relaxation**: Côté, along with several other scholars, encourages **mental practice** at an early age, particularly teaching children the skills needed to relax and the ability to use **imagery**.

The techniques are the stock-in-trade of sport psychologists, and several other types of **intervention**, for example **goal setting**, complement them. The interest in the present context is in how Côté and others believe that mental toughness may be *taught* in childhood, the presumption being that it will carry through to adulthood. Whether mental toughness is just an ability to stay calm and relaxed and retain a degree of emotional **control** throughout a contest is another issue. The wider definition favored here includes five other criteria that may well be learned, though perhaps not in such a structured environment as the ones suggested by Côté.

For example, Michael Schumacher presents an epitome of mental toughness, one incident in particular showcasing this. In 1996 at the Circuit de Catalunya near Barcelona, he won an astonishing race in treacherous hard rain that forced several of his rivals, including Damon Hill, to retire. Hill said: 'I'm happy to be in one piece. You could not see the track. You are putting your life on the line more than normal.' Hill's response seemed rational. Schumacher, trailing in sixth place, defied the poor visibility and slick track by driving with a total disregard for his own safety. At one point, he lapped at five seconds faster than the rest of the field. His eventual victory prompted Jacques Villeneuve later to conclude 'he is now out of touch with reality.' This appraisal did not take account of Schumacher's mental toughness: his refusal to accept defeat did not arise spontaneously, but was honed by his early exploits in karting (he was German Junior karting champion in 1984 and 1985 when 15/16).

This single illustration includes most of the salient features of mental toughness. Schumacher remained unfazed in a life-threatening situation, his resolve to win superseding other considerations, particularly those about his own safety. The **risk** to his life was enormous, yet he showed no **fear**. He maintained an appropriate level of arousal, managing **emotion** and bringing his skill to bear while several rivals either spun off the track or simply resigned themselves to defeat. Schumacher's refusal to be intimidated by the circumstances and his determination to complete the course demonstrated an exemplary mental toughness.

Historically, there have been a great many other instances of facets of mental toughness, some athletes manifesting them regularly. Pete Sampras often salvaged seemingly impossible situations when most other players would have succumbed. John Elway's famed **composure** in the most alarming circumstances distinguished him from his peers. Tiger Woods' preparedness to take seemingly irrational chances to secure improbable victories established him as the premier golfer of his generation. English soccer player Stuart Pearce's routine defiance of **injury** to prolong his playing career into his late thirties exposed his trademark mental toughness.

Conversely, there are several other athletes with obvious physical proficiencies who are liable to fold, panic, **choke**, surrender or simply absent themselves from competition in discouraging circumstances. Physical and mental toughness have no necessary relationship.

Further reading

Côté, J. (2001) 'Coach and peer influence on children's development through sport,' pp. 520–40 in Silva, J.M. and Stevens, D.E. (eds) *Psychological Foundations of Sport* Boston MA: Allyn & Bacon.
Smith, R.E. and Smoll, F.L. (1996) *Way to Go, Coach* Portola Valley CA: Warde.

METAMOTIVATION

According to Kurt Frey, metamotivation is 'the way in which a person's motives can change and fluctuate during the course of activities and daily life.' The state in which the person finds him or herself 'sets' what that person wants and this is liable to change as an interaction progresses. Frey gives the example of a pick-up game of basketball at a local gym: a player may start simply wanting to have fun, dribbling, showboating and trash-talking fellow players. In contrast, he or she may also be in a more serious frame of mind, anxious about personal performance and determined to win, however insignificant the game. 'These opposite states are operative in everyone and entail distinctive motives, perceptions and emotions,' writes Frey, an adherent of **reversal theory**.

Reversal theory states that metamotivational states occur in couples of opposites, so that when one state is active, its opposite is inactive. Humans alternate or reverse back and forth between these oppositions. The perspective challenges more conventional accounts of **motivation** which typically claim that motives revolve around a single optimal point. The prefix *meta*, from the Greek for 'after' or 'beyond' and meaning, in this instance, a change of position or condition to another order (as in 'metabolism'), suggests how the concept of a single energizer of action is replaced by a duality: a duality that changes through a course of action. At the heart of this lies a model of the human being as inconsistent, self-contradictory and endlessly capricious, devoid of a stable **personality** and animated by competing states rather than a single **drive** or impulsion.

Further reading

Frey, K.P. (1999) 'Reversal theory: basic concepts,' pp. 3–17 in Kerr, J.H. (ed.) *Experiencing Sport: Reversal theory* London: Wiley.

MIMETIC

From the Greek *mimesis*, for imitation, mimetic is an adjective meaning of or relating to mimicry. Mimetic activities, according to Joe Maguire, 'provide a "make-believe" setting which allows emotions to **flow** more easily and which elicits excitement of some kind, imitating that produced by real-life situations, yet without its dangers or risks.' All sports are, in effect, mimetic activities: they create tensions and drama and evoke **emotion** of high **intensity**; and, while they some-times involve the actual rather than imagined **risk** of harm or even death, this is deliberately minimized.

Obviously, the moods elicited by participation in sports are different from those elicited by actual situations. Yet there is a resemblance. The **adrenaline rush** experienced in flight-or-fight situations is often replicated in sports, particularly high-risk activities such as Xtreme sports. States of **arousal** and, indeed, **anxiety** achieved through sports bear resemblance, at least in a quantitative sense, to states experienced in stressful predicaments. The point of sport is to stimulate what Maguire calls the 'pleasurable excitement' that comes from 'achieve-ment sports.'

The mimetic properties of much contemporary sport are clear. All Olympic events, for example, have an obvious ancestry in hunting or combat activities that predate even the Games of Ancient Hellas (Greece) in 4000 BCE. Desmond Morris has described many of today's team sports, such as football and hockey, as 'ritual hunts.' Morris writes of the elements of the primeval hunting sequence reappearing in contempor-ary sports, with danger or the risk of serious **injury** ever present.

In a sense, argues Morris, every **competition** is a 'stylized battle' and, as such, involves strategy, fitness, **concentration**, stamina, vision and imagination. Many others have argued that sports resemble warfare. Greek and Roman competitions either side of the Christian era were explicitly designed to prepare competitors for combat and often concluded in death or wounding. The **control** of **violence** that accompanied the civilizing process ensured that sports incorporated measures to minimize hazards, though Murphy *et al.* point out that the medieval and early modern British 'mock fights' bore 'a greater resemblance to real fighting than their modern-day equivalents.'

Further reading

Maguire, J. (1992) 'A sociological theory of sport and the emotions: a process-sociological perspective,' pp. 96–120 in Dunning, E. and Rojek, C. (eds) *Sport and Leisure in the Civilizing Process: Critique and counter-critique* Houndmills, England: Macmillan.
Morris, D. (1981) *The Soccer Tribe* London: Jonathan Cape.
Murphy, P., Sheard, K. and Waddington, I. (2000) 'Figurational sociology and its application to sport,' pp. 92–105 in Coakley, J. and Dunning, E. (eds) *Handbook of Sports Studies* London: Sage.

MODELING

Observing another's behavior, retaining an image of it and, later, attempting to imitate it is known as modeling, from the Latin *modulus*, meaning exemplary or ideal. In sports, as in many other realms, modeling is a significant means of learning and, as such, is a basic component of the **socialization** process. Obviously, the process is not automatic: the conditions under which the observation takes place, the characteristics of the model being observed and other situational factors affect how effectively the behavior is learned. As such, modeling suggests an alternative to theories predicated on the importance of **instinct** or **drive** in determining behavior, and those stressing a passive role for humans in reacting to **stimuli** in the environment. **Cognition** plays a crucial part in modeling: the subject can think and represent situations, anticipate probable consequences of behavior and interpret stimuli rather than just react to them.

Modeling, or vicarious learning as it is sometimes called, is not confined to literal imitation of behavior but occurs with the acquisition of information from another person, visually or verbally. **Emotion** can also be learned by watching the **emotional** responses of others as they undergo painful or pleasurable experiences. A child who observes another child contorting and screaming in a dentist's chair may feel **fear** when he or she approaches a dental appointment. One of the classic experiments in modeling by Albert Bandura and Richard Walters involved nursery school children who observed an adult expressing various forms of aggressive behavior toward an inflated doll. After watching, both boys and girls mimicked the adult, punching, kicking and striking the doll with a hammer. Subsequent research indicated that children were most likely to imitate the behavior when they observed models being positively reinforced for their behavior, a process called vicarious **reinforcement**. The consequences of behavior played an important part in shaping the behavior of the children. Relatively new behaviors could be acquired with this method.

Similar processes operate during other types of learning, including **skill acquisition**. In his *Social Learning Theory*, Bandura advanced a four-stage theory in which: (1) a subject *attends* to a performance, taking note of key features; (2) the subject *retains* or remembers vital material, coding and storing information to the **memory**; (3) the subject attempts to *reproduce* the **skill performance**, perhaps recruiting help from others initially; (4) the subject must have requisite **motivation** to keep repeating the performance, and in this respect positive reinforcement is important. While Bandura's process was somewhat linear, later research embellished it, adding that the **sex** of the model being imitated made a difference: same-sex modeling works most effectively. Also, observing a peer performing a task more proficiently than oneself can underline a **skill** discrepancy and de-motivate a learner.

Learning through modeling is cumulative, building from simple to more complex tasks. Playing ice hockey, for instance, requires basic skills such as skating and controlling the puck, but the proficient player must integrate these and other learnt behaviors into a more complex repertoire. In this way, a beginner develops **self-efficacy** and the **confidence** that grows from repeated **skill performance**. This, in itself, is not sufficient to account for creativity and the imaginative use of skill, but the point about modeling is that it is generalizable: once basic units of skill are augmented by the repertoires, subjects can extend and enlarge skills that were not initially observed.

Modeling has been used to account for the learning of sports-related skills, yet it may have application to some aspects of **deviance**. For example, athletes might observe, encode information about **doping** and witness the vicariously reinforcing consequences of others' success. If the subject imitates others' behavior by taking performance-enhancing drugs and is not discovered, the lack of punishment is likely to reinforce further rule-breaking. From this perspective, cheating is modeled.

Further reading

Bandura, A. (1977) *Social Learning Theory* Englewood Cliffs NJ; Prentice-Hall.

Bandura, A. and Walters, R.H. (1963) *Social Learning and Personality Development* New York: Holt, Rinehart & Winston.

MOMENTUM

Used originally in mechanics to describe the quantity of motion (*mass + velocity*) and the impetus gained by movement, 'momentum' (the word is actually from the Latin for move, *movimentum*) in sports refers to shift in the **flow** of a contest that affects either the perceptions of the competitors or, perhaps, the outcome of the **competition**. In psychological terms, momentum arises from a perception associated with a sense of **control** in the pursuit of a **goal** and can lead to increased **confidence, motivation**, focusing ability and, according to Scott Kerick *et al.*, 'mind–body synchrony.'

'Momentum acts like water – flowing backwards and forwards, sometimes faster or slower, or at times not moving at all,' writes tennis coach Alistair Higham in his 2000 book *Momentum: The hidden force in tennis*. As a stone thrown into water makes ripples, a precipitating event initiates psychological momentum, or PM. A late touchdown may give the come-from-behind team momentum in overtime; a break of serve at 4–4 in the fourth set to lead for the first time in the match; a fielding error; a mis-hit; a flash knockdown – potentially any event can introduce or change momentum.

Precisely how psychological momentum affects performance is open to dispute. In Taylor and Demick's 1994 *multidimensional model*, an event works as a catalyst, prompting a response from the athlete. Cognitive, physiological and behavioral changes combine to produce a driving force that affects the athlete's behavior and, in turn, elevates his or her performance. Change in perceptions (in particular, of **self-efficacy** and control) and **arousal** translates into performance. Conversely, losing momentum, or experiencing negative momentum, can prove detrimental to performance, especially if a lead has been depleted and one's opponent is coming from behind. This may change the outcome of a competition.

According to *antecedents–consequences* theory, antecedents, like a steal or a dunk, affect perceptions which can lead to an improved performance, or the opposite process if one is on the receiving end of the event. PM can influence performance, though this depends on circumstances. For example, in a sport requiring low levels of arousal, such as putting or free throw shooting, psychological momentum may be of no benefit. R.M. Adams, who in 1995 discovered that improvements in **concentration** followed momentum shifts in pool, has disputed this.

In contrast to the first two approaches, the *projected performance model* proposed by Allen Cornelius *et al.* in 1997 suggests that momentum has little impact on performance. Perceptions of momentum are typically short-lived and can encourage a competitor to coast; this is known as 'positive inhibition.' Also, a player who has performed poorly and witnessed his or her opponent catch up or go into a lead may be stung into action and become more energized than ever, a process known as 'negative facilitation.'

Stéphane Perrault *et al.* conducted experiments that gave partial support to all three theories, finding evidence that coming from behind 'can have a profound effect on perceptions of PM,' and this facilitates competitive performance, particularly in sports that need a great deal of effort. They also discovered that the negative facilitation suggested by Cornelius could work to influence the performance of athletes who have seen their initiative slip away.

Despite disagreement about the mechanics of momentum, evidence of its presence in sport is beyond dispute. It manifests dramatically in team sports, when games often turn on a single event. For example, in the twenty-first minute of his team's crucial World Cup qualifying game against England in 2001, Germany's Sebastian Deisler missed a simple goal for a 2–1 lead; instead, the score remained 1–1. Had Deisler scored, the whole German team would surely have gained momentum. His error gave his opponents the momentum they needed to surge to a 5–1 win.

While changes in perceptions of momentum may influence competitors during contests, the question of sustained momentum's impact on the future of successive contests is open to doubt. Roger Vergin's 2000 research on winning and losing **streaks**, for example, undermined the 'almost universal belief by athletes, sports fans and media observers' that a winning (or losing) sequence affects future results. As an objective causal agent in the outcome of contests 'momentum is mostly myth,' concludes Vergin.

Further reading

Kerick, S.E., Iso-Ahola, S.E. and Hatfield, B.D. (2000) 'Psychological momentum in target shooting: cortical, cognitive-affective, and behavioral responses,' *Journal of Sport & Exercise Psychology* vol. 22, pp. 1–20.

Perreault, S., Vallerand, R.J., Montgomery, D. and Provencher, P. (1998) 'Coming from behind: on the effect of psychological momentum on sport performance,' *Journal of Sport & Exercise Psychology* vol. 20, pp. 421–36.

MOOD

Unlike **emotion**, mood is a pervasive, lingering subjective state that is usually diffuse, in the sense that it has no focus. A mood may be evaluative: for example, a subject may simply be in a good or bad mood without being pleased or angry with anyone or anything. The word is from the Old English *mod*, meaning mind or thought.

Mood swings usually refer to relatively swift and unexpected vacillations between **depression** and elation without obvious antecedents. When such swings become so excessive that they interfere with normal functioning, they become *bipolar* mood disorders, or the less extreme *cyclothymic* disorders in which the swings occur in relatively consistent cycles. Mood disorders cover a variety of other conditions.

In sports, persistent depression and unreasonable, enduring **anxiety** are mood disturbances (rather than disorders). Research on the effect of physical exercise on mood disturbances has been documented by, among others, LaFontaine *et al.* in 1992 and Cox in 1998, with the conclusion that there is an association between participating in exercise and the moderating of depression and anxiety. This does not establish that exercise in itself affects mood. Other mediating factors might include: the interaction with other exercisers; the **self-efficacy** that emerges from training; and the distracting effects of exercise in taking a subject's **attention** away from their mood. Still other possibilities are that the increased secretion of neurotransmitters has a positive effect on mood and the production of **endorphins** improves feelings of wellbeing.

Further reading

Cox, R.H. (1998) *Sport Psychology: Concepts and applications*, 4th edition, Boston MA: McGraw-Hill.
LaFontaine, T.P., DiLorenzo, T.M., Frensch, P.A., Stucky-Ropp, R.C. Bargman, E.P. and McDonald, D.G. (1992) 'Aerobic exercise and mood: a brief review, 1985–1990,' *Sports Medicine* vol. 13, pp. 160–70.

MOTIVATION

Formed from a Latin source *motus*, for move, motivation refers to prompting movement. Beyond this elementary definition of motivation, there is little agreement on the precise meaning of a concept that is absolutely central to sport psychology. A sample of the various interpretations available includes: Silva and Weinberg's (1984) 'the intensity and direction of behavior'; Green's (1996) 'processes involved in the initiation, direction, and energization of individual behavior'; Reber's (1995) 'an intervening process or an internal state of an organism that impels or drives it to action'; Alderman's (1974) 'the tendency for the direction and selectivity of behavior to be controlled by its connections to consequences, and the tendency of this behavior to persist until a **goal** is achieved'; and Hill's (2001) 'the desire to engage and persist in sport, often despite disappointments, sacrifice, and encouragement.' Distilling these, we are left with: *an internal state or process that energizes, directs and maintains goal-directed behavior.*

While some analysts prefer to approach motivation as a generalized **drive**, others, particularly those concerned with sports, argue that motivation is specific to particular objectives and directions. Motivation functions as a kind of mainspring for action, directing it toward identifiable ends; obviously, the resulting behavior is intentional, though the consequences of the behavior may not be. Where there is no link between action and outcome, there is usually no motivation (captured in the term *amotivation* – if weight training has no connection with improving chess skills, the chess player will have no motivation to lift weights, unless for another purpose). The anticipated outcomes, effects or consequences of a motivated behavior are vital to the maintenance of motivation. This is illustrated in Mark Anshel's breakdown of motivation in a sports context.

Anshel's treatment is inspired by Alderman's conception and involves five component parts: (1) direction of motivation – 'the motivated athlete is energized to engage in a purposeful and meaningful task'; (2) selectivity of behavior – behavior is rarely automatic or random and needs direction, often selected by a coach; (3) connections to consequences – the tangible results of motivated action must be available for inspection; (4) goals – these provide 'the **incentive** to persist at a task until a new **skill** or performance **mastery** has been achieved'; (5) **expectancy** – for motivation to continue to energize, there must be a reasonable expectation that efforts will lead to desired results. (We should note the resemblance between this and the perspective offered by Maehr and Brascamp in 1986: motivation comprises direction, persistence, behavioral **intensity** and performance, which is the final outcome of motivation.)

While this formalization is useful, it leaves an important question unanswered: what induces a person to act? In other words, from where does motivation come? Abraham Maslow's answer in the 1950s was based on his celebrated *hierarchy of needs*, which was a structure based on human imperatives, the primary one of which was biological (hunger, thirst, temperature maintenance and so on). Above the basic needs were tiers of ever more cultivated needs, including the need for affiliation with others, aesthetic needs and the need for **self-actualization** to find fulfillment in realizing one's own potential. Our initial motivation derives from the satisfaction of needs at the lower end of the hierarchy, and once these are met we ascend upwards, striving to satisfy the more sophisticated needs. Motivation, in this model, has origins in human needs, or drives, some of which have organic sources.

Freud too believed humans are motivated by primal drives, in his case **sex** and **aggression**. In childhood, parents forbid the free expression of sex and aggression and these become repressed, remaining in the unconscious. For Freud, these unconscious motives manifest in later life, exercising an influence over conduct though in disguised ways, such as in illness, accidents, mannerisms or Freudian slips (of the tongue). The motive, or the power behind the behavior, is not immediately available to the senses, as it lurks in the unconscious. In their different ways, Maslow and Freud offered interesting accounts of motivation, both premised on the presence of drives or instincts that govern human conduct.

Presuming the existence of such drives proved unsatisfactory for other analysts who believed that both motivation and the responses it engenders are shaped by circumstances. Action is governed not by unconscious or unknown forces, but by the way we envisage the consequences. This approach diverges from not only drive-based or **instinct** theories, but also from those of behaviorists, most of whom avoid all reference to consciousness, subjectivity, ideas or other cognitive processes (i.e. activities concerned with thinking, knowing, reasoning, insight, intention, etc.). Stuart Biddle's essay 'Cognitive theories of motivation and the physical self' documents several theories, all in some way subscribing to the view that 'people are motivated to action in areas of their lives in which they are likely to experience positive feelings of competence and esteem.' The opposite is also presumed: that motivation is reduced in activities that yield feelings of **negativity**.

'Self-based' approaches fall within the framework of cognitive theory in the sense that they explore the ways in which behavior is motivated and, indeed, shaped by self-evaluations. If a person desires to look like a supermodel and they see themselves as overweight, then their motivation may be to exercise and eat less as a way of closing up the discrepancy between what they are currently like and what they want to be. Competence is not high, but the desire for improved competence, or in this case appearance, is sufficient to provide the motivation. Whether or not the equation is accurate is not relevant; in fact, many **eating disorders** are precipitated by flawed judgements of this kind. What counts is the person's subjective evaluation of their likely success: in this sense, the desire for **self-efficacy**, perceptions of personal control and **confidence** in ability are likely to feature. There is no presumption that we are rational decision-makers. Working in this vein, Susan Harter in 1978 argued that we are motivated in domains in which we feel we can demonstrate our competence, especially if we also feel intrinsically attracted toward that domain and discern an internal locus of control in our **attribution** of success or failure. Many of the approaches to motivation that focus on **cognition** engage with the **achievement motive** debate, which was originally started by the argument that we are all impelled by the motive to achieve success and the motive to avoid failure.

Research in the 1970s by Edward Deci highlighted the difference between *intrinsic* and *extrinsic* motivations, the former deriving from feelings of satisfaction and fulfillment, the latter referring to factors that involve reward or punishment (or both) from outside forces. Deci's work with children who were set puzzle-solving tasks indicated that those who did receive a reward spent less free time working on puzzles than those who received no reward. In other words, being paid for an intrinsically interesting activity decreased intrinsic motivation. This has obvious relevance for professional athletes, all of whom will have been originally motivated by intrinsic factors, but whose motivation probably becomes purely extrinsic once they begin to earn money from sports: extrinsic incentives undermine intrinsic rewards – which helps explain why an NFL player might choose to sit out his contract, even though ten years before he would probably have played football endlessly for pure enjoyment.

In line with cognitive approaches, Deci assumed that we are motivated by the urge toward self-mastery and competence in dealing with the environment. So individuals are intrinsically motivated to perform activities that enhance their sense of accomplishment. 'Any event that enhances perceived competence will tend to enhance intrinsic motivation,' declared Deci and Ryan in their 1985 book *Intrinsic Motivation and Self-Determination in Human Behavior.*

When extrinsic rewards displace intrinsic factors as the primary reason for engaging in an activity, individuals experience a loss of **control**: instead of determining for themselves how and when to participate in an activity, they feel controlled. This is not confined to professional spheres. For example, young athletes are sometimes pressured by parents to participate in a sport, so that the line between intrinsic and extrinsic motivation is blurred: while they may enjoy competing, they may also feel the burden of having to respond to parents imploring them to succeed. The conflict helps account for the high rate of **burnout** among young tennis pros: they sense a loss of control – and a corresponding loss of self-efficacy – from an early age, rarely enjoying the intrinsic satisfactions of their sport. Extrinsic rewards carry with them the potential to wrest control from the individual. Turning pro often implies surrendering part of one's ability to decide one's own destiny.

Perhaps the starkest illustration of this in sports is corruption: the bribe, or 'bung,' as it is often known in Britain, is an extrinsic reward that motivates an athlete *not* to perform to the best of his or her ability and so not exhibit competence. Any residual intrinsic motivation to engage in a sport is sacrificed in the interests of pursuing money and **competition** is reduced to exhibition.

While the cognitive approach to motivation in many ways supplanted earlier theories which rested on assumptions that drives lay at the source of motivations, they also made untestable assumptions, particularly about the human endeavor to demonstrate competence and aspire to self-determination and esteem. **Reversal theory**'s alternative account replaces motivation with the term **metamotivation**, which is intended to capture the sense of a constant movement in and out of different psychological states. There is no single motivation: individuals' motives change before and during activities, *reversing* back and forth. This fluidity makes theories of motivation based on a single drive or a desire to improve and demonstrate competence too linear, according to reversal theory. Action is propelled by the interplay between several often conflicting motives.

Further reading

Biddle, S.J.H. (1997) 'Cognitive theories of motivation and the physical self,' pp. 59–82 in Fox, K.R. (ed.) *The Physical Self: From motivation to well-being* Champaign IL: Human Kinetics.

Deci, E.L. and Ryan, R.M. (1985) *Intrinsic Motivation and Self-determination in Human Behavior* New York: Plenum Press.

Hill, K.L. (2001) *Frameworks for Sport Psychologists: Enhancing sport performance* Champaign IL: Human Kinetics.

Silva, J.M. and Weinberg, R.S. (1984) 'Motivation,' pp. 171–6 in Silva, J.M. and Weinberg, R.S. (eds) *Psychological Foundations of Sport* Champaign IL: Human Kinetics.

NEGATIVITY

If a subject consistently contradicts, disproves, rejects or refuses to accept positive, assuring advice or counsel, he or she is said to exhibit negativity, from Latin *negare*, to deny (*neg* denotes not). There are several dimensions to this: the subject's **cognition** (including beliefs and opinions), **emotion**, interpretations of events and dispositions to act will all be influenced by a negative orientation. An athlete's negativity can initiate what Ziegler once called a 'negative thought–anxiety cycle,' in which the experience of **stress** prior to or during a **competition** leads to above-optimal **arousal** and an increase in **anxiety**. These in turn lead to further physiological changes, such as muscular tension or 'tightening,' which contribute toward an error. The experience of making an error cycles back in the form of even more anxiety, which precedes decrements in **concentration**, a loss of **composure** and the probability that more errors will follow. At vital parts of a contest, this can lead to **choking**.

Negativity afflicts all manner of athletes, regardless of **personality** and can be addressed with several types of **intervention**, including **cognitive–behavioral modification** and progressive **relaxation**.

Negativity is close in meaning to *passive negativism*, which is an attitude characterized by a resistance to the suggestions of others. It should be distinguished from active negativism, which is a tendency to behave in ways contrary to rules or directions, even when there is no obvious reason for doing so. In **reversal theory**, this is known as proactive negativism, aimed at achieving excitement only. It counterpoints reactive negativism, which is an **emotional** reaction to frustration or disappointment.

Further reading

Ziegler, S.G. (1980) 'An overview of anxiety management strategies in sport,' pp. 257–64 in Straub, W.F. (ed.) *Sport Psychology: An analysis of athlete behavior* Ithaca NY: Mouvement Publications.

NERVOUS

Originally used to describe conditions and disorders connected with the **nervous system**, the adjective 'nervous' was later used to describe any set of symptoms with **emotional** rather than organic sources. 'Nervous' has tended to slip out of popular usage, being replaced by 'stressed' (an all-purpose term to describe almost any form of discomfort), 'hyper' (agitated or excited), 'highly strung' (irritable or touchy) or 'anxious' (as in **anxiety** attack) as well as other imprecise but commonplace expressions. The term has evolved from the Latin *nervus* and the Greek *neuron* (a word now used for the cell that constitutes the basic unit of the nervous system).

In sports, 'nervous' is typically reserved for persons with a propensity to become tense on important occasions or **choke** as they approach victory, or those who favor experiencing nervousness prior to **competition** (some athletes use **fear** to their advantage, of course).

Batsmen in cricket are famously vulnerable after scoring 89 runs: with the prospect of a symbolic century (100 runs) ahead, batsmen frequently make crass errors in what cricket calls the 'nervous nineties.' Phlegmatic athletes who manage to retain **confidence** and **composure** regardless of circumstances are sometimes labeled *nerveless*.

'Nervous' prefixes terms that are still used popularly, such as 'nervous breakdown,' which covers a variety of emotional disorders – many severe enough to incapacitate – and 'nervous habit,' again covering a variety of tendencies, some relatively harmless (nail-biting, nose-scratching), others symptoms of a **dependency**. In a formal sense, 'nervous' forms part of the term 'nervous system.'

Further reading

Kremer, J. and Scully, D. (1994) *Psychology in Sport* London: Routledge.

NERVOUS SYSTEM

The physical arrangement of neural tissue in vertebrates is the nervous system, and its basic function is to receive information about the environment, process, store, retrieve and respond to it in appropriate ways. In sports, responses to change in the environment, to be effective, have to be swift and definite. Possessing a **skill** means being able to respond relevantly to surrounding changes and maintain **control** over one's body.

The human nervous system comprises: (1) the central nervous system (CNS), which is the control center of the brain and its message conduit, the spinal cord; and (2) the peripheral nervous system (PNS), which is the network of nerves originating in the brain and spinal cord and which is responsible for picking up messages from the skin and sense organs (sensory nerve cells) and carrying messages from the CNS to muscles (motor nerve cells).

While humans exert a large degree of control over their bodies through the CNS, many vital activities, such as heartbeat, peristalsis and functioning of the kidneys, are regulated by a secondary system of nerves called the autonomic nervous system (ANS). Many of the cell bodies of the ANS lie outside the brain and spinal cord and are massed together in bunches called ganglia, which receive information from receptors in the various organs of the body and then send out appropriate instructions to muscles, such as the heart, and glands, such as salivary glands. Activation of organs and mechanisms under the control of the ANS will affect levels of **arousal**, which are crucial to athletes.

The ANS is divided into two strata: the sympathetic system (more centrally located in the body and responsible for changes associated with arousal) and the parasympathetic system (more dispersed). The parasympathetic system constricts the pupils of the eyes, increases the **flow** of saliva, expands the small intestine and shrinks the large intestine; the sympathetic system has the opposite effect and is much slower. This is why bodily changes that occur after a sudden fright are rapid, but the process whereby they resume normal functioning is gradual.

The name 'autonomic nervous system' implies that it is independent and self-regulated, whereas in fact the centers that control ANS activity are in the lower portions of the brain and usually below the threshold of conscious control. In sports, the appeal of bringing ANS functions under conscious control is obvious: the potential, particularly in the areas of **relaxation**, recovery from **injury** and perhaps even **skill acquisition** (among others) is great.

Further reading

Wilmore, J.H. and Costill, D.L. (1999) *Physiology of Sport and Exercise*, 2nd edition, Champaign IL: Human Kinetics, part one.

NOMOTHETIC

From the Greek *nomos*, meaning laws, nomothetic theories or conceptual approaches strive for abstract knowledge that can be generalized across a range of phenomena. In effect, the knowledge generates laws that apply not simply to one situation, but to a great many.

Much of the output of sport psychology is oriented toward generating knowledge that is widely applicable. **Social facilitation** theory or **reversal theory** are examples. One famous inverted-U theory of **arousal** included *law* in its name (the **Yerkes–Dodson law**). Even theories that rely on the central role of **cognition** strive for enlightenment that is not confined to one particular case or even cluster of situations, but which may be used generally. Lisa Van Landuyt *et al.* warn against use of nomothetic models in sport psychology, arguing that, while they have 'intuitive appeal,' they 'provide poor accounts of the diversity encountered in real-life.' The contrasting approach is **idiographic**.

Further reading

Cashmore, E. and Mullan, B. (1983) *Approaching Social Theory* London: Heinemann Educational.

Van Landuyt, L.M., Ekkekakis, P., Hall, E.E. and Petruzzello, S.J. (2000) 'Throwing the mountains into the lakes: on the perils of nomothetic conceptions of the exercise–affect relationship,' *Journal of Sport & Exercise Psychology* vol. 22, pp. 208–34.

OBEDIENCE

Submitting to rules, norms, orders, commands, directions, prescriptions, mandates or any other kind of injunction is an act of obedience. In many respects the equivalent of compliance, obedience carries the additional implied meaning that the person behaving obediently does so without actually believing in or understanding what he or she is doing. They do it because they feel obliged to do so. The application in sports is transparent: athletes are frequently charged by coaches to perform tasks for which they see no purpose, logic or meaning. Sometimes they may violently disagree with coaches' or managers' instructions. Ideally, coaches or others with comparable responsibilities want athletes to agree with their operational decisions. In practice, methods must be found of exacting obedience, regardless of whether they agree or disagree. (The word is from the Latin *obedientia*.)

Interestingly, obedience is not as difficult to institute as common sense might suggest. Studies by Muzafir Sherif in the 1930s and, later, Solomon Asch showed how relatively easy it was to create conditions under which conformity to norms occurred. Sherif took subjects into a darkened room individually and asked them to make judgements about how far and in what direction a light was moving. The evaluations were wildly diverse. When the subjects were taken back in, this time in a group, the judgements converged, indicating that individuals tended to conform to the judgements of the group. Asch took the ambiguity out of the situation by making subjects decide which of several lines was longer. Although the correct answer was obvious, Asch planted subjects who had been instructed to give an obviously wrong answer, just to discover whether the genuine subjects would provide manifestly wrong answers. They did. Asch concluded that the forces to conform to others overpowered a person's ability to make simple sensory judgements. Dissenting from majority opinions was too much for Asch's subjects.

These and lesser-known studies highlighted the force of collectivities in influencing both the thought and the behavior of individuals, even in the face of often bizarre, conflicting evidence. Individuals were more comfortable when conforming to group norms than they were in challenging majority views. The study that brought out the more ominous implications of these findings was Stanley Milgram's *Obedience to Authority*. Inspired by Hannah Arendt's 1963 thesis on 'the banality of evil' – which raised the possibility that the atrocities of the Second World War were not brought about by 'monsters' but by ordinary people following orders – Milgram's experiments involved 'ordinary' people who were asked to perform extraordinary, cruel deeds.

Subjects were told they were being paid to participate in learning experiments: 'learners' were strapped into an electrically wired chair and had electrodes attached to their bodies. The subjects were told to test them and administer electric shocks when the learners got their answers wrong. Actually, the learners were 'insiders' and did not receive the shocks; they just reacted dramatically to convince the subjects that the situation was real. Milgram's important finding was that the so-called ordinary people were quite prepared to keep upping the electric shocks, even when the learners were thought to be in considerable **pain**. Each time the subject would object, a researcher would snap back: 'Please continue!' or 'You *must* go on.' Milgram found that 65 per cent of the subjects obeyed, progressing all the way to the maximum voltage of 450 volts. Subjects surrendered their autonomy to the experiment, believing it to be conducted in the spirit of 'science,' which in this case functioned as an overarching ideology. One presumes that the state and military imperatives function similarly in times of mass conflict, supplying the individual with a 'greater good' to justify immediate evils.

There are several mediating factors to consider when we consider the relevance of these findings to sports. The more direct the person's experience with the victim, the less the obedience. In other words, obedience is enhanced when there are several buffers. For example, a coach who tells a football player to try to injure a rival team's key player will have only a limited chance of getting his player to carry out the instruction: the player would have direct physical contact with the opponent and would witness firsthand the effects of the **injury**.

Also, the credibility of the communicator is vital: if players in a team doubt the wisdom of the coach or manager, they are unlikely to obey commands. If, on the other hand, they have implicit faith in the coach, they will follow instructions even if they do not know the reason for them. They may not even like the coach: they will obey as long as they believe that the coach's judgements can be trusted. This is why so many advertisers sign athletes to endorse their products: because consumers trust their judgement – they are credible. Another reason is that they identify with them. This too affects obedience. People often seek to identify with or be like people whom they like and admire, though they will not necessarily obey that person in defiance of their own principles (buying a sports drink or pizza is unlikely to raise inner conflicts). This may explain why coaches rarely seek to be liked, and in some cases seem to go out of their way to be disliked. Credibility is a more potent resource when trying to establish obedience among players.

A further factor is **attribution**: often in sports athletes interpret success and failure in terms of internal and external factors. In team sports especially, relinquishing a degree of personal **control** and judgement to an external source serves to protect **self-esteem**. A defeat can be explained as due to the coach's faulty tactics rather than the athlete's ability; while a success can be understood as a triumph for both the coach's tactics and the individual's ability to operationalize them perfectly. Obedience affords the individual athlete something of a shield.

Further reading

Asch, S. (1955) 'Opinions and social pressures,' *Scientific American* vol. 193, pp. 31–5.

Milgram, S. (1974) *Obedience to Authority: An experimental view* New York: Harper & Row.

Sherif, M. (1936) *The Psychology of Social Norms* New York: Harper & Row.

OBSESSION

From the Latin *obsessio* for haunt, beleaguer or surround, obsession is a condition under which ideas persist unreasonably in the consciousness of a subject. The inappropriateness of an obsession may not always be recognizable to the subject, and even if it is, the subject may either be unable or unwilling to address it. Sports or physical exercise is often talked of as an obsession and its devotees as obsessive, though this is only rarely the case. Yet there are instances of participants and fans who have been obsessed.

Health food or exercise 'junkies' is the colloquialism for those obsessed with physical fitness to the point where they structure their lives around its pursuit, eating obsessively and working out frequently to the point of **overtraining**. The term 'orthorexia nervosa' was coined in 2001 by Bratman and Knight to describe the condition of people overwhelmed by the 'obsession of healthy eating,' which is itself an **eating disorder**. Obsessive exercising may become a **dependency**: claims of persistent 'natural highs' presumably achieved through the secretion of **endorphins** often issue from gym habitués and incessant runners. While exercise habits rarely become 'pathological,' some have known to be disruptive of family relationships.

Sports **fandom** is a diverse collection of individuals, and occasionally followers of individual athletes have become obsessed to the point of stalking the object of their fixation. While many rock and movie stars have been involved in life-threatening situations, Monica Seles was stabbed by a devotee of Steffi Graf in 1993, and in 1991 a fan of multiple world snooker champion Stephen Hendry threatened to shoot him. The dividing line between fixated admirers and dangerous predators is a very fine one, as David Giles notes: 'The obsessive fan who camps on the star's doorstep has the potential to become either a murderer or a marriage partner.'

Further reading

Bratman, S. and Knight, D. (2001) *Health Food Junkies – Orthorexia Nervosa: Overcoming the obsession of healthy eating* New York: Bantam Doubleday Dell.
Giles, D. (2000) *Illusions of Immortality: A psychology of fame and celebrity* New York: St Martin's Press.

OPERANT CONDITIONING *see* **reinforcement**

OVERTRAINING

When the **intensity** and frequency of training exceeds the body's capacity to respond positively to it, overtraining occurs. Its symptoms, according to Julia Dalgleish and Stuart Dollerty include: tiredness, decreased immune system efficiency, nausea, excessive weight loss, aching joints and muscles, nausea, repetitive loading injuries (such as shin splints), reduction in bone density and an increased length of time to reach fitness goals (the 'plateau effect'). At least the first four of these symptoms may be described as psychophysiological in **character**, having both psychological and physical components.

Jonathan Metzler argues that overtraining is part of the training **stress** syndrome: 'Athletes who have training stress greater than their ability to adapt to that stress may experience a plateau or a decrease in performance.' For instance, competitors across a wide range of sports include weight training in their preparations. A 158lb rower may bench press 225lb one week and increase this to 235lb three weeks later. 'Initially, athletes also may observe increases in self-confidence and motivation to train; this may catalyze further increases in training stress imposed by the athletes themselves,' writes Metzler.

A combination of overenthusiasm and determination to improve produces more strenuous labors to maintain progress but, as anyone who has worked with weights has discovered, training gains do not accrue at a steady pace. The plateau arrives and the athlete experiences a type of law of diminishing returns, or even a law of non-existent returns: expenditures of effort beyond a certain point do not yield proportionate returns.

The experience leads to a decline in **motivation** and a corresponding drop in **confidence**; in other words, the athlete becomes *stale*. Metzler warns: 'Staleness should not be confused with being in a **slump**' (which happens when there is a decrease in performance). Among the adaptations available to athletes in a condition of staleness is to rest, change or to train even more. The final option produces overtraining and possibly even **burnout** among some athletes. Another maladaptive strategy is to consume less: **eating disorders** are common among athletes trying to combat staleness.

Dalgleish and Dollerty represent the process as a *dose–response curve*, each dose of training generating a positive response, but only up to a certain point. 'As the level of exercise becomes excessive the body fails to adapt positively to the stress placed on the body,' they observe. 'When this optimal level is exceeded, the risks overtake the benefits and overuse injuries and reduced immune system efficiency results in illness.'

Further reading

Dalgleish, J. and Dollerty, S. (2001) *The Health and Fitness Handbook* Harlow, England: Pearson Education.

Metzler, J. (2002) 'Applying motivational principles to individual athletes,' pp. 80–106 in Silva, J.M. and Stevens, D.E. (eds) *Psychological Foundations of Sport* Boston MA: Allyn & Bacon.

Raglin, J.S. and Wilson, G.S. (2000) 'Overtraining in athletes,' pp. 191–208 in Hanin, Y.L. (ed.) *Emotions in Sport* Champaign IL: Human Kinetics.

PAIN

From the Latin *poena*, for penalty, pain refers to suffering in its generic sense. While physical pain is cited most commonly, artists may suffer for their art, lovers may suffer for their loved ones and prisoners may suffer for their deeds or perhaps their conscience. In sports, pain most frequently refers to the physical feelings experienced because of **injury** or the sensation of crossing certain thresholds of endurance, i.e. the pain barrier. Fans sometimes talk of the painful experience of witnessing their team lose, though this metaphorical use is in jest (mostly).

Crossing the pain barrier relates to pain tolerance, and training for endurance events particularly is geared to instilling in an athlete the ability to tolerate pain for long periods. The pain in question is not chronic, of course, but it is a dispersed and persistent discomfort that distance runners especially have to assimilate. Tolerance to pain may have a biological component, but its variability and susceptibility to change indicate that it also has a significant psychological component. In training, athletes are implored to 'bite the bullet' or similar when approaching the pain threshold. Bodybuilders famously remind others of the 'no pain, no gain' principle. The Gracie dynasty of jiu-jitsu fighters prepared its members for contests by a type of pain inoculation, inducing pain in training so as to safeguard against it during **competition**.

Summarizing the various types of **intervention** used, Anshel observes: 'Elite athletes tend to use one of two mental techniques in coping with physical discomfort, *association* and *dissociation*.' The **goal** of the first is to remain 'in touch with one's body' and maintain the necessary **motivation** to meet challenges: weight lifters 'associate with' their muscles as they lift; runners concentrate on planting their feet with each stride. This strategy can backfire if the athlete's **concentration** wavers and he or she begins focusing on the area of pain rather than the bodily functions that enhance performance. Dissociation entails externalizing or projecting feelings and sensations outward to surrounding events rather than inward to internal experiences.

Further reading

Anshel, M.H. (1997) *Sport Psychology: From theory to practice*, 3rd edition, Scottsdale AZ: Gorsuch Scarisbrick.
Rushall, B.S. (1979) *Psyching in Sport* London: Pelham Books.

PARENTING

From the Latin *parere*, to bring forth, parenting is the entire process of giving birth to, feeding, nurturing, providing a secure environment for and facilitating the growth and maturation of offspring. Its meaning in the context of sports has an accent. As well as nourishing children's physical, intellectual and **emotional** development, parenting involves encouraging the young's athletic progress in a variety of ways, some of which may ultimately prove detrimental. For every Richard Williams or Earl Woods – both of whom urged, supported and prepared their children for abundantly successful sports careers – there are countless other parents whose pushiness and overbearing zeal have been ruinous for their children.

Parents are key figures in a child's **socialization**, of course. In the primary socializing phase, they present a child with uniquely influential agents for **modeling** language, behavior and, later, values. The child's integration as a member of society and sense of distinct personal **identity** are accomplished while in the custody of parents. Styles of parenting are predictably diverse: *authoritarian* families uphold **discipline** and restrict a child's autonomy, while, at the other end of the continuum, *complex* families permit or even facilitate more individuality and spontaneity. There are also degrees of involvement. Some parents tend to be deeply involved in their children's sports or other pursuits, while others prefer to steer clear, allowing complete independence.

Reviewing the copious literature on parents' involvement in their children's sport, Woolgar and Power in 1993 identified three criteria. The first is support, whether emotional (such as providing comfort in times of **stress**), informational (dispensing technical advice) or tangible (money for equipment, traveling, etc.). Striking the right balance is crucial to the child's experience in sport. The second is modeling, which is one of the potential sources of **self-efficacy**: vicarious and actual **reinforcement** (like watching fathers or mothers perform tasks successfully, imitating them and then being rewarded). The third is expectations, which are the most problematic feature of parents' involvement with their children in the context of sports. If parents' expectations are too high or too low, children can become either demoralized or indifferent: to be conducive to a child's continued involvement in sport, expectations have to be congruent with children's abilities.

Parenting in sports has led to too many stories of premature **burnout**, emotional vacuums and **deviance** to be treated as anything but dubious. Often the motives of parents are open to doubt. One of the most graphic illustrations of this is in the 1995 documentary *Hoop Dreams*, in which the central characters are effectively beasts of burden, freighting not only personal ambitions but also those of their parents. Echoes of this were to be found in the relationship between former heavyweight champion Joe Frazier and his son Marvis, a fighter far less redoubtable than his father, who suffered a torrid and punishing professional career.

The previously mentioned Richard Williams was not a sportsman, but pushed his daughters Venus and Serena into tennis at an early age and encouraged them to follow a strict training regime. His authoritarian approach stemmed from his own experiences as a boy in Louisiana, where he was racially abused (he and his mother were made to flee to Compton, Los Angeles). The rationale behind his maneuvers was to prevent his daughters from enduring similar experiences. By contrast, Earl Woods believed he was acting out a divine plan when he propelled his son Eldrick into golf. 'The Almighty entrusted this precocious child to me,' wrote Earl in his book *Training a Tiger: A father's guide to raising a winner in both golf and life*. Interestingly, black athletes generally were more likely to receive support and encouragement from peers, coaches and teachers rather than parents, according to research by Harris in 1994.

'Sports parents' are often criticized for pursuing **vicarious achievement**: transposing their ambitions on to their children, becoming over-protective and, occasionally, even tyrannical in efforts to shelter their children. Damir Dokic, father of Jelena, exemplified this: confrontations with journalists, tournament officials and coaches were commonplace as the custodial Dokic followed his daughter around the pro tennis circuit. His sometimes boorish behavior earned him a six-month ban from the WTA, and in 2000 he prevented Jelena from competing for Australia, where the family had lived since 1994. While his presence was considered pernicious by the world's media, Jelena defiantly maintained it was beneficial: 'It makes a difference when you have someone out there who works with you all the time, someone you've had with you your whole life.' The example serves to demonstrate that parental influences cannot always be judged from an outsider's perspective. Mary Pierce and, to a lesser extent, Steffi Graf had parents known for their misdemeanors, yet both remained loyal and enjoyed successful sports careers. The role of parents in shaping children's **achievement motivation, cognition** and self-efficacy has been confirmed by Brustad's research.

There is also a **gender** issue to consider: a study by Colley *et al.* in 1992 found that having parents active in and enthusiastic about sports was an important factor in young females' involvement in sport (before and after adolescence) but not with young males. Another study (by Jacobs and Eccles, 1992) concluded that mothers' 'gender-role stereotypic beliefs' were likely to affect their children's chances of participating in sports.

The question is: should parenting be evaluated on the degree of success or the quality of the sporting experience, or does one go with the other? Power and Woolgar's 1994 research indicated that children who reported most enthusiasm (for swimming, in this study) had parents with only moderate levels of 'directiveness' and performance outcome goals. More concretely, Mark Anshel in his *Sport Psychology: From theory to practice* asserts that, for young athletes: 'Winning is among the least important reasons for participating.'

On the other hand, self-efficacy is considered a welcome outcome of sports participation and achievement is one of the factors that encourage this. According to some research on tennis by Leff and Hoyle in 1995, the association between parental support or even pressure and involvement in achievement-oriented activities, enjoyment of such activities and enhanced self-perception is strong and valuable.

Further reading

Colley, A., Eglinton, E. and Elliott, E. (1992) 'Sport participation in middle childhood: association with styles of play and parental participation,' *International Journal of Sport Psychology* vol. 23, pp. 193–206.

Côté, J. and Hay, J. (2002) 'Family influences on youth sport performance and participation,' pp. 503–19 in Silva, J.M. and Stevens, D.E. (eds) *Psychological Foundations of Sport* Boston MA: Allyn & Bacon.

Woolgar, C. and Power, T.G. (1993) 'Parent and sport socialization: views from the achievement literature,' *Journal of Sport Behavior* vol. 16, pp. 171–89.

PARTICIPATION MOTIVATION

Participation motivation is the collective term given to the explanations of children for being involved with or withdrawing from sports. Studies in participation motivation typically use a self-report approach, inviting young people to address the reasons why they became interested in, continued in or left sports. The focus is on the personal dispositions of the subjects rather than on external factors that may affect **motivation** and **commitment**.

Reasons typically given for participating include: achievement; challenge; companionship; fun; health and fitness; **skill acquisition** and motives associated with a task **goal orientation** and intrinsic motivation. Summarizing the ample research on this subject, Weiss and Chaumeton conclude that certain reasons, such as fun, **competition** and fitness crop up consistently, regardless of children's ages, **sex** or experience. Later studies, reported by Diane Gill, offered a more complicated scenario with differences related to **gender**, age, parents' education and geographic region: 'the relevance of motivational dimensions varies according to sociocultural and geographic factors.'

Further reading

Gill, D.L. (2000) *Psychological Dynamics of Sport and Exercise*, 2nd edition, Champaign IL: Human Kinetics.

Weiss, M.R. and Chaumeton, N. (1992) 'Motivational orientations in sport,' in Horn, T.S. (ed.) *Advances in Sport Psychology* Champaign IL: Human Kinetics.

PEAK PERFORMANCE

A peak performance is one of the highest value or quality, the word 'peak' probably being a variation on the Middle English *pike*, meaning the top of a hill or a wooden shaft with a pointed metal head. Athletes are often said to be 'hitting a peak,' or 'peaking,' of course. The inference is the same: a maximum level feat. A peak performance more usually describes a feat that is *experienced* as maximal, even though objectively it may not be at or even near the athlete's best effort in quantifiable terms.

Abraham Maslow used the term 'peak experience' to describe a moment in people's lives when they feel in harmony with all things about them and momentarily lose track of time and space. Similarly, Karen Lee Hill states that 'the importance of other people to the outcome of the [peak] transaction is relegated to the background of the athlete's attention.' So outside evaluations, measurable or otherwise, are not important; experience is. While there is often congruence between feelings of peaking and actually peaking objectively, there is no necessary relationship. Athletes have been known to report a peak subjective performance, even though their measurable performance was not their best (and vice versa: athletes often reflect on how they did not feel themselves to be playing well, when observers considered them to be performing at or near a peak).

By definition, peaking in sport is not an everyday occurrence, nor is it long-lasting. While athletes and coaches work sedulously at 'peaking at the right time,' there is no formula for achieving a peak: preparation can only establish the conditions under which peaking is both possible and probable; it cannot guarantee it. In fact, if the work of Kenneth Ravizza is to be accepted, once the conditions are established, the athletes 'must surrender the usual thinking–evaluating self to the experience.'

Ravizza's interpretation of peaking is a highly subjective one and accentuates the 'intrinsic satisfaction' rather than the objective referents. But the conditions he stipulates seem applicable to both senses: **centering**, focusing, narrowing **attention**, 'being totally in-volved in the task at hand' and losing **fear**. These appear to be conducive to producing exceptional performances in an objective way. Anshel adds to the desirable conditions: 'feelings of being in an envelope'; states of physical and mental **relaxation**; an acute awareness of one's body; **confidence**; and encouraging 'no sense of imposing **control**,' i.e. **automaticity**. These, he suggests, form a 'mental game checklist' which is 'very helpful in preparing the athlete for **com-petition**.' These are culled from the subjective reports of athletes after feelings of peak performance. Anshel's checklist is an instrument designed to replicate them in other athletes.

Discussions of peaking and how to fulfill it are intricately meshed with studies of **flow**, staying **focused** and being in the **zone** – each of which, in some way, involves subjects in a peak performance.

Further reading

Anshel, M.H. (1997) *Sport Psychology: From theory to practice*, 3rd edition, Scottsdale AZ: Gorsuch Scarisbrick.

Hill, K.L. (2001) *Frameworks for Sport Psychologists* Champaign IL: Human Kinetics.

Ravizza, K. (1984) 'Qualities of the peak experience in sport,' pp. 452–61 in Silva, J.M. and Weinberg, R.S. (eds) *Psychological Foundations of Sport* Champaign IL: Human Kinetics.

PERCEPTION

Perception refers to the processes by which we apprehend or become aware of objects, qualities or other items of sensory input and organize them into coherent units of experience. This is an inclusive definition of a term that stems from the Latin *perceptio*: it covers the entire series of actions, from the physical presentation of stimulus to the subjective sensations. Although sensory content is always present in perceptual processes, perception is not a passive or automatic process in which **stimuli** impress themselves on consciousness: it is an active operation in which **memory**, expectations and surroundings are influences.

This can be illustrated by the way we perceive distance or depth perception. Stereoscopic vision is the term to describe how each of our eyes picks up slightly different information. The eyes work to compare the images and the slight lack of correspondence between them produces an experience of distance and depth. But several studies have indicated that such perception is not innate in humans and probably not in other animals: perception can be modified by experience, a phenomenon known as perceptual plasticity.

Research on previously blind people who, having had their sight restored, had initial difficulty in their perception of distance, length and color, showed that only over time were they able to perceive 'normally.' In another case, a member of an Equatorial African tribe, who had lived most of his life amid trees and foliage, when taken into open country mistook a distant herd of buffalo for insects and a boat some way offshore as a piece of wood. Again, it took time before normal perceptual functioning occurred. The point is that perception is learned through experience, at first through **socialization** and, later, through training.

Athletes train in perception, particularly depth perception. A bowler in cricket or a baseball pitcher needs an acute perception of depth to be able to deliver accurately and consistently. Fielders in both games need perception of distance and motion to be able to retrieve balls and return them without hesitation. Once struck by the bat, the ball appears as a tiny speck traveling through space: to field it successfully, a player needs to judge its variable distance, its speed and its likely direction. In this sense, perception is a **skill** and is refined by much the same processes as other skills. As in any sport, perceptual cues in the environment are used; this is especially intricate in fielding because of the lack of physical coordinates as the ball moves at great speed through space and the player is looking upwards.

In such situations, the size of the retinal image (the image of the visual scene formed on the retina at the back of the eye) depends on the distance between the eye and the ball. Of course, the perceived size does not vary markedly: the ball does not suddenly appear to be the size of a meteor. While the retinal image may grow, the player's actual experience (the phenomenology) of it does not. This *perceptual constancy*, as it is called, occurs not only for size, but also for shape, color, brightness, etc. So a cricket ball or a baseball does not appear to the players to change color as the darkness falls and floodlights are switched on, even though the stimulation reaching the retina is different. The perceptual world remains stable, especially to athletes who must judge distance, trajectory and so on in markedly different environmental conditions. The stability is a result of the fact that most of our percepts (objects of perception) are *overdetermined*, meaning that visual, auditory and tactile and other types of cues about the environment mutually reinforce each other, yielding information that provides a consistent representation of the world.

Not all perception is immediately apparent. Subliminal perception (from *sub*, beneath, and *limen*, threshold) involves a stimulus of very short duration that can be shown to have been perceived without conscious awareness. So it is possible to perceive an image, sound or any other kind of information from the environment without actually being aware of it. Fears about the misuses of this by, for instance, advertisers and politicians (to manipulate tastes and change opinions) have been largely unfounded.

Further reading

Banks, W.P. and Krajicek, D. (1991) 'Perception,' *Annual Review of Psychology* vol. 42, pp. 305–31.

Turnbull, C.M. (1961) 'Some observations regarding the experiences and behavior of the Ba Mbuti pygmies,' *American Journal of Psychology* vol. 74, pp. 304–8.

PERFORMANCE ENHANCEMENT

While the term 'performance enhancement' has migrated into popular usage as a synonym for **doping**, it actually refers to any method, legal or illegal, of heightening, intensifying or exaggerating the qualities or value of an athlete's performance (the word 'enhance' is from the Old French *enhaucier,* which may be distantly related to *altus,* Latin for high). To be pedantic, a more accurate term would be 'training enhancement' because most aids are ergonomic in effect: they help athletes work more efficiently in their environments. Most performance enhancers enable an athlete to train harder and longer.

The competitive performance is the ultimate demonstration of value, of course; but, in several respects, this reflects the quality and perhaps quantity of training accomplished by an athlete prior to a contest. Performance enhancement is a process that begins long before an actual **competition**. Many athletes favor **autogenic** and related forms of progressive **relaxation**, including **hypnotism**. **Applied sport psychology** is a resource used widely by athletes. It could even be argued that believing in God is a type of performance enhancement: after all, a devotee of a **religion** who believes he or she is being guided toward victory by an omniscient being enjoys a competitive edge!

Certainly, ergonomically designed apparel is a form of performance enhancement. Aerodynamic body suits have been worn legally by many runners, as have swimming outfits made from a synthetic fiber modeled on sharkskin (which has striations to allow rivulets of water to run across it); and, of course, running shoes with air-inflated modules in their soles have been used since Nike launched its 'Tailwind' in 1978.

Less obviously, it could be argued that contact lenses or even eyeglasses enhance performance. The user who has less than 20/20 vision would not be able to perform as efficiently without them. While this is not seen as conferring an unfair advantage on the wearer of lenses or spectacles, some might argue that there is a difference of degree rather than kind between this kind of aid and the taking of painkillers to ease **injury**.

While it stretches the point unreasonably, training itself is performance enhancement, and a form which at times during the nineteenth century, just before the rise of organized sport, would have been considered tantamount to cheating. It suggested the athlete was trying to procure an advantage over those who chose not to train.

Further reading

Cashmore, E. (2000) *Making Sense of Sports*, 3rd edition, London: Routledge.

PERSONALITY

The singular, unique and distinguishing **character** of a sentient being is its personality. Beyond this most rudimentary definition, there is no agreement on what constitutes a personality, what purposes it serves, what consequences it has and, indeed, whether it exists at all. Against this absolute lack of accord on a definition, it is impossible to draw a coherent statement on the question of what impact personality has on sports. Are certain personality types attracted to sports? Do some personalities excel at sports? Will some personality types inevitably fail? An approach to these and related questions is to consider how the term 'personality' has been conceptualized in various theories. These theories cluster into four main groups: psychodynamic; trait; behaviorist; and constructivist.

Psychodynamic theories of personality derive from the classic work of Freud and Jung and have been refined by the likes of Adler, Fromm, Horney and Laing, among many others. Fundamental differences forbid a neat summary, though there is agreement on the existence of an entity called the personality that develops over time and is significantly affected by childhood experiences. Conflicts below the threshold of consciousness are a considerable motivating force in psychological development and how the individual deals with such conflicts contributes toward the integration of the distinct personality. In a sense, the way we repress, displace or in other ways adapt to opposing desires and controls shapes the personality.

Assumptions about the existence of a personality structure (id, ego and superego) were anathema to later psychologists who insisted on studying only observable phenomena. Trait theorists, in particular, concentrated on how personality is expressed through behavior. Stable patterns observed over time revealed consistent properties, or traits, that collectively provided a picture of an individual's personality. The guiding idea behind the trait approach was to formulate a matrix of identifiable personality factors. Hans Eysenck's theory of universal personality types exemplifies this: according to Eysenck, everyone can be located somewhere on his schema, which includes the now-famous introvert–extravert dimensions. Eysenck's theory is firmly in the hereditarian tradition in that personality traits are inherited rather than produced through social exchange.

Both these theories hypothesized that there was an entity called a personality, something that affected the way subjects thought and behaved; it was a permanent feature of a person's psychological makeup. By contrast, other theoretical approaches either cast doubt on the existence of a personality or regarded it as a protean concept, changing constantly to suit different environments.

Behaviorists, in particular, spurned any reference to what they regarded as an obscure internal entity, the existence of which could only be inferred from observable behavior. Consistent patterns of behavior, tendencies and tastes were the outcome of contingencies of **reinforcement**. In other words, the environment determines who we are and what we become. There are variations on this, one being that we are originally *tabula rasa*, blank tablets on which experience is inscribed. In this view, humans have a largely passive role. 'Softer' versions of the approach assign a greater role for **cognition**: human beings, unlike other creatures, can actively select **stimuli** in their environments and choose how they will respond to them.

The behaviorist approach broke from the conventional wisdom that personality originates in individuals and remains with them, in some form, for life. Constructivist approaches accepted the emphasis on environment or context, but explored the pivotal role of social interaction. Our personality, or, more accurately, personalities (we may have several) are constructed through day-to-day, moment-to-moment exchanges with others, who function as audiences. The subject is an actor, envisioning herself as she (we will assume it's a female) imagines others see her and adjusting her language and behavior in such a way as to pull off a successful impression. This impression management is made possible by a 'reciprocity of perspectives': humans constantly try to see themselves not only as others see them, but also as others see them imagining how they see them. This is what we mean when we refer to self-awareness – not just an awareness of ourselves, but of how others are seeing and thinking about us. Personality, in this theory, is not a fixed entity but a process that is forever being negotiated between the subject and the people she mixes with (her audience).

Even this extremely brief and undeveloped summary of the main theoretical groups suggests profound differences in the concept of personality. The differences militate against any conclusions on whether it has an effect on recruitment, involvement and performance in sports. If personality is a relatively permanent entity that produces certain patterns of thought and behavior, then there is a possibility that it affects participation in sports. Heather Deaner and John Silva, who have tried to disentangle the theories in their essay 'Personality and sport performance,' dismiss many of the mooted relationships, including 'the idea that certain individuals are born with psychological characteristics that predispose them to select into certain sports.'

Deaner and Silva consider a number of other theories, including Silva's own 'Personality and performance pyramid' that proposes that all sorts of personality types enter sport. But as athletes move up the pyramid toward elite levels, only those with 'adaptive personality characteristics' advance. Physical abilities are more evenly matched at higher levels, so personality becomes significant. The authors argue that those athletes with patience, **emotional** control and **confidence** are better able to make the transition upwards because their personalities equip them well when making adjustments, even after setbacks. Athletes who clearly lack patience as well as **control** but still make it to the top are exceptions, according to Deaner and Silva. This theory as well as several others is based on mapping features of personalities. The 'iceberg profile,' for example, predicts that athletes who have low scores on tension, depression, **anger**, fatigue and confusion but a high score on vigor are likely to be successful. The premise of both theories is the trait model of personality.

A judgement that research on the mooted link between personality and performance is 'inconclusive' is not surprising. There is so little agreement on what personality actually is that it would be astonishing if any link could be found. While the trait theory is serviceable and lends itself to research on personality and performance, a constructivist account would contend that the personality is actually in a process of construction during an athlete's career in sports and that, far from being a fixed entity, the personality is a negotiated process that continues through a career and beyond. Such is the disparity between conceptions of personality. Inadequate as it seems, the only safe and credible conclusion is: sports attract a diversity of personalities, and while those that ascend to elite levels may exhibit certain consistent features, or traits, it remains uncertain whether they possessed them at early stages or acquired them as they progressed.

Further readings

Deaner, H. and Silva, J.M. (2002) 'Personality and sport performance,' pp. 48–65 in Silva, J.M. and Stevens, D.E. (eds) *Psychological Foundations of Sport* Boston MA: Allyn & Bacon.

Hampson, S. (1996) 'The construction of personality,' pp. 602–21 in Colman, A.M. (ed.) (1996) *Companion Encyclopedia of Psychology*, vol. 2, London: Routledge.

PERSONALITY ASSESSMENT

While there is historical and contemporary debate about what exactly constitutes a **personality**, attempts have been made to appraise, evaluate and measure this elusive concept by means of instruments known collectively as personality assessment. Although it is often assumed that top athletes have the right personality for success while lesser ones do not, personality assessments have proved poor indicators of athletic performance.

Many personality assessments are based on an **inventory**: a list of items to which the subject is asked to respond by indicating those that apply to him or herself, for example, 'yes,' 'no,' 'questionable.' Or the subject is presented with two pairs of statements and invited to choose which one best applies to him or her. Likert Scale testing involves asking subjects to reply to statements, usually with choices such 'agree,' 'uncertain,' 'strongly disagree' and so on.

First used in 1942, the Minnesota Multiphasic Personality Inventory became one of the most popular personality assessments, consisting originally of 550 statements about feelings and behavior. Subjects were asked to indicate the ones with which they agreed/ disagreed. Several different scales, each designed to assess different personality facets were spawned from the original test. The Cattell Sixteen Personality Factor Questionnaire (16PF) used a factor analysis that facilitated the identification of the sixteen 'first order' factors of personality. From these 'second order' or surface traits could be traced: these included **anxiety**, independence and several other traits that appeared to be important to success in sports.

This approach was adapted for sports: the Athletic Motivation Inventory attempted to measure personality traits associated with sports performance. **Aggression**, **drive**, **leadership**, **emotional control** and **mental toughness** were among the traits used in the instrument, though the results were inconclusive, underscoring the fact that, if there is a cluster of personality traits linked to success in sports, a way of discovering them has not yet been found.

'Sport personology' is the term used by Morgan to characterize the search for a personality that provides a predictor of athletic performance. There is a fundamental disagreement between those who continue the search and those who believe it is futile. Many contemporary researchers take the middle ground, accepting that evidence from personality assessment reveals that there are certain personality features shared by successful athletes. But these cannot be used to identify those who will ultimately become successful because personality is only one of a great many factors that contribute to athletic success.

Further reading

Morgan, W.P. (1980) 'Sport personology: the credulous–skeptical argument in perspective,' pp. 330–9 in Straub, W.F. (ed.) *Sport Psychology: An analysis of athlete behavior*, 2nd edition, Ithaca NY: Mouvement.
Tutko, T.A. and Richards, J.W. (1972) *Coaches' Practical Guide to Athletic Motivation* Boston MA: Allyn & Bacon.

POISE *see* **composure**

PREMACK PRINCIPLE

In the 1950s, David Premack advanced a proposition that **reinforcement** is relative, not absolute: it became known as the Premack principle. While reinforcers were conventionally regarded as **stimuli** which, when presented, strengthened the preceding response, Premack postulated that it was more helpful to conceptualize reinforcers as the responses or activities themselves. So, for example, a British soccer player may be contracted to receive a cash bonus of £1,500 per **goal** (not an uncommon arrangement): it is not the cash **incentive** (a stimulus) that reinforces the player's scoring of goals, but the spending of the money (an activity). Any activity a human (or for that matter any organism) performs can reinforce any other activity the organism engages in less frequently.

Premack arrived at his conclusions after an experiment in which he offered children the choice of operating a pinball machine or eating candy. The children who liked candy increased their rate of operating the pinball machine if playing the machine led to eating candy. So eating candy reinforced playing the machine: one behavior reinforced the other. But the children who preferred playing pinball to eating candy ate more candy only if this enhanced their chances of playing pinball.

Among Premack's conclusions was that there was a hierarchy of reinforcement and, for any given subject, any activity in the hierarchy may be reinforced (i.e. made more probable) by any activity above it and may *itself* reinforce any activity below it. Parents intuitively, and perhaps unwittingly, subscribe to the principle when they allow their children to play computer games or watch videos, but only after they have completed homework.

The hierarchy is not static. Premack discovered that the children who liked playing pinball more than eating candy eventually became hungry, at which point the 'reinforcement relation' reversed itself. Eating candy reinforced playing pinball. Another experiment involved rats: food reinforced running for a hungry rat, but running reinforced eating if the rats were fully fed, but had been locked up and unable to run around for a long time. Our soccer player may eventually become so wealthy that he becomes like the satiated rat; but his scoring rate tails off (!), causing his pride to suffer. The example is strained, but he might seek the private counsel of a professional yogi with expensive fees to help him rediscover the goal touch. Scoring goals would then reinforce spending money.

Further reading

Premack, D. (1959) 'Toward empirical behavior laws: I. Positive reinforcement,' *Psychological Review* vol. 66, pp. 219–33.
Premack, D. (1962) 'Reversibility of the reinforcement relation,' *Science* vol. 136, pp. 255–7.

PROFILE

A psychological profile is a figurative representation of a person or thing constructed by selecting salient characteristics and integrating these into a coherent image that may guide inquiry and understanding (the origins of the term are obscure, but may lie in the Italian *profilare*, to draw in outline). The process of construction which is called profiling was popularized by films such as Michael Mann's *Manhunter* and Jonathan Demme's *The Silence of the Lambs*, both of which featured psychological profilers assisting police investigations in detecting killers by building a conceptual picture of the killer.

The purpose of profiling in sports is less dramatic: it builds a metaphorical sketch of an athlete based on his or her physical, technical, tactical and psychological competencies and moods and applies this in several ways, all designed to enhance performance. Profiles have been used to interesting effect in the assessment of **emotion**. For example the Profile of Mood States (POMS) was used to build a representation of an athlete's **emotional** state just prior to **competition**. The subject would be asked to describe his or her state in terms of: tension, **depression**, **anger**, vigor, fatigue and confusion.

In one of the more successful applications of **personality assessment** research, W.P. Morgan used POMS with Olympic wrestlers and found members typically exhibited an *iceberg profile*: they tended to score highly on vigor, lower on anger and fatigue and much lower on tension, depression and confusion. Expressed graphically, with the states defining a horizontal axis, an iceberg shape surfaces. Aspiring or less proficient athletes would probably show other variations, such as having too much tension or too little vigor. Profiles help establish a representation of an optimal set of states, moods or properties. From this, deviations can be measured to assess how far individuals need to change before they approach the desired profile.

Further reading

McNair, D.M., Lorr, M. and Droppleman, L.F. (1992) *Profile of Mood States Manual* San Diego CA: Educational and Industrial Testing Services.

Morgan, W.P. (1979) 'Prediction of performance in athletics,' pp. 173–86 in Klavora, P. and Daniels, J.V. (eds) *Coach, Athlete and the Sport Psychologist* Champaign IL: Human Kinetics.

PSYCHING

Seeking to gain an advantage by either overawing, discouraging or intimidating an opponent prior to a **competition** by fair (if occasionally disputable) means, *or* by rousing oneself, has become known as 'psyching.' The expression came into popular use during the 1970s when the application of psychology to sports was being discussed in scholarly and practical circles. Psyching emphasized the importance of mental as well as physical preparation in gaining an edge, however slight, either through initiating **anxiety** in one's opponent – psyching *out* – or heightening one's own **arousal** to an optimum state – psyching *up*.

Some athletes had intuitively used psyching techniques for years before: Sonny Liston, for example, pioneered a method of psyching out opponents by staring them down during pre-fight preliminaries. Liston's famous **eyeballing** virtually challenged opponents to glare back or, as was often the case, avert their gaze. Even Muhammad Ali, who took the world title away from Liston in 1964 and gave the impression of being brash, later admitted: 'Just before the fight, when the referee was giving us instructions, Liston was giving me that stare. And I won't lie; I was scared.'

Vince Lombardi ruled his formidable Green Bay Packers team of the 1960s with a rod of iron: his strict disciplinarian approach completely subordinated players to his command. While his domineering style may not have met success in later years, Lombardi's quasi-military system was perfect for his time. Today, a Lombardi-style approach would be considered somewhat crude: coaches run the **risk** of making athletes anxious by 'pumping' (or hyping) them up. Psyching an athlete for an event frequently involves allaying anxiety by downplaying the seriousness of an occasion or the importance of the winning rather than the opposite. In other words, **relaxation** is as much a part of psyching up as arousal.

Perhaps the finest example of a psyching strategy that backfired was that of Butch Lewis, manager of boxer Michael Spinks, who in 1988 prepared to fight Mike Tyson. As is customary in world title matchups, a representative of the opponent is permitted to watch as a fighter bandages his hands. In his book *Tyson*, Peter Heller recounts how Lewis noticed a lump in Tyson's bandage and insisted the whole hand be unwrapped and re-bandaged. It was a tactic Lewis believed would irritate Tyson and gain an advantage for Spinks. Instead, Tyson grew furious. After Lewis left the locker room, Tyson promised 'I'm gonna hurt this guy.' He did: with barely controlled **anger**, Tyson dismantled his opponent in only 91 seconds.

Further reading

Hauser, T. (1997) *Muhammad Ali: His life and times* London: Pan Books.
Heller, P. (1990) *Tyson* London: Pan Books.
Tosches, N. (2000) *Night Train: The Sonny Liston story* London: Hamish Hamilton.
Wells, R. (1997) *Lombardi: His life and times* Madison WI: Prairie Oak Press.

PSYCHOLOGICAL MOMENTUM *see* **momentum**

PSYCHOLOGICAL SKILLS INVENTORIES

Instruments designed to measure the psychological expertise associated with sports are psychological skills inventories, an **inventory** being a detailed list of properties (from *inventorium*, Latin for things discovered). As the name suggests, the skills to be discovered are not, for example, deftness, footwork, timing, etc., but **achievement motivation**, **control**, **concentration**, **motivation**, team orientation and so on.

Many of the inventories measure how well athletes cope with **anxiety** and **stress**, while others assess receptivity to coaching advice and ability to fit into a coherent team structure (i.e. becoming a **team player** rather than remaining an individual). Among the most discussed are Mahoney *et al.*'s Psychological Skills Inventory for Sports, Smith *et al.*'s Athletic Coping Skills Inventory and Thomas *et al.*'s Test of Performance Strategies (TOPS). TOPS was one of the most ambitious instruments that assessed athletes in **competition** as well as in training. The eight factors that measured psychological behavior during practice were: activation, attentional **control, automaticity, emotional** control, **goal setting, imagery, relaxation** and **self-talk**. More specific measures include the Sport Competition Anxiety Test, which, as its name suggests, was devised to measure the tendencies to become anxious during competition.

As with other forms of **skill**, psychological skills can be studied and learned and athletes can become adept at **intervention** techniques that help them adjust levels of **arousal** and use imagery and **gating** procedures.

Further reading

Mahoney, M.J., Gabriel, T.J. and Perkins, T.S. (1987) 'Psychological skills and exceptional athletic performance,' *The Sport Psychologist* vol. 1, pp. 181–99.

Smith, R.E., Schultz, R.W., Smoll, F.L. and Ptacek, J.T. (1995) 'Development and validation of a multidimensional measure of sport specific psychological skills: the athletic coping skills inventory – 28,' *Journal of Sport & Exercise Psychology* vol. 17, pp. 379–98.

Thomas, P.R., Hardy, L. and Murphy, S. (1996) 'Development of a comprehensive test of psychological skills for practice and performance,' *Journal of Applied Sport Psychology* vol. 8, supplement S119.

RACE

Once accepted as an objective biological category, the concept of race, or 'race' as many prefer (quotation marks denoting its indefinite status), is now usually considered as a belief held by those who consider the world's human population divisible into discrete, natural units. The units are known as 'races' and the inference is that these units are ordered hierarchically, some 'races' occupying a position of pre-eminence over others – such a belief and the action it precipitates is racism. This is a definition that avoids the controversies over the ontology of race: accepted by some as a fact and rejected by others as a fiction, the concept has engaged scholars and politicians for decades, even centuries. (The origins of 'race' in this sense are unclear, but are not the same as those of race in the sense of **competition**; this is from the Old English *ræs*, for running.)

One thing is certain: that the belief in race has been one of the great motivating and bedeviling doctrines of modern times. 'We do not define races because biological data compels us so to do,' writes Kenan Malik in his *The Meaning of Race: Race, history and culture in western societies*. 'Rather, society begins with a prior division of humanity into different races for which it subsequently finds a rationale in certain physical characteristics.' In sports, as well as elsewhere, beliefs about the existence and effects of races and the guiding rationale behind such beliefs have precipitated debates and conflicts.

In an essay published in 1973 to introduce his edited volume *Psychology and Race*, Peter Watson identified two central areas of interest to the psychologist: (1) prejudiced attitudes and discriminatory behavior; (2) **intelligence** and race. Thirty years on, and the fundamental questions remain. Why does racism persist in a context where it is discouraged and condemned? Are some populations designated races endowed naturally with less intelligence than others? Both questions have relevance in sports. Stanley Eitzen adds a third: 'Does sport reduce or exacerbate racial tensions?'

Psychology, sociology, political science and the panoply of other disciplines that have tried to answer why prejudice exists have concluded that it is learned through childhood **socialization** and peer group interaction, which are in turn influenced by the overall social context. Some arguments suggest that, as a species, we are predisposed to discriminate, if only for purposes of adaptive survival. Exactly *how* we discriminate, for example because of skin color or other phenotypical (observable) characteristics, is learned, often from an early age. This may be reinforced if we move in circles that prevent or limit actual experience of groups/things that are the object of prejudice. Remember, the word 'prejudice' means literally that: a judgement made before ('pre') experience.

Debates over whether intelligence is inherited rather than learned have a history that dates back to the early twentieth century. In the 1960s and 1970s, the research of Arthur Jensen (1969) in the USA and Hans Eysenck (1971) in Britain linked this to race by asserting that 'Negroes' scored less well than whites in IQ tests and that this was due primarily to genetic, rather than social, factors. The argument gained fresh impetus in the 1990s with the publication of Herrnstein and Murray's *The Bell Curve: Intelligence and class structure in American life*.

Both these issues were reflected in sports. Arguments about 'stacking,' or allocating certain ethnic minorities to particular playing positions, came to the fore in the 1970s. It was argued by many that teachers, coaches, administrators and other, mainly white, groups assigned black players to playing positions that required speed and power rather than tact and ingenuity. Basing evaluations on stereotypes (images based on false or incomplete information) rather than firsthand knowledge, those responsible for **decision making** would 'ghettoize' African Americans and Britain's African Caribbeans on the sports field.

A justification for this was the 'natural ability' argument: black people had for long been known to possess sporting prowess and its source was presumed to be natural. The symmetry between this and the race–IQ argument is readily apparent. As Marek Kohn writes: 'One consequence of admitting that human groups may have significant bodily differences … is that it implies the possibility of differences in the brain.' The assumptions underlying this argument were racist: they were based on the premise that races existed and that some races were naturally suited to some tasks rather than others.

John Hoberman's book *Darwin's Athletes* bears the subtitle *How sport has damaged black America and preserved the myth of race*: in it, he unravels the racist logic that maintains that blacks are natural athletes. He also shows how this entraps in low-level jobs all but the few black athletes who make it to elite levels, *and* provides continuing evidence for the view that blacks are ill equipped for more intellectual activities. Black athletic achievement is 'haunted by the Law of Compensation,' as Hoberman calls it, 'an inverse relationship between mind and muscle, between athletic and intellectual development.'

Hoberman supplies an answer of sorts to Eitzen's question about whether sport reduces or exacerbates racial tensions: it glosses over them. Every new black superstar appears to be a triumph for black people, but in reality just conforms to the Law of Compensation. The majority of black people continue to struggle.

Because race has been such a contested concept, its meaning has changed and will, according to Kohn, continue to change: it is 'malleable.' Contemporary scientists who subscribe to beliefs in distinct genetic distributions continue to lend credibility to the notion that there are races. Other analysts emphasize the power of culture in shaping population differences. Approaching the concept of race as a culturally sustained belief does not deny the possibility of actual variations, variations that may have genetic sources. It acknowledges that there is a relationship between biological variation and cultural belief, at the same time suggesting that it is belief rather than difference that makes most impact on human conduct.

Further reading

Eitzen, D.S. (1999) *Fair and Foul: Beyond the myths and paradoxes of sport* Lanham MD: Rowman & Littlefield.

Hoberman, J. (1997) *Darwin's Athletes: How sport has damaged black America and preserved the myth of race* New York: Houghton Mifflin.

Kohn, M. (1996) *The Race Gallery: The return of racial science* London: Vintage.

Malik, K. (1996) *The Meaning of Race: Race, history and culture in western societies* London: Macmillan.

REACTION TIME

The minimum time that elapses between the moment a stimulus is presented to a subject and when that subject responds is known as the reaction time, or simply RT. This is a generic term to cover several different types, the most common in sports being the *disjunctive* reaction time, which covers situations in which there are complex **stimuli** and responses available. It includes *choice* reaction time. In many competitive situations, athletes are presented, at unpredictable times, with not simply a single stimulus and one response but a variety of distinct, fast-changing stimuli and a range of responses. The athlete has decisions to make: he or she must select an appropriate response to each of the stimuli. The choice reaction time describes how long it takes the athlete to make and implement the appropriate selections.

Closely related to this is the *discrimination* reaction time. In some situations, the athlete must respond to some and desist from responding to the others. In other words, a rapid discrimination between the various stimuli must be made. In most sports, deception or faking is so commonplace that skilled athletes need to be able to refrain from responding needlessly to dummy stimuli.

Another variant of RT applicable to sports is *complex* (sometimes called *compound*) reaction time, where two or more stimuli are available and two or more responses are employed in quick succession or simultaneously. This is common in ball sports, where the release or the contact with the ball usually corresponds with other responses.

When the term RT is not qualified by any of the above, it usually refers to *simple* reaction time, in which a single stimulus requires a single response, and describes the times between the two. These are rare in sports: a tip-off in basketball in which a tossed ball works as a stimulus for a single response might serve as an example.

In the early 1950s, research by W.E. Hick found that the more choices we are presented with, the more time we need to react appropriately. Alternatively, P.M. Fitts indicated that if RT remained constant when the volume of stimuli went up, then accuracy was sacrificed. It was thought that humans had a 'capacity-limited **information processing** channel' and that there would inevitably be a sort of trade-off: speed for accuracy or vice versa. More recently, other accounts of the **skill acquisition** process have indicated that RT is not so fixed and can be changed through extended repetition in training. At elite levels, RTs are typically at their quickest during actual **skill performance**: that is, under competitive conditions.

Further reading

Abernethy, B. and Sparrow, W.A. (1992) 'The rise and fall of dominant paradigms in motor behaviour research,' pp. 3–54 in Summers, J.J. (ed.) *Approaches to the Study of Motor Control and Learning* Amsterdam: Elsevier.

Fitts, P.M. (1954) 'The information capacity of the human motor system in controlling the amplitude of movement,' *Journal of Experimental Psychology* vol. 47, pp. 381–91.

Hick, W.E. (1952) 'On the rate of gain information,' *Quarterly Journal of Experimental Psychology* vol. 4, pp. 11–26.

REHABILITATION

The process by which someone, or something, is restored either to effectiveness or to a previous condition by training is rehabilitation, a term that comes from the Latin *re*, for again, and *habilitare*, ability. In sport psychology, the restoration to effectiveness rather than previous condition is usually the implied meaning.

Every **injury** is accompanied by some degree of psychological upheaval and the recovery process necessarily involves restoring, for example, **confidence**, **self-efficacy** and the inclination to compete with **intensity** rather than ritualistically (i.e. to prevent a recurrence of the injury). Psychological **intervention** in rehabilitation involves healing, in the correct sense of the word – to make whole (from the Old English *hælen*). This proceeds on several fronts, including **goal setting**. Often, injuries result in loss of capacities and a diminution of **skill**. Setting goals for the recovery of skill is often used in conjunction with others, such as acquiring new skills relating to judgement and strategy.

Imagery is also often used. Williams *et al.* reported how **goal** setting and **emotional** rehearsal (envisioning what is happening to the injury internally during rehabilitation) facilitates the healing process. To this we might add **biofeedback** training, **relaxation** and **stress management** suggested by Cupal. Despite this, Cornelius cautions that the 'majority of rehabilitative studies have **focused** on athletes with knee injuries and little is known about the success of interventions with other types of injuries.' Nevertheless, he concludes that: 'After an injury, athletes experience a wide range ... serious disturbances in **mood**, including **depression, anger,** frustration and tension.' The rehabilitative process should take account of these as well as the more tangible physical injury.

Further reading

Cornelius, A. (2002) 'Psychological interventions for the injured athlete,' pp. 224–46 in Silva, J.M. and Stevens, D.E. (eds) *Psychological Foundations of Sport* Boston MA: Allyn & Bacon.

Cupal, D.D. (1998) 'Psychological interventions in sport injury prevention and rehabilitation,' *Journal of Applied Sport Psychology* vol. 10, pp. 103–23.

Williams, J.M., Rotella, R.J. and Heyman, S.R. (1998) 'Stress, injury, and the psychological rehabilitation of athletes,' pp. 409–28 in Williams, J.M. (ed.) *Applied Sport Psychology: Personal growth to peak performance,* 3rd edition, Mountain View CA: Mayfield.

REINFORCEMENT

The process of strengthening or supporting a piece of behavior, or indeed anything, is reinforcement, a term that is embedded in learning theory. As such, the use of the concept implicitly harbors assumptions about the mechanisms involved in learning, and ultimately about the nature of the human animal. Its application in sports is diffuse: virtually all coaches use rewards to reinforce **skill acquisition** and punishment to deter improper behavior. Whether they know it or not, they are using reinforcement.

Positive reinforcement describes **stimuli** that, when presented following a response, increase the probability that the same response will be repeated; the rewards accruing to successful athletics performances are examples. Related to this is *negative* reinforcement, including painful stimuli, like electric shocks or deafening noise, which when withdrawn emit the desired response. Negative reinforcement is not the same as punishment. The former involves an active deterrent, such as removing the physical distress resulting from a shock, while the latter entails denial of, or withdrawal from, access to rewards and decreases the probability of a response. For example, giving an animal an electric shock every time it presses a lever will weaken, not reinforce, the response – this punishes pressing the lever.

The term 'reinforcement' has origins in Ivan Pavlov's early twentieth-century experiments with dogs that were inadvertently conditioned to salivate in response to a signal as much as they did to the presence or smell of food. At first, the dogs salivated only when their food arrived – what Pavlov called an unconditioned response (UR) to an unconditioned stimulus (US) – but the continual accompaniment of the signal forged an association, so that even in the absence of food the dogs salivated when the signal sounded. This was a *conditioned* response: the food (US) functioned as a reinforcer of the conditioned stimulus (CS)–US bond. Take the food away and eventually the UR becomes extinct. The food satisfies a need or a desire.

In this sense, the reinforcer is a reward. Later experiments demonstrated that similar simple rewards could be used to induce rats to push levers and pigeons to perform often elaborate behavior, like 'playing' ping-pong. The conditioning process described is instrumental and it works on the basic idea that the reinforcer is *contiguous* to the action: in other words, the reinforcement must take place quickly after the appropriate response. When every response is reinforced in sequence, there is a *schedule* of reinforcement. This is a little too straightforward, however.

Some human behavior does appear to operate according to the same principle. Fan adulation, cash and sincere congratulations from a coach reinforce an athlete's successful performance. These may seem like functional equivalents of food for rats: the rats continue to press the right bar, while the athlete attempts to reproduce the same behavior that brought him or her success – though, of course, they may not do so. Building a cash **incentive** into contracts, raising prize monies or awarding medals and extravagant gifts such as luxury cars or gold bars to winners work as reinforcers. Humiliation, exclusion from honors and the **emotion** associated with failure may negatively reinforce, or punish, the behavior that brought defeat. Obviously, reinforcement in sports does not work in this regular and predictable fashion.

Athletes do not win every **competition**; gamblers do not win every bet. Yet athletes continue to play and gamblers continue to gamble, at least until the losses are so consistent or punishing that they can no longer be sustained. While schedules of reinforcement are effective in developing, modifying and maintaining many types of behavior, complex human behavior is more difficult. B.F. Skinner's extensive work on variable interval, compound and other sorts of variations in schedules of reinforcement established him as a pioneer in the field of behaviorist psychology. His operant conditioning is one of the most comprehensive explanations available. An 'operant' is any instance of behavior that effects a change in the environment, whether it is a rat pushing a lever or a football player scoring a touchdown; when the operant is brought under the **control** of a specific stimulus or combination of stimuli, operant conditioning has happened. This is different from simple respondent behavior, which is a direct response to a stimulus, such as Pavlov's dogs' salivation. Operant behavior is controlled by its own consequences. For instance, left alone, a baby may kick out or cry spontaneously in the absence of stimuli. Once the behavior occurs, the likelihood it will be repeated depends on the consequences. Similarly, a baseball hitter who accidentally changes grip and immediately scores a home run is likely to use the same grip again. In both cases, the consequences dictate the future responses.

One of the premises of this approach is that the human being is plastic, capable of being molded (the Greek, *plastikos*, means precisely this). Behavior can be modified as long as the necessary schedules of reinforcement can be identified – and technically they can be, though in practice they are not. Skinner, in particular, has been characterized as basing his theories on the view that the human is a passive receptor of stimuli rather than an active creator of his or her own environment. The tradition dates back to the seventeenth-century philosopher John Locke and his *tabula rasa* conception of mind as a 'blank tablet' with no innate ideas. Yet in Skinner's theory – and, for that matter, Locke's – the human being is far from passive: in responding to stimuli in the environment, subjects *operate* actively, discriminating, comparing and combining.

For Skinner, understanding human and, indeed, any animal behavior requires no reference to internal states such as **cognition**, consciousness, motive or **perception**. All behavior is subject to the same principle of stimulus–response: as long as the pertinent stimuli and the appropriate schedules are known, any type of behavior is subject to operant conditioning. The emphasis for Skinner and for all those who subscribe to the explanatory power of reinforcement is on the environment – that which lies outside the organism.

Accordingly, applications of reinforcement theory have **focused** on changing environmental contingencies, or circumstances, as a way of shaping and maintaining behavior. Desirable behavior is palpable: the chances of making it happen repeatedly can be enhanced by reinforcing it. The results are observable. Inner states, by contrast, are neither palpable nor observable, so followers of reinforcement theory are not interested. Instead, they concentrate on encouraging expedient and discouraging inexpedient behavior. Many coaches, perhaps intuitively, do this: even something as simple as complimenting athletes after good moves and reprimanding them after errors is reinforcement. More extreme negative reinforcements include benching or not selecting players in team games; punishments might include fining athletes for misdemeanors on or off the province of play. Positive reinforcements are numerous, of course: in addition to the obvious ones already mentioned, there are the less direct rewards that accrue from successful performance: endorsement deals, **celebrity** status and the media exposure coveted by so many athletes.

Suppose a successful basketball player is offered the opportunity to host a television talk show, due to start in eight weeks' time at the season's end. His contract with his club stipulates that he needs permission and the club allows him to do the TV work, but only if he can finish with 3,000 points, a tough though not impossible task to which he rises splendidly, producing some of his best performances ever. Without realizing it, our player is demonstrating the **Premack principle**. Named after David Premack, this states that reinforcement is a relative, not an absolute, phenomenon. Chocolate will reinforce children with a sweet tooth, but if they need to run around the block as fast as they can to get the chocolate, they will run hell for leather. Eating chocolate reinforces running. One activity works as reinforcement for another. The activity of having his own TV show reinforces points scoring for the basketball player.

Unlike this example, much of reinforcement's application in sports has been geared toward the learning of desirable behavior, such as **skill**, and the maintenance of habits that will either improve or preserve that skill. In 1997, Scott et al. disclosed how a laser beam that let off a beep functioned as a positive reinforcer, signaling a successful pole vault, which eventually led to a modification of vaulting technique. Rewards were used to great effect in a study of golfers' performances by Simek et al. (1994): in this study, the golfers behaved rather like satiated rats: after responding to rewards with good play for a while, they came to expect the rewards, and their performance deteriorated abruptly when the rewards were withdrawn.

Further reading

Scott, D., Scott, L. and Goldwater, B. (1997) 'A performance improvement program for an international-level track and field athlete,' *Journal of Applied Behavior Analysis* vol. 30, pp. 573–5.

Simek, T., O'Brien, R. and Figlerski, L. (1994) 'Contracting and chaining to improve the performance of a college golf team: improvement and deterioration,' *Perceptual and Motor Skills* vol. 78, pp. 1,099–105.

Skinner, B.F. (1938) *The Behavior of Organisms* New York: Appleton-Century-Croft.

Smith, R.E. 'A positive approach to sport performance enhancement: principles of reinforcement and performance feedback,' pp. 28–40 in Williams, J. (ed.) *Applied Sport Psychology: Personal growth to peak performance*, 3rd edition, Mountain View CA: Mayfield.

RELAXATION

From the Latin *re*, once more, and *laxis*, loose, relaxation involves a diminution of levels of emotions, especially **anger**, **anxiety** and **fear**; somatically, there is an absence of activity in voluntary muscles, a slowing down of respiratory rate and a reduction of body temperature when the subject is relaxed. In sports, the benefits of relaxation have been recognized either as part of an athlete's preparation for a contest, or as a winding-down technique after **competition** and, less often, a way of restoring **composure** during a contest.

In many ways, relaxation is the opposite of 'flight-or-fight': the individual is calm, possibly tranquil, though not necessarily in repose. The benefits to some athletes include **confidence**, serenity and a lessening of pre-competition anxiety. Not all sports performers favor relaxation as a preparatory technique: some believe **self-talk** or moderate exercise to be more effective responses to **stress** or the various unpleasant conditions and emotions that may occur before competition. Involuntary relaxation may be a troublesome condition for athletes; for it to be effective, it must be a voluntarily induced **emotional** and bodily state.

Techniques for inducing relaxation are many and include **autogenic**, or self-induced, **hypnosis**, transcendental meditation and mental **imagery**, though perhaps the most influential is *progressive relaxation* devised in the 1929 and modified in 1938 by Edmund Jacobson. The procedure involves thinking of muscle groups separately, contracting and tensing the muscles, holding for a few seconds then relenting so that the tension disappears and the muscles go lax and limp. Thought then transfers to other muscle groups – for example from the left arm to the right – so that groups of muscles are relaxed progressively. As muscle tension is released, so heart and breathing rates decline, a process that is accompanied by what Mark Anshel, in his *Sport Psychology: From theory to practice*, calls an 'un-clenching of the mind.'

The technique is methodical and needs practice, though experienced exponents can progress through the muscle groups so quickly that, within minutes, they are unable even to grip something as light as a golf tee between their fingers. Relaxing prior to a competition is often seen as a method of reaching optimal performance, though there are instances of athletes consciously relaxing during a contest. Tennis players are often seen with their eyes closed or with a towel draped over their heads during changeovers. Sebastian Coe, the 800 and 1,500 meter runner, advocated relaxing during a race: maintaining one's form (i.e. running style, technique and plan) is facilitated by remaining calm and unruffled regardless of the circumstances.

By contrast, boxers are often doused with water, slapped across the face and roused by their corner – an approach designed to engender more **aggression** and deter relaxation. Boxers and many other athletes favor relaxation before a contest but need **arousal** during it.

As an **emotion**, relaxation can coexist with others and is compatible with, for example, excitement. Members of a team which is leading an important game may enjoy their imminent win and feel satisfied with their performance: they relax as they coast toward victory but are excited by the prospect of winning a big one. But two late scores by the opposition can quickly lead to anxiety and anger as they are made to cling on desperately in the dying minutes. Like other emotional responses, relaxation during a contest is situational: the proficient athlete tries to maintain and control levels throughout the vagaries of a contest.

Further reading

Anshel, M.H. (1997) *Sport Psychology: From theory to practice*, 3rd edition, Scottsdale AZ: Gorsuch Scarisbrick, pp. 395–402.
Jacobson, E. (1974) *Progressive Relaxation*, 2nd edition, Chicago: University of Chicago Press.

RELIGION

As its root *religionis* suggests, religion is an internally coherent system of beliefs that binds a believer to a pattern of worship, **obedience** to a superordinate being and **commitment** to a specific doctrine that purports to explain problems that are germane to the human condition. *Religionis* is Latin for obligation or bond. While religions typically include belief in a transcendental entity, for example a deity or divinely ordained prophets, some religions, such as Buddhism, do not. Some scholars have analyzed sport as if it were a functional equivalent of a religion: its **fandom** is like a body of believers, its symbols and rituals resemble religious ceremonies and, perhaps most importantly, it supplies meaning and significance to its followers.

Sporting contests dating from 2000 BCE formed part of religious festivals. Greek culture incorporated **competition** into civic and religious life (there was no hard and fast distinction between the two). The Greeks' pursuit of *agõn,* as it was called, was not simply a striving for athletic supremacy but a quest for recognition in the eyes of the gods. Victory was an accomplishment of literally heroic proportions. We can only imagine what impact this made on **motivation**.

The tradition of linking competition with religion persisted through the eighteenth century. English folk games, which were precursors to football, were played on designated Holy Days. In the nineteenth century, sports and exercise in Britain and North America were regarded as godly activities, united by the creed of muscular Christianity, a development documented by Tony Money, in his 1997 *Manly and Muscular Diversions: Public schools and the nineteenth-century sporting revival.*

At the level of the individual, religion has inspired many athletes. Countless winners, when interviewed after a contest, acknowledge the role of God in their victory; losers typically cite more mundane factors when apportioning blame. Evander Holyfield, a Christian, rarely missed the opportunity to thank God for guiding him safely through contests. Goran Ivanisevic entered Wimbledon 2001 as a wild card and emerged as champion, pronouncing throughout that his progress was guided by God.

Whether or not deities intervene in the earthly matter of sports cannot be known, of course. What can be known is the motivating power of *believing* that a god is 'in your corner,' so to speak. This can work in several possible ways, not all of them helpful. In Ivanisevich's case, he became convinced after his unlikely successes in the opening rounds of the competition. This enhanced his **confidence**, so that by the time he reached the final he was composed and certain of victory. He was even able to quell his short burst of **anger** midway through the final. The benefits of believing that victory is preordained are that the athlete can approach a competition with an **expectancy** of winning; **relaxation** levels will be appropriate and **anxiety** may not mar the performance. The dangers are that an athlete may become over-confident and lack **intensity**; when the **momentum** of the contest swings against him or her, a trailing athlete may have difficulty getting **focused** and lose motivation as the match drifts away.

Some rivals of Ayrton Senna, a Roman Catholic, say his belief in an afterlife influenced his devil-may-care style, which won him four world motor racing F1 championships but was also responsible for his death in 1994, when aged 34. Open appeals to God may also inspire opponents. In approaching the ring for his second fight against Mike Tyson, Frank Bruno, a Roman Catholic, crossed himself repeatedly, as if invoking the talismanic powers of God to protect him. The gesture was less a confirmation of faith, more a frantic appeal for salvation in the face of impending disaster. Tyson would not have been slow to spot this.

Coaches often discourage appeals to God, a notable example coming from Bob Knight. In John Feinstein's *A Season on the Brink*, the then Indiana Hoosiers coach confronts player Steve Alford, a believer: 'Steve, you always talk about God. Well, I'm gonna tell you something, Steve, God is not going to provide any **leadership** on this basketball team. He couldn't care less if we win or not. He is not going to parachute in through the roof of this building and score when we need points.' As an afterthought, Knight, who had been raised in a Methodist home and had gone to church every Sunday, asks: 'Do you really think that God is going to help a team that *I'm* coaching?'

Religion has also played a part in the fan **violence** in Britain. The first serious outbursts of hooliganism were witnessed in Glasgow, where fans of the Protestant club, Rangers, clashed with the Catholic fans of Celtic in the 1960s. Similar sectarian patterns emerged in Liverpool when rival fans of the city's two main clubs, Liverpool and Everton, fought. These fights were among the first instances of a phenomenon that was to spread and continue for the following decades.

Further reading

Feinstein, J. (1989) *A Season on the Brink: A year with Bob Knight and the Indiana Hoosiers* New York: Fireside.
Hoffman, S.J. (ed.)(1992) *Sport and Religion* Champaign IL: Human Kinetics.
Hubbard, S. (1998) *Faith in Sports: Athletes and their religion on and off the field* New York: Doubleday.

REM

REM is an acronym for the rapid eye movements, which characterize a particular stage of sleep when the eyeballs move in the sockets and there is a relative absence of delta brainwaves (the slow, large-amplitude waves), flaccid musculature, fluctuating heartbeat, erratic respiration, genital changes and, in the vast majority of cases, vivid and

emotional dreaming. It is contrasted with NREM sleep, which is divided into four stages based on the amount of delta wave activity. REM sleep typically occurs in cycles every ninety minutes. There is also a tendency known as *REM rebound*, meaning that subjects who are deprived of REM sleep on one night experience disproportionate amounts of it on subsequent nights. This is why many athletes report that they do not sleep well the night before an important event, but still perform at or near their peak.

This observation is lent some support by research from Mougin *et al.* which focused on how sleep deprivation affects athletes' recovery process when working out the following day. The conclusions indicated only minor alterations in hormonal responses.

Further reading

Hobson, J.A. (1996) 'Sleep and dreaming,' pp. 109–32 in Colman, A.M. (ed.) (1996) *Companion Encyclopedia of Psychology*, vol. 1, London: Routledge.

Mougin, F., Bourdin, H., Simon-Rigaud, M.L., Nguyen Nhu, U., Kantelip, J.P. and Davenne, D. (2001) 'Hormonal responses to exercise after partial sleep deprivation and after a hypnotic drug-induced sleep,' *Journal of Sports Sciences* vol. 19, pp. 89–97.

RETIREMENT

Withdrawal from active participation is retirement, a word taken from *re*, again, and the French *tirer*, to draw. 'Retirement from sport: social death or rebirth?' is a question raised by Andrew Yiannakis *et al.* in their edited collection, which offers contrasting perspectives on the subject.

Considering an athletic career typically begins in childhood and may end, possibly because of **injury** or axing or erosion of **skill**, any time from the early twenties, an athlete invests a substantial portion of time in sport. The power of sport as an agency of secondary **socialization** suggests that the **identity** of athletes is shaped by their involvement in training and **competition**. Yiannakis *et al.* argue that 'an element of both psychological and physical addiction may also be present.' Certainly, the number of athletes who embark on at least one **comeback** (often more) after announcing their retirement provides at least inferential evidence of the **dependence** many develop. This is particularly acute for **celebrity** athletes who have become inured to media **attention** and the idolatry of a hysterically reverent **fandom**. Only a minority transfer seamlessly into media work as pundits and maintain their public **profile**. Of the others, many stay in sports as, for example, managers, coaches and scouts and, less often, owners. A full-time career in sports equips its participants with specialist knowledge but only limited applications.

For those who do not succeed in gaining jobs in sport, or who fail in their new capacities, or who simply do not want to stay in sport, adjustment may be 'traumatic,' according to Barry McPherson, who argues that '**personality** disorders appear as reflected in attempted or successful suicides, alcohol or drug addiction and a general orientation to the past rather than to the present or future.' McPherson also points out that **deviance** of one kind or another is not uncommon among ex-pros. Apart from the obvious lack of skills, their **self-esteem** has been structured around athletic performance. Once detached from a culture that has been such a source of identity cues, the retiree approaches an uncertain future in which horizontal or downward mobility is likely. Most athletes earn less and experience a drop in status in retirement. Even those who transfer to movie careers are usually best known for past athletic deeds.

McPherson writes of 'skidding,' a process in which athletes who rarely if ever think about their futures extend their competitive careers for as long as possible, far beyond their peak years, simply because they have no conception of life outside sports. Eventually, they are involuntarily taken out of sports and undergo an abrupt decline in status and earning capacity. Often, they have mismanaged their earnings and have little **emotional** support from peers or employers once they retire.

The drop in standing following retirement has prompted some writers to call it a social death, meaning that an athlete's status degrades, either suddenly or slowly – some star athletes are sometimes allowed longer periods to rediscover form, like a patient given a realistic chance of recovery. Stars are encouraged to indulge in illusions about their career longevity, while less distinguished athletes are simply cut.

Research on college and amateur athletes, on the other hand, indicates that their retirement is less troublesome. In fact, many look forward to the relief from **stress** and pressure to perform involved in sports. Their adjustment is 'mild' rather than severe, according to research by Susan Greendorfer and Elaine Blinde in 1987. Jay Coakley complicates this picture by arguing that: 'Leaving sport is not inevitably stressful or identity-shaking, nor is it the source of serious adjustment problems.' Obviously, adjustments are necessary, but the majority of ex-athletes successfully negotiate them. The more serious problems are experienced by those athletes who have not sought credentials outside sport, have restricted their relationships to other athletes, whose families have provided little support for them in nonsports activities and/or who lack gratifying relationships and activities away from sports. Ethnic and class backgrounds and **gender** all factor into the equation, according to Coakley. For an extreme example, a black athlete from a poor background who has not handled her earnings wisely and restricted friends and contact to within sports circles is likely to have a problematic adjustment.

Further reading

Coakley, J.J. (1987) 'Leaving competitive sport: retirement or rebirth?', pp. 311–17 in Yiannakis, A., McIntyre, T.D., Melnick, M. and Hart, D.P. (eds) *Sport Sociology: Contemporary themes*, 3rd edition, Dubuque IA: Kendall/Hunt.
McPherson, B.D. (1987) 'Retirement from professional sport: the process and problems of occupational and psychological adjustment,' pp. 293–301 in Yiannakis, A., McIntyre, T.D., Melnick, M. and Hart, D.P. (eds) *Sport Sociology: Contemporary themes*, 3rd edition, Dubuque IA: Kendall/Hunt.

REVERSAL THEORY

As its name suggests, reversal theory focuses on how the needs and desires that guide human behavior alternate from one psychological state to another and then back again, reversing to and fro as individuals engage in action throughout the course of a day. In recent years, its application to sports has become influential, posing an alternative to psychological theories that **stress** consistency and stability in human behavior. Reversal theory presumes humans are inconsistent, unstable and in the process of constant change.

The theory is concerned centrally with **motivation** and experience, the latter referring specifically to 'how one interprets and responds emotionally to, a given situation,' according to Kurt Frey, whose essay 'Reversal theory: basic concepts' provides a clear introduction to the approach. Frey gives an example of reversal: in a particular state, a person may want to feel aroused, while in another state that person may want to feel calmness or **relaxation**. 'However, if one desires to experience high **arousal**, but does not, one will feel anxious,' Frey observes. 'Thus different states represent opposite ways of experiencing the same level of a particular psychological variable, such as arousal.'

A person's motives can change throughout the course of activity, a process described as **metamotivation**. According to reversal theory, metamotivational states occur in pairs of opposites, involving opposite desires and subjective responses. There are four pairs, and at any given time a person is experiencing a total of four states, one from each pair, though normally one state is 'salient.' The four active states determine what the person wants, how he or she thinks and acts and the kinds of **emotion** he or she experiences.

The first two pairs of metamotivational states are *somatic* and refer to the process of experiencing one's own body. These consist of the *telic* and *paratelic* states. A soccer player at the kickoff would be in a **telic state**: narrowly goal-oriented with a specific aim in mind. In training, or perhaps playing with children, the same person will be much more playful and unfocused, attaching little importance to what he or she is doing, and so experiencing a paratelic state. In a serious game, the competitors may start intimidating and fouling each other to the point where players experience **anxiety**. In a pickup game, the action may become so slow and placid that they become bored.

The second pair of somatic states are *conformist* and *negativist* and these relate to means *v.* ends: in other words, how a person regards rules and conventions that guide behavior in particular circumstances. In a conformist state, a person wishes to stick within the rules of a game; in a negativist state, the person wants to break free of any restrictions at all. During **competition**, athletes need to observe rules or **risk** censure, of course; at the same time, they commit fouls and perhaps infringe other points of etiquette.

The other two pairs of states are known as *transactional* and describe a person's interactions with the immediate environment, including people. The first pair comprise **mastery** and sympathy states. A person in mastery state interprets an interaction as conflictual power struggle: in any competitive sport, this would be the salient state of athletes. When an athlete is generous, considerate, even caring toward an opponent or teammate (for example, after an **injury**) there is evidence of a sympathy state. More usually, the sympathy state manifests in the *esprit de corps* and cooperation of teammates. Perhaps the most famous example of a sympathy state expressing itself in an otherwise aggressive sport came in 1980 when Larry Holmes, then heavyweight champion of the world, battered the 38-year-old Muhammad Ali for ten sickeningly one-sided rounds. Over the final rounds, Holmes visibly eased up, at times inviting the referee to intervene to spare his opponent the punishment.

The other pair of transactional states are called *autic* and *alloic*, both concerned with outcomes. In an autic state, an individual is concerned with his or her own outcomes from an interaction, whereas in a alloic state the individual is concerned with others' outcomes.

The metamotivational reversal refers to the switch from any one state to its opposite in any one pair; the result is often a dramatic change in outlook and **emotional** experience. During an NBA game, players may jostle then jokingly make up, suggesting a movement from telic to paratelic reversal; as competitive action resumes, players reverse once more to telic states. Frustration at the failure to achieve one's goals can precipitate a reversal: Mike Tyson's astonishing switch from conformist to negativist states involved his taking a bite from Evander Holyfield's ear in their 1997 fight.

The premise of reversal theory is that any form of behavior, including competitive behavior, needs to be analyzed in terms of the motivations that underlie it. This is complicated by the fact that there is never a one-to-one correspondence between motivation and behavior, nor a direct link between behavior and experience. Identical behavior may be observed in two individuals, yet those individuals may be in contrasting metamotivational states and have totally different experiences. Reversal theory is based on a conception of human beings as inconsistent, self-contradictory and capable of sometimes paradoxical changes during short periods of time.

Further reading

Apter, M.J. (1989) *Reversal Theory: Motivation, emotion and personality* London: Routledge.

Frey, K.P. (1999) 'Reversal theory: basic concepts,' pp. 3–17 in Kerr, J.H. (ed.) (1999) *Experiencing Sport: Reversal theory* Chichester, England: Wiley.

RIGHT STUFF, THE *see* character

RINGELMANN EFFECT

When individual performances are inhibited by the presence of others, the Ringelmann effect is said to have transpired. The implications in sport are evident: individuals' performances should decrease as the size of the team in which they are competing increases.

Interest in the way in which individual performances are affected negatively by the presence of others was sparked by an experiment conducted by an engineer named Max Ringelmann, who was a professor at the French National Institute of Agronomy between 1870 and 1900. His research **focused** on the relative work efficiency of oxen, horses and men, and involved elementary tasks such as rope pulling, measuring the amount of force exerted per person. As each new person was added to the group, so the amount of force for each individual diminished: it was found that, as the number of participants in a work task increased, so the individual performances decreased. For example, if one individual standing on a track and told to exert maximum effort at pulling a rope could be reasonably expected to pull 200lb (or 91kg), then three should pull 600lb, five 1,000lb and so on.

Contrary to expectations, there was a steady, progressive shortfall in the effort expended by the individuals as the size of the group increased. At first, Ringelmann thought that this was because of a loss of teamwork and coordination. In any cooperative task, members of groups have to coordinate their efforts to achieve maximum joint output. As with any team effort, there were person-to-person links that needed to be coordinated. The number of links increased exponentially with every added member: two people – one link; three people – three links; four people – six links; five people – ten links; eight people – twenty-eight links, etc. The formula is: $(n^2 - n) \div 2$.

Coordination links helped explain the performance loss in some group activities, but not others. In some team games, especially ball games, cooperative operations are central and performance has to be socially organized throughout a **competition**. By contrast, the cooperative links in a relay race occur only between two members at a time and only at the handover of the baton. Later studies, including that of Ingham *et al.*, minimized the coordination losses and still found decrements in performance with additional group members. The suspicion was that mechanical problems were not the source of the Ringelmann effect. The cause may be motivational loss.

Ringelmann's original research was conducted prior to Norman Triplett's 1897/8 study of cyclists who pedaled with greater speed when they rode in teams rather than individually, though it was not published until after. While Triplett had found a **social facilitation** of **motivation** in which performance was enhanced by the presence of others, Ringelmann found that it was inhibited. Under some conditions the presence of others led to motivational gains, while under others it produced motivational losses. Ringelmann's work stimulated later research into what became known as **social loafing**, a process in which performance is inhibited by the presence of others.

Impressionistic corroboration for Ringelmann's study comes from soccer and hockey: when a player is given a red card or sent to the sin bin, the team is reduced and fellow team players typically respond by sinking more effort into their play, often making it tough for the opposition to capitalize. While this does not constitute direct support for Ringelmann, the inference is that reducing group size delivers greater motivation and performance from individuals. The added value of the performance of fewer players is what Ivan Steiner, in his *Group Process and Productivity*, called the 'assembly bonus.'

Further reading

Ingham, A.G., Levinger, G., Graves, J. and Peckham, V. (1974) 'The Ringelmann effect: studies of group size and group performance,' *Journal of Experimental Social Psychology* vol. 10, pp. 371–84.

Kravitz, D. and Martin, B. (1986) 'Ringelmann rediscovered: the original article,' *Journal of Personality and Social Psychology* vol. 37, pp. 936–41.

Triplett, N. (1898) 'The dynamogenic factors in pacemaking and competition,' *American Journal of Psychology* vol. 9, pp. 507–33.

RISK

Exposure to jeopardy is, of course, risk, from the Italian *risco*, for danger (a word that derives interestingly from the Old French *dangier*, descended from *dominarium*, Roman for lord). Paradoxically, the effort to minimize the element of danger in mainstream sports over the past century has been accompanied by attempts to invent competitive activities that are unsafe by design. The proliferation of sports in which risk is paramount suggests a desire to seek out perilous situations combined with a wish to escape what some writers regard as an oversafe culture in which personal security, public protection and environmental management have become priorities. This contradicts the commonly held view that people avoid taking risks, even when they carry a potential gain, and submit to them only when trying to avert a certain loss – a phenomenon known as *risk aversion*.

Frank Furedi argues that societies all over the world have become preoccupied by safety: nothing that is potentially controllable is left to chance in the effort to limit risks. But as the search for safety has gained **momentum**, the ways to escape it have become more ingenious. Established practices like mountain climbing, stunt cycling and potholing continue as newer adaptations flourish. Zorbing, bungee-jumping, whitewater rafting and other Xtreme sports contain ersatz dangers: they offer thrills, though under controlled conditions, and give the impression that followers are motivated by a **death wish**.

Other responses, such as hang gliding and kayaking off waterfalls, are less amenable to **control**.

The title of Furedi's book *Culture of Fear* describes an environment in which people panic over things that would have been taken for granted in previous times: drinking water; the nuclear family, technology; all are now viewed as secreting previously unknown perils. While people avoid risks that lie outside their control, they are quite prepared to take voluntary lifestyle risks, such as smoking, drinking, driving and using cellular phones. Sports present manufactured risks that are actually constructed to preserve natural dangers or build in new ones. Furedi cites the example of rock climbing, which had some of its risks reduced by the introduction of improved ropes, boots, helmets and other equipment: 'The fact that young people who choose to climb mountains might not want to be denied the *frisson* of risk does not enter into the calculations of the safety-conscious professional, concerned to protect us from ourselves.'

Ulrich Beck believes that advances in science and technology have expanded our knowledge not only of how the world works, but also of the perils it holds. Many of the perils have actually been fostered by our desire to know more. In other words, much of the **anxiety** that pervades society is produced by knowledge, not ignorance. A preoccupation with safety has come about through a 'tendency for society to fragment,' itself the result of economic dislocation and a weakening of social institutions, according to Furedi. We have become *individuated*: survival has become a personal concern, not a social one. In the midst of this transformation of the relationship between the individual and society, tradition and **cohesion** have been lost. The problem, as Furedi and others see it, is that risk is still an important element in human life: we can become too secure and lose what has been historically a vital, heroic trait.

Michael Bane suggests: 'In our personal lives, we accept the government's (and the legal system's) position that life should be free of risks.' Yet the more people find ways of controlling or even eliminating danger, the more they find ways of reintroducing it. John Adams believes that we have inside us a *risk thermostat* which we can set to our own tastes, according to our own particular culture. 'Some like it hot – a Hell's Angel or a Grand Prix racing driver, for example; others like it cool,' writes Adams. 'But no one wants absolute zero.' Most people would not go to a restaurant declared unsafe by state sanitary inspectors, but some of those same people might ski off-piste, scuba or go on survivalist expeditions.

Further reading

Adams, J. (1995) *Risk* London: UCL Press.

Bane, M. (1997) *Over the Edge: A regular guy's odyssey in extreme sports* New York: Gollancz.

Furedi, F. (1997) *Culture of Fear: Risk-taking and the morality of low expectation* London: Cassell.

SELF-ACTUALIZATION

The process of becoming all that one is capable of being is known as self-actualization, from the Latin *actualitas*, for real or existing in fact. At least, that is the definition offered in the 1950s by Abraham Maslow, who advocated developing a unique self while moving through the famous hierarchy of needs from survival (hunger, thirst, temperature maintenance and so on) to cultivated needs, including the need for affiliation with others, aesthetic needs and the need for self-actualization to find fulfillment in realizing one's own potential. **Motivation**, in this model, has origins in human needs or drives, some of which have organic sources. Maslow's theory built on that of the physician/psychiatrist Kurt Goldstein, for whom self-actualization was *the* prime motive, all others being by-products.

Especially relevant to sports is the interpretation of Carl Rogers, who regarded all human beings as striving productively for fulfillment and development. For Rogers, humans are set at birth to grow: humans are active and forward moving and, if the conditions are permissive, attempt to develop potential to the maximum; this is the process of self-actualization. The specifics of human growth vary from person to person. One individual may choose to become intensely involved in family life and the rearing of children, heightening his or her experiences in that context, whereas another may immerse him or herself in an occupation, improving competence without domestic bliss. Yet, for Rogers, they may both share the same motive: the actualizing tendency.

Although the form of actualization differs from one individual to another and from one population to another, there are some common features: flexibility rather than rigidity is sought; openness rather than restrictedness; freedom from external **control** rather than submission to control. The conditions must be conducive to such developments, and in sports there are contradictions. Rigidity in learning may be a condition of flexibility in expression. Applying such ideas to aspirant athletes, it could be said that when conditions are not conducive to their actualization in the spheres of education and work, they may turn to sport as the vehicle for actualization. Certainly the fulfillment many derive from sports in terms of expression and **identity** is suggestive of this.

The empirical research on the subject is equivocal: while several studies suggest that participation in sports does not promote or impede self-actualization, others indicate that it does, but for males only, and still other studies maintain that all athletes tend to be more self-actualized than nonathletes. Compounding the situation is the question of level: at some levels of **competition** participation may encourage self-actualization, while at other levels it does not. In spite of that, Karen Lee Hill concludes: 'Although attempts to quantitatively prove that sport is a positive path toward self-development and actualization have not been successful, the hypothesis that self is impacted in lasting ways by sports participation remains viable.'

Further reading

Hill, K.L. (2001) *Frameworks for Sport Psychologists* Champaign IL: Human Kinetics.
Rogers, C.R. (1977) *Carl Rogers on Personal Power* New York: Delacourt Press.

SELF-CONCEPT *see* identity

SELF-CONFIDENCE *see* confidence

SELF-EFFICACY

Albert Bandura's term to describe a person's or team's belief in their capacity to produce desired results under specific conditions is 'self-efficacy.' As conditions change, so might someone's belief in their competence to reach a certain level of performance, as might the strength of their certainty as well as the generality of their self-efficacy (s-e). The word 'efficacy' shares a common root with 'efficiency,' the Latin *efficax* which means, essentially, bringing a desired outcome.

For example, a triathlete may have high s-e when competing in domestic events, but not so high at Olympic or Iron Man levels; the triathlete may be 100 per cent certain of winning with **home advantage** but only 50 per cent certain of winning overseas. The triathlete's strongest disciplines may be swimming and cycling, and in these s-e may be high compared to running. Yet an impressive swim and a better-than-expected cycle may increase s-e for the run.

So s-e is not constant and mediates between **skill** or proficiency and actual outcomes, or performance. In this regard, it is more fluid than **confidence** and is susceptible to change in four ways: (1) performance – repeated success raises s-e; lack of success depresses it; (2) vicarious experiences – watching fellow team members playing well, for instance; (3) verbal persuasion – which is why coaches will always tell athletes they are doing well (even when they are not); and (4) **emotional** arousal – which is the most vague, yet arguably the most interesting; studies show that athletes who experience high **arousal** or even **fear** can be persuaded that their aroused state is beneficial, in which case their s-e is raised (other studies suggest athletes with **anxiety** are not so amenable to such persuasion).

While s-e is changeable, some athletes have relatively stable levels. Those with high s-e will relish challenges, persevere at meeting them, show resolution and achieve at consistently high levels. When athletes are evenly matched, self-efficacy can often prove a crucial difference, especially over longer competitions (involving overtime, extra time, tiebreakers, etc.). It is interesting to speculate how s-e might play a significant part in boxing if the judges' scores were revealed at the end of each round instead of at the end of the fight, as they now are. The s-e of a boxer who knows he or she is winning rounds would rise, while the opponent's would decline. Not that this would necessarily lead to onesided contests: vital incidents, like knockdowns, would still have dramatic effects on a boxer's s-e.

Further reading

Bandura, A. (1986) *Social Foundations of Thought and Action: A social cognitive theory* Englewood Cliff NJ: Prentice-Hall.

Haggar, M.S., Chatzisarantis, N. and Biddle, S.J.H. (2001) 'The influence of self-efficacy and past behavior on the physical activity intentions of young people,' *Journal of Sports Sciences* vol. 19, pp. 711–25.

Lan, L.Y. and Gill, D.L. (1984) 'The relationships among self-efficacy, stress responses, and a cognitive feedback manipulation,' *Journal of Sport Psychology* vol. 6, pp. 227–38.

SELF-ESTEEM

How worthy or valuable a person considers him or herself is self-esteem. Conceptually, this is very close to other terms, such as *self-image*, which is how one imagines oneself or supposes one to be, and *self-concept*, which means all the elements that make up a person's view of him or herself and which includes self-image. The cognate term *idealized self* is a characterization of what one would like to be or become. *Self-presentation* – or sometimes 'presentation of the self' – is behavior designed to influence the impressions of the self formed by others. The various concepts are intertwined.

It has been argued that self-esteem is, in part, a product of **parenting**, fathers and mothers giving a high level of **emotional** support to their children contributing significantly to how those children evaluate themselves. Similarly, coaches and teachers can use **reinforcement** to boost athletes' evaluations of themselves. The actual experience of **competition** is also likely to affect self-esteem, though exactly how is unclear. Competing in sport would appear to increase an athlete's self-esteem. On the other hand, those subjects with high self-esteem may gravitate toward sports competition.

Coaches sometimes encourage subjects to strive toward establishing a degree of congruence between their actual selves and their idealized selves – how they would like to imagine themselves. At entry level, the basic **mastery** of new tasks can induce a heightened sense of **control**, an enhanced feeling of **self-efficacy** and an all-round enlargement of self-esteem. Even the most basic exercising can have positive effects on self-esteem, though a **dependence** on exercise, like any other form of dependence, can ultimately damage self-esteem. The loss of form that results from **overtraining** can be especially harmful in this respect.

Within sports there are various levels of self-esteem, and this has an impact on the competitive experience. There is a relationship between self-esteem and **attribution**: subjects who place low value on themselves are more ready to blame themselves for failure. When they do so, every failure negatively impacts on self-esteem. On the other hand, internal attributions for success increase feelings of **confidence**, pride and all-round self-esteem. Self-esteem is never static and varies throughout an athlete's career. **Aging** affects the self-esteem of men and women differently, according to a 1992 study by Bond and Nideffer: as female athletes grow older their self-esteem decreases, yet as male athletes age their self-esteem increases.

Further reading

Côté, J. and Hay, J. (2002) 'Family influences on youth sport performance and participation,' pp. 503–19 in Silva, J.M. and Stevens, D.E. (eds) *Psychological Foundations of Sport* Boston MA: Allyn & Bacon.

Mutrie, N. (1997) 'The therapeutic effects of exercise on the self,' pp. 287–314 in

Fox, K.R. (ed.) *The Physical Self: From motivation to well-being* Champaign IL: Human Kinetics.

SELF-HANDICAPPING

Many athletes tend, consciously or not, to behave in ways that undermine or subvert their own ability to function optimally when competing, or even in training, and this is known as self-handicapping. While it may seem a wholly destructive maneuver, the athlete provides him or herself with a convenient subsequent explanation, or perhaps excuse, for failure and so affords a degree of self-protection. Failure to beat a rival or break a record can be discounted, being attributable to, for example, an **injury** or adverse weather conditions.

Self-handicapping can help preserve **self-efficacy** by blaming a defeat or lackluster performance on factors other than one's own ability, so any discussion of its causes and impact relates to patterns of **attribution**. Group **cohesion** has been shown to moderate the effects of self-handicapping.

Further reading

Leary, M.R. (1995) *Self-Presentation: Impression management and interpersonal behavior* Boulder CO: Westview.

SELF-TALK

As the term suggests, this is a method of verbalizing or silently affirming to oneself before or during a contest. Athletes use it to invoke feelings of empowerment and **confidence** and to achieve optimal **arousal**. Like **biofeedback** and the use of **imagery**, self-talk is also useful in assisting **relaxation**.

Typically, performers will focus inwardly, reminding themselves of their strengths and deflecting **attention** away from those of the opponent. The locus of causality may feature in the self-talk; in other words, they might repeat something like 'It's in your own hands,' or 'You **control** your own destiny.'

Another purpose in self-talk is to reflect and analyze during a contest. 'That touchdown was due to my slack coverage of the wide receiver,' a defense player might utter under his breath, adding: 'That's not gonna happen again.' A related function of the technique is to facilitate **gating**. This is featured in Sam Raimi's 1999 movie *For Love* *of the Game*, in which Kevin Costner's pitcher is able to summon an inner silence and attend selectively to his task by quietly uttering, 'Clearing the mechanism': the crowd noise is obliterated and he sees nothing but the hitter. In this instance, the self-talk is a scripted sequence of words that serve as a cue to elicit **cognition** and behavior.

While it was not featured in the film, one can imagine the hitter self-talking at the same time, perhaps with a different purpose: 'I nearly always foul out against this guy. *Not this time*: the ball's going out of the park,' might work as a way of changing self-doubts into positive thoughts. In contrast to the cue mechanism, the self-talk in this case works to re-frame a situation. It counters negative images and thoughts and perhaps negative self-talk.

Negative self-talk afflicts some athletes because it has a self-perpetuating quality. A golfer might feel positive about all aspects of his or her game apart from putts just outside the 'gimme' range. 'I hate these three-feet shots,' the golfer may say silently as he or she approaches the hole. 'Such self-talk reinforces a negative, ineffective self-concept and evokes images and emotions that reinforce the fear,' writes Jack Lesyk in his *Developing Sport Psychology within Your Clinical Practice: A practical guide for mental health professionals*, suggesting that similar situations will begin to evoke the same negative self-talk, so that each successive outcome will be unfavorable. Positive affirmations can help break this cycle.

Sometimes, argues Lesyk, they can be written on cue cards: 'I can putt successfully from this range.' Although it is hard to imagine a pro golfer being handed index cards by a caddie, the point is a valid one: the words are intended to evoke a specific, practiced response in competitive situations. This is an example of **cognitive–behavioral modification**: using mental dexterity to change the way the athlete approaches material situations and producing actual changes in the way he or she executes a putt, or any other maneuver for that matter. Self-talk is designed to alter not only the way competitors view a task, but also the way they respond to it – which in turn controls arousal levels and, ultimately, thoughts. The negatively self-perpetuating cycle is broken and replaced by an affirmative loop.

Limitations on the value of self-talk have been raised from various quarters. Van Raalte *et al.* discovered variations in the uses and consequences of strategies, pointing out that in their study it was possible that 'negative self-talk was harmful to the performance of only some of these athletes and that it served a motivational function for others.' Prior to his second successive Wimbledon final in 2001, Pat Rafter reflected on how the previous year, when he lost to Pete

Sampras, he had tightened, despite self-talking 'Relax, relax.' 'So this time I'll be saying "**choke**, choke," ' said Rafter, who lost in five sets to Goran Ivanisevic.

Further reading

Hardy, J., Hall, C.R. and Alexander, M.R. (2001) 'Exploring self-talk and affective states in sport,' *Journal of Sports Sciences* vol. 19, pp. 469–75.

Van Raalte, J.L., Cornelius, A.E., Brewer, B.W. and Hatten, S.J. (2000) 'The antecedents and consequences of self-talk in competitive tennis,' *Journal of Sport & Exercise Psychology* vol. 22, pp. 245–56.

Zinsser, N., Bunker, L. and Williams, J.M. (1998) 'Cognitive techniques for building confidence and enhancing performance,' pp. 270–95 in Williams, J.E. (ed.) *Applied Sport Psychology: Personal growth to peak performance* Mountain View CA: Mayfield.

SEX

Biological differences between males and females are subject to classification, and the main way in which contemporary culture determines differences is according to sex, a term derived from the Old French *sexe*. Distinctions between men and women which have a natural, as opposed to social, origin and which relate to reproductive capabilities and hormonal characteristics, as well as anatomical structures, are sexual differences – as contrasted with **gender** differences, which involve the cultural responses to natural distinctions.

While common sense dictates that there is a sharp division between males and females and this is self-evident, this is in fact a relatively recent conception. Thomas Laqueur's studies of historical medical texts indicates that the male/female dichotomy is a product of only the past 300 years: for 2,000 years before this, bodies were not visualized in terms of differences. Plainly expressed, there were people, some of whom could have children, others of whom could not. Sexual difference was not a concept so it was impossible to conceive of a distinct bifurcation of types. Even physical differences that today seem obvious were not so obvious without a conceptual understanding of sexual difference. In some periods, a woman's clitoris was thought to be a minuscule protuberance, an underdeveloped version of a penis. This vision complemented a male-centered worldview in which, as Laqueur puts it, 'man is the measure of all things, and woman does not exist as an ontologically distinct category.'

The tradition of physical similarities came under attack, particularly from anatomists, who argued that sex was not restricted to reproductive organs but affected every part of the body. Londa Schiebinger's medical history traces how nineteenth-century anatomists searched for the sources of women's difference and apparent inferiority. In the process, the concept of sexual difference was integrated into the discourse, so that, by the end of the century, female and male bodies were understood in terms of opposites, each having different organs, functions and **emotion**.

In the eighteenth and early nineteenth centuries, intellectual curiosity centered on the dissimilarities between men and women: in what respects are they different? While this may seem perfectly clear, the fact that it was not illustrates just how dramatically understanding of sex can change. Nelly Oudshoorn's research on how sex hormones were discovered shows how the female body only became conceptualized in terms of its unique sexual **character** in the 1920s and 1930s. In these decades, sex endocrinology created a completely new understanding of sex based on hormones. Eventually, hormonal differences became accepted as natural facts.

Once women were conceived as different from men in a sexual and so the most categorical and unchangeable way, they were discouraged from all types of practices, including sports (they were also encouraged in others, such as nurturing and domestic duties), which were considered harmful to their reproductive capacities and liable to affect their sexual characteristics (one theory held that any woman who competed strenuously risked becoming a **transsexual**).

Even in the late twentieth century – and possibly to the present day – questions of sex differences persist in sports. The concept of psychological **androgyny** dispelled the idea that emotion, **intelligence, personality** and other features were not linked to biological sex. Despite the grand explanatory power conventionally attributed to sex, many of the differences – particularly psychological differences – ascribed to men and women owe more to cultural than to natural processes.

Further reading

Laqueur, T. (1990) *Making Sex: Body and gender from the Greeks to Freud* Cambridge MA: Harvard University Press.

Oudshoorn, N. (1994) *Beyond the Natural Body: An archaeology of sex hormones* London: Routledge.

Schiebinger, L. (1989) *The Mind Has No Sex: Women in the origins of modern science* Cambridge MA: Harvard University Press.

SKILL

The competence to perform elaborate, planned sequences of behavior efficiently and repeatedly in order to achieve a predetermined objective with economy of effort is known as a skill. The word is from the Old Norse *skil*, meaning distinction. While skill is often described as 'instinctual' or even 'God-given,' it is actually learned, and as such is developed, improved and refined through training. Skill is acquired or achieved rather than ascribed or attributed, much less an **instinct**.

There are three basic types of skill, all of which come into play in sports: (1) motor skills, which are responsible for the production of complex sequences of physical movement, and which figure in every sport; (2) perceptual skills, which involve receiving information about the environment via the senses, and which are particularly important in many sports where, for instance, peripheral vision is called for (pitching in baseball being an obvious example); (3) cognitive skills, which relate to thinking: again, important skills in many sports, particularly chess, bridge and sports in which superior performance depends on anticipation and decision making. In all three types, extended practice reduces the need for involvement as performance becomes automatic. Different sports demand different permutations of the three types of skill, a **discipline** such as weight lifting requiring few perceptual or cognitive skills but a lot of motor skills to perform a task successfully. Success in golf depends on choosing and carrying out strokes that are appropriate to particular conditions, and so involves all three types of skill. Skill in this instance lies as much in the strategy of the game as in the making of accurate individual strokes, or in muscular strength.

There is a relationship between skill, aptitude and ability. For example, an individual's *potential* to perform a task is aptitude: this describes the possibility that an individual may be trained. If an individual can perform a certain task without any training at all, we refer to his or her *ability* – the unlearned qualities, faculties or talents that enable them to complete the task without instruction or practice. Training will enhance their ability to perform the task with greater degrees of proficiency. In other words, skill is made possible by a person's aptitude and builds on their ability (**talent** is a somewhat uncertain property).

Returning to weight lifting, this is a sport that involves *gross motor* abilities, including dynamic strength (in exerted force), explosive strength (short bursts of muscular effort) and gross body coordination (while the lift is in motion). Other sports involve *psychomotor* abilities: for example, manual dexterity in manipulating objects, aiming at targets and rapid reaction to **stimuli**, such as the bang of a starter's pistol. A person's aptitude is the potential they have to convert these abilities into skills.

The skills developed through training in weight lifting are clearly very different from the skills honed by a chess player, golfer, gymnast or many other types of athletes. Whereas weight lifting involves a *discrete* skill with a sharply defined beginning and end, other sports such as cycling or rally driving are *continuous* and progress in long series without a clear finish. The latter involves the performer in continually varying responses to continuously varying stimuli. Beyond this basic bifurcation of skills, there are many ways of subdividing types of athletic skills. The competitive environment often determines the precise manner in which we classify skills.

Time is an important criterion. In some situations, an athlete may operate in an environment which affords him plenty of time: *self-paced* skills are called for. A basketball player may stand and compose herself when preparing to take a free shot; there is no interference from other players and she has complete **control** over the pace at which the skill is brought about. That same player will then employ *externally paced* skills: her movements will be affected by the speed and direction of the ball and other players, both teammates and rivals – these constitute external factors that will impinge on the execution of skills and introduce pressure to move quickly. While basketball players need to employ both self- and externally paced skills, some sports, such as golf, require self-paced skills exclusively. Most sports that need externally paced skills include an element for self-paced skills; even fast sports like soccer and hockey have interludes when self-pacing is essential.

The competitive environment will also dictate whether the athlete can use *closed* skills: the exact conditions under which the skill is to be performed is established in advance for all competitors and incalculable factors are minimized. Typically, closed skills are exhibited in sports that emphasize esthetic as well as athletic qualities: synchronized swimming, ice dancing and gymnastics are obvious cases. By contrast, *open* skills are practiced in environments in which change, incon-sistency and indeterminacy are the norm. All sports in which confrontation or collision are ingredients need open skills: athletes have to make quick decisions and react to movements, either of other athletes or of missiles, in order to perform the skill. Open skills typically incorporate all three basic skills, motor, perceptual and cognitive.

Most sports do not involve one distinct skill but a great many that are linked together in the execution of an athletic performance. Coaching skills usually involves digesting sequences of activity, reducing them to a convenient number of small movements. Sprint coaches often make their athletes work exclusively on their starts before switching to the pickup and then moving to finishing. The skills that contribute to a 100 meter sprint are linked together in an unbroken chain, so that the whole motion is continuous.

Further reading

Fischman, M.G. and Oxendine, J.B. (1998) 'Motor skill learning for effective coaching and performance,' pp. 13–27 in Williams, J.M. (ed.) *Applied Sport Psychology: Personal growth to peak performance*, 3rd edition, Mountain View CA: Mayfield.

Griffin, L.L., Mitchell, S.A. and Oslin, J.L. (1997) *Teaching Sport Concepts and Skills* Champaign IL: Human Kinetics.

SKILL ACQUISITION

As conventionally understood, **skill** acquisition refers to the process through which we experience the environment and learn to perform activities that are refined into skills. This suggests that acquired skills depend on critical experiences rather than innate, species-specific properties. Some scholars doubt whether we possess such properties at all.

In his *Wolf Children and the Problem of Human Nature*, Lucien Malson argued that the study of feral children 'reveals the absence of these dependable *a priori*, of adaptive schemata peculiar to the species.' Deprived of human contact and reared in the wild by animals in their formative years, feral children who have been discovered by humans were mute quadrupeds, who began to stand erect only after painstaking tutoring. Some eventually spoke, though not competently. One boy could use his hands only for picking up objects between his thumb and index finger. Yet many were adept at tree climbing and other dexterous acts not usually associated with humans, such as lapping up water or fighting with hands and teeth. Their perceptual skills were also different: some had acute senses of smell and hearing while others could not judge distance or even distinguish between paintings and reality. Children who had been raised by nocturnal animals had photophobia, an extreme sensitivity to light. Malson encouraged a conception of humans as having 'an *acquired nature* ... a structure of possibilities ... which are only realized in some specific social context.'

Any analysis of skill acquisition should be informed by this observation: even the most elementary of tasks, ones that are commonly regarded as 'natural,' are learned. Some are adaptations to the environment, others are developed through imitation and tuition. Fitts and Posner formulated an early model that identified three stages to the acquisition. The *cognitive stage* involves understanding a task and its demands: lack of familiarity means that there will be clumsiness and plenty of errors. Progressing to an *intermediate* and *associative stage*, the learner begins to identify strategies that allow quick **perception** and retrieval of information pertinent to the task at hand; the subject learns appropriate responses, errors decrease and speed increases. The final stage is *late or autonomous*: the skilled performer is able to execute the skill or skills efficiently and with the minimum of errors, without much cognitive involvement.

But the question this raises is: precisely how does the acquisition process work? Several theories have purported to answer this, many resting on the idea that the results of our engagement with the material world feed back to us in the form of valuable information, which we in turn use to modify our behavior. **Knowledge of results** accomplished through previous actions is fed back to the individual, the more precise and direct the more effective. In the early cognitive stage, the information needs to be exact and detailed, but as the athlete improves and reaches the associative stage he or she is able to modify behavior in accordance with the knowledge fed back. Eventually, less conscious **attention** needs to be paid and the performance of the skills becomes automatic.

At this autonomous stage, when the basic skills have been conquered, each item of information covers a larger unit of performance. For example, a cricket batsman will not need **feedback** on grip, posture and positioning, as he does not need to be consciously aware of these features. He may still require information on how to play a particular type of bowler on a particular type of surface, and that information may result in his using a mixture of unorthodox reverse sweeps and pulls with conventional driving. Because fewer units of performance need to be adjusted, the modification will appear smoother. Highly skilled performers are not only efficient, but also versatile. An efficient yet inflexible batsman may have acquired technique but may be unable to adapt to unusual conditions.

Skill acquisition is often very specific and does not transfer to other skills, though it can carry the potential for transference to related domains. This means that the strategies and knowledge picked up in acquiring one skill may be applied to other areas. Mathematics students famously apply the skills acquired during their studies to chess playing. Bo Jackson and Dennis Compton were both adept at ostensibly very different sports, in Jackson's case football and baseball, in Compton's, soccer and cricket. But each pair of sports shared perceptual and cognitive skills, if not motor skills. The strategies employed to master one of the sports were presumably used to master the other.

Typically, improvements in skill acquisition are rapid at first, then slow down to a gradual pace. Simple repetition and **reinforcement** is the key mechanism at first, but improvement requires new knowledge and strategies. An improvement in accuracy and coordination is not achieved by performing the same skill over and over again, but by introducing new, related skills. Athletes improve by taking on new and possibly unfamiliar challenges. This does not mean that highly proficient performers will lose their original skills. Quite the contrary: once the skill has been attained, it is secure for many, many years, though, of course, fine edges may be dulled without continual practice. Even after prolonged inactivity enforced by injury, athletes can usually recapture skills in a relatively short period of time. **Injury**, loss of ambition or lack of physical condition rather than the erosion of skill ends careers.

Further reading

Fitts, P.M. and Posner, M.I. (1967) *Human Performance*, 2nd edition, Belmont CA: Brooks/Cole.
Holding, G.H. (ed.) (1988) *Human Skills* London: Wiley.

SKILL PERFORMANCE

The execution of learned abilities under testing conditions is skill performance. In sports, the most testing conditions are, of course, actual **competition**. The performance involves: (1) memorizing features of previous performances, or rehearsals (such as in training) – including sensory input (how the body felt); (2) interpreting information from the present environment; and (3) exercising judgement in choosing actions appropriate to particular circumstances, which may change suddenly.

So skill performance involves the three tenses of past, present and future. It requires the performer to draw on experiences accumulated from practice and *past* performance and combine these with knowledge of *immediate* situations, while *anticipating* the probable results of lines of action. All the time, adjustments must constantly be made to take account of **feedback** from the here-and-now. An obvious example: a golfer might discover midway through a round that a strong wind necessitates a modification of technique. Information from the present environment impels a change, familiarity with similar past situations influences the decision and an evaluation of the likely outcomes of the decision informs the response. Other situations in different sports may demand that the performer responds more quickly than a golfer, but the components of the process are likely to be similar.

The successful performance of **skill** in sports usually depends on responding to swift and definite changes in the environment. Both components of the **nervous system** – the central nervous system (CNS) and the peripheral nervous system (PNS) – need to direct changes and issue instructions to relevant parts of the body in order that they react quickly. The quickest communication system is based on electrical impulses. Simply put, the CNS comprises the **control** center of the brain and its message conduit, the spinal cord, and the PNS is the network of nerves originating in the brain and spinal cord and is responsible for picking up messages from the skin and sense organs (sensory nerve cells) from the CNS to the muscles (motor nerve cells).

It is probable that athletes and nonathletes alike can pick up roughly equivalent quantities and qualities of information from the environment. Sense organs enable us to take in information through eyes, ears and other body parts. What separates highly skilled performers from lesser beings is how they interpret information and adjust their behavior accordingly. Interpreting information received through the senses involves several cognitive processes. Very briefly, data received, whether visual, auditory or tactile, is stored before it is either sent to the short-term **memory** or discarded. For example, a basketball player will momentarily store the sound of the official's whistle before attempting a free shot; or a quarterback will fleetingly hold the image of a moving wide receiver before releasing a pass. In both these and myriad other cases in sports, the athlete is busy screening out irrelevant information, or **gating**, and selectively attending to the job at hand.

Athletes often interpret, or make sense of, sensory input in highly specialized ways: a cricketer can use tactile information about the surface of a cricket ball; a tennis player will hit the heel of a hand with the racket to assess the tension of the strings. Disabled athletes often compensate for the loss of sense organs with others that are highly developed, such as a sense of equilibrium or an acute sense of hearing. In all cases, initial movements provide sensory feedback which facilitates adjustment and control of future actions – which, in turn, provide further information.

Perhaps the most critical phase in the performance of skill is **decision making**. Once information from the environment has been received and interpreted, an athlete is faced with a range of possibilities about what to do. Skilled athletes typically make appropriate choices. How do they arrive at their decisions? It is tempting to imagine that they consider the various actions available to them, project ahead to possible outcomes and assign probabilities and utilities to these outcomes. In other words, this would be a completely rational decision-making process based on systematic principles. In practice the process is less rational.

Research by Kahneman *et al.* indicated that athletes make use of experiences to devise rules of thumb, or *heuristics*. For instance, an experienced, skilled boxer might base a provisional fight strategy against southpaw opponents on his or her recollection of previous similar opponents and, assuming the memory is sound and that the experiences were representative, then there is sufficient for a judgement. This may serve the boxer well in this fight; but it may also lead to error if the opponent is unlike previous southpaw opponents (i.e. unrepresentative), or if the boxer has fought so few southpaws that previous experiences are not readily available. Heuristics may prove reliable in most circumstances, but they are imperfect, especially in circumstances filled with uncertainty – as sports are, of course. Highly skilled performers are those who can estimate the probabilities of outcomes and respond appropriately on a regular basis, though not on every single occasion.

It is often said that older athletes make up in experience what they lack in youth. Effectively, they can draw on such a vast repository of information when making decisions that they compensate for the erosion of speed or agility brought about by **aging**. Training, diet, conditioning and all-round lifestyle can contribute to the continuing capacity to perform a skill. There are, however, limits: no amount of preparation or temperate living can prevent the slowing down of **reaction time**, often abbreviated to just RT – the minimum time between the presentation of a stimulus and a subject's response to it. Technically, there are several different kinds of RT. For example: simple reaction time, where there is a single stimulus and a single, simple response; complex (or compound), where two or more **stimuli** and responses are involved; or choice reaction time, where there are more than one stimuli and the subject has to respond to one but refrain from responding to the others, which is often the case in competition. Timing and the fine judgement that comes of years of practical experience may balance out the effects of a decelerating RT, but eventually the performance of skills will be adversely affected.

Further reading

Butler, R.J. (ed.) (1997) *Sport Psychology in Performance* Oxford: Butterworth.

Kahneman, D., Slovic, P. and Tversky, A. (1982) *Judgement under Certainty: Heuristics and biases* Cambridge: Cambridge University Press.

SLUMP

A sudden decline or a gradual subsidence in form that extends beyond normal fluctuations is known as a slump. If it persists, an athlete is said to be slumping, the word possibly being taken from a seventeenth-century English word, 'slumpy' (from the German *schlump*), for a bog, marsh or muddy place.

'An unexplained drop' in performance, is how Taylor defined slump, suggesting that potentially anything can cause decrements in performance. A recurrent **injury**, a defeat leading to changes in **self-efficacy**, or a distracting new **goal** unrelated to sport are common conditions that can undermine performance.

The most unwelcome quality of a slump is that it can become self-perpetuating: **anxiety** over one poor performance can affect the next performance, which leads to more anxiety and perhaps even **fear** of competing. Slumping can eventually undermine an athlete's **motivation**, but even if it does not, increasing efforts does not always yield improvements. Compensating by working harder in training can lead to **overtraining** and a deeper slump. Often **cognitive–behavioral modification** is used, **relaxation** being a key resource in allaying an athlete's anxiety, restoring **confidence** and allowing a resumption of more typical form. 'Slump-related coping' was studied in 1998 by Eklund *et al.*

Further reading

Goldberg, A. (1998) *Sports Slump Busting: 10 steps to mental toughness and peak performance* Champaign IL: Human Kinetics.

Taylor, J. (1988) 'Slumpbusting: a systematic analysis of slumps in sports,' *The Sport Psychologist* vol. 2, pp. 39–48.

SOCIAL FACILITATION

Any activity is facilitated in some way by the presence of others: fully fed chickens carry on eating when surrounded by other chickens which are eagerly devouring feed; children will play more enthusiastically when their friends are around; and athletes perform differently when in the company of other athletes or spectators. The effect is known as social facilitation, and in sports it was first documented in the pioneering research of Norman Triplett who, in the late nineteenth century, observed the differences in cycling records set under different conditions. 'Facilitate' is from the Latin *facilis*, for easy or unconstrained, and the research suggested that company can have the effect of removing constraints on performance.

Triplett compared cyclists riding alone with those paced by the clock and those racing against each other. There was a pronounced improvement across the three situations, leading Triplett to conclude: (1) the presence of others aroused the 'competitive instinct' which, in turn, released hidden reserves of energy; (2) the sight of others' movements had the effect of making the subject speed up.

Speed was important to the research tradition started by Triplett. In 1924, Floyd H. Allport argued that the presence of others facilitated enhanced quantity or quickness of movement, but that it also led to decrements in precision or quality of performance. Greater speed came at the cost of accuracy. In this and subsequent research, the role of others' presence in facilitating behavioral changes in athletes, whether individuals or in teams, became ever clearer.

Robert Zajonc is credited with providing most clarity to social facilitation with his research, published in 1965. A follower of the variant of learning theory advanced by Clark Hull, known as **drive** reduction hypothesis (which maintains that **goal** motivated behavior is directed toward the reduction of drive states), Zajonc argued that the sheer presence of others, either as spectators or as fellow participants (coactors), increased drive or **arousal** level. If the subject is well practiced and has **mastery** over a **skill**, or the skill itself is relatively simple, then the increased drive benefits performance and the appropriate response is dominant. If, on the other hand, the subject is a beginner or the skill is difficult, then the performance will be hindered. This would account for why young or inexperienced athletes sometimes 'freeze' in their first outing at a big venue.

Contradictory research findings followed. For example, some studies showed that rookies were less affected by audiences than experienced competitors and that their performance did not suffer; other studies showed that social facilitation worked for simple skills, but not always where complex skills were needed. There were also conceptual criticisms leveled at Zajonc. Whereas Hull had used 'drive' as a theoretical construct to explain motivated behavior, Zajonc conflated it with arousal, which may be operationalized empirically, using palmar sweating, heart rate increases, self reports and so on. In this way, Zajonc produced a theory that could be tested and challenged. (In using 'drive' to explain behavior, Zajonc used a precise operational definition and specified quantifiable behavioral referents as measures of the construct.)

Doubts were raised about the 'mere presence factor': is the mere presence of others enough to arouse athletes, or are there other causal factors, such as the type of crowd or the athletes' awareness of the crowd? For instance, if athletes interpret the spectators as having the potential to evaluate them, then this may give rise to **anxiety**, which leads to decrements in performance. If nothing turns on the performance and the consequences of the crowd's evaluation are of no significance, then there is unlikely to be any 'evaluation apprehension,' as Cottrell called it.

There have been several attempts to modify Zajonc's formulation, one of the most interesting by Leonard Wankel, whose 1984 essay moved beyond what he called the 'mechanistic drive theory' toward 'more complex models which place greater emphasis on **cognition** and how the individual interprets the information in the social situation.' It is this subjective social situation that constitutes the reality to which the individual reacts,' wrote Wankel, who introduces features such as age, **gender**, previous experience and **personality** into the mix to show that there are many surprising findings in social facilitation. Less experienced competitors experience less **stress** and distraction at big championship events than more experienced athletes, presumably because they feel they have 'nothing to lose.' Audience effects on female competitors were changing when Wankel wrote his paper: the gender of the audience and that of the competitor, as well as the nature of the task, were all factors. But values have changed and it is less likely that gender of performers or observers has as much influence.

The composition, size, density, expectations and general **character** of the crowd also have relevance: bellicose and boisterous fans urging competitors to play more aggressively may influence performance. Crowds are often thought to 'get behind' teams, especially when at home. This is one among other factors in **home advantage**, though we should also allow for the possibility that officials as well as athletes are subject to social facilitation and their performance will affect outcomes.

The impact of **group dynamics** is manifold: experiments with **obedience** have illustrated how behavior, if not attitudes, can be manipulated. **Leadership** studies have shown how individuals in the appropriate context can almost 'bend' the will of individuals, again underlining the influence of the group.

Further reading

Cottrell, N.B. (1972) 'Social facilitation,' pp. 185–236 in McClintock, G. (ed.) *Experimental Social Psychology* New York: Holt, Rinehart & Winston.

Turner, J.C. (1991) *Social Influence* Milton Keynes, England: Open University Press.

Wankel, L. (1984) 'Audience effects in sport,' pp. 293–314 in Silva, J.M. and Weinberg, R.S. (eds) *Psychological Foundations of Sport*, Champaign IL: Human Kinetics.

SOCIAL LOAFING

Not to be confused with just loafing – spending time idly or acting at a leisurely pace – *social* loafing is the inclination to reduce effort when working toward a common **goal** with others. In other words, individuals tend to slacken off when trying to accomplish something with a group. This is by no means confined to sports: it has implications for any collective endeavor. Yet it does have particular effects in team sports where the potential for individuals to reduce effort under some conditions is high.

A research team led by Latané in 1979 questioned the adage 'many hands make light work.' The team discovered that there was a 'motivational loss' when individuals worked in groups, and this led to a decrease in performance. Exploring what had previously been called the **Ringelmann effect**, the team was interested in the apparent loss in **motivation** of group members as the size of the group increased. The tasks assigned were relatively simple – clapping and shouting – but the finding was significant: people who thought they could get 'lost in the crowd' did not try as hard as they would if they thought they could be identified as individuals. A comparison would be people singing hymns in a church: if the church is relatively empty, they might sing more vigorously than if it was crowded. The potential for being identified and appraised decreases with increases in the size of the group.

It follows that social loafing is unlikely to occur when performers know or suspect their performances are being evaluated or even compared with those of others. Research by Harkins and Jackson indicated that social loafing is least likely to happen when individual performances can be clearly monitored, giving rise to **anxiety** about evaluation. The potential for social loafing is highest when all team members are not only trying to achieve a common goal but also performing the same task. A tug-of-war is the most obvious example, because every team member is doing exactly the same thing – pulling the rope. Rowing is another sport in which all members of the crew, apart from the cox, are working in unison. Athletes are unlikely to believe they are accountable for their individual performances in these kinds of contests.

In 1983, N.L. Kerr argued that this creates two types of competitor. The 'free rider' thinks there is a good chance that other members of the group will perform better than him or her and he or she will still get the same amount of credit. So the cost–benefit equation is simple: do less work for the same approval. The problem is that the others will get the same idea and, rather than being the 'suckers' who do all the work while others slack off, they reduce their own efforts as a way of balancing out what might otherwise be an unequal distribution of effort. In this light, social loafing appears to be less the result of a reduction in motivation and more an avoidance of doing more than one's fair share of the work for only the same amount of credit.

Minimizing social loafing in team sports is obviously crucial, and Harkins and Szymanski provide a clue as to how coaches might do this: merely reminding individuals in a group of a personal performance standard was enough in itself to stop social loafing. In most team sports, there is a division of labor that ensures that individual performances can be monitored. In baseball and cricket, two team sports in which statistics are tabulated on individuals' batting, fielding, etc., the possibilities for social loafing are slim. In most professional team sports, the financial incentives for team success are sufficient to ensure that individuals do not hold back on effort.

Further reading

Harkins, S.G. and Jackson, J.M. (1985) 'The role of evaluation in eliminating social loafing,' *Personality and Social Psychology Bulletin* vol. 11, pp. 457–65.

Harkins, S.G. and Szymanski, K. (1989) 'Social loafing and self-evaluation with an objective standard,' *Journal of Experimental Psychology Bulletin* vol. 24, pp. 354–65.

Karau, S.J. and Williams, K.D. (1993) Social loafing: a meta-analytic review and theoretical integration,' *Journal of Personality and Social Psychology* vol. 65, pp. 681–706.

SOCIALIZATION

The process by which humans learn to become members of a culture is known as socialization, from the Latin *socius*, company, and *izare*, meaning method or way. As humans grow in the company of other humans, they learn the characteristics that actually make them human. Studies of feral children reared outside human society have shown that, while they were biologically *Homo sapiens*, the children had no faculty of speech and behaved much as the animals with which they were raised. Reviewing two such cases, Harold Kerbo concluded: 'These children are in a sense not human.'

Defined in its broadest sense, culture is everything that is learned (rather than inherited genetically); it is transmitted from one generation to the next primarily through language, then elaborated on for future transmission. As humans grow in groups of other humans, they learn the characteristics that actually make them human: for example, their **personality**, convictions and behavioral traits. Obviously, human development depends on a combination of biological, psychological and social factors, and much of the argument on the precise balance of influences in the socialization process involves the nature *v.* nurture discourse. Recognizing that there are biological limits or, perhaps more accurately, biological timing in maturation does not preclude the substantial impress of culture in, for example, cognitive development, including **intelligence**, **identity** formation and self-concept.

Clearly, certain aspects of us are not conferred by nature. We have no biological predisposition to speak English rather than Punjabi any more than we have to like garage more than classical music. Even gifted artists are probably not literally 'gifted,' as in having natural endowments, but may have basic propensities that are nurtured and molded by significant others. **Modeling** enables a person to refine his or her abilities by imitating and perhaps innovating on the accomplishments of others. This has obvious applicability in sports, where aspirant athletes participate in what some theorists call *secondary* socialization, *primary* socialization being the initial process in which language, personality and basic cultural competence are achieved.

Secondary socialization involves the learning of specialist skills and capacities. Immersion into competitive sports means that the subject acquires a new vocabulary, a new circle of significant others and probably a new set of goals as well as a new repertoire of behavioral habits. Socialization in sports may introduce a subject to **discipline** and will almost certainly confer some degree of **achievement motivation**. It may also introduce a developing athlete to **doping**, **stress** and a miscellany of other unwelcome facets of the sporting experience, including **deviance**. Sports will almost certainly involve *anticipatory* socialization: learning a future role to which a subject aspires, whether it is that of a champion or a routine healthy competitor.

Some people experience a kind of biographical hiatus and change their entire conception of themselves and the world. Converts to a new **religion**, particularly a cult, are frequently implicated in what is often called a *resocialization*. This means learning sometimes the most fundamental 'facts' over again: even domain assumptions, such as loving one's parents and believing in God, can be undermined during resocialization. A retrospective interpretation of her 'former life' enables a convert to look back and render her life intelligible in terms of the new conceptual framework. To a lesser extent, being imprisoned or joining the armed forces both involve a resocialization of sorts because new values, codes and behaviors are imposed and need to be learned.

Agents of socialization are varied. While family, close peers and sometimes the Church are instrumental in primary phases, the media, particularly television, and the school become more prominent later. In secondary socialization, any number of agencies can figure. This is not to suggest that the various agencies exert a one-way influence: the socialization process should be understood as negotiated, i.e. a productive interaction between the subject and the agencies involved. All socialization takes place in face-to-face interaction, yet at the same time both primary and secondary socialization relate the individual to the wider world. 'The attitudes which the individual learns in socialization usually refer to broad systems of meaning and of values that extend far beyond his immediate situation,' wrote Peter and Brigitte Berger in what remains one of the best examinations of the process: 'Socialization enables the individual to relate to specific individual others; subsequently, it enables him to relate to an entire social universe. For better or worse, being human entails having such a relationship on a lifelong basis.'

Further reading

Berger, P. and Berger, B. (1981) *Sociology: A biographical approach* New York: Penguin, ch. 3.
Kerbo, H.R. (1989) *Sociology: Social structure and social conflict* New York: Macmillan, ch. 7.

STIMULI

Events, occurrences or changes that evoke behavioral responses from organisms are stimuli, the plural of 'stimulus,' a term drawn from the Latin *stimulare*, meaning animate or goad.

Stimuli are typically defined as objectively describable, but it has been argued that an **incentive** is a stimulus: it is possible for concepts or percepts to function as stimuli when they excite a person to action or to more vigorous action. Stimuli may be outside or inside the organism as long as they are within receptive range. 'A 40,000Hz tone may be a stimulus for a bat but not for a human,' writes Arthur Reber in his *Dictionary of Psychology.*

Pavlov's experiments showed how it is possible to create, manipulate and shape stimuli, and his theories of classical conditioning were crucial to the understanding of the ways in which **reinforcement** works.

Further reading

Domjan, M. and Burkhardt, B. (1986) *The Principles of Learning and Behavior* Pacific Grove CA: Brooks/Cole.

STREAKS

Uninterrupted sequences of recent results are known as streaks, from the Gothic word *striks*, meaning strokes (e.g. of pens or swords). A popular notion in sports is that winning or losing streaks have an effect on ensuing contests: going into a matchup on a five-game hot streak is preferable to coming off five straight defeats, for example. The idea is that the rise in **confidence** and **self-esteem** that accompanies a succession of good results affects the positive **momentum** of an individual or entire team. Yet in contrast to accepted wisdom, Roger

Vergin found that the statistical chances of winning are not dependent on the results of recent contests, and so the streak has no causal connection with future outcomes.

Vergin's findings tend to undermine athletes' own commonsense ideas about the impetus precipitated by winning runs and the self-perpetuating qualities of a **slump**: 'The probability of winning a game is independent of the results of recent games' – though it should be pointed out that much of the research on momentum focuses on athletes' **perception** of the impetus rather than its objective effects.

Further reading

Vergin, R.C. (2000) 'Winning streaks in sports and the misperception of momentum,' *Journal of Sport Behavior* vol. 23, pp. 181–97.

STRESS

Although it is commonly associated with almost any form of discomfort, stress is, strictly speaking, a constraining or propelling force or pressure that causes a significant change in a system; alternatively, it may be approached as the *responses* of a system to the force; or even the relationship between the two. Robert Gatchel captures aspects of all three when he defines stress as 'the process by which environmental events threaten or challenge an organism's well-being and by which that organism responds to this threat.' The term 'stress' is taken from 'distress,' originally *destresser*, an Anglo-French word meaning to vex or make unhappy.

Athletes are said to be under stress when expectations of them are, as they see them, too high or, less commonly, too low. The effects of stress include **anxiety**, such as when the situation facing a competitor is seen as threatening, or too much **arousal**, possibly precipitated by intense preparation for a contest. In both cases, stress is typically accompanied by behavioral and physiological changes.

Stress is one of the most over-used and misunderstood terms in the lexicon: people complain of being 'stressed out' by their work, their domestic situation and even their leisure activities. In this sense, stress is considered an effect, consequence of or response to underlying forces, rather than the forces themselves. This still fits in with the above definition, though sports analysts have tried to be more precise in examining the relationship between stress as an antecedent of effects and stress as a reflection of other conditions.

Richard Lazarus, for example, has argued that stress should properly be examined as a transaction between the human being and the environment, the force being produced by their interaction rather than residing in either. This moves away from more straightforward cause→effect models in which stress is the causal agent: for Lazarus, the process is *recursive*, the individual and the environment affecting and changing each other in a sort of rebounding interaction. For instance, the two members of a beach volleyball team preparing for an important game may face exactly the same kind of task but respond differently. One may look forward eagerly to a demanding game she believes she will enjoy. The other may be daunted by the prospect, and her uneasiness may manifest in errors during training. In an effort to compensate for this, she may train even harder, though without much improvement in form. This apparent loss of form at a crucial stage makes her even uneasier, possibly causing her to tighten up during training and commit even more errors. So the errors keep recurring and compound her situation. (The word 'recursive' is from the Latin *re*, as in again, and *curs*, run.)

So there are no absolutes in the stress process: the response to a situation depends on the cognitive appraisal of it and the consequences of the appraisal. To change the scenario slightly: the overawed player may put extra effort into training and see some improvements in her form; rather than tightening up, she may use some **cognitive–behavioral modification**, relax and grow easier with the prospect of the big game. The stress disappears following an appropriate **intervention**.

Not all types of stress are negative. Hans Selye proposes that we experience **eustress** when we are euphoric or pleasantly thrilled. On the other hand, tension and apprehension manifest in the form of *distress*. There are two other types of stress, according to Selye: *hyperstress*, which occurs when we are overloaded with too much stress, and *hypostress* when we do not have enough, such as when we are waiting for hours at an airport with nothing to do.

The enforced inactivity of a sports performer recovering from a long-term **injury** in the prime of his or her career may bring on hypostress, which may then lead to heavy drinking and, eventually, to a **dependence** of some kind. This is quite common among professional athletes who have probably not experienced a long period away from active **competition** since childhood. An example of hyperstress would be a football **team player** who is given the added responsibility of captaincy and finds the additional demands too taxing. By contrast, another player may accept the **leadership** role with relish, ridding him or herself of the hypostress of not having sufficient responsibility to occupy his or her full capacities.

Further reading

Gatchel (1996) 'Stress and coping,' pp. 560–77 in Colman, A.M. (ed.) *Companion Encyclopedia of Psychology*, vol. 1, London: Routledge.
Lazarus, R.S. (1993) 'From psychological stress to the emotions: a history of changing outlooks,' *Annual Review of Psychology* vol. 44, pp. 1–21.
Selye, H. (1983) 'The stress concept: past, present and future,' pp. 1–20 in Cooper, C.L (ed.) *Stress Research* New York: Wiley.

STRESS INOCULATION TRAINING

As its name suggests, stress inoculation training is a program of treatment that involves the use of **stress** itself to protect against its more serious attacks. To inoculate is to treat a person or animal with the agent of a disease to induce a milder form of it. Pioneered by Meichenbaum, the program exposes athletes to situations of progressively greater stress, the idea being that this will eventually work as a safeguard.

It has three phases.

1 Conceptualization phase: this involves encouraging the athlete to recognize and address the **character** of his or her stress and the effects it has on his or her performance.
2 Skills acquisition phase: **relaxation**, deep breathing, **imagery**, problem solving and other **coping strategies** are developed. The emphasis is on controlling negative thoughts and reinforcing effort.
3 Application and follow through phase: the athlete translates the coping skills into programs of practical action.

Once the agent of the subject's stress is identified, modest and controllable amounts of stress are introduced in much the same way as an *inoculum* (substance used for an inoculation) is injected. For example, an athlete may be induced into a relaxed state, then encouraged to imagine stressful encounters before rehearsing ways of coping with them. Role-playing and videos of imaginary situations are used. Once this is well practiced, the athlete may be plunged into a real stressful situation so that he or she can experience first hand a low level of stress. As the subject becomes skilled at coping, the level of stress is upped and a more intimidating situation is created. This continues until the athlete is adept at coping in even highly stressful circumstances. Ultimately, the athlete is able to confront and overcome the original problem in actual **competition**.

Stress inoculation training is an alternative to Ronald Smith's **stress management training**, which differs in its focus only on highly stressful situations. While it shares with the inoculation approach several coping strategies, outlined above (2), its main effort is to create extremely high levels of **emotional arousal** in subjects by urging them to imagine a situation of maximum stress, while practicing coping skills.

Further reading

Meichenbaum, D. (1977) *Cognitive Behavior Modification: An integrative approach* New York: Plenum.
Meichenbaum, D. (1985) *Stress Inoculation Training* New York: Pergamon Press.

STRESS MANAGEMENT TRAINING

Aimed at equipping subjects with the ability to cope with **anxiety**, stress management training is predicated on the view that there must be active cognitive involvement from the subject. Whereas earlier approaches to anxiety reduction involved subjects passively, the cognitive–affective orientation of stress management training means that 'the client plays a far more active role and assumes more personal responsibility for developing and applying new modes of thinking about problem situations,' according to Ronald Smith.

While Smith's method resembles that of **stress inoculation training**, it differs in an important respect: rather than practicing under low levels of **stress**, a technique known as induced affect is employed to allow rehearsal of coping responses while experiencing strong **emotion**. Subjects are typically encouraged to imagine an intensely stressful situation, then to experience the feelings that the scene elicits in them. By conjuring a worst case scenario, the subjects are imaginatively immersing themselves in a worse situation than they will actually encounter. When subjects reach a very high state of **arousal**, they are told to 'turn it off,' using **coping strategies**, such as deep breathing or task-relevant **self-talk**, that induce physical **relaxation**.

The premise of the method is that learning to manage high levels of stress ensures that lower levels can also be managed in real situations;

stress inoculation proceeds from the other direction. For example, an ice skater was asked to vividly imagine a scene in which she skated on to the ice and fell down during her routine. This would be unlikely to happen in actuality. Having generated a high level of arousal, the skater was then advised to go through her repertoire of coping strategies, such as deep inhalation and mental commands ('I can do no more than give my best, so relax') during exhalation. After perfecting this, the skater discovered that she could use the strategies to reduce high levels of anxiety both in training and in **competition**. The long-term benefits of the approach include a continuing ability to **control** high arousal and an enhancement in **self-efficacy**. There is also the possibility of generalizing the results from sports-specific situations. For instance, the skater, having developed a capacity for managing competitive stress, may be able to use coping strategies to deal with a wide range of other potentially stressful situations and grow in **confidence** as a result.

Like other forms of cognitive–affective training, stress management seeks to influence new patterns of behavior by introducing subjects to the value of relaxation, **imagery** and other cognitive techniques. Although some of these techniques are used in behavioral approaches, they are conceived rather differently – as silent behaviors. The **goal** of behavioral approaches is to modify the subject's behavior, not necessarily to equip him or her with the cognitive ability to control the anxiety.

Further reading

Smith, R.E. (1980) 'A cognitive–affective approach to stress management training for athletes,' pp. 54–72 in Nadeau, C., Halliwell, W., Newell, K. and Roberts, G. (eds) *Psychology of Motor Behavior and Sports – 1979* Champaign IL: Human Kinetics.

Smith, R.E. (1984) 'Theoretical and treatment approaches to anxiety reduction,' pp. 157–70 in Silva, J.M. and Weinberg, R.S. (eds) *Psychological Foundations of Sport* Champaign IL: Human Kinetics.

SUPERSTITION

A belief, practice or opinion based on an uncritically held notion of cause and effect is a superstition, a word taken from the Latin *super*, denoting above, and *stat*, for stand. Superstition is common in sports: athletes subscribe to often obscure rituals and gestures in their efforts to secure good **luck**. Peculiar charms, complex dressing routines and bizarre procedures form parts of athletes' superstitions. Common to them all is the complete absence of anything resembling what others would recognize as adequate evidence that they work. Yet athletes are, in all probability, no more susceptible to magic, chance and erroneous conceptions of causation than the rest of the population. Myriad historical and anthropological studies support the conclusion that ritualistic and superstitious practices have existed in all cultures in all ages.

The way superstition comes into being may be explained in behaviorist terms. Say a hurdler inadvertently puts on her left sock inside out, then produces a personal best while winning her race. Later, in the locker room, she discovers the reversed sock, so resolves to wear the same sock that way for all subsequent races, some of which she wins, others she does not. Winning the first race when the sock was worn strengthened the likelihood that it would be worn like this again. In other words, the behavior was reinforced. This raises the frequency of the sock-wearing in the next several races, so that, next time the athlete records a good win, the probability is that she will be wearing the sock the same way. That serves as the next **reinforcement**, which in turn strengthens the frequency of the sock being worn in future. Over time, the athlete will probably display a superstitious inside-out sock-wearing response, even though the response has no direct relationship to the reinforcement being received. The sock does not cause good performances, but is merely reinforced adventitiously and irregularly. An assessment of cause and effect is not necessary for the hurdler, nor for any other athlete who has stumbled on a superstition.

Once the superstition appears to bring desired results, the athlete's **confidence** may be affected, her **composure** may improve and her **expectancy** may change; reductions in **anxiety** may follow. The athlete's feelings of **control** over performance may offer a perceived way of minimizing the uncertainty inherent in **competition**. In this sense, the superstition can function as a placebo. When the superstition is not followed by the right results and this occurs consistently, the strength of the reinforcement will disappear and the ritual will be abandoned. Or the athlete may create an **obsession** out of the ritual, in which case **dependence** is possible. Instead of concentrating on more palpable forms of preparation, athletes can become preoccupied with observing the minutiae of the ritual.

Van Raalte *et al.* hypothesized that superstitions are more apt to develop among people who believe they can exert some control over chance outcomes through their own actions. Thirty-seven subjects completed the Levenson Chance Orientation Scale, which measures belief in maintaining control over chance events. Subjects attempted fifty putts on an artificial putting green turf. Those who believed their actions could control chance events were more likely to select a 'lucky ball' after making a successful putt. The level of anxiety increased the more ego-involved an athlete was in sport: the level of importance one attaches to task performance measures ego-involvement. Ego-involvement would make the athlete more likely to develop superstitions to cope with anxiety in sport. The more subjects believed their actions allowed an element of control over chance events, the more likely they were to choose the same ball or 'lucky ball' following a successful putt.

Amy Shepper summarized research into the prevalence of superstition in a variety of sports, concluding that the extraordinary beliefs and practices of fans matched meaningless behavior or abstinence from behavior (including **sex**) of competitors. 'Participation [in superstitious behavior] may add an element of empowerment for televised sports viewers by creating a dynamic in which the fan interacts with the people/sports event on the other end of the television screen,' she writes. Whether fans actually believe they influence the course of a contest is less relevant than the sense of vicarious involvement enhanced by the rituals.

Further reading

Shepper, A.I. (2000) 'Superstition,' pp. 392–7 in Cashmore, E. (ed.) *Sports Culture: An A–Z guide* London: Routledge.
Van Raalte, J.L., Brewer, B.W., Nemeroff, C. and Linder, D. (1991) 'Chance orientation and superstitious behavior on the putting green,' *Journal of Sport Behavior* vol. 14, pp. 41–50.

TALENT

From the Greek *talanton*, a weight or sum of money, talent is conventionally defined as a possession of special desirable gifts, faculties or aptitude (for music, for art, etc.). Athletes are frequently described as 'talented' or even 'multi-talented,' meaning they are highly proficient in a particular **skill** or set of skills.

While the term is often used uncritically to suggest a genetic basis for skill (such as **instinct**), more considered appraisals of the **skill acquisition** process avoid the inference and prefer terms such as 'aptitude' (potential for achievement), 'competency' (sufficiency of means to perform tasks), 'capability' or 'capacity' (both meaning un-developed faculty). None of these terms implies a natural source for human skill, or, more obscurely, a 'God-given talent.'

Further reading

Domjan, M. and Burkhardt, B. (1986) *The Principles of Learning and Behavior* Pacific Grove CA: Brooks/Cole.

Entine, J. (2000) *Taboo: Why black athletes dominate and why we're afraid to talk about it* New York: PublicAffairs.

TEAM PLAYER

A team player is one who is prepared to combine his or her efforts with those of others for the group's purposes rather than for individual benefit. In the process, he or she may need to subordinate personal interests, possibly forfeiting individual accomplishments and honor for the sake of the team of which he or she is part. The word *team* is key: its origins probably lie in the Germanic word *taug*, which means pull and which, over time, became *taumr*, Norse for bridle (to restrain horses). As a verb, 'to team' is to harness (horses, etc.) into a common action. So the team player is one who works (or 'pulls') in an organized and cooperative way. (The word 'team' later came to mean family or offspring.)

Playing in a team is a **skill** in itself. It involves accepting and playing according to team norms, performing a role in a division of labor and assisting others in ways that will facilitate the achievement of team goals. There is no necessary incompatibility between being a team player and an individual: in fact, individual excellence is often realized in the context of a team – a point made by basketball coach Pat Riley in his *The Winner Within: A life plan for team players*. Many outstanding individual athletes have prospered in the framework of teams that scored high on **cohesion** and operated in a way that allowed virtuosity to flourish. Wayne Greztsky, Michael Jordan and Zinedine Zidane were all exceptional individual athletes and distinguished team players ('I had to convince Michael that the route to greatness was in making others better,' Jordan's coach Phil Jackson reflected). These and other team players did not simply coexist with other members, but contributed to a synergy. Other players with great technical proficiency may be capable of performing at a high level, but only as individuals rather than as members of a unit.

Often coaches despair at players who show aptitude and **motivation** but little conception of how to integrate into a team. The **Ringelmann effect** may be a factor: an individual's performance may be inhibited by the very presence of other team members. The team player, on the other hand, benefits from the presence of others, a process known as **social facilitation**. Changes in the conditions of **competition** can change this. For instance, delegating the captaincy of a team to an individual can both grant that player autonomy and induce him or her to exercise effective **leadership** and align his or her skills with those of other members. Empowering a player with more authority and responsibility is a common method of making him or her more responsive to the **group dynamics** of the team (or, conversely, it could introduce unwelcome **stress**).

The concept of *team efficacy* (as opposed to **self-efficacy**) is sometimes used to capture the collective sense of self-belief that can transform some teams of individually modest players into effective units. Winning games obviously helps team efficacy, especially when opponents are favored to succeed.

Further reading

Feltz, D.L. and Lirgg, C.D. (1998) 'Perceived team and player efficacy in hockey,' *Journal of Applied Psychology* vol. 83, pp. 557–64.
Riley, P. (1994) *The Winner Within: A life plan for team players* New York: Berkeley.

TELIC STATE

From the Greek word *telos*, meaning end, 'telic' describes a state in which ends, goals or objectives are sought. It contrasts with a *paratelic* state, which is playful and pleasurable in its own right. The term has been used in several ways by sports scholars trying to understand the transformations of motivational states, changes in levels of **arousal** and wholesale cultural shifts. The term is associated principally with two theories: **reversal theory** and *figurational theory*, both of which are concerned with sports.

Reversal theory concentrates on **metamotivation**, 'the way in which a person's motives can change and fluctuate.' A subject in a telic motivational state sees a particular objective as being more important than whatever means are used to achieve it. A **goal**, once met, is often seen as another means, i.e. to a higher goal, which in turn leads to another goal (e.g. winning a game, leading to a qualification for a playoff spot, leading to a title win, etc.). The theory suggests that high arousal in a telic state will be interpreted as disagreeable and may be experienced as **anxiety**, while comparable levels of anxiety in a paratelic state will be understood as beneficial, uplifting and pleasurably exciting. As Kurt Frey writes: 'Although the telic person wants to be energized enough to pursue his or her objective, he or she does not want to be unnecessarily "worked up" ... A common (though less precise) word to describe being telic is "serious".'

In a different way, figurational theory offers a historical account of the development of sports in the nineteenth century, in which activities that were once engaged in for the purposes of gaining pleasure underwent fundamental changes. The civilizing process brought with it the establishment of definite objectives and rational planning so that those objectives could be met. The change was accompanied by transformations in **personality** and *habitus* (the schemes, values and practices of groups): rationality, planning and foresight became features of the civilizing process. These changes were reflected in pastimes and other leisure pursuits: the accent on pleasure diminished as **competition** grew in popularity. Ends were prioritized while an **achievement ethic** came to prominence. So the 'expressive' use of **violence** so integral to folk games was replaced by the 'instrumental use,' and activities that were once engaged in for the purposes of gaining pleasure mutated to become 'serious' goal-oriented competitions.

In this conception, the dichotomy between individual and society is meaningless. For Norbert Elias, the founder of the figurational approach, the two are inseparable. 'Since people are more or less dependent on each other first by nature and then through social learning,' wrote Elias, 'they exist ... only as pluralities, only in figurations.' The shift to a telic state is to be understood not at two levels but as a single process in which individuals, being parts of a figuration, experience and exhibit more rational calculation and more pronounced **goal orientation**.

Frey and other followers of reversal theory understand the telic state as a fluctuating experience that is evidenced most clearly in the shift from fun activities to more serious competition and which has consequences on individuals. Elias and figurational theorists see the telic state as a general condition describing the tendency of whole populations to think and behave in more instrumental ways – ways that were reflected in the structure of competitive sports.

Further reading

Elias, N. (1986) 'An essay on sport and violence,' pp. 150–74 in Elias, N. and

Dunning, E. (eds) *Quest for Excitement: Sport and leisure in the civilizing process* Oxford: Blackwell.

Frey, K.P. (1999) 'Reversal theory: basic concepts,' pp. 3–17 in Kerr, J.H. (ed.) (1999) *Experiencing Sport: Reversal theory* Chichester, England: Wiley.

TEMPERAMENTAL

'Temperamental' is an adjective typically applied to persons who exhibit an unusual sensitivity to certain **stimuli** – in plain English, they are 'easily upset.' Athletes with a reputation for being temperamental are known for their erratic, impetuous and sometimes aggressive behavior. This is thought to reflect permanent – some would argue genetically constituted – dispositions to react to particular types of situations. In this sense, they are far from unpredictable: if the stimuli are identifiable, then the response evoked by them can be anticipated. This is why opponents of temperamental athletes will intentionally try to perturb them as a way of breaking their **concentration** and prevent effective focusing.

If, as Peter Crocker *et al.* suggest, *temperament* 'refers to stable individual differences in how people experience and express emotions,' then a temperamental player is one who experiences an **emotion** and has few inhibitions about responding to it without a cautionary period for rational reflection. The response, in other words, is rash. Often, temperamental athletes are creative, as if possessed of an artistic temperament: they may perform indifferently in some, perhaps the majority of, competitions, yet flourish in others, prompting observers to detect an 'inspiration.' Such inspiration is, on analysis, a particular type of **motivation** that energizes the player under certain conditions, or a stimuli that elicits an appropriate behavioral response.

By contrast, a *temperate* athlete is moderate, self-restrained and hardly ever liable to respond incautiously to even obvious provocation. The temperate player remains unfazed by what he or she regards as poor officiating decisions, unpunished foul play or the incitement of rivals. An example of a temperamental *v.* temperate matchup might be Marat Safin against Pete Sampras.

Further reading

Crocker, P.E., Kowalski, K.C., Graham, T.R. and Kowalski, N.P. (2002) 'Emotion in sport,' pp. 107–31 in Silva, J.M. and Stevens, D.E. (eds) *Psychological Foundations of Sport* Boston MA: Allyn & Bacon.

THERAPY

From the Greek *therapeia*, for healing, therapy is the treatment of any form of disorder. Psychological therapy refers to treatment by psychological rather than biological or physical means. The term serves as an umbrella for many different types of techniques, all of which are intended to assist subjects in modifying their behavior and **cognition** and perhaps their **emotional** responses to particular circumstances. Therapy for athletes may be directed at any source of **anxiety** or **stress** experienced by a performer at any level of **competition**.

Different types of therapy rest on different assumptions. For example, some believe that the modification of behavior is dependent on the subject's understanding of his or her motives, while others feel that subjects can learn **coping strategies**, without exploring motives and just by changing their behavior. Still others approach therapy through a combination of techniques sometimes known as **cognitive–behavioral modification**.

Beyond differences, most therapy is predicated on the alliance or communion between the principals: the therapist and the client. The client is expressly reminded that, to be effective, the alliance relies on his or her total honesty. In return, a nonjudgemental atmosphere is maintained as the therapist offers guidance designed to support the client and promote independence rather than indefinite reliance.

Sport psychology therapist Jack Lesyk recounts how, in the 1980s, athletes 'seemed to **fear** a stigma if it were known that they were seeing a "shrink".' By 1990, the 'trickle down' was taking place and younger athletes were taking note of the endorsements of elite performers who had sought therapy of one kind or another to improve their competitive performance.

Despite the countless athletes who seek the therapy of sport psychology, the term 'therapy' retains a certain infamy, if not a stigma. Television programs, especially HBO's *The Sopranos*, and movies like *Antz* (in which a worker ant, voiced by Woody Allen, consults his therapist complaining that he feels 'insignificant' – 'That's because you *are*,' his therapist reassures him) have perpetuated this.

Infamy also surrounded Eileen Drury, a faith healer who was appointed by Glenn Hoddle, then manager of the England soccer team, to issue therapeutic guidance to players, some of whom were incredulous. While the choice of therapist was unorthodox, the basic motive was essentially that of any coach or manager who believes in the value of therapy – to offer understanding and insight, reassure and support and to suggest adaptive responses, perhaps using **reinforcement** to strengthen appropriate attitudes and behavior.

Further reading

Lesyk, J.L. (1998) *Developing Sport Psychology within Your Clinical Practice: A practical guide for mental health professionals* San Francisco CA: Jossey-Bass.

TRANSSEXUAL

A subject who has the physical characteristics of one **sex** and psychological characteristics of another is known as a transsexual. The term is taken from the Latin *trans*, for across, and *sexualis*, and should be distinguished from *transvestite*, which is a person who clothes him or herself in garments conventionally associated with the opposite sex but who may do so without any sexual purpose. Male athletes who have worn clothes regarded in western culture as women's, such as outer garments undivided below the waist, include Dennis Rodman, David Beckham and boxer Chris Eubank. The Thai boxer Parinya Kiatbusaba, known as Tum, dressed in women's clothing outside the ring and wore makeup when fighting: he attracted a **gay** following in Bangkok.

The most renowned transsexual in sports is Renee Richards, who played on the women's tennis tour before it was discovered that she was formerly Richard Raskind, a 6ft 2in, 147lb player who had been active on the men's circuit without achieving much of note. Raskind had undergone surgery to remove his penis and then resumed his/her tennis-playing career. The United States Tennis Association (USTA) and the Women's Tennis Association (WTA) introduced a Barr bodies sex test, which Richards refused to take. She was excluded from **competition**. In 1977, the New York Supreme Court ruled that requiring Richards to take the Barr test was 'grossly unfair, discriminatory and inequitable, and violative of her rights.'

During the *Richards v. USTA* case, the WTA and the US Open Committee opposed Richards' right to compete as a woman because 'there is a competitive advantage for a male who has undergone "sex-change" surgery as a result of physical training and development as a male.' Effectively, the argument did not revolve around whether or not Richards was a man or a woman, but on the issue of **gender** and fairness. Richards won the right to enter the 1977 US Open but was beaten in the first round, and thereafter pursued a less controversial career as a middle-order professional, retiring at age 47 to become Martina Navratilova's coach.

Transsexualism can also work the other way. Heidi Krieger, of the former German Democratic Republic, who won the European shot title in 1986, revealed that she had been on a **doping** program which included anabolic steroids since the age of 17. After turning 19, she felt a growing urge to be a man and, in 1997, underwent surgery to have her female sex organs, including breasts, ovaries and womb, removed. Krieger legally changed her name to Andreas and became officially a man, though he did not pursue a further operation that would have involved reconstructing male organs.

Further reading

Birrell, S. and Cole, C. (1990) 'Double fault: Renee Richards and the construction and naturalization of difference,' *Sociology of Sport Journal* vol. 7, pp. 1–21.

Raymond, J. (1979) *The Transsexual Empire* London: Beacon Press.

VICARIOUS ACHIEVEMENT

Imaginatively experiencing success through other persons, particularly one's children, is vicarious achievement, the term derived from the Latin *vicarius*, meaning substitute (the same root of the word vicar: originally, a clergyman deputizing for another). Its most obvious application in sports is in relation to **fandom**, in which collections of people take satisfaction or pleasure vicariously from the success of teams or individuals (or **pain** from their failure). Less obviously, but perhaps more interestingly, it has relevance to **parenting**.

The issue of parents' displacing of their own, perhaps thwarted, sporting ambitions on to their children is vexatious: fabulous success stories sit side by side with tales of misspent childhood, domineering parents and physical and psychological **burnout**. Parents who burden their children with the weight of their own expectations expose to **risk** not only themselves but other parents, as one case in particular illustrates.

Thomas Junta and Michael Costin both had sons who played hockey in Reading, Massachusetts. In July 2001, Costin supervised a practice session, while Junta watched. After seeing his son get checked and struck by an elbow, Junta complained to and, later, attacked and killed Costin in front of Costin's three sons. Reporting on this and the several other cases of **violence** among parents of maturing athletes,

William Nack and Lester Munson observed how 'the fields and arenas of youth sports in North America have become places where a kind of psychosis has at times prevailed with parents and coaches screaming and swearing at the kids, the official or each other, and fights breaking out among adults.' The authors concoct the term *parentis vociferous* to describe the species of 'loud, intrusive moms and dads unable to restrain themselves.'

There is an incongruity between the primary **goal** of young people and that of many parents who believe their children are, as Nack and Munson put it, 'Mozart in cleats.' The parents pursue tangible success much more zealously than the children do. In fact, there is evidence to support the view that young people participate in sports for a variety of reasons, the least of which is actually winning (for example, Power and Woolgar's 1994 study; other evidence is summarized by Mark Anshel, 1997).

Nack and Munson quote psychologist Joel Fish: 'Something deep down inside happens in moms and dads when they see their kid up there with the bases loaded.' There is actually a technical term, *intermittent explosive disorder*, that describes what Fish alludes to: when other psychiatric disorders associated with loss of **control** of aggressive impulses are ruled out, subjects prone to episodes of assaults on people or property are said to manifest symptoms of this type of impulse control disorder. We should, however, understand this disorder not in isolation but as part of a culture closely identified with and driven by an **achievement ethic** that has its roots in the sixteenth century. When the subject striving to achieve success through another sees that other person defeated or stymied in some way, their reactions may be more explosive than if they were beaten themselves.

Further reading

Nack, W. and Munson, L. (2001) 'Out of control,' *Sports Illustrated* vol. 93 pp. 86–95.
Power, T.G. and Woolgar, C. (1994) 'Parenting practices and age-group swimming: a correlational study,' *Research Quarterly for Exercise and Sport* vol. 65, pp. 59–66.

VIOLENCE

Action involving the exercise of physical force to hurt, injure or disrespect another human, or property, is violence, from the Latin *violare*, which has essentially the same meaning. In sports, as in many other areas, violence is equated with the unlawful use of force, though many sports either tacitly condone or explicitly encourage violence. Hockey is an example of the former and boxing the latter, of course. In both sports, however, the transgression of boundaries is still punishable, as this constitutes a rule *violation* (from the same Latin root). Violence among fans is prevalent, especially in soccer's **fandom**.

Violence should be distinguished from **aggression**, which is behavior, or a propensity to behave in a way, that is either intended or carries with it a recognizable possibility that a living being will be harmed, though no action or harm *necessarily* materializes. Aggression is considered legitimate under many conditions. **Aggressiveness** is not only legitimate but a *sine qua non*, a requirement, of numerous sports. Only combat sports officially approve of violence, and even then within strictly determined frameworks of rules that ostensibly protect competitors from sustaining unnecessary punishment. Even retaliation to acts of violence, which may be justified as self-defense in many quarters, is punishable in sports. In **competition**, much aggressive behavior is instrumental rather than hostile (i.e. intended to procure an advantage through intimidation). 'The closest parallels may be found between athletes and military personnel, who also follow strongly institutionalized regulatory structures,' argues Kevin Young, perhaps overlooking the more spontaneous eruptions of violence that lack any calculation.

Young's overview of the types of violence in sport encompasses player and fan violence: explanations of their causes often link the two, spectators **modeling** their behavior on that of competitors. The role of the media in disseminating − and, indeed, sensationalizing − accounts of player violence has also been acknowledged, if not in stimulating violence, in legitimating it. Soccer hooliganism, in particular, has proved the most resilient and enduring type of fan violence that has resisted all attempts to eradicate it. Clampdowns on player violence throughout the world made little impact on violent disorder among crowds. Soccer violence embodies elements of spontaneity and calculation: while the actual episodes may be catalyzed by unexpected events, confrontations are frequently planned beforehand.

Hooliganism has been approached as a ritualistic pattern of fighting behavior, as, for example, wildebeests defend their territory in a stylized horn-locking standoff. There are certainly rituals involved in fan violence, as there are in many other forms of violent behavior in and out of sports. Even the seemingly unpremeditated and impulsive rages common in public places have formulaic elements that suggest the presence of **mimetic** processes. There also appears to be a propensity for perpetrators of violence to repeat their actions, presumably because they experience **reinforcement**. To understand the appeal of violence – and anyone who doubts the existence of a vicarious appeal is referred to the popularity of action movies with triple digit bodycounts – we might examine what happens to those who engage in violence.

An assailant, in and out of sports, experiences **arousal** that has been likened to sexual excitement. Subjects have reported responses that resemble an **adrenaline rush** when engaging in a violent act. Often there is a dehumanization of the target person: the perpetrator either involuntarily loses or abandons the ability to empathize and treats the victim as an object. This is consistent with a binary mode of thinking in which the antagonist conceives the action only in terms of right/ wrong, good/bad, justifiable/unjustifiable, etc. The violence is typically understood as right, good, justifiable, etc.

Perhaps most interestingly, subjects recount feelings of empowerment and **control** while attacking, at the same time sensing they are out of control ('I just snapped'). This squares with an argument first advanced by Fontana in 1978 in which even impetuous displays of violence are rendered comprehensible in terms of an increasingly fragmented and impersonal society. Fragmentation prompted a 'return to primitive sensation,' violence being a way of reasserting individuality and personal distinctness. Far from being at the mercy of uncontrollable impulses, the perpetrator uses violence as a resource to restore a subjective feeling of power.

Further reading

Fontana. A. (1978) 'Over the edge: a return to primitive sensation in play and games,' *Urban Life* vol. 7, pp. 213–29.
Young, K. (2000) 'Sport and violence,' pp. 382–407 in Coakley, J. and Dunning, E. (eds) *Handbook of Sports Studies* London: Sage.

VISUALIZATION *see* imagery

VISUO-MOTOR BEHAVIORAL REHEARSAL

VMBR, as it is often abbreviated, is a **cognitive–behavioral modification** that uses **relaxation** and **imagery**. It was originally designed in the 1950s to treat phobias by exposing patients to a series of approximations to the **stimuli** they feared. For example, someone with a phobia about feathers would be introduced to a feather which would be moved progressively toward him or her.

VMBR encourages athletes progressively to relax and imagine typical competitive situations that involve **stress** and discomfort. Practicing prior to **competition** reduces the effects of state **anxiety** and enhances performance. Other cognitive–behavioral interventions include **stress inoculation training** and **stress management training**.

Further reading

Suinn, R.M. (1972) 'Removing emotional obstacles to learning and performance by visuo-motor behavior rehearsal,' *Behavioral Therapy* vol. 31, pp. 308–10.

WEIGHT CONTROL

Using a variety of activities, techniques or appliances to maintain body weight within certain limits is known as weight control, or weight management. While this appears to be a contemporary phenomenon – a byproduct of cultural changes that have granted status to thinness and stigmata to fatness – it is actually not so new. During the days of empire, Romans built *vomitoria*, passages in their amphitheaters where they would deliberately puke up their food. Given the importance of **body image** to **identity**, role and status, it is hardly surprising people are concerned about maintaining what Angela Page and Kenneth Fox call 'a culturally acceptable body shape.' Adolescent females, in particular, 'see weight loss as worth seeking simply because the potential social rewards are high. They experiment with dietary practices such as laxatives, appetite suppressants, and vomiting in attempts to find easy solutions to weigh loss.'

Some attempts to **control** weight grow from body dissatisfaction. This may begin before puberty: various studies show 60-plus per cent of young females consistently express dissatisfaction with their bodies, with 40-plus per cent of males feeling similarly. In 1997, Caroline Davis reported: 'Body weight (most frequently represented as Body Mass Index [BMI]: weight [kg]/height^2) and body fat content have consistently been found, particularly among women, to correlate positively with measure of body dissatisfaction.'

According to Julia Stuart writing in the *Independent* Review section (6 September 2001), some 8-year-old girls are on diets. **Self-esteem** is related to perceptions of one's own body, suggesting that concern over physical appearance borders on an **obsession**. Yet even allowing for inconsistencies in assessment, about 30 per cent of women and 65 per cent of men in Europe and the USA are technically overweight. About 10 per cent of children under 11 are overweight. Accompanying this is a proliferation of 'fad' dieting, a trend encouraged by a diet industry comprising plans, books, videos and magazines, replacement drinks, etc.

Some sports, such as boxing and judo, demand rigorous weight control, of course. The esthetic emphasis of others, such as gymnastics and ice dancing, necessitates a certain vigilance. Body weight is typically managed with a combination of diet and exercise. Yet exaggerated efforts to manage weight have led to the spread in **eating disorders** among athletes, as well as the general population.

Further reading

Davis, C. (1997) 'Body image, exercise, and eating behaviors,' pp. 143–74 in Fox, K.R. (ed.) *The Physical Self: From motivation to well-being* Champaign IL: Human Kinetics.

Page, A. and Fox, K.R. (1997) 'Adolescent weight management and the physical self,' pp. 229–56 in Fox, K.R. (ed.) *The Physical Self: From motivation to well-being* Champaign IL: Human Kinetics.

YERKES–DODSON LAW

First published in 1908, the principle established by Robert Yerkes and J.D. Dodson stated that there is a relationship between **arousal** and task performance that, when plotted on a graph, defines an inverted-U shape. Its application to sports is: there is an optimum level of arousal that accompanies successful task performance and deviations from this – increases or decreases in **stress** level – result in a decline in performance.

On intricate tasks, low levels of arousal improve performance relative to high levels, but on straightforward tasks the reverse holds: high arousal levels facilitate performance relative to low levels. Golf putting, for example, requires considerably less arousal than weight lifting, which, research shows, can be improved by the experience of **emotion**, such as **anger**.

Further reading

Yerkes, R.M. and Dodson, J.D. (1908) 'The relation of strength and stimulus to rapidity of habit formation,' *Journal of Comparative and Neurological Psychology* vol. 18, pp. 459–82.

ZEN

From the Japanese *zenna*, which means 'quiet mind,' Zen refers to the school of Mahayana Buddhism that emphasizes meditation and personal awareness as ways of approaching illumination (*satori*). Drawn by its accent on hard work, concentrated practice and **discipline**, some sports practitioners, including basketball coach Phil Jackson, have adopted its principles selectively and refined them as part of preparation.

In traditional western conceptions, the mind is regarded as a motor of **cognition** and **perception**. Zen, however, treats the mind as a facility that needs to be trained for specific purposes. As such, there is compatibility between elements of Zen philosophy and methods of preparing athletes for **self-actualization** and **competition**. The almost universally approved benefits of **relaxation**, for example, have clear resonance with the teachings of Zen. **Autogenic** techniques also share features with Zen. There is also some symmetry between Zen and the metamotivational states that are so crucial to **reversal theory**: a 1997 study by Kerr *et al.* suggested that **metamotivation** may be manipulated by various means to achieve an appropriate level of **arousal** in a **telic state**. This invites comparison with Zen methods of achieving desired states of awareness.

Further reading

Kerr, J.H., Yoshida, H., Hirata, C., Takai, K. and Yamazaki, F. (1997) 'Effects on archery performance of manipulating metamotivational state and felt arousal,' *Perceptual and Motor Skills* vol. 84, pp. 818–28.

Lazenby, R. (2000) *Mind Games: Phil Jackson's long, strange journey* New York: McGraw Hill.

Low, A. (1992) *Zen and Creative Management* Rutland VT: Tuttle.

ZONE

The metaphor of the zone is used to describe a mental state in which athletes believe they can perform to peak levels. In this conceptual space, athletes acquire an enhanced capacity to focus and, in some cases, a level of consciousness that facilitates exceptional **composure**. They also report blissful feelings and an agreeable loss of their sense of time and space, complemented, on occasion, by almost otherworldly sensations. While the term 'zone' is commonly used in sporting circles, it has also been appropriated by Yuri Hanin and followers of the **IZOF (individual zones of optimal functioning)** approach to studying the relationship between **arousal, emotion** and athletic performance.

When 'in the zone,' athletes have related passages of *peak experience* (a term originally used by **motivation** theorist Abraham Maslow), or **peak performance**, when they abandon all **fear** and inhibition and perform to the best of their ability, at the same time enjoying their perceptions and feelings. This is a subjective experience and may or may not occur with an objectively verifiable peak performance. Research on the subject by, among others, Privette and Bundrick, shows that athletes who report heightened awareness, joyfulness and even transcendence during an athletic event do not – contrary to their own impressions – always perform to their peak. They just feel that they are.

Kenneth Ravizza's research on peak performance records experiences of '**focused** awareness, complete **control** of self and the environment and transcendence of self' and, while Ravizza does not cite the zone, his reference to an athlete's ability 'to exclude external variables (e.g. the crowd)' suggests that he was studying the same phenomenon under a different name. According to Ravizza, there are several elements to the peak performance. These include a 'centered present focus,' meaning that 'all [the athlete's] consciousness is channeled into the present moment' and outside distractions are eliminated. **Concentration** yields a narrow focus of **attention** exclusively on the object of the athlete's **perception**. There is also 'complete absorption' in the task at hand, and often athletes lose track of time and space.

Once in the zone, athletes feel no pressure and need no encouragement; they have no fear, **stress** or restraints as they strive for excellence. Ravizza's subjects reported feelings of *harmony and oneness* in which 'total self is integrated physically and mentally' and fatigue and **pain** disappear. The experiences are *noncritical* and *effortless*, meaning that athletes surrender themselves to the experiences rather than exerting themselves. In sum, the peak experience constitutes a 'higher state of consciousness.' One of the most astonishing instances of this was in the 1981 cricket test match between England and Australia at Headingley. England bowler Bob Willis produced the performance of his life, taking eight wickets for 43 runs, and later reflected on how he was in 'a cocoon of concentration,' spurning the encouragement and congratulations of teammates. 'Once I was in it, I didn't want any distractions,' said Willis, whose interlude is rated as one of the finest spells of bowling at test level in history.

The emphasis on awareness, **automaticity**, effortlessness and bliss suggests strong comparisons with the concept of **flow**, a state in which athletes lose self-consciousness, self-judgement and self-doubts and just allow themselves to be carried along by the performance – they just go with the flow. The differences between 'peak experience' and 'flow' are so minor as to be insignificant and, in turn, the differences between these and the more popularly used 'zone' are hard to discern. All seem to involve tasks completed with great **centering**, yet without great exertion; they also accord athletes rewarding feelings, such as wellbeing, power and potency. And, of course, they all leave the athletes with the – sometimes inaccurate – sense that they have performed to their highest level.

Sometimes the two do coincide. Consider this account: 'It felt like your whole mind, your whole body, was either in space or in the middle of the ocean, with no traffic, with no noise. Everything was as calm and quiet as could be.' The words were those of Ben Johnson, reflecting on his 9.79 seconds 100 meters at the Seoul Olympics of 1988. The time was subsequently expunged when Johnson was found guilty of **doping**. But the singular experience he described is as lucid a depiction of being in a zone as imaginable. Of course, his passage into the zone was chemically assisted. (Johnson recounted his experience on BBC2/A&E television's *Reputations: Lost Seoul*.)

Entering the zone, experiencing a peak performance or getting in flow seem to share many characteristics. To the ones we have identified, we might add one more: evanescence – they fade quickly. Being in zone may be a lustrous and vivid encounter; but it is a short-lived one. Whether or not it is possible to create conditions under which athletes can enter zones is an open question. Some believe **relaxation**, **self-talk** and related strategies can maximize the chances of zone entry. **Hypnosis** has also been used as a route to the sought-after zone. Subjects in Susan Jackson's 1992 study of flow believed that, while the state was not available on demand, it could be approached through mental and physical preparation (reported in Jackson and Csikszentmihalyi's *Flow in Sports: The keys to optimal experiences and performances*). On the other hand, other studies – such as Cooper's – suggest that the zone and analogous experiences are spontaneous and probably random.

Further reading

Cooper, A. (1998) *Playing in the Zone: Exploring the spiritual dimensions of sport* Boston: Shambhala.

Jackson, S.A. and Csikszentmihalyi, M. (1999) *Flow in Sports: The keys to optimal experiences and performances* Champaign IL: Human Kinetics.

Ravizza, K. (1984) 'Qualities of the peak experience in sport,' pp. 452–61 in Silva, J.M. and Weinberg, R.S. (eds) *Psychological Foundations of Sport* Champaign IL: Human Kinetics.

BIBLIOGRAPHY

Abernethy, B. and Sparrow, W.A. (1992) 'The rise and fall of dominant paradigms in motor behaviour research,' pp. 3–54 in Summers, J.J. (ed.) *Approaches to the Study of Motor Control and Learning* Amsterdam: Elsevier.

Adams, J. (1995) *Risk* London: UCL Press.

Adams, J.A. (1971) 'A closed loop theory of motor learning,' *Journal of Motor Behavior* vol. 3, pp. 111–50.

Adams, R.M. (1995) 'Momentum in the performance of professional tournament pocket billiards players,' *International Journal of Sport Psychology* vol. 26, pp. 580–7.

Ajzen, I. (1991) 'The theory of planned behavior,' *Organizational Behavior and Human Decision Processes* vol. 50, pp. 179–211.

Alderman, R.B. (1974) *Psychological Behavior in Sport* Philadelphia PA: Saunders.

Allport, F.H. (1924) *Social Psychology* Boston MA: Houghton Mifflin.

Andrews, D.L. and Jackson, S.J. (2001) *Sports Stars: The cultural politics of sporting celebrity* London: Routledge.

Annett, J. (1969) *Feedback and Human Behavior* Harmondsworth: Penguin.

Anonymous (1997) 'Sinister origins,' *The Economist* (15 February) vol. 342, p. 80–1.

Anshel, M.H. (1997) *Sport Psychology: From theory to practice*, 3rd edition, Scottsdale AZ: Gorsuch Scarisbrick.

Apter, M.J. (1989) *Reversal Theory: Motivation, emotion and personality* London: Routledge.

Arendt, H. (1963) *Eichmann in Jerusalem: A report on the banality of evil* New York: Viking Press.

Arms, R., Russell, G. and Sandilands, M. (1987) 'Effects on the hostility of spectators of viewing aggressive sports,' pp. 259–64 in Yiannakis, A. McIntyre, T., Melnick. M. and Hart, D. (eds) *Sport Sociology*, 3rd edition, Dubuque IA: Kendall/Hunt.

Asch, S. (1955) 'Opinions and social pressures,' *Scientific American* vol. 193, pp. 31–5.

Atkinson, R.L, Atkinson, R.C. and Hilgard, E. (1983) *Introduction to Psychology*, 8th edition, New York: Harcourt, Brace, Jovanovich.

Atkinson, R.L., Atkinson, R.C., Smith, E.E., Bem, D.J. and Hilgard, E.R. (1990) *Introduction to Psychology*, 10th edition, New York: Harcourt, Brace, Jovanovich.

Austed, S.N. (1997) *Why We Age: What science is discovering about the body's journey through life* New York: Wiley.

Baddeley, A. (1996) 'Memory,' pp. 281–301 in Colman, A.M. (ed.) (1996) *Companion Encyclopedia of Psychology*, vol. 1, London: Routledge.

Baillie, P.H.F. and Danish, S.J. (1992) 'Understanding the career transition of athletes' *The Sport Psychologist* vol. 6, pp. 77–98.

Balague, G. and Reardon, J.P. (1998) 'Case studies of a clinical nature,' pp. 227–44 in Thompson, M.A., Vernacchia, R.A. and Moore, W.E. (eds) *Case Studies in Applied Sport Psychology: An educational approach* Dubuque IA: Kendall/Hunt.

Balmer, N.J., Nevill, A.M. and Williams, A.M. (2001) 'Home advantage in the Winter Olympics (1908–1998),' *Journal of Sports Sciences* vol. 19, pp. 129–39.

Bamberger, M. and Yaeger, D. (1997) 'Over the edge: aware that drug testing is a sham, athletes seem to rely more than ever on banned performance enhancers,' *Sports Illustrated*, 14 April, p. 6.

Bandura, A. (1973) *Aggression: A social learning analysis* Englewood Cliffs NJ: Prentice-Hall.

——(1977) *Social Learning Theory* Englewood Cliffs NJ: Prentice-Hall.

——(1986) *Social Foundations of Thought and Action: A social cognitive theory* Englewood Cliffs NJ; Prentice-Hall.

Bandura, A. and Walters, R.H. (1963) *Social Learning and Personality Development* New York: Holt, Rinehart & Winston.

Bane, M. (1997) *Over the Edge: A regular guy's odyssey in extreme sports* New York: Gollancz.

Banks, W.P. and Krajicek, D. (1991) 'Perception,' *Annual Review of Psychology* vol. 42, pp. 305–31.

Baron, J. (1988) *Thinking and Deciding* Cambridge: Cambridge University Press.

Baumeister, R.F. and Showers, C.J. (1986) 'A review of paradoxical performance effects: choking under pressure in sports and mental tests,' *European Journal of Social Psychology* vol. 16, pp. 361–83.

Beisser, A. (1967) *The Madness in Sport* New York: Appleton-Century-Crofts.

Bem, S.L. (1974) 'The measurement of psychological androgyny,' *Journal of Consulting and Clinical Psychology* vol. 42, pp. 155–62.

Benedict, J. and Klein, A. (1997) 'Arrest and conviction rates for athletes accused of sexual assault,' *Sociology of Sport Journal* vol. 14, pp. 86–94.

Berger, P. and Berger, B. (1981) *Sociology: A biographical approach* New York: Penguin.

Berkowitz, L. (1989) 'Frustration–aggression hypothesis: examination and reformulation,' *Psychological Bulletin* vol. 106, pp. 1,135–44.

Biddle, S.J.H. (1997) 'Cognitive theories of motivation and the physical self,' pp. 59–82 in Fox, K.R. (ed.) *The Physical Self: From motivation to well-being* Champaign IL: Human Kinetics.

——(2000) 'Exercise, emotions and mental health,' pp. 267–92 in Hanin, Y.L. (ed.) *Emotions in Sport* Champaign IL: Human Kinetics.

Birrell, S. and Cole, C. (1990) 'Double fault: Renee Richards and the construction and naturalization of difference,' *Sociology of Sport Journal* vol. 7, pp. 1–21.

Blanchard, K. (1995) *The Anthropology of Sport*, revised edition, Westport CN: Bergin & Garvey.

Bond, J.W. and Nideffer, R.M. (1992) 'Attentional and interpersonal characteristics of elite Australian athletes,' *Excel* vol. 8 (June), pp. 101–10.

Boutcher, S.H. and Zinsser, N.W. (1990) 'Cardiac deceleration of elite and beginning golfers during putting,' *Journal of Sport & Exercise Psychology* vol. 12, pp. 37–47.

Bratman, S. and Knight, D. (2001) *Health Food Junkies – Orthorexia Nervosa: Overcoming the obsession of healthy eating* New York: Bantam Doubleday Dell.

Bray, S.R. and Widmeyer, W.N. (2000) 'Athletes' perception of home advantage: an investigation of perceived causal factors,' *Journal of Sport Behavior* vol. 23, pp. 1–10.

Brettschneider, W.-D. and Heim, R. (1997) 'Identity, sport and youth development,' pp. 205–27 in Fox, K.R. (ed.) *The Physical Self: From motivation to well-being* Champaign IL: Human Kinetics.

Brill, A.A. (1929) 'The why of a fan,' *North American Review* part 228, pp. 428–35.

Brown, D.R. (1992) 'Physical activity, ageing and psychological well-being: an overview of the research,' *Canadian Journal of Sports Sciences* vol. 17, no. 3, pp. 185–92.

Brustad, R.J. (1992) 'Integrating socialization influences into the study of children's motivation in sport,' *Journal of Sport & Exercise Psychology* vol. 14, pp. 59–77.

Bull, P. and Frederikson, L. (1996) 'Non-verbal communication,' pp. 852–72 in Colman, A.M. (ed.) *Companion Encyclopedia of Psychology*, vol. 2, London: Routledge.

Bullock, A., Stallybrass, O. and Trombley, S. (eds) (2000) *New Fontana Dictionary of Modern Thought* London: Fontana.

Burton, D. (1989) 'Winning isn't everything: examining the impact of performance goals on collegiate swimmer's cognitions and performance,' *The Sport Psychologist* vol. 2, pp. 105–32.

——(1992) 'The Jekyll/Hyde nature of goals: reconceptualizing goal setting in sport,' pp. 267–97 in Horn, T.S. (ed.) *Advances in Sport Psychology* Champaign IL: Human Kinetics.

——(1993) 'Goal setting in sport,' pp. 467–91 in Singer, R.N., Murphey, M. and Tennant, L.K. (eds) *Handbook of Research on Sport Psychology* New York: Macmillan.

Butler, R.J. (ed.) (1997) *Sport Psychology in Performance* Oxford: Butterworth.

Cannon, W.B. (1927) 'The James–Lange theory of emotions: a critical examination and an alternative theory,' *American Journal of Psychology* vol. 39, pp. 106–24.

——(1929) *Bodily Changes in Pain, Hunger, Fear and Rage*, 2nd edition, New York: Appleton.

Cantu, R.C. and Mueller, F.O. (1999) 'Fatalities and catastrophic injuries in high school and college sports, 1982–1997: lessons for improving safety,' *Physician and Sports Medicine* vol. 27, pp. 35–48.

Carron, A.V. (1982) 'Cohesiveness in sport groups: interpretations and considerations,' *Journal of Sport Psychology* vol. 4, pp. 123–38.

Carron, A.V. and Dennis, P.W. (1998) 'The sport team as an effective group,' pp. 127–41 in Williams, J.M. (ed.) *Applied Sport Psychology: Personal growth to peak performance*, 3rd edition, Mountain View CA: Mayfield.

Cash, T.C. and Henry, P.E. (1995) 'Women's body images: the results of a national survey in the USA,' *Sex Roles* vol. 33, pp. 19–28.

Cash, T.C. and Pruzinsky, T. (1990) *Body Images: Development, deviance and change* New York: Guilford.

Cashmore, E. (1982) *Black Sportsmen* London: Routledge.

——(2000) 'Adrenaline rush,' pp. 5–6 in Cashmore, E. (ed.) *Sports Culture: An A–Z guide* London: Routledge.

——(2000) 'Death,' pp. 80–2 in Cashmore, E. (ed.) *Sports Culture: An A–Z guide* London: Routledge.

——(2000) *Making Sense of Sports*, 3rd edition, London: Routledge.

——(2000) *Sports Culture: An A–Z guide* London: Routledge

——(2000) 'The *Angels with Dirty Faces* effect,' pp. 20–5 in Cashmore, E. (ed.) *Sports Culture: An A–Z guide* London: Routledge.

Cashmore, E. and Mullan, B. (1983) *Approaching Social Theory* London: Heinemann Educational.

Chelladurai, P. (1993) 'Leadership,' pp. 647–71 in Singer, R.N., Murphey, M. and Tennant, L.K. (eds) *Handbook of Research in Sport Psychology* New York: Macmillan.

Coakley, J.J. (1987) 'Leaving competitive sport: retirement or rebirth?', pp. 311–17 in Yiannakis, A., McIntyre, T.D., Melnick, M. and Hart, D.P. (eds) *Sport Sociology: Contemporary themes*, 3rd edition, Dubuque IA: Kendall/Hunt.

——(1992) 'Burnout among adolescent athletes: a personal failure or social problem?', *Sociology of Sport Journal* vol. 9, pp. 271–85.

——(2001) *Sport in Society: Issues and controversies*, 7th edition, New York: McGraw-Hill.

Coakley, J.J. and Dunning, E. (eds) (2000)*Handbook of Sports Studies* London: Sage.

Colley, A., Eglinton, E. and Elliott, E. (1992) 'Sport participation in middle childhood: association with styles of play and parental participation,' *International Journal of Sport Psychology* vol. 23, pp. 193–206.

Colman, A.M. (ed.) (1996) *Companion Encyclopedia of Psychology*, 2 volumes, London: Routledge.

Cooper, A. (1998) *Playing in the Zone: Exploring the spiritual dimensions of sport* Boston MA: Shambhala.

Cooper, C.L (ed.) (1983) *Stress Research* New York: Wiley.

Cooper, P.J. (1996) 'Eating disorders,' pp. 930–49 in Colman, A.M. (ed.) *Companion Encyclopedia of Psychology*, vol. 1, London: Routledge.

Coren, S. and Halpern, D.F. (1991) 'Left-handedness: a marker for decreased survival fitness,' *Psychological Bulletin* vol. 109, pp. 90–106.

Cornelius, A. (2002) 'Intervention techniques in sport psychology,' pp. 197–223 in Silva, J.M. and Stevens, D.E. (eds) *Psychological Foundations of Sport* Boston MA: Allyn & Bacon.

——(2002) 'Introduction of sport psychology interventions,' pp. 177–96 in Silva, J.M. and Stevens, D.E. (eds) *Psychological Foundations of Sport* Boston MA: Allyn & Bacon.

——(2002) 'Psychological interventions for the injured athlete,' pp. 224–46 in Silva, J.M. and Stevens, D.E. (eds) *Psychological Foundations of Sport* Boston MA: Allyn & Bacon.

Cornelius, A., Silva, J.M., Conroy, D.E. and Petersen, G. (1997) 'The projected performance model: relating cognitive and performance antecedents of psychological momentum,' *Perceptual and Motor Skills* vol. 84, pp. 475–85.

Côté, J. (2002) 'Coach and peer influence on children's development through sport,' pp. 520–40 in Silva, J.M. and Stevens, D.E. (eds) *Psychological Foundations of Sport* Boston MA: Allyn & Bacon.

Côté, J. and Hay, J. (2002) 'Family influences on youth sport performance and participation,' pp. 503–19 in Silva, J.M. and Stevens, D.E. (eds) *Psychological Foundations of Sport* Boston MA: Allyn & Bacon.

Cottrell, N.B. (1972) 'Social facilitation,' pp. 185–236 in McClintock, G. (ed.) *Experimental Social Psychology* New York: Holt, Rinehart & Winston.

Courneya, K.S. and Carron, A. (1992) 'The home advantage in sport competitions: a literature review,' *Journal of Sports Exercise Psychology* vol. 14, pp. 13–27.

Cox, R.H. (1998) *Sport Psychology: Concepts and applications*, 4th edition, Boston MA: McGraw-Hill.

Crocker, P.E., Kowalski, K.C., Graham, T.R. and Kowalski, N.P. (2002) 'Emotion in sport,' pp. 107–31 in Silva, J.M. and Stevens, D.E. (eds) *Psychological Foundations of Sport* Boston MA: Allyn & Bacon.

Csikszentmihalyi, M. (1990) *Flow: The psychology of optimal experience* New York: Harper & Row.

Cupal, D.D. (1998) 'Psychological interventions in sport injury prevention and rehabilitation,' *Journal of Applied Sport Psychology* vol. 10, pp. 103–23.

Dalgleish, J. and Dollerty, S. (2001) *The Health and Fitness Handbook* Harlow, England: Pearson Education.

Darwin, C. (1998) *On the Origin of the Species by Means of Natural Selection* (introduction by Jeff Wallace) first published 1859, Wane, England: Wordsworth.

Davis, C. (1997) 'Body image, exercise, and eating behaviors,' pp. 143–74 in Fox, K.R. (ed.) *The Physical Self: From motivation to well-being* Champaign IL: Human Kinetics.

Dawson, K.A., Brawley, L.R. and Maddux, J.E. (2000) 'Examining the relationships among concepts of control and exercise attendance,' *Journal of Sport & Exercise Psychology* vol. 22, pp. 131–44.

Deaner, H. and Silva, J.M (2002) 'Personality and sport performance,' pp. 48–65 in Silva, J.M. and Stevens, D.E. (eds) *Psychological Foundations of Sport* Boston MA: Allyn & Bacon.

Deci, E.L. (1971 'Effects of externally mediated rewards on intrinsic motivation,' *Journal of Personality and Social Psychology*, vol. 8, pp. 105–15.

——(1975) *Intrinsic Motivation* New York: Plenum Press.

Deci, E.L. and Ryan, R.M. (1985) *Intrinsic Motivation and Self-Determination in Human Behavior* New York: Plenum Press.

Del Rey, P. and Sheppard, S. (1981) 'Relationship of psychological androgyny in female athletes to self-esteem,' *International Journal of Sport Psychology* vol. 12, pp. 165–75.

Dollard, J., Doob, L.W., Miller, N.E., Mowrer, O.H. and Sears, R.R. (1939) *Frustration and Aggression* New Haven CT: Yale University Press.

Domjan, M. and Burkhardt, B. (1986) *The Principles of Learning and Behavior* Pacific Grove CA: Brooks/Cole.

du Maurier, D. (1992) *Rebecca* London: Arrow.

Duda, J.L. (1993) 'Goals: a social-cognitive approach to the study of achievement motivation in sport,' pp. 421–36 in Singer, R.N., Murphey, M. and Tennant, L.K. (eds) *Handbook of Research on Sport Psychology* New York: Macmillan.

Dunn, S. (1996) 'Thrills and chills,' *Shape* vol. 15, pp. 116–19.

Dweck, C.S. (1980) 'Learned helplessness in sport,' pp. 1–11 in Nadeau, C.H., Halliwell, W.R., Newell, K.M. and Roberts, G.C. (eds) *Psychology of Motor Behavior and Sport – 1979* Champaign IL: Human Kinetics.

Eaton. W.O., Chipperfield, J.G., Ritchot, F.M. and Kostiuk, J.H. (1996) 'Is a maturational lag associated with left-handedness? A research note,' *Journal of Child Psychology and Psychiatry and Allied Disciplines* vol. 37, pp. 613–17.

Eitzen, D.S. (1999) *Fair and Foul: Beyond the myths and paradoxes of sport* Lanham MD: Rowman & Littlefield.

Eklund, R.C., Grove, R. and Heard, N.P. (1998) ' "The measurement of slump-related coping": factorial validity of the COPE and modified-COPE inventories,' *Journal of Sport & Exercise Psychology* vol. 20, pp. 421–36.

Ekman, P. and Friesen, W.V. (1969) 'Non-verbal leakage and clues to deception,' *Psychiatry* vol. 32, pp. 88–106.

Elias, N. (1986) 'An essay on sport and violence,' pp. 150–74 in Elias, N. and Dunning, E. (eds) *Quest for Excitement: Sport and leisure in the civilizing process* Oxford: Blackwell.

Elias, N. and Dunning, E. (eds) (1986) *Quest for Excitement: Sport and leisure in the civilizing process* Oxford: Blackwell.

Entine, J. (2000) *Taboo: Why black athletes dominate and why we're afraid to talk about it* New York: PublicAffairs.

Erikson, E. (1963) *Childhood and Society* New York: Norton.

Etnier, J.L. and Landers, D. M. (1996) 'The influence of procedural variables on the efficacy of mental practice,' *The Sport Psychologist* vol. 10, pp. 48–57.

Eysenck, H.J. (1970) *The Structure of Human Personality* London: Methuen.

——(1971) *Race, Intelligence and Education* London: Maurice Temple Smith.

Eysenck, M.W. (1996) 'Attention,' pp. 302–18 in Colman, A.M. (ed.) *Companion Encyclopedia of Psychology,* vol. 1, London: Routledge.

Fazey, J. and Hardy, L. (1988) *The Inverted-U Hypothesis: A catastrophe for sport psychology?* British Association of Sports Sciences, Monograph No. 1, Leeds: National Coaching Foundation.

Feinstein, J. (1989) *A Season on the Brink: A year with Bob Knight and the Indiana Hoosiers* New York: Fireside.

Feltz, D.L. and Landers, D.M. (1983) 'The effects of mental practice on motor skill learning and performance: a meta-analysis,' *Journal of Sport Psychology* vol. 5, pp. 25–57.

Feltz, D.L. and Lirgg, C.D. (1998) 'Perceived team and player efficacy in hockey,' *Journal of Applied Psychology* vol. 83, pp. 557–64.

Fiedler, F.E. *A Theory of Leadership Effectiveness* New York: McGraw-Hill.

Finch, L. (2002) 'Understanding individual motivation in sport,' pp. 66–79 in Silva, J.M. and Stevens, D.E. (eds) *Psychological Foundations of Sport* Boston MA: Allyn & Bacon.

Fischman, M.G. and Oxendine, J.B. (1998) 'Motor skill learning for effective coaching and performance,' pp. 13–27 in Williams, J.M. (ed.) *Applied Sport Psychology: Personal growth to peak performance,* 3rd edition, Mountain View CA: Mayfield.

Fiske, S.T. and Taylor, S.E. (1991) *Social Cognition* New York: McGraw-Hill.

Fitts, P.M. (1954) 'The information capacity of the human motor system in controlling the amplitude of movement,' *Journal of Experimental Psychology* vol. 47, pp. 381–91.

Fitts, P.M. and Posner, M.I. (1967) *Human Performance* Belmont CA: Brooks/Cole.

Fontana, A. (1978) 'Over the edge: a return to primitive sensation in play and games,' *Urban Life* vol. 7, pp. 213–29.

Foucault, M. (1977) *Discipline and Punish: The birth of the prison* New York: Pantheon.

Fox, K.R. (1997) 'Introduction – let's get physical!', pp. vii–xiii in Fox, K.R. (ed.) *The Physical Self: From motivation to well-being* Champaign IL: Human Kinetics.

——(ed.) (1997) *The Physical Self: From motivation to well-being* Champaign IL: Human Kinetics.

Freud, S. (1978) 'Why war?,' pp. 197–218 in Strachey, J. (ed.) *The Standard Edition of the Complete Psychological Work of Sigmund Freud*, vol. 23, London: The Hogarth Press.

Frey, K.P. (1999) 'Reversal theory: basic concepts,' pp. 3–17 in Kerr, J.H. (ed.) (1999) *Experiencing Sport: Reversal theory* Chichester, England: Wiley.

Frijda, N.H. (1986) *The Emotions* Cambridge: Cambridge University Press.

Furedi, Frank (1997) *Culture of Fear: Risk-taking and the morality of low expectation* London: Cassell.

Gatchel, R.J. (1996) 'Stress and coping,' pp. 560–77 in Colman, A.M. (ed.) (1996) *Companion Encyclopedia of Psychology*, vol. 1, London: Routledge.

Geschwind, N. and Galaburda, A.M. (1987) *Cerebral Lateralization* Cambridge MA: MIT Press.

Giles, D. (2000) *Illusions of Immortality: A psychology of fame and celebrity* New York: St Martin's Press.

Gill, D.L. (2000) *Psychological Dynamics of Sport and Exercise*, 2nd edition, Champaign IL: Human Kinetics.

Gill, D.L., Dowd, D.A., Williams, J., Beaudoin, C.M. and Martin, J.J. (1996) 'Competitive orientation and motives of adult sport and exercise participants,' *Journal of Sport Behavior* vol. 19, pp. 307–18.

Goldberg, A. (1998) *Sports Slump Busting: 10 steps to mental toughness and peak performance* Champaign IL: Human Kinetics.

Goldstein, K. (1939) *The Organism: A holistic approach to biology* New York: American Book.

Gordin, R.D. (1998) 'Composure: arousal and anxiety dynamics,' pp. 37–62 in Thompson, M.A., Vernacchia, R.A. and Moore, W.E. (eds) *Case Studies in Applied Sport Psychology: An educational approach* Dubuque IA: Kendall/Hunt.

Gould, D., Udry, E., Tuffey, S. and Loehr, J. (1996) 'Burnout in competitive junior tennis players: I. A quantitative psychological assessment'/'Burnout in competitive junior tennis players: II. Qualitative psychological assessment,' *The Sport Psychologist* vol. 10, pp. 322–40.

Grant, R.W. (1988) *The Psychology of Sport: Facing one's true opponent* Raleigh NC: McFarland Jefferson.

Graves, R. (1989) *I, Claudius: From the autobiography of Tiberius Claudius, born 10 BC, murdered and deified AD 54* New York: Vintage.

Green, R.G. (1996) 'Social motivation,' pp. 522–41 in Colman, A.M. (ed.) *Companion Encyclopedia of Psychology*, 2 volumes, London: Routledge.

Greendorfer, S.L. and Blinde, E.M. (1987) ' "Retirement" from intercollegiate sports: theoretical and empirical considerations,' pp. 301–6 in Yiannakis, A., McIntyre, T.D., Melnick, M. and Hart, D.P. (eds) *Sport Sociology: Contemporary themes*, 3rd edition, Dubuque IA: Kendall/Hunt.

Gregory, R.L. (1987) *The Oxford Companion to the Mind* Oxford: Oxford University Press.

Griffin, L.L., Mitchell, S.A. and Oslin, J.L. (1997) *Teaching Sport Concepts and Skills* Champaign IL: Human Kinetics.

Griffin, P. (1998) *Strong Women, Deep Closets: Lesbians and homophobia in sport* Champaign IL: Human Kinetics.

Haggar, M.S., Chatzisarantis, N. and Biddle, S.J.H. (2001) 'The influence of self-efficacy and past behavior on the physical activity intentions of young people,' *Journal of Sports Sciences* vol. 19, pp. 711–25.

Hampson, S. (1996) 'The construction of personality,' pp. 602–21 in Colman, A.M. (ed.) (1996) *Companion Encyclopedia of Psychology*, vol. 2, London: Routledge.

Hanin, Y.L. (ed.) (2000) 'Introduction: an individualized approach to emotion in sport,' pp. ix–xii in Hanin, Y.L (ed.) *Emotions in Sport* Champaign IL: Human Kinetics.

——(ed.) (2000) *Emotions in Sport* Champaign IL: Human Kinetics.

Hardy, J., Hall, C.R. and Alexander, M.R. (2001) 'Exploring self-talk and affective states in sport,' *Journal of Sports Sciences* vol. 19, pp. 469–75.

Harkins, S.G. and Jackson, J.M. (1985) 'The role of evaluation in eliminating social loafing,' *Personality and Social Psychology Bulletin* vol. 11, pp. 457–65.

Harkins, S.G. and Szymanski, K. (1989) 'Social loafing and self-evaluation with an objective standard,' *Journal of Experimental Psychology Bulletin* vol. 24, pp. 354–65.

Harris, C. (1998) 'A sociology of television fandom,' pp. 41–54 in Harris, C. and Alexander, A. (eds) *Theorizing Fandom: Fans, subculture and identity* Cresskill, NJ: Hampton Press.

Harris, C. and Alexander, A. (eds) (1998) *Theorizing Fandom: Fans, subculture and identity* Cresskill, NJ: Hampton Press.

Harris, L.J. (1993) 'Do left-handers die sooner than right-handers? Commentary on Coren and Halpern's (1991) "Left-handedness: a marker for decreased survival fitness,"' *Psychological Bulletin* vol. 114, pp. 203–32.

Harris, O. (1994) 'Race, sport and social support,' *Sociology of Sport Journal* vol. 11, pp. 40–50.

Harter, S. (1978) 'Effectance motivation reconsidered: toward a developmental model,' *Human Development* vol. 21, pp. 94–104.

——(1981) 'The development of competence motivation in the mastery of cognitive and physical skills: is there still a place for joy?', pp. 3–29 in Roberts, G.C and Landers, D.M. (eds) *Psychology of motor behavior and sport – 1980* Champaign IL: Human Kinetics.

Harwood, C., Hardy, L. and Swain A. (2000) 'Achievement goals in sport: a critique of conceptual and measurement issues,' *Journal of Sport & Exercise Psychology* vol. 22, pp. 235–55.

Hauser, T. (1997) *Muhammad Ali: His life and times* London: Pan Books.

Heaton, A.W. and Sigall, H. (1989) 'The "championship choke" revisited: the role of fear of acquiring a negative identity,' *Journal of Applied Social Psychology* vol. 19, pp. 1,019–33.

Heider, F. (1958) *The Psychology of Interpersonal Relations* New York: Wiley.

Heil, J. (2000) 'The injured athlete,' pp. 245–65 in Hanin, Y.L. (ed.) *Emotions in Sport* Champaign IL: Human Kinetics.

Heller, P. (1990) *Tyson* London: Pan Books.

Hemery, D. (1986) *Sporting Excellence* Champaign IL: Human Kinetics.

Hepworth, J. (1999) *The Social Construction of Anorexia Nervosa* London: Sage.

Herrnstein, R. and Murray, C. (1994) *The Bell Curve: Intelligence and class structure in American life* New York: Free Press/Simon & Schuster.

Hersey, P. and Blanchard, K.H. (1977) *Management of Organizational Behavior*, 3rd edition, Englewood Cliffs NJ: Prentice-Hall.

Hick, W.E. (1952) 'On the rate of gain information,' *Quarterly Journal of Experimental Psychology* vol. 4, pp. 11–26.

Hicks, R.A. Pass, K., Freeman, H. Bautista, J. and Johnson, C. (1993) 'Handedness and accidents with injury,' *Perceptual and Motor Skills* vol. 77, pp. 1,119–24.

Higham, A. (2000) *Momentum: The hidden force in tennis* Leeds, England: 1st4sport/ Meyer&Meyer.

Hilgard, E.R. (1986) *Divided Consciousness: Multiple controls in human thought and action* New York: Wiley.

Hill, K.L. (2001) *Frameworks for Sport Psychologists* Champaign IL: Human Kinetics.

Hinshaw, K. (1991) 'The effects of mental practice on motor skill performance: critical evaluation and meta-analysis,' *Imagination, Cognition and Personality* vol. 11, pp. 3–35.

Hird, J.S., Landers, D.M., Thomas, J.R. and Horan, J.J. (1991) 'Physical practice is superior to mental practice in enhancing cognitive and motor task performance,' *Journal of Sport and Exercise Performance* vol. 13, pp. 281–93.

Hoberman, J. (1997) *Darwin's Athletes: How sport has damaged black America and preserved the myth of race* New York: Houghton Mifflin.

Hobson, J.A. (1996) 'Sleep and dreaming,' pp. 109–32 in Colman, A.M. (ed.) *Companion Encyclopedia of Psychology*, vol. 1, London: Routledge.

Hoch, P. (1972) *Rip Off the Big Game: The exploitation of sports by the power elite* New York: Anchor Doubleday.

Hoffman, S.J. (ed.)(1992) *Sport and Religion* Champaign IL: Human Kinetics.

Hoffmann, P. (1997) 'The endorphin hypothesis,' pp. 163–77 in Morgan, W.P. (ed.) *Physical Activity and Mental Health* Washington DC: Taylor & Francis.

Holding, G.H. (ed.) (1988) *Human Skills* London: Wiley.

Horn, T.S. (ed.) (1992) *Advances in Sport Psychology* Champaign IL: Human Kinetics.

Hornby, N. (1996) *High Fidelity* London: Indigo.

Horner, M.S. (1972) 'Toward an understanding of achievement-related conflicts in women,' *Journal of Social Issues* vol. 28, pp. 157–76.

Hubbard, S. (1998) *Faith in Sports: Athletes and their religion on and off the field* New York: Doubleday.

Hull, C.L. (1943) *Principles of Behavior* New York: Appleton-Century-Crofts.

Humphrey, J.H. (ed.) (2000) *Stress in College Athletics: Causes, consequences, coping* Binghamton NY: Haworth Half-Court.

Humphrey, J.H., Yow, D.A. and Bowden, W.W. (2000) 'Reducing stress through biofeedback,' pp. 141–5 in Humphrey, J.H. (ed.) *Stress in College Athletics: Causes, consequences, coping* Binghamton NY: Haworth Half-Court.

Husman, B.F. and Silva, J.M. (1984) 'Aggression in sport: definitional and theoretical considerations,' pp. 246–60 in Silva, J.M. and Weinberg, R.S. (eds) *Psychological Foundations of Sport* Champaign IL; Human Kinetics.

Ingham, A.G., Levinger, G., Graves, J. and Peckham, V. (1974) 'The Ringelmann effect: studies of group size and group performance,' *Journal of Experimental Social Psychology* vol. 10, pp. 371–84.

Isberg, L. (2000) 'Anger, aggressive behavior, and athletic performance,' pp. 113–33 in Hanin, Y.L. (ed.) *Emotions in Sport* Champaign IL: Human Kinetics.

Jackson, S.A. (1996) 'Toward a conceptual understanding of the flow experience in elite athletes,' *Research Quarterly for Exercise and Sport* vol. 67, no. 1, pp. 76–90.

Jackson, S.A. and Csikszentmihalyi, M. (1999) *Flow in Sports: The keys to optimal experiences and performances* Champaign IL: Human Kinetics.

Jackson, S.A., Ford, S.K., Kimiecik, J.C. and Marsh, H.W. (1999) 'Psychological correlates of flow in sport,' *Journal of Sport & Exercise Psychology* vol. 20, pp. 358–78.

Jacobs, J.E. and Eccles, J.S. (1992) 'The impact of mothers' gender-role specific stereotypic beliefs on mothers' and children's ability perceptions,' *Journal of Personality and Social Psychology* vol. 63, pp. 932–44.

Jacobson, E. (1974) *Progressive Relaxation*, 2nd edition, Chicago: University of Chicago Press.

James, W. (1884) 'What is an emotion?' *Mind* vol. 9, pp. 188–205.

Janelle, C.M., Singer, R.N. and Williams, A., (1999) 'External distribution and attentional narrowing: visual search evidence,' *Journal of Sport & Exercise Psychology* vol. 21, pp. 70–91.

Jenkins, H. (1992) *Textual Poachers: Television fans and participatory culture* London: Routledge.

Jensen, A. (1969) 'How much can we boost IQ and scholastic achievement?', *Harvard Educational Review* vol. 39, pp. 1–123.

Jones, G. and Swain, A. (1995) 'Predispositions to experience debilitative and facilitative anxiety in elite and nonelite performers,' *The Sport Psychologist* vol. 9, pp. 201–11.

Jones, R.L. and Armour, K.M. (eds) (2000) *Sociology of Sport: Theory and practice* Harlow, Essex: Longman.

Kahneman, D., Slovic, P. and Tversky, A. (1982) *Judgement under Certainty: Heuristics and biases* Cambridge: Cambridge University Press.

Kandel, E.R. (1991) 'Brain and behavior,' pp. 5–17 in Kandel, E.R., Schwartz, J.H. and Jessell, T.M. (eds) *Principles of Neural Science*, 3rd edition, New York: Elsevier.

Kandel, E.R., Schwartz, J.H. and Jessell, T.M. (eds) (1991) *Principles of Neural Science*, 3rd edition, New York: Elsevier.

Karau, S.J. and Williams, K.D. (1993) 'Social loafing: a meta-analytic review and theoretical integration,' *Journal of Personality and Social Psychology* vol. 65, pp. 681–706.

Kauss, D.R. (2001) *Mastering Your Inner Game: A self-guided approach to finding your unique sports performance keys* Champaign IL: Human Kinetics.

Kelley, B.C., Eklund, R.C. and Titter-Taylor, M. (1999) 'Stress and burnout among collegiate tennis coaches,' *Journal of Sport & Exercise Psychology* vol. 22, pp. 113–30.

Kendon, A. (1985) 'Some uses of gesture,' pp. 215–34 in Tannen, O. and Saville-Troika, M. (eds) *Perspectives on Silence* Norwood NJ: Ablex.

Kerbo, H.R. (1989) *Sociology: Social structure and social conflict* New York: Macmillan.

Kerick, S.E., Iso-Ahola, S.E. and Hatfield, B.D. (2000) 'Psychological momentum in target shooting: cortical, cognitive–affective, and behavioral responses,' *Journal of Sport & Exercise Psychology* vol. 22, pp. 1–20.

Kerr, J.H. (ed.) (1999) *Experiencing Sport: Reversal theory* Chichester, England: Wiley.

Kerr, J.H., Yoshida, H., Hirata, C., Takai, K. and Yamazaki, F. (1997) 'Effects on archery performance of manipulating metamotivational state and felt arousal,' *Perceptual and Motor Skills* vol. 84, pp. 818–28.

Kerr, N.L. (1983) 'Motivation losses in small groups: a social dilemma analysis,' *Journal of Personality and Social Psychology* vol. 45, pp. 819–28.

Klavora, P. and Daniels, J.V. (eds) (1979) *Coach, Athlete and the Sport Psychologist* Champaign IL: Human Kinetics.

Kohn, M. (1996) *The Race Gallery: The return of racial science* London: Vintage.

Koukouris, K. (1994) 'Constructed case studies: athletes' perspectives of disengaging from organized competitive sport,' *Sociology of Sport Journal* vol. 18, pp. 114–39.

Kraemer, R.R., Dzewaltowskj, D.A., Blair, M.S., Rinehardt, K.F. and Castracane, V.D. (1990) 'Mood alteration from treadmill running and its relationship to betaendorphine, corticotrophine, and growth hormone,' *Journal of Sports Medicine and Physical Fitness* vol. 30, pp. 241–6.

Kravitz, D. and Martin, B. (1986) 'Ringelmann rediscovered: the original article,' *Journal of Personality and Social Psychology* vol. 37, pp. 936–41.

Kremer, J. and Scully, D. (1994) *Psychology in Sport* London: Routledge.

Kyllo, L.B. and Landers, D.M. (1995) 'Goal setting in sport and exercise: a research synthesis to resolve the controversy,' *Journal of Sport & Exercise Psychology* vol. 17, pp. 117–37.

LaFontaine, T.P., DiLorenzo, T.M., Frensch, P.A., Stucky-Ropp, R.C. Bargman, E.P. and McDonald, D.G. (1992) 'Aerobic exercise and mood: a brief review, 1985–1990,' *Sports Medicine* vol. 13, pp. 160–70.

Lainson, S. and Sportstrust (1997) 'Comebacks,' *The Creative Athlete* issue 18, pp. 1–2, www.onlinesports.com/sportstrust/creative18.html.

Lan, L.Y. and Gill, D.L. (1984) 'The relationships among self-efficacy, stress responses, and a cognitive feedback manipulation,' *Journal of Sport Psychology* vol. 6, pp. 227–38.

Laqueur, T. (1990) *Making Sex: Body and gender from the Greeks to Freud* Cambridge MA: Harvard University Press.

Latané, B., Williams, K.D. and Harkins, S.G. (1979) 'Many hands make light work: the causes and consequences of social loafing,' *Journal of Personality and Social Psychology* vol. 37, pp. 823–32.

Lazarus, R.S. (1991) *Emotion and Adaptation* New York: Oxford University Press.

——(1993) 'From psychological stress to the emotions: a history of changing outlooks,' *Annual Review of Psychology* vol. 44, pp. 1–21.

Lazarus, R.S. and Lazarus, B. (1994) *Passion and Reason: Making sense of our emotions* New York: Oxford University Press.

Lazenby, R. (2000) *Mind Games: Phil Jackson's long, strange journey* New York: McGraw-Hill.

Le Unes, A. and Nation, J. (1996) *Sport Psychology* Chicago, IL: Nelson Hall Publishers.

Leary, M.R. (1995) *Self-Presentation: Impression management and interpersonal behavior* Boulder CO: Westview.

Lee, M.J., Whitehead, J. and Balchin, N. (2000) 'The measurement of values in youth sport: development of the youth sport values questionnaire,' *Journal of Sport & Exercise Psychology* vol. 22, pp. 307–26.

Leff, S.S. and Hoyle, R.H. (1995) 'Young athletes' perceptions of parental support and pressure,' *Journal of Youth and Adolescence* vol. 24, pp. 187–203.

Leith, L.M. (1988) 'Choking in sports: are we our own worst enemies?, *International Journal of Sport Psychology* vol. 19, pp. 59–64.

Lenskyj, H. (1986) *Out of Bounds: Women, sport and sexuality* Toronto: Women's Press.

Lesyk, J.L. (1998) *Developing Sport Psychology within Your Clinical Practice: A practical guide for mental health professionals* San Francisco CA: Jossey-Bass.

Lewin, K. (1948) *Resolving Social Conflicts* New York: Harper.

Liggett, D.R. (2000) *Sport Hypnosis* Champaign IL: Human Kinetics.

Locke, E.A. and Latham, G.P. (1990) *A Theory of Goal Setting and Task Performance* Englewood Cliffs NJ: Prentice-Hall.

Lorenz, K. (1966) *On Aggression* New York: Harcourt Brace Jovanovich.

Low, A. (1992) *Zen and Creative Management* Rutland VT: Tuttle.

Lowe, G. (1996) 'Alcohol and drug addiction,' pp. 950–68 in Colman, A.M. (ed.) *Companion Encyclopedia of Psychology* vol. 2, London: Routledge.

Lukes, S. (1973) *Individualism* Oxford: Blackwell.

McAuley, E. and Duncan, T.E. (1990) 'Cognitive appraisal and affective reactions following physical achievement outcomes,' *Journal of Sport & Exercise Psychology* vol. 11, pp. 187–200.

McClelland, D.C., Atkinson J.W., Clark R.A. and. Lowell, E.C. (1953) *The Achievement Motive* New York: Appleton-Century-Crofts.

McClintock, G. (ed.) (1972) *Experimental Social Psychology* New York: Holt, Rinehart & Winston.

MacFarland, D.J. (1987) 'Instinct,' pp. 374–5 in Gregory, R.L. (ed.) *The Oxford Companion to the Mind* Oxford: Oxford University Press.

McGowan, R.W. and Schultz, B. (1989) 'Task complexity and affect in collegiate football,' *Perceptual and Motor Skills* vol. 69, pp. 671–4.

McGuigan, J. (1999) *Modernity and Postmodern Culture* Philadelphia PA: Open University Press.

McNair, D.M., Lorr, M. and Droppleman, L.F. (1992) *Profile of Mood States Manual* San Diego CA: Educational and Industrial Testing Services.

McPherson, B.D. (1987) 'Retirement from professional sport: the process and problems of occupational and psychological adjustment,' pp. 293–301 in Yiannakis, A., McIntyre, T.D., Melnick, M. and Hart, D.P. (eds) *Sport Sociology: Contemporary themes*, 3rd edition, Dubuque IA: Kendall/Hunt.

Maehr, M.L. and Brascamp, L.A. (1986) *The Motivation Factor: A theory of personal investment*, Lexington MA: Lexington Books.

Maehr, M.L. and Nicholls, J.G. (1980) 'Culture and achievement motivation: a second look,' pp. 221–67 in Warren, N. (ed.) *Studies in Cross-Cultural Psychology* New York: Academic Press.

Maguire, J. (1992) 'A sociological theory of sport and the emotions: a process – sociological perspective,' pp. 96–120 in Dunning, E. and Rojek, C. (eds) *Sport and Leisure in the Civilizing Process: Critique and counter-critique* Houndmills, England: Macmillan.

Mahoney, M.J., Gabriel, T.J. and Perkins, T.S. (1987) 'Psychological skills and exceptional athletic performance,' *The Sport Psychologist* vol. 1, pp. 181–99.

Malik, K. (1996) *The Meaning of Race: Race, history and culture in western societies* London: Macmillan.

Malson, L. (1972) *Wolf Children and the Problem of Human Nature*, New York: Monthly Review Press.

Manzo, L. (2002) 'Enhancing sport performance: the role of confidence and concentration,' pp. 247–71 in Silva, J.M. and Stevens, D.E. (eds) *Psychological Foundations of Sport* Boston MA: Allyn & Bacon.

Martens, R. (1987) 'Science, knowledge, and sport psychology,' *The Sport Psychologist* vol. 1, pp. 29–55.

Martin, K.A. and Hall, C.R. (1995) 'Using mental imagery to enhance intrinsic motivation,' *Journal of Sport & Exercise Psychology* vol. 13, pp. 149–59.

Martin, L. (1976) 'Effects of competition upon the aggressive responses of college basketball players and wrestlers,' *Research Quarterly* vol. 47, pp. 388–93.

Masani, P.R. (1989) *Norbert Wiener, 1894–1964* Boston MA: Birkha.

Meggyesy, D. (1970) *Out of Their League* Berkeley CA: Ramparts Press.

Meichenbaum, D. (1977) *Cognitive Behavior Modification: An integrative approach* New York: Plenum.

——(1985) *Stress Inoculation Training* New York: Pergamon Press.

Metzler, J. (2002) 'Applying motivational principles to individual athletes,' pp. 80–106 in Silva, J.M. and Stevens, D.E. (eds) *Psychological Foundations of Sport* Boston MA: Allyn & Bacon.

Milgram, S. (1974) *Obedience to Authority: An experimental view* New York: Harper & Row.

Miller, P.H. (1983) *Theories of Developmental Psychology* San Francisco CA: Freeman.

Money, T. (1997) *Manly and Muscular Diversions: Public schools and the nineteenth-century sporting revival* London: Duckworth.

Moore, W. (1998) 'Confidence,' pp. 63–88 in Thompson, M.A., Vernacchia, R.A. and Moore, W.E. (eds) *Case Studies in Applied Sport Psychology: An educational approach* Dubuque IA: Kendall/Hunt.

Moran, A.P. (1996) *The Psychology of Concentration in Sport Performers: A cognitive analysis* East Sussex: Psychology Press.

Morgan, W.J. (1994) *Leftist Theories of Sport* Urbana IL: University of Illinois Press.

——(2000) 'The philosophy of sport: a historical and conceptual overview and a conjecture regarding its future,' pp. 204–12 in Coakley, J.J. and Dunning, E. (eds) *Handbook of Sports Studies* London: Sage.

Morgan, W.P. (1979) 'Prediction of performance in athletics,' pp. 173–86 in Klavora, P. and Daniels, J.V. (eds) *Coach, Athlete and the Sport Psychologist* Champaign IL: Human Kinetics.

——(1980) 'Sport personology: the credulous–skeptical argument in perspective,' pp. 330–9 in Straub, W.F. (ed.) *Sport Psychology: An analysis of athlete behavior,* 2nd edition, Ithaca NY: Mouvement.

Morris, D. (1981) *The Soccer Tribe* London: Jonathan Cape.

Morrison, B. (2001) 'Jordan, me, and the lure of the comeback,' *Independent on Sunday,* 'Focus,' 20 April, p. 15.

Mougin, F., Bourdin, H., Simon-Rigaud, M.L., Nguyen Nhu, U., Kantelip, J.P. and Davenne, D. (2001) 'Hormonal responses to exercise after partial sleep deprivation and after a hypnotic drug-induced sleep,' *Journal of Sports Sciences* vol. 19, pp. 89–97.

Mueller, F.O. and Ryan, A. (eds) (1991) *The Sports Medicine Team and Athletic Injury Prevention* Philadelphia PA: Davis.

Mummery, W.K. and Wankel, L.M. (1999) 'Training adherence in adolescent competitive swimmers: an application of the theory of planned behavior,' *Journal of Sport & Exercise Psychology* vol. 21, pp. 313–28.

Muris, P., Kop. W.J., Merckelbach, H. (1994) 'Handedness, symptom reporting and accident susceptibility,' *Journal of Clinical Psychology* vol. 50, pp. 389–92.

Murphy, P., Sheard, K. and Waddington, I. (2000) 'Figurational sociology and its application to sport,' pp. 92–105 in Coakley, J.J. and Dunning, E. (eds) *Handbook of Sports Studies* London: Sage.

Murphy, S.M. (1994) 'Imagery interventions in sport,' *Medicine and Science in Sports and Exercise* vol. 26, pp. 486–94.

Mutrie, N. (1997) 'The therapeutic effects of exercise on the self,' pp. 287–14 in Fox, K.R. (ed.) *The Physical Self: From motivation to well-being* Champaign IL: Human Kinetics.

Nack, W. and Munson, L. (2001) 'Out of control,' *Sports Illustrated* vol. 93 pp. 86–95.

Nadeau, C.H., Halliwell, W.R., Newell, K.M. and Roberts, G.C. (eds) (1980) *Psychology of Motor Behavior and Sport – 1979* Champaign IL: Human Kinetics.

Nauright, J. and Chandler, T.J.L. (eds) (1996) *Making Men: Rugby and the masculine identity* London: Frank Cass.

Nicholls, J.G. (1984) 'Achievement motivation: conceptions of ability, subjective experience, task choice and performance,' *Psychological Review* vol. 91, pp. 328–46.

Nideffer, R.M. (1976) 'Test of attentional and interpersonal style,' *Journal of Personality and Social Psychology* vol. 34, pp. 394–404.

——(1992) *Psyched to Win* Champaign IL: Human Kinetics.

Nideffer, R.M. and Sagal, M.-S. (1998) 'Concentration and attention control training,' pp. 296–315 in Williams, J. (ed.) *Applied Sport Psychology: Personal growth to peak performance*, 3rd edition, Mountain View CA: Mayfield.

Nisbett, R.E. and Wilson, T.D. (1977) 'The halo effect: evidence for unconscious alteration of judgements,' *Journal of Personality and Social Psychology* vol. 35, pp. 250–6.

Nixon, H.L. (1993) 'Accepting the risks of pain and injury in sport: mediated cultural influences on playing hurt,' *Sociology of Sport Journal* vol. 10, no. 2 (June), pp. 183–96.

Ogilvie, B. and Tutko, T.A. (1966) *Problem Athletes and How to Handle Them* London: Pelham.

Olsen, J. (1968) *The Black Athlete* New York: Time Life.

Ostrow, A.E. (1996) *Dictionary of Psychological Tests in the Sport and Exercise Sciences* Morgantown WV: Fitness Information.

Oudshoorn, N. (1994) *Beyond the Natural Body: An archaeology of sex hormones* London: Routledge.

Page, A. and Fox, K.R. (1997) 'Adolescent weight management and the physical self,' pp. 229–56 in Fox, K.R. (ed.) *The Physical Self: From motivation to well-being* Champaign IL: Human Kinetics.

Parkinson, B. (1996) 'Emotion,' pp. 485–505 in Colman, A.M. (ed.) *Companion Encyclopedia of Psychology*, 2 volumes, London: Routledge.

Partridge, J. and Stevens, D.E. (2002) 'Group dynamics: the influence of the team in sport,' pp. 272–90 in Silva, J.M. and Stevens, D.E. (eds) *Psychological Foundations of Sport* Boston MA: Allyn & Bacon.

Perreault, S., Vallerand, R.J., Montgomery, D. and Provencher, P. (1998) 'Coming from behind: on the effect of psychological momentum on sport performance,' *Journal of Sport & Exercise Psychology* vol. 20, pp. 421–36.

Petruzzello, S.J., Landers, D.M. and Slazar, W. (1991) 'Biofeedback and sport/exercise performance: applications and limitations,' *Behavior Therapy* vol. 22, pp. 379–449.

Piaget, J. (1952) *The Origins of Intelligence in Children*, New York: International Universities Press.

Power, T.G. and Woolgar, C. (1994) 'Parenting practices and age-group swimming: a correlational study,' *Research Quarterly for Exercise and Sport* vol. 65, pp. 59–66.

Premack, D. (1959) 'Toward empirical behavior laws: I. Positive reinforcement,' *Psychological Review* vol. 66, pp. 219–33.

——(1962) 'Reversibility of the reinforcement relation,' *Science* vol. 136, pp. 255–7.

Privette, G. and Bundrick, C. (1987) 'Measurement of experience: constructs and content validity of the experience questionnaire,' *Perceptual and Motor Skills* vol. 65, pp. 315–32.

Pronger, B. (1990) *The Arena of Masculinity: Sports, homosexuality and the meaning of sex* New York: St Martin's Press.

Quilliam, S. (1996) *Making Love Work* London: Thorsons.

Radcliffe Richards, J. (2000) *Human Nature after Darwin: A philosophical introduction* London: Routledge.

Raglin, J.S. and Hanin, Y.L. (2000) 'Competitive anxiety,' pp. 93–111 in Hanin, Y.L. (ed.) *Emotions in Sport* Champaign IL: Human Kinetics.

Raglin, J.S. and Wilson, G.S. (2000) 'Overtraining in athletes,' pp. 191–208 in Hanin, Y.L. (ed.) *Emotions in Sport* Champaign IL: Human Kinetics.

Rail, G. (ed.) *Sport and Postmodern Times* Albany NY: State University of New York Press.

Rakos, R.F. (1991) *Assertive Behavior* London: Routledge.

Ravizza, K. (1984) 'Qualities of the peak experience in sport,' pp. 452–61 in Silva, J.M. and Weinberg, R.S. (eds) *Psychological Foundations of Sport* Champaign IL: Human Kinetics.

Raymond, J. (1979) *The Transsexual Empire* London: Beacon Press.

Raymond, M., Pontier, D., Dufour, A. and Moller, A.P. (1996) 'Frequency-dependent maintenance of left-handedness in humans,' *Proceedings of the Royal Society of London* Series B, 263, pp. 1,627–33.

Reber, A.S. (1995) *Dictionary of Psychology*, 2nd edition, Harmondsworth: Penguin.

Redhead, S. (1997) *Post-Fandom and the Millennial Blues: The transformation of soccer culture* London: Routledge.

Reiterer, W. (2000) *Positive: An Australian Olympian reveals the inside story of drugs and sport* Sydney: Pan Macmillan Australia.

Rescher, N. (1995) *Luck: The brilliant randomness of everyday life* New York: Farrar Straus Giroux.

Riley, P. (1994) *The Winner Within: A life plan for team players* New York: Berkeley.

Rinehart, R. (1998) 'Born-again sport: ethics in biographical research,' pp. 33–46 in Rail, G. (ed.) *Sport and Postmodern Times* Albany NY: State University of New York Press.

Roberts, G.C. (ed.) (1992) *Motivation in Sport and Exercise* Champaign IL: Human Kinetics.

Rogers, C.R. (1977) *Carl Rogers on Personal Power* New York: Delacourt Press.

Rojek, C. (2001) *Celebrity* London: Reaktion.

Rushall, B.S. (1979) *Psyching in Sport* London: Pelham Books.

Ryan, E. (1970) 'The cathartic effect of vigorous motor activity on aggressive behaviour,' *Research Quarterly* vol. 41, pp. 542–51.

Ryan, J. (1998) *Little Girls in Pretty Boxes: The making and breaking of elite gymnasts and figure skaters* London: Women's Press.

Salmoni, A.W. , Schmidt, R.A. and Walter, C.B. (1984) 'Knowledge of results and motor learning: a review and critical appraisal,' *Psychological Bulletin* vol. 95, pp. 355–86.

Sandford, B. (1987) 'The "adrenaline rush," ' *Physician and Sportsmedicine*, vol. 15, no. 12, p. 184.

Schachter, S. (1964) 'The interaction of cognitive and physiological determinants of emotional state,' pp. 27–48 in Festinger, L. (ed.) *Advances in Experimental Social Psychology*, vol. 1, New York: Academic Press.

Schachter, S. and Singer, J.E. (1971) 'Cognitive, social and physiological determinants of emotional state,' *Psychological Review* vol. 69, pp. 379–99.

Schiebinger, L. (1989) *The Mind Has No Sex: Women in the origins of modern science* Cambridge MA: Harvard University Press.

Scott, D., Scott, L. and Goldwater, B. (1997) 'A performance improvement program for an international-level track and field athlete,' *Journal of Applied Behavior Analysis* vol. 30, pp. 573–5.

Seligman, M.E.P. (1975) *Helplessness: On depression, development and death* San Francisco CA: W.H. Freeman.

Selye, H. (1983) 'The stress concept: past, present and future,' pp. 1–20 in Cooper, C.L. (ed.) *Stress Research* New York: Wiley.

Shepper, A.I. (2000) 'Superstition,' pp. 392–7 in Cashmore, E. (ed.) *Sports Culture: An A–Z guide* London: Routledge.

Sherif, M. (1936) *The Psychology of Social Norms* New York: Harper & Row.

Silva, J.M. (1982) 'Competitive sport environments: performance enhancement through cognitive intervention,' *Behavior Modification* vol. 6, pp. 443–63.

——(1990) 'An analysis of the training stress syndrome in competitive athletics,' *Journal of Sport Psychology* vol. 8, pp. 5–20.

——(2002) 'The evolution of sport psychology,' pp. 1–26 in Silva, J.M. and Stevens, D.E. (eds) *Psychological Foundations of Sport* Boston MA: Allyn & Bacon.

Silva, J.M. and Hardy, C.J. (1991) 'The sport psychologist: psychological aspects of injury in sport,' pp. 114–32 in Mueller, F.O. and Ryan, A. (eds) *The Sports Medicine Team and Athletic Injury Prevention* Philadelphia PA: Davis.

Silva, J.M. and Stevens, D.E. (eds) (2002) *Psychological Foundations of Sport* Boston MA: Allyn & Bacon.

Silva, J.M. and Weinberg, R.S. (1984) 'Motivation,' pp. 171–6 in Silva, J.M. and Weinberg, R.S. (eds) *Psychological Foundations of Sport* Champaign IL: Human Kinetics.

——(eds) (1984) *Psychological Foundations of Sport* Champaign IL: Human Kinetics.

Simek, T., O'Brien, R. and Figlerski, L. (1994) 'Contracting and chaining to improve the performance of a college golf team: improvement and deterioration,' *Perceptual and Motor Skills* vol. 78, pp. 1,099–105.

Simons, J. (1998) 'Concentration,' pp. 89–114 in Thompson, M.A., Vernacchia, R.A. and Moore, W.E. (eds) *Case Studies in Applied Sport Psychology: An educational approach* Dubuque IA: Kendall/Hunt.

Singer, R.N., Murphey, M. and Tennant, L.K. (1993) (eds) *Handbook of Research on Sport Psychology* New York: Macmillan.

Skinner, B.F. (1938) *The Behavior of Organisms* New York: Appleton-Century-Crofts.

Smith, R.E. (1980) 'A cognitive–affective approach to stress management training for athletes,' pp. 54–72 in Nadeau, C., Halliwell, W., Newell, K. and Roberts, G. (eds) *Psychology of Motor Behavior and Sports – 1979* Champaign IL: Human Kinetics.

——(1984) 'Theoretical and treatment approaches to anxiety reduction,' pp. 157–70 in Silva, J.M. and Weinberg, R.S. (eds) *Psychological Foundations of Sport* Champaign IL: Human Kinetics.

——(1986) 'Toward a cognitive–affective model of athletic burnout,' *Journal of Sport Psychology* vol. 8, pp. 36–50.

——(1998) 'A positive approach to sport performance enhancement: principles of reinforcement and performance feedback,' pp. 28–40 in Williams, J.M. (ed.) *Applied Sport Psychology: Personal growth to peak performance*, 3rd edition, Mountain View CA: Mayfield.

——(2000) 'Generalization in coping skills training,' *Journal of Sport & Exercise Psychology* vol. 20, pp. 358–78.

Smith, R.E. and Smoll, F.L. (1990) 'Measurement and correlates of sport-specific cognitive and somatic trait anxiety: the sport anxiety scale,' *Anxiety Research* vol. 2, pp. 263–80.

——(1996) *Way to Go, Coach* Portola Valley CA: Warde.

Smith, R.E., Schultz, R.W., Smoll, F.L. and Ptacek, J.T. (1995) 'Development and validation of a multidimensional measure of sport specific psychological skills: the athletic coping skills inventory – 28,' *Journal of Sport & Exercise Psychology* vol. 17, pp. 379–98.

Spanos, N.P. (1982) 'A social psychological approach to hypnotic behavior,' pp. 231–71 in Weary, G. and Mirels, H.L. (eds) *Integrations of Clinical and Social Psychology* New York: Oxford University Press.

Sparkes, A.C. (2000) 'Illness, premature career-termination, and the loss of self: a biographical study of an elite athlete,' pp. 14–32 in Jones, R.L. and Armour, K.M. (eds) *Sociology of Sport: Theory and practice* Harlow, Essex: Longman.

Stainback, R.D. (1997) *Alcohol and Sport* Champaign IL: Human Kinetics.

Steiner, I.M. (1972) *Group Process and Productivity* New York: Academic Press.

Sternberg, Robert J. (1987) 'Intelligence,' pp. 375–9 in Gregory, R.L. *The Oxford Companion to the Mind* Oxford: Oxford University Press.

——(1996) 'Intelligence and cognitive styles,' pp. 583–601 in Colman, A.M. (ed.) *Companion Encyclopedia of Psychology*, vol. 2, London: Routledge.

Strachey, J. (ed.) (1978) *The Standard Edition of the Complete Psychological Work of Sigmund Freud*, vol. 23, London: The Hogarth Press.

Straub, W.F. (ed.) (1980) *Sport Psychology: An analysis of athlete behavior*, 2nd edition, Ithaca NY: Mouvement Publications.

Strean, W.B. and Roberts, G.C. (1992) 'Future directions in applied sport psychology research,' *The Sports Psychologist* vol. 6, pp. 55–65.

Suinn, R.M. (1972) 'Removing emotional obstacles to learning and performance by visuo-motor behavior rehearsal,' *Behavioral Therapy* vol. 31, pp. 308–10.

Sulloway, F. (1980) *Freud, Biologist of the Mind* London: Fontana.

Summers, J.J. (ed.) (1992) *Approaches to the Study of Motor Control and Learning* Amsterdam: Elsevier.

Sundgot-Borgen, J. (1994) 'Eating disorders in female athletes,' *Sports Medicine* vol. 17, pp. 176–88.

Sundgot-Borgen, J. (1994) 'Risk and trigger factors: the development of eating disorders in female elite athletes,' *Medicine and Science in Sports and Exercise* vol. 26, pp. 414–19.

Tannen, O. and Saville-Troika, M. (eds) (1985) *Perspectives on Silence* Norwood NJ: Ablex.

Taub, D. and Benson, R. (1992) 'Weight concerns, weight control techniques, and eating disorders among adolescent competitive swimmers: the effects of gender,' *Sociology of Sport Journal* vol. 9, pp. 76–86.

Tavris, C. (1989) *Anger* New York: Touchstone.

Taylor, J. (1988) 'Slumpbusting: a systematic analysis of slumps in sports,' *The Sport Psychologist* vol. 2, pp. 39–48.

Taylor, J. and Demick, A. (1994) 'A multidimensional model of momentum in sports,' *Journal of Applied Sport Psychology* vol. 6, pp. 51–70.

Therberge, N. (2000) 'Gender and sport,' pp. 322–33 in Coakley, J.J. and Dunning, E. (eds) *Handbook of Sports Studies* London: Sage.

Thomas, P.R., Hardy, L. and Murphy, S. (1996) 'Development of a comprehensive test of psychological skills for practice and performance,' *Journal of Applied Sport Psychology* vol. 8, supplement S119.

Thompson, M.A. (1998) 'A charge,' pp. 257–60 in Thompson, M.A., Vernacchia, R.A. and Moore, W.E. (eds) (1998) *Case Studies in Applied Sport Psychology: An educational approach* Dubuque IA: Kendall/Hunt.

Thompson, M.A., Vernacchia, R.A. and Moore, W.E. (eds) (1998) *Case Studies in Applied Sport Psychology: An educational approach* Dubuque IA: Kendall/Hunt.

Tofler, I., Styer, B., Micheli, L. and Herman, L. (1996) 'Physical and emotional problems of elite female gymnasts,' *New England Journal of Medicine* vol. 335, pp. 281–3.

Tosches, N. (2000) *Night Train: The Sonny Liston story* London: Hamish Hamilton.

Triplett, N. (1897) 'The dynamogenic factors in pacemaking and competition,' *American Journal of Psychology* vol. 9, pp. 507–33.

Tulving, E. (1972) 'Episodic and semantic memory,' pp. 381–403 in Tulving, E. and Donaldson, W. (eds) *Organization of Memory* New York: Academic Press.

Tulving, E. and Donaldson, W. (eds) (1972) *Organization of Memory* New York: Academic Press.

Turnbull, C.M. (1961) 'Some observations regarding the experiences and behavior of the Ba Mbuti pygmies,' *American Journal of Psychology* vol. 74, pp. 304–8.

Turner, J.C. (1991) *Social Influence* Milton Keynes, England: Open University Press.

Tutko, T.A. and Richards, J.W. (1972) *Coaches' Practical Guide to Athletic Motivation* Boston MA: Allyn & Bacon.

Van Landuyt, L.M., Ekkekakis, P., Hall, E.E. and Petruzzello, S.J. (2000) 'Throwing the mountains into the lakes: on the perils of nomothetic conceptions of the exercise–affect relationship,' *Journal of Sport & Exercise Psychology* vol. 22, pp. 208–34.

Van Raalte, J.L., Brewer, B.W., Nemeroff, C. and Linder, D. (1991) 'Chance orientation and superstitious behavior on the putting green,' *Journal of Sport Behavior* vol. 14, pp. 41–50.

Van Raalte, J.L., Cornelius, A.E., Brewer, B.W. and Hatten, S.J. (2000) 'The antecedents and consequences of self-talk in competitive tennis,' *Journal of Sport & Exercise Psychology* vol. 22, pp. 245–56.

Van Schoyck, S. and Grasha, A. (1981) 'Attentional style variations and athletic ability: the advantages of a sports-specific test,' *Medicine and Science in Sport and Exercise* vol. 26, pp. 495–502.

Varca, P.E. (1980) 'An analysis of home and away game performance of male college basketball teams,' *Journal of Sport Psychology* vol. 2, pp. 245–57.

Vealey, R.S. (1986) 'Conceptualization of sport-confidence and competitive orientation: preliminary investigation and instrument development,' *Journal of Sport Psychology* vol. 8, pp. 221–46.

Vergin, R.C. (2000) 'Winning streaks in sports and the misperception of momentum,' *Journal of Sport Behavior* vol. 23, pp. 181–97.

Vernacchia, R.A. (1998) 'Making the case for case study research,' pp. 7–18 in Thompson, M.A., Vernacchia, R.A. and Moore, W.E. (eds) (1998) *Case Studies in Applied Sport Psychology: An educational approach* Dubuque IA: Kendall/Hunt.

Vroom, V.H. (1964) *Work and Motivation* New York: Wiley.

Vroom, V.H. and Jago, A.G. (1988) *The New Leadership: Managing participation in organizations* Englewood Cliffs NJ: Prentice-Hall.

Waddington, I. (1996) 'The development of sports medicine,' *Sociology of Sport Journal* vol. 19, pp. 176–96.

——(2000) *Sport, Health and Drugs: A critical sociological perspective* London: Spon.

Wagstaff, G.F. (1996) 'Hypnosis,' pp. 991–1,006 in Colman, A.M. (ed.) *Companion Encyclopedia of Psychology*, vol. 2, London: Routledge.

Wankel, L. (1984) 'Audience effects in sport,' pp. 293–314 in Silva, J.M. and Weinberg, R.S. (eds) *Psychological Foundations of Sport* Champaign IL: Human Kinetics.

Wann, D.L, Melnick, M.J., Russell, G.W. and Pease, D.G. (2001) *Sports Fans: The psychology and social impact of spectators* London: Routledge.

Warren, N. (ed.) (1980) *Studies in Cross-Cultural Psychology* New York: Academic Press.

Watson, P. (1973) 'Introduction – psychologists and race: the "actor factor",' pp. 13–19 in Watson, P. (ed.) *Psychology and Race* Harmondsworth: Penguin.

Weary, G. and Mirels, H.L. (eds) (1982) *Integrations of Clinical and Social Psychology* New York: Oxford University Press.

Weinberg, R.S. (1981) 'The relationship between mental preparation strategies and motor performance: a review and critique,' *Quest* vol. 33, pp. 195–213.

——(1992) 'Goal setting and motor performance: a review and critique,' pp. 177–97 in Roberts, G.C. (ed.) *Motivation in Sport and Exercise* Champaign IL: Human Kinetics.

Weiner, B. (1972) *Theories of Motivation: From mechanism to cognition* Chicago IL: Markham.

——(1986) *An Attributional Theory of Motivation and Emotion* New York: Springer-Verlag.

Weiss, M.R. and Chaumeton, N. (1992) 'Motivational orientations in sport,' in Horn, T.S. (ed.) *Advances in Sport Psychology* Champaign IL: Human Kinetics.

Wells, R. (1997) *Lombardi: His life and times* Madison WI: Prairie Oak Press.

Widmeyer, W.N., Dorsch, K.D., Bray, S.R. and McGuire, E.J. (2002) 'The nature, prevalence, and consequences of aggression in sport,' pp. 328–51 in Silva, J.M. and Stevens, D.E. (eds) *Psychological Foundations of Sport* Boston MA: Allyn & Bacon.

Wiggins, D.K. (1984) 'The history of sport psychology in North America,' pp. 9–22 in Silva, J.M. and Weinberg, R.S. (eds) *Psychological Foundations of Sport* Champaign IL: Human Kinetics.

Williams, J.M. (ed.) (1998) *Applied Sport Psychology: Personal growth to peak performance*, 3rd edition, Mountain View CA: Mayfield.

Williams, J.M. and Harris, D.V. (1998) 'Relaxation and energizing techniques for regulation of arousal,' pp. 324–37 in Williams, J.M. (ed.) *Applied Sport Psychology: Personal growth to peak performance*, 3rd edition, Mountain View CA: Mayfield.

Williams, J.M. and Straub, W.F. (1998) 'Sport psychology: past, present and future,' pp. 1–10 in Williams, J.M. (ed.) *Applied Sport Psychology: Personal growth to peak performance*, 3rd edition, Mountain View CA: Mayfield.

Williams, J.M, Rotella, R.J. and Heyman, S.R. (1998) 'Stress, injury, and the psychological rehabilitation of athletes,' pp. 409–28 in Williams, J.M (ed.) *Applied Sport Psychology: Personal growth to peak performance*, 3rd edition, Mountain View CA: Mayfield.

Wilmore, J.H. and Costill, D.L. (1999) *Physiology of Sport and Exercise*, 2nd edition, Champaign IL: Human Kinetics.

Wolf, N. (1991) *The Beauty Myth: How images of beauty are used against women* New York: Morrow.

Woodman, T., Albinson, J.G. and Hardy, L. (1997) 'An investigation of the zones of optimal functioning hypothesis within a multidimensional framework,' *Journal of Sport & Exercise Psychology* vol. 19, pp. 131–40.

Woods, E. and McDaniel, P. (1997) *Training a Tiger: A father's guide to raising a winner in both golf and life* New York: HarperCollins.

Woolgar, C. and Power, T.G. (1993) 'Parent and sport socialization: views from the achievement literature,' *Journal of Sport Behavior* vol. 16, pp. 171–89.

Yerkes, R.M. and Dodson, J.D. (1908) 'The relation of strength and stimulus to rapidity of habit formation,' *Journal of Comparative and Neurological Psychology* vol. 18, pp. 459–82.

Yesalis, C. and Cowart, V. (1998) *The Steroids Game: An expert's look at anabolic steroid use in sports*, Champaign IL: Human Kinetics.

Yiannakis, A., McIntyre, T.D., Melnick, M. and Hart, D.P. (1987) (eds) *Sport Sociology: Contemporary themes*, 3rd edition, Dubuque IA: Kendall/Hunt.

Young, K. (2000) 'Sport and violence,' pp. 382–407 in Coakley, J.J. and Dunning, E. (eds) *Handbook of Sports Studies* London: Sage.

Zajonc, R. (1965) 'Social facilitation,' *Science* vol. 149, pp. 269–74.

Ziegler, S.G. (1980) 'An overview of anxiety management strategies in sport,' pp. 257–64 in Straub, W.F. (ed.) *Sport Psychology: An analysis of athlete behavior*, 2nd edition, Ithaca NY: Mouvement Publications.

Zillman, D., Katcher, A.H. and Day, K.D. (1972) 'Provoked and unprovoked aggressiveness in athletes,' *Journal of Research in Personality* vol. 8, pp. 139–52.

Zinsser, N., Bunker, L. and Williams, J.M. (1998) 'Cognitive techniques for building confidence and enhancing performance,' pp. 270–95 in Williams, J.M. (ed.) *Applied Sport Psychology: Personal growth to peak performance*, 3rd edition, Mountain View CA: Mayfield.

INDEX